The Cambodian Wars

MODERN WAR STUDIES

Theodore A. Wilson
General Editor

Raymond A. Callahan
J. Garry Clifford
Jacob W. Kipp
Allan R. Millett
Carol Reardon
Dennis Showalter
David R. Stone
Series Editors

The Cambodian Wars

Clashing Armies and CIA Covert Operations

Kenneth Conboy

UNIVERSITY PRESS OF KANSAS

Published by the University Press of Kansas (Lawrence, Kansas 66045), which was organized by the Kansas Board of Regents and is operated and funded by Emporia State University, Fort Hays State University, Kansas State University, Pittsburg State University, the University of Kansas, and Wichita State University

Library of Congress Cataloging-in-Publication Data

Conboy, Kenneth J.
The Cambodian wars : clashing armies and CIA covert operations/ Kenneth Conboy.
pages cm. — (Modern war studies)
Includes bibliographical references and index.
ISBN 978-0-7006-1900-9 (cloth : alkaline paper)
1. Cambodia—History, Military—20th century. 2. Armies—Cambodia—History—20th century. 3. Political violence—Cambodia—History—20th century. 4. Espionage, American—Cambodia—History—20th century. 5. Paramilitary forces—Cambodia—History—20th century. 6. United States. Central Intelligence Agency—History—20th century. 7. United States—Foreign relations—Cambodia. 8. Cambodia—Foreign relations—United States. 9. United States—Military relations—Cambodia. 10. Cambodia—Military relations—United States. I. Title.
DS554.8.C65 2013
327.1273059609'045—DC23

2013000730

British Library Cataloguing in Publication Data is available.

Printed in the United States of America

10 9 8 7 6 5 4 3 2 1

The paper used in this publication is recycled and contains 30 percent postconsumer waste. It is acid free and meets the minimum requirements of the American National Standard for Permanence of Paper for Printed Library Materials Z39.48-1992.

Contents

Illustrations

Maps

Photographs

Preface and Acknowledgments

This book has been nearly three decades in the making. To be fair, my focus during the initial decade was toward the war in Laos, where I was documenting a massive and extended paramilitary campaign conducted by the Central Intelligence Agency (CIA). Over the course of interviewing dozens of CIA officers who had served in Laos, I encountered many who had spent shorter stints in neighboring Cambodia. I dutifully jotted down their Cambodian anecdotes and filed them away.

Years later when researching a book on covert operations in North Vietnam, I once more came across CIA officers who had done Cambodian tours. Then when I wrote a book on the CIA operation in Tibet, again I interviewed officers who had Cambodian experience. Collectively, their tales were gaining critical mass.

It is perhaps fitting that I came to writing this book while researching others. After all, it has become cliché to call the conflict in Cambodia a "sideshow." During the Second Indochina Conflict, this was not an unfair characterization. Although Cambodia sometimes carried the headlines, the battles there were usually secondary to, or in support of, the main struggle in neighboring Vietnam.

This did not remain the case. By the time of the Vietnamese invasion of Democratic Kampuchea in 1978, and the subsequent war through 1991, Cambodia moved from sideshow to center stage. It was the main issue that defined the Association of Southeast Asian Nations (ASEAN) for more than a decade. It also came to symbolize the faultline between the socialist camps, with China and the Khmer Rouge on one side and the Soviets, with their Vietnamese proxies, on the other.

Throughout this period of events, and for different reasons, the United States had difficulty responding to the troubles in Cambodia. During the 1960s, limits largely followed from Cambodia's nonaligned foreign policy. During the first half of the 1970s, a larger American role was proscribed by congressional restraints. Then during the 1980s, lingering effects of the Vietnam Syndrome led even the most hawkish members of President Ronald Reagan's administration to downplay direct involvement in Cambodian affairs.

Enter the CIA. During those times when the Pentagon and Foggy Bottom were constrained with regard to what they could do in Cambodia, CIA covert operations were a pragmatic and attractive alternative. On several occasions, the CIA cooperated with intelligence counterparts from regional states, who for their own reasons also sought to keep their involvement in Cambodia discrete.

This book attempts to pull back the veil on the CIA's involvement in Cambodia, first during the Khmer Republic and then after the Vietnamese invasion, when it was largely channeled through the noncommunist Cambodian resistance. Although there are a modest number of titles covering recent Cambodian history, this is the first one to investigate at length CIA operations in that country. And aside from a single monograph in 1991, there are no English-language books on the noncommunist resistance. This book will hopefully be an important source for students of contemporary Southeast Asian history, the Second Indochina Conflict, and CIA paramilitary operations.

In one sense, this is really two separate stories separated by time, though not geography. And perhaps not surprisingly, most of the primary characters—from Cambodian royalty to Thai generals to CIA case officers—maintained their roles throughout these periods. To them, Cambodia might have had chapters spread over a quarter of a decade, but they were always part of a continuing saga. They are treated as such in this book.

Among the many who contributed to this work, I would like to single out some who were especially generous with their help and support. In the United States, thanks go out to Andy Antippas, Alan Armstrong, Kenton Clymer, Doan Huu Dinh, Jim Dunn, Dennis Elmore, Denny Lane, Jim Parker, and Nate Thayer. Warm thanks go to Barry Broman for sharing his thoughts over some delicious bowls of *khao soi*.

In Singapore, I would like to acknowledge the assistance offered by the library staff at the Institute of Southeast Asian Studies.

In Thailand, Tony Davis, Mike Eiland, Bertil Lintner, Sorachai Montrivat, Roland Neveu, Veera Star, and Mac Thompson have my gratitude. Special thanks goes to the late Lieutenant Colonel Manit Nakajitti, who never failed to amaze me with his photographic memory and network of contacts.

In Cambodia, I have received constant encouragement and help from Chea Chheang, Sieng Lapresse, and Leng Sochea. I would like to thank Hassan Kasem, Hul Sakada, and Kong Thann for their assistance with translations and interviews. My warmest appreciation goes as well to Dien Del, Sam Oum, Hun Phoeung, Tepi Ros, and Riem Sarin, with whom I shared many meals and conversations. I would especially like to thank Dr. Gaffar Peang-Meth and General Suon Samnang for their patient recollections over the years.

The author reserves special thanks to Merle Pribbenow for his remarkable translations and infectious enthusiasm for Southeast Asian military history.

And finally, the author would like to thank his editor, Mike Briggs, for years of support in seeing this through.

Ken Conboy
Jakarta, Indonesia
November 2012

Acronyms

AFIOC — Armed Forces Intelligence Operations Center
ANKI — National Army for an Independent Cambodia (Armées Nationale pour Khmer Independent)
ANS — Sihanoukist National Army (Armée Nationale Sihanoukienne)
APPCO — Armed Political, Psychological, and Clandestine Operations
ASA — Army Security Agency
ASEAN — Association of Southeast Asian Nations
BIRD — Bureau of Intelligence, Research, and Documentation
CGDK — Coalition Government of Democratic Kampuchea
CIA — Central Intelligence Agency
CIDG — Civilian Irregular Defense Group
COS — Clandestine Operations Service
CPK — Communist Party of Kampuchea
CPT — Communist Party of Thailand
CRTs — Commando Raider Teams
DCM — Deputy Chief of Mission
DDRS — Declassified Document Reference System
DPPU — Displaced Persons Protection Unit
DRV — Democratic Republic of Vietnam
Exco — Executive Coordinating Committee
FANK — National Cambodian Armed Forces (Forces Armées Nationales *Khmères*) [beginning April 1970]
FARK — Royal Cambodian Armed Forces (Forces Armées Royales *Khmères*) [before April 1970]
FBIS — Foreign Broadcast Information Service
FRUS — *Foreign Relations of the United States*
FULRO — United Front for the Liberation of Oppressed Races (Front Uni de Lutte des Races Opprimées)
Funcinpec — Independent, Neutral, Peaceful, and Cooperative Cambodia (Front Uni National pour un Cambodge Indépendant, Neutre, Pacifique, et Coopératif)
FUNK — National United Front of Kampuchea (Front Uni National du Kampuchea)

GRUNK	Royal Nation United Government of Kampuchea (Gouvernement Royal d'Union Nationale du Kampuchea)
JCS	Joint Chiefs of Staff
JMC	Joint Military Command
KEG	Khmer Emergency Group
Khmer Rouge	the Cambodian Communist movement
KISA	Khmer Information and Security Agency
KKK	Khmer Kampuchea Krom
KPNLAF	Khmer People's National Liberation Armed Forces (Forces Armées Nationale de Libération du Peuple Khmer)
KPNLF	Khmer People's National Liberation Front
KPRP	Khmer People's Revolutionary Party
MACV	U.S. Military Assistance Command in Vietnam
MACVSOG	[U.S. Military Assistance Command Vietnam] Special Operations Group
Moulinaka	National Movement for the Liberation of Kampuchea (Mouvement pour la Libération Nationale du Kampuchea)
OMZ	operational military zone
PARU	Police Aerial Reinforcement Unit
PAVN	People's Army of Vietnam
PCCS	Provisional Central Committee of Salvation
Permico	Permanent Military Committee for Cooperation
PLANA	Department of Planning and Analysis
PRC	People's Republic of China
PRG	Provisional Revolutionary Government
PRK	People's Republic of Kampuchea
PRKAF	PRK Armed Forces
PS	Pakse Site
RCAF	Royal Cambodian Armed Forces
RTA	Royal Thai Army
SAS	Special Air Service
SEATO	Southeast Asia Treaty Organization
SEPES	Social and Political Studies Service (Service des Etudes Politiques et Sociales)
SGU	Special Guerrilla Unit
SID	Security and Intelligence Division
SNC	Supreme National Council
SOC	State of Cambodia

SRV	Socialist Republic of Vietnam
TOC	Tactical Operations Center
UNAMIC	United Nations Advance Mission in Cambodia
UNTAC	United Nations Transitional Authority in Cambodia
USAID	U.S. Agency for International Development
USSF	U.S. Army Special Forces
Viet Cong	National Liberation Front [Vietnam]
VPAF	Vietnam People's Air Force
WSAG	Washington Special Action Group

The Cambodian Wars

1. Springtime in Cambodia

In the water, crocodiles; on land, tigers. So goes the Khmer proverb that describes the historically rough neighborhood found on mainland Southeast Asia, the neighborhood where a litany of Cambodian fiefdoms found themselves wedged between a figurative rock and a hard place. At the start of the Middle Ages, a few of these principalities in the Mekong Delta, growing rich while brokering trade between China and India, congealed for a time into the Hindu kingdom of Funan. Then in the seventh century, some Cambodian royals added more real estate around the Dangrek Mountains and briefly united as the Kingdom of Chenla.

But it was not until the start of the ninth century that a Khmer Empire beat back encroaching neighbors and rose to regional domination across Southeast Asia. Showing their mettle, legions of Cambodian infantry, cavalry, and war elephants pushed north to Vientiane and south to the Kra Isthmus. To the east, they held at bay their perennial rivals in what is now central and southern Vietnam.

The centerpiece of the Khmer Empire was the capital of Angkor. Roughly the size of Los Angeles, Angkor supported half a million residents at a time when Tokyo was still only a village. Its irrigation system extended 25 kilometers from the city's center, allowing for three crops a year. And its magnificent temples—erected by thousands of coolies at the behest of kings that purported divine lineage—remain the largest religious buildings ever constructed.

Through the fourteenth century, the Khmer basked in such opulence. Part of the empire's staying power resided in Angkor's strategic location: With enemies channeled up the Mekong, they were relatively easy to interdict. Part, too, was grounded in the adulation ladled upon the king; as a self-professed intermediary with the gods, he mobilized the masses to build vast elevated reservoirs, cut extensive irrigation channels, realize grand palaces and temples, and fill the expanding ranks of his infantry.

But as with all empires, rot eventually set in. Theories abound for the decline of Angkor's glory. Excessive manpower was siphoned off for the army, goes one, and away from more substantive economic endeavors. The road network built around Angkor proved a double-edged sword, goes another, as it abetted movement of the enemy as much as it did Khmer troops. Perhaps the biggest reason, however, was the adoption of Theravada Buddhism as the state religion; with its emphasis on introspection and inner Truth, it undercut dedication to the god-kings and their megaprojects. Angkor's infrastructure, especially its irrigation system, eventually fell into disrepair, and productivity plummeted.

To the west, Ayutthaya, a Thai kingdom that was exceptionally savvy toward foreign traders, was on the ascent. Sensing weakness in the faltering Khmer, the Thai surged east in 1431 and sacked Angkor. The Khmer capital, once the gold standard for urban sprawl prior to the Industrial Revolution, was abandoned to the jungle.

After that, history was less than kind to the Cambodians. From the heights of Angkorian splendor, the Khmer entered into one of Southeast Asia's longest unbroken losing streaks. Situated on the fault line between surging Thai and Vietnamese states, Cambodia leached territory—and dignity—for the next four centuries as it was reduced to a vassal of one or the other, or both.

Ironically it was the French, who had arrived in Indochina and declared protectorate status over Cambodia in 1863, that provided a reprieve. Recognizing the benefit of a buffer between its lucrative Vietnamese holdings and the expansion-minded Thai, France spared Cambodia from further territorial erosion and fixed its borders to an area roughly the size of Oklahoma.[1]

As far as protectorates go, Cambodia offered the French few headaches. Eighty percent of the populace were peasants who, more often than not owning their own plots of land, appeared genuinely content. Of the minority that lived in urban centers, ethnic Chinese, and to a lesser extent ethnic Vietnamese, dominated the business sector; Cambodians themselves placed a distant third.

Perched at the top of all this was the Cambodian monarch and his court. Kings had long since devolved into little more than figureheads, with true power residing in the French resident-general. When King Sisowath Monivong died in April 1941, however, the French saw special urgency in finding a suitable successor. This was because by that time Nazi Germany had installed the puppet Vichy government in France. The Vichy regime, which tacitly controlled France's Indochinese colonies, was in turn beholden to Germany's Axis partner, Imperial Japan. With such a tenuous toehold over its Southeast Asian territories, the French understandably desired the next Cambodian king to be especially malleable.

Eventually getting the nod was Monivong's grandson, eighteen-year-old Norodom Sihanouk. He was a good choice on two accounts. First, Sihanouk—with a father from the Norodoms and mother from the Sisowaths—reconciled the two royal houses that were in perpetual competition. Second, the youthful royal, who was attending high school in Saigon at the time, was said to most enjoy philosophy and music. Such benign interests, calculated the French, pointed toward a monarch with little backbone.

Initially, Sihanouk lived up to such low expectations. In 1945, when the Japanese shunted aside the Vichy and pressured Cambodia to declare independence near the close of World War II, the king was agreeable. A few months later, when the French returned to Indochina and professed their intent to reclaim their Asian colonies, Sihanouk just as quickly returned to the fold.

Shortly thereafter, however, Sihanouk began to show a nationalist streak and act against typecast. As background to this, by the close of the 1940s a violent independence struggle against the French had started to gain momentum in Vietnam. Although guerrillas of various political persuasions had also taken root in Cambodia, they rarely resorted to violence, and at no point did they ever seriously threaten French hold. This did not deter the emboldened Sihanouk, who began agitating for France's departure not only from Cambodia but also from all of Indochina.

Confronted by Sihanouk's shrill orating, the French opted for a surprising yet pragmatic retreat. In November 1953, they embraced the king's demands and summarily granted Cambodia its independence ahead of all the other Indochinese states. By appeasing Sihanouk in this manner, the French felt they could retain Cambodia's goodwill while simultaneously redoubling efforts at defeating the far more serious communist insurgency spreading across the Vietnamese countryside. In the end, the French did remain on cordial terms with Sihanouk, but they were still forced to make a humiliating departure from the rest of Indochina the next year.

Following France's withdrawal, the political landscape of mainland Southeast Asia was fluid. Vietnam was partitioned near the 17th Parallel between a communist Democratic Republic of Vietnam (DRV) in the north and a pro-West Republic of Vietnam in the south; elections to reunite the two were supposed to take place in 1956 but did not occur, setting the stage for the superpowers' proxy conflict. Laos was ostensibly neutral with a royal family symbolically on top, but communist and noncommunist factions remained very much vying for control underneath.

In Cambodia, the situation was somewhat less confusing as Sihanouk consolidated his grip over the kingdom. On a personal level, the monarch, who had married six women over eight years and had twelve children with four of them, had settled down with his seventh consort by 1955.[2] On a professional level, Sihanouk abdicated that same year and handed the crown to his father. Now demoted to a prince and with a freer hand to enter politics, he served short, almost annual stints as prime minister and formed his own party, which won all ninety-one National Assembly seats in a cooked 1955 election.[3]

From that point onward, Sihanouk's idiosyncrasies grew more pronounced. A man of impossibly thin skin, Sihanouk was increasingly convinced of his own indispensability. As a U.S. military officer assigned to Phnom Penh wrote in January 1964:

> A highly emotional individual, he had an insatiable appetite for praise, and appeared incapable of tolerating criticism. When under the spell of his own voice, he was prone to making ill-considered statements which later came back to plague him. . . . He has been a shrewd politician and consummate actor, capable of changing his mood to fit the moment.[4]

Sihanouk's moods changed so often, in fact, that it became cliché to call him mercurial. One result of this was a penchant for cutting diplomatic relations with noncommunist neighbors. By 1961, he had twice closed the embassy in Bangkok; in 1963 he severed relations with Saigon; and in May 1965 he broke ties with Washington.[5]

By contrast, and despite lip service to maintaining nonaligned status, Sihanouk had little problem courting the socialist world. By the mid-1960s, he counted among his closest allies the DRV, the People's Republic of China (PRC), and North Korea. He also saw common cause with Indonesia's Sukarno, a fellow self-declared neutralist who took pleasure tweaking the nose of the West.

On some occasions, Cambodia's left-leaning nonalignment was obnoxious but otherwise benign. In 1962, for example, Sihanouk and Sukarno took exception to the apolitical nature of the Olympics and formed an alternative international sporting competition—the Games of the Newly Emerging Forces—that openly embraced (largely socialist) politics. The following year, Sihanouk delivered a speech during which he implied that the assassinated President John Kennedy was languishing in hell.[6]

Far more serious was Cambodia's internecine role in the Vietnam War. Since the early 1960s, the DRV's armed forces, known as the People's Army of Vietnam (PAVN), had been striking at South Vietnam from Cambodian border sanctuaries. Through sins of omission, Phnom Penh elected not to interfere with this affront to its national sovereignty. It also took the extra step of condemning, and sometimes interdicting, any attempts by the United States or South Vietnam to pursue communist guerrillas into their Cambodian havens.

In November 1965, Cambodia crossed the line and laid the groundwork for sins of commission. That month, the head of the Cambodian army, Lieutenant General Lon Nol, flew to Beijing to confirm a secret treaty already approved by

Sihanouk for use of Sihanoukville's port to transship Chinese arms and supplies to PAVN sanctuaries along the border. Chinese shipments were passing through Sihanoukville by the following year; these were carried by the Hak Ly Trucking Company, a Phnom Penh–based entity that was actually led by an officer from PAVN's General Rear Services Department.[7] In return, the Cambodian military received at least 10 percent of all weapons shipments, as well as hefty port and transportation fees.[8] The Cambodians also reportedly allowed PAVN to make use of a military hospital in Kompong Cham.[9]

On the economic front, Sihanouk's policies were no less slanted and, in hindsight, misguided. Much of Cambodia's nonagrarian sectors were nationalized; what little private sector that remained was stifled by Sihanouk's own shocking neglect and blind eye toward rampant corruption—which in many cases was tied to the family of his seventh wife.[10] Worse, American largesse—amounting to nearly $410 million in economic grant aid from 1955 to 1963, plus another $84 million in military assistance—came to a halt after U.S. aid was summarily renounced in November 1963; this shortfall was never filled by similar levels of assistance extended by Cambodia's socialist allies.

As the Cambodian economy faltered, so, too, did Sihanouk's apparent grasp on reality. Between 1966 and 1969, the prince spent inordinate amounts of time writing scripts, composing music, and sometimes acting in nine extremely amateurish films. Showing his skewed priorities, he mobilized air force helicopters during the filming of one, forcing a one-day delay in the evacuation of casualties during a border clash with Thailand. As Cambodia's educated class tried to hide their embarrassment, he organized international film festivals in Phnom Penh during 1968 and 1969—and awarded himself the grand prize both times.[11]

There were other excesses are well. Showing little sense for conserving limited government resources, Sihanouk pushed for ten new universities or campuses to be built around the country—despite some of them never having more than 100 students apiece. And even when crucial government decisions had to be made, every other year he took extended leave of his kingdom for a rest cure on the French Riviera.

Yet despite economic stagnation, severely limited political expression, and Sihanouk's mounting personal quirks, there was no denying the prince remained popular in some quarters. Topping this list was the Cambodian peasantry. Such adulation was, in a sense, hard to explain. In his domestic speeches the prince would often refer to the Cambodian farmer in paternalistic tones that were pandering at best, insulting at worst. Moreover, when farmers rose up in 1967 after the government imposed stringent—and disadvantageous—regulations affecting rice sales, Sihanouk sent paratroopers to Battambang province to brutally quell the uprising. This seemed to matter little, however, as the peasantry continued to adore the accessible prince.

On an international level, too, it was sometimes difficult to fathom Sihanouk's appeal among socialist nations. After all, his periodic crackdowns on Cambodia's leftist intellectuals and politicians had sent them by the end of the 1960s to the grave or fleeing into the jungle. Also, Sihanouk's bourgeoisie proclivities should theoretically have made him fair game for condemnation among socialist ideologues. But reflecting Cold War pragmatism, the affable prince remained in their good graces.[12]

Others, not surprisingly, were less forgiving. Cambodian businessmen increasingly saw little benefit from Sihanouk's nationalization efforts that suppressed commerce and lined the pockets of his entourage. And while Sihanouk had long made little secret of his contempt for the urban elite, by the close of the decade the educated class was returning the sentiment. Some royals, especially the ambitious Prince Sisowath Sirik Matak, had even gone from trusted allies to guarded rivals.

Sitting on the fence was Sihanouk's enigmatic military chief, Lon Nol. The son of a minor government official from Prey Veng province, Lon Nol was a Khmer Krom, a reference to the ethnic Khmer found in the lower reaches of the Mekong Delta. Split by shifting borders, the bulk of the Khmer Krom lived inside Cambodia, but a half-million more could be found on the Vietnamese side of the frontier. Historically the Khmer Krom had been afforded better access to French education and, as Lon Nol could attest, had landed government posts disproportionate to their numbers.

Lon Nol hardly fit the stereotype of a military man. Quiet, unpretentious, and an uninspiring orator, he had initially entered the police force under the French colonial administration. After rising through the police ranks, he was named a provincial governor and later joined Sihanouk as a novice politician when the king began agitating for independence. It was not until 1952, at age thirty-nine, that Lon Nol transferred to the kingdom's fledgling army and was on hand the following December when a Khmer military column was sent to Battambang on one of its first postindependence forays. The French were actually in charge of the operation but, catering to Sihanouk's ego, allowed him to take command on paper. In the end, the French kept the enemy at a distance and the battle was a nonevent, barely rating as a skirmish. But showing tact, Lon Nol wrote up an after-action account that glowingly praised Sihanouk's supposed military prowess.[13]

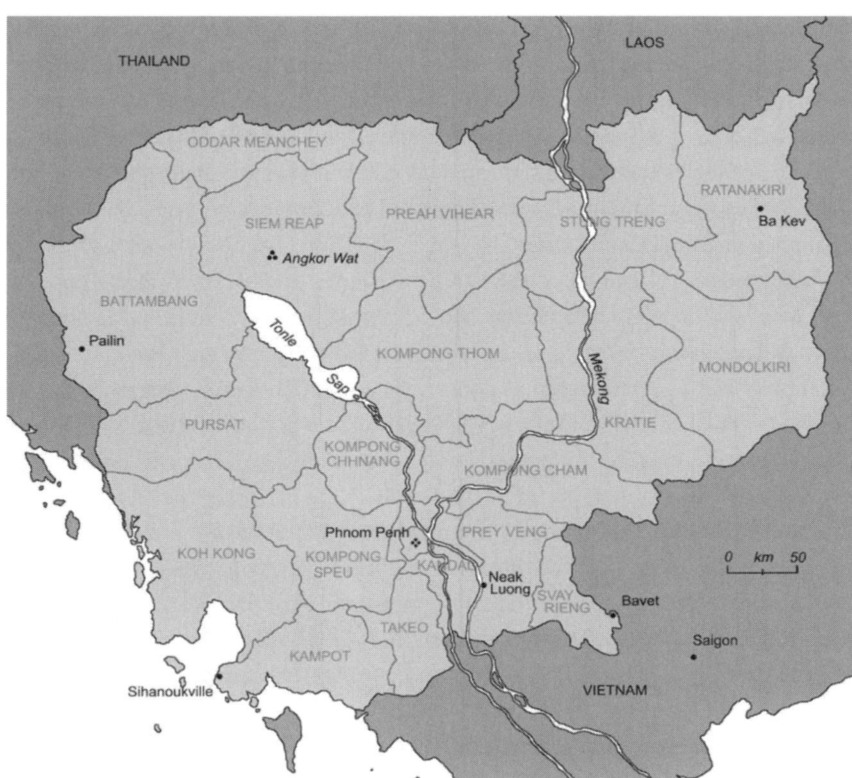

The Khmer Republic

From that point forward, Sihanouk allowed Lon Nol's career to go from strength to strength. In 1955, he was named army chief; five years later, he became chief of the General Staff as well as defense minister. Adding hats outside of the armed forces, he was chosen deputy premier in 1963 and in 1966 did a brief turn as prime minister.

As with other senior officials, Lon Nol owed all to the prince. Still, the general had quietly built his own constituencies. As he himself started out as a lowly government functionary, he held a positive rating among civil servants. The monks, too, favored him—even though his take on Buddhism was heavily laced with mysticism and the supernatural. Not surprisingly, soldiers liked Lon Nol, especially given his folksy, unassuming lifestyle. He was even something of a populist, his dark-bronze complection much closer to the color of the peasantry than to that of the other, paler members of the Sino-Khmer elite.[14]

Hedging Cold War bets, Lon Nol had courted favor among foreign nations as well. When Sihanouk slammed the door on further U.S. military aid in late 1963, the general showed diplomatic savvy when he warmly thanked members of the American mission for their efforts, then expressed hope that U.S. assistance would again flow in the future.[15] The very next year, however, he flew to China to secretly authorize communist military supplies to transit Sihanoukville. While there, he vowed to the Chinese that he would use his military to combat any U.S. aggression against Cambodia.[16]

When needed, Lon Nol could also be a calculating schemer. He reportedly kept extensive dossiers at his home about friends and foes alike. He also showed skill at fomenting trouble in neighboring South Vietnam. Back in 1959, Sihanouk, fuming over Saigon's support of Cambodian rebels, ordered his army chief to strike back in kind. Lon Nol's response was nuanced and unconventional. Using a handful of trusted army associates, he organized two underground organizations opposed to the South Vietnamese regime. The first, the Front de Libération du Champa (Champa Liberation Front), was established in 1960 ostensibly to support the rights of the ethnic Cham and highland tribes that had once constituted the formidable Kingdom of Champa. The Cham has since been reduced to pockets strung between Cambodia's Kompong Cham province (where they were primarily Muslim) and central Vietnam (where many were Hindu).

Although there is no evidence any ethnic Cham took up arms against the Saigon authorities, the highland tribes, which populated the mountainous spine running down South Vietnam, were a different matter. With discrete moral support coming from Phnom Penh, tribesmen from the Champa front staged a series of armed uprisings against the Saigon government in late 1964.[17]

The second underground organization created by Lon Nol in 1960 sought to stir discontent among the Khmer Krom living in South Vietnam's Mekong Delta. Using the nom de guerre Chau Dara, Lon Nol named himself leader of the Front de Libération du Kampuchea Krom (Khmer Krom Liberation Front), also known as the White Scarves.[18] This underground movement openly agitated for ethnic Cambodians in the lower Mekong to secede from Saigon's rule. With prompting from Chau Dara, the Front recruited sympathizers among the ethnic Cambodian population in the Delta; these members occasionally crossed the border to report their findings to Cambodian government handlers.[19] What's more, an armed wing known as the Khmer Kampuchea Krom (KKK) took root at the instigation of Lon Nol; KKK guerrillas mounted sporadic attacks in the Delta through the mid-1960s, though the movement had devolved into little more than a handful of bandits by that decade's end.[20]

Throughout that time, Lon Nol gave every indication he was loyal to Sihanouk. “He was a staunch royalist,” confirmed Dien Del, the general’s aide-de-camp during the early 1960s, “and he was especially respectful toward Queen Kossamak.”[21]

But by 1969, change was in the offing. For years Sihanouk had been staging a highwire act both among international players and domestic politicians. Although it was increasingly apparent he did not have the requisite skills needed to pull off such risky brinkmanship, the prince did not seem to have problems with polarizing the Cambodian body politic or driving neighboring states beyond frustration. The moribund Cambodian economy, however, was something that could no longer be overlooked. Making matters worse, the kingdom’s economic crisis sharpened in July due to expectations of a bad harvest.

Out of options, Sihanouk did the unthinkable—he relinquished center stage. Acquiescing to a vote by the National Assembly in August, he watched as Lon Nol was chosen to become prime minister for a second time. Even more remarkable was the assembly’s selection for deputy premier: Sisowath Sirik Matak, the urbane prince whose great-grandfather had been king near the start of the century. Although from different social strata—Lon Nol was born to a minor government official, Sirik Matak was born into privilege near the palace—they had been friends ever since attending the same high school in Saigon. Both entered the civil service, both eventually became governors, and both joined the same political party during Cambodia’s tame independence struggle. After that, both gravitated toward the military, with Sihanouk naming Sirik Matak as the first defense minister after independence.

Despite similar career paths, the two could not have had more different personalities. Lon Nol was the inscrutable Asian, emotions kept in check while he obediently did mental gymnastics to keep pace with Sihanouk’s fluctuating diplomatic whims. Sirik Matak was more sophisticated and opinionated, taking vocal exception to Sihanouk’s skewed nonalignment. Not surprising given Sihanouk’s inability to weather criticism, he eventually shunted off his cousin to a string of ambassadorial postings in Beijing, Manila, and Tokyo.

Now that he was back in Phnom Penh and wielding real influence in government, Sirik Matak pounced on the opportunity for change. Long an advocate of renewing U.S. aid and expanding commerce, he almost immediately laid out a program to denationalize and deregulate the economy from the stifling state controls imposed by Sihanouk.

Changes were also forthcoming in foreign policy. To be fair, Sihanouk had already started easing his nonaligned policies back toward the center. In January

1969, for example, he had allowed the army to launch sporadic attacks against PAVN and Cambodian communist guerrillas in the remote northeastern province of Ratanakiri.[22] Then, in August, he had normalized diplomatic relations with the United States after a four-year hiatus. That same month, he held frank discussions with U.S. Senate majority leader Mike Mansfield and admitted that the biggest threat to Cambodia was Vietnamese communists violating its borders.[23]

This last admission was more than a little disingenuous. After all, it was Sihanouk who had not only tolerated the Vietnamese border sanctuaries for years but also approved Chinese military supplies transiting Sihanoukville on the way to the sanctuaries. Those supplies were still flowing as of mid-1969, with regular Sunday coordination sessions in Phnom Penh between members of PAVN and the Cambodian army. Senior military officers, including Lon Nol, were reportedly lining their pockets with the generous proceeds from resultant port fees.

But now with Lon Nol and Sirik Matak at the helm, Phnom Penh signaled an even tougher line toward communism. Some of the steps taken were discrete. In September, for example, Lon Nol sent an emissary to make secret contact with Sihanouk's bête noire, Son Ngoc Thanh. A fellow Khmer Krom five years Lon Nol's senior, Son Ngoc Thanh made an early mark by establishing the first Khmer-language newspaper in 1936. A proponent of right-wing politics, he quickly soured toward the monarchy and became an opponent of Sihanouk upon his coronation.

By the time of World War II, Son Ngoc Thanh had worked his way to the top of Cambodia's small political elite. When Imperial Japan pressured Sihanouk to abruptly declare independence from France in 1945, he even briefly served as prime minister. This did not sit well when the French returned after the war; they promptly arrested him as a collaborator before packing him off to exile in Paris.

After a decent interval, Son Ngoc Thanh was allowed to return to Phnom Penh. If the French thought he was suitably chastened during exile, they were mistaken. He soon took to the jungle, where he became a leader among the assortment of insurgents opposed to French rule. He remained there after independence, molding his loyal guerrillas—which came to be known as the Khmer Serei, or Free Cambodians—into an armed anticommunist movement opposed to Sihanouk's royal government.

As insurgencies go, the Khmer Serei were a tame bunch that never seriously threatened Phnom Penh. Operating from South Vietnam, Son Ngoc Thanh fielded two pockets of guerrillas: one strung along the South Vietnamese border—which consisted largely of Khmer Krom—and the other just inside Thailand along the Dangrek Mountains. After a dormant period, they grew marginally more active in 1963 following an injection of covert military aid from Saigon and Bangkok. They also ran a pair of weak radio transmitters that sniped at Sihanouk over the airwaves.[24]

Even though largely ineffectual, the Khmer Serei left Sihanouk livid and prone to overreaction. In November 1963, for example, a Khmer Serei member was lured to Phnom Penh with a safe conduct pass—only to be arrested and locked in a cage at the National Assembly. Sihanouk later had his slow execution filmed—it lasted more than 15 minutes—and made it required viewing in cinemas for a month.[25]

Sihanouk's hysterics aside, the Khmer Serei ranks were plunging into a downward spiral. This was largely due to economic realities. In search of proper employment, hundreds of members joined the paramilitary forces of the South Vietnamese government.[26] Most of the remainder, especially those in the Dangrek Mountains, began defecting in droves to the Cambodian government during the first half of 1969 and were inducted into the army.

By the time Lon Nol contacted Son Ngoc Thanh in September 1969, the Khmer Serei had ceased to be an irritant. Still, it was a step rife with symbolism: Despite being vilified by Sihanouk for decades, and indeed sentenced to death in absentia, Cambodia's highest profile anticommunist now appeared to be mending fences with Phnom Penh's new management.

Other steps taken by Lon Nol's government were equally substantial. By October 1969, Cambodian militiamen were initiating occasional attacks against Vietnamese communist units—dubbed "armed bandits" in the Cambodian media—in places like Kandal, the province adjacent to Phnom Penh.[27] The following month, Sirik Matak, ignoring the counsel of Sihanouk, ordered a wider military operation in Ratanakiri.[28] Located in the triborder region where Laos, South Vietnam, and Cambodia converged, Ratanakiri was significant for a couple of reasons. First, the majority of its sparse population comprised tribesmen that largely operated outside of Phnom Penh's writ; many, in fact, were sympathetic to Cambodia's small but growing armed communist movement. Second, offshoots of the Ho Chi Minh Trail logistical corridor fed from Laos into PAVN cache sites spread across the jungles of Ratanakiri. Between the tribesmen and PAVN troops, Phnom Penh's grip over the province was shaky at best.

The military operation into Ratanakiri intended to address both issues. Not only would the troops literally plant the flag, and thus extend the central government's influence, but more important they would begin to plot the size and locations of PAVN units. Dispatched for this mission would be three tactical groups assembled from the ranks of some of the army's best infantry battalions, as well as armor and paratroopers.[29]

Ironically, among the tactical group commanders was Lieutenant Colonel Um Savuth. One of the country's first airborne officers, Savuth had married an attractive Eurasian woman—only to be driven to drink over her suspected dalliances. During one such binge, he decided to re-create the William Tell legend by having a junior officer shoot a can off his head. The officer, understandably nervous, missed his mark and instead sent the shot into Savuth's cranium. Though he survived, he was forced to walk with a cane and keep the alcohol flowing to dull the pain.

Despite his physical impediment and frequent inebriation, Savuth remained a skilled officer and was promoted to head the Brigade de Palaise, the strategic Palace Brigade that guarded Phnom Penh. As a confidante of Lon Nol, he was also given the sensitive assignment of cochairing the Special Transportation Committee that coordinated the PAVN supplies that flowed through Sihanoukville. Now, after ably abetting the PAVN logistical corridor for more than three years, he was selected to spearhead one of the tactical groups mobilizing against the Vietnamese.[30]

As had been the case with the Cambodian troops that entered Ratanakiri at the beginning of the year, the tactical groups inevitably clashed with the PAVN interlopers. Small numbers of casualties were inflicted on both sides, and some Vietnamese prisoners were taken.[31] Upping the ante, the Cambodian government cut an airfield at Labang Siek and began staging a handful of interdiction runs with its fleet of aging fighter-bombers.[32] Although PAVN was under orders to avoid instigating any confrontations with the Cambodian military, Moscow was sufficiently irate with Phnom Penh that it halted the flow of spare parts and ammunition for the MiG-17 fighters it had given Cambodia earlier in the decade.

Effectively sidelined, Sihanouk had no choice but to watch his kingdom veer farther away from its erstwhile socialist allies. All of this had apparently taken a toll on his health, as the fatigued prince decided during the first week of January 1970 that it was the right time to take his customary extended medicinal cure on the French Riviera. Before boarding his plane for France, he assured his countrymen over the radio that he would be back by April in time to plow the "first furrow of the agricultural year."[33]

This promise proved overly optimistic. In the prince's absence, decades of pent-up frustration over his misguided rule came to the fore and the ranks of anti-Sihanouk conspirators began to swell. Taking the lead was the brooding, ambitious Sirik Matak. Lon Nol, who returned from his own extended medical treatment in France on 18 February, was also agreeable (albeit more cautiously) to Sihanouk's ouster.

The day after Lon Nol's return, another conspirator, In Tam, was enticed into taking a key step. With a career path not unlike Lon Nol and Sirik Matak, the portly In Tam had risen through the police ranks before switching to politics (he was elected to the National Assembly in 1966) and serving time as a governor. Though he was derided for occasionally displaying a wicked temper in public, he was renowned for his scrupulous honesty. Probably because of this, Sirik Matak on 19 February tapped In Tam to form a commission in the assembly to weed out corruption. Immediately, four assemblymen, all pro-Sihanoukists, were implicated in smuggling and drummed out of office. One of the resultant openings was filled by In Tam himself, who thereafter became deputy president of the assembly. This was critical because if Sihanouk were to be dismissed in a vote of no-confidence, the assembly president would replace the prince as chief of state and In Tam would become president of the assembly.

With that vital procedural step out of the way, the conspirators ratcheted up pressure against the Vietnamese communists and, by association, Sihanouk. In late February, plans were hatched to stage anti-Vietnamese demonstrations in the border province of Svay Rieng. This hardly needed any prompting. As one of Cambodia's driest and most impoverished provinces, its populace was renowned for their socially crass, often martial nature. And as they had had to endure the presence of PAVN sanctuaries—and resultant cross-border attacks from South Vietnam—for the better part of a decade, they were begging to lash out at the squatters. Aided by students driven in from Phnom Penh, Svay Rieng residents on 8 March initiated three days of raucous anti-Vietnamese protests.

This was tame compared to what happened next. On 11 March, Sirik Matak arranged for a large student rally, spearheaded by four dozen soldiers, which resulted in the sacking of the embassies of the DRV and communist Provisional Revolutionary Government (PRG) of the Republic of Vietnam.[34] Not willing to ease up, the following day Lon Nol publicly demanded—unrealistically—that all PAVN sanctuaries be vacated within three days. Sirik Matak, meantime, nullified trade agreements with the PRG.

Frightened of getting caught in the backlash, army officers who had been close to PAVN grew worried. One lieutenant colonel who had coordinated the Sihanoukville shipments hid all of his private vehicles except one jeep parked in front of his residence. The manager of the Hak Ly Trucking Company, meantime, disappeared from Phnom Penh on the evening of 12 March; the remainder of his staff went into hiding.[35]

Monitoring events from France, Sihanouk was devastated. Heading from the Riviera to Paris, he addressed a small audience at the Cambodian embassy. In a vintage moment of rage, the prince vented against the government he left behind in Phnom Penh, going so far as to say he would put most of the leadership to death upon his return. Though he had shown himself capable of flashes of brutality against regime opponents in the past, these latest comments could most likely be written off as hyperbole. Trouble was, they were tape-recorded and a copy reached Cambodia—and Lon Nol's ear—by the end of the second week of March.

Compounding matters, Sihanouk made another critical misstep. On 13 March, after initially hinting that he was going to curtail his trip and come home quickly, he instead decided to reroute his return journey with five days each in the Soviet Union and PRC. This would delay his landing in Phnom Penh—originally scheduled for 18 March—by an additional six days. Still a believer in his own brinkmanship and indispensability, Sihanouk intended to use his Moscow and Beijing visits to urge both countries to pressure Hanoi to reduce its PAVN presence in Cambodia.[36] And in a late bit of wishful thinking, the prince was reportedly considering asking Moscow to provide Cambodia with a squadron of MiG-21 jets.[37] Even a novice student of international diplomacy could predict he was likely to be disappointed on all counts.

Worse for Sihanouk, his delay allowed his opponents more time to conspire. With their plan nearly reaching full boil, In Tam and his fellow assemblymen on 16 March made an initial, rather timid attempt to sanction Sihanouk. By this point, virtually no effort was being made to camouflage their intent to seek Sihanouk's ouster. Rising to her son's defense, Queen Kossamak summoned Lon Nol and Sirik Matak that same day and ordered the two to cease their scheming. Despite Lon Nol's reverence toward the queen, her plea fell on deaf ears.

That night, Oum Mannorine, the chief of police and Sihanouk's brother-in-law, began an eleventh-hour attempt to mobilize diehard royalists. Word leaked from their camp, however, and Lon Nol, for once showing gritty determination, moved decisively over the course of 17 March to detain more than two-dozen high-ranking Sihanouk sympathizers in the armed forces and government.

The next day, the National Assembly took its cue. During a morning plenary session, they railed against the prince, ladling charges of corruption against him and his cohorts. Immediately after lunch, they held a secret ballot to determine whether Sihanouk should be removed as chief of state. When the tally was counted, the results were unanimous: Sihanouk was out of a job. In accordance with provisions contained in the 1960 constitution, he was temporarily replaced by President of the Assembly Cheng Heng pending an election. Though the move was to be commonly described as a coup d'état in the media, the overthrow followed legislative procedures and was more accurately an engineered vote of no-confidence.

Sihanouk, of course, did not see it that way. He was en route to the Moscow airport when Soviet premier Alexei Kosygin broke news of the putsch. Boarding his flight for Beijing via Siberia, Sihanouk was seething. With no more tightropes to walk, the gloves were about to come off.

2. Finger in the Dike

It is said that Cambodians enjoy a good conspiracy, and the events of 18 March provided extremely fertile territory. The dust had barely settled in Phnom Penh when a chorus, led by Sihanouk himself, blamed Washington—and especially the Central Intelligence Agency (CIA)—for orchestrating the change in governments. To be sure, the sacking of Sihanouk had been telegraphed by the main conspirators to the point where even casual observers could plot the general trajectory of events. But to say that the United States was pulling the strings was almost certainly not the case.

This was true for several reasons. First, the U.S. government could not but have been generally satisfied with the direction Cambodian foreign policy had taken over the previous year with Sihanouk at the helm. After all, the fickle prince had mended fences to the point of restoring diplomatic ties in August 1969. In December of that year, Sihanouk penned an article in the official journal *Sangkum* in which he stated that the United States could not afford to withdraw from Southeast Asia and went on to make a thinly disguised appeal for the resumption of American aid to Cambodia.[1] During his rest cure in France at the start of 1970, he hinted that he wanted Chinese and Soviet help to get the North Vietnamese to greatly reduce, if not evacuate, their Cambodian sanctuaries. Though one might anticipate yet another about-face given his mercurial nature, and acknowledging the fact that many things were happening in Phnom Penh in spite of him and not because of him, from Washington's perspective Sihanouk seemed more palatable than perhaps at any time in half a decade.

Second, President Richard Nixon's White House papers reveal that Cambodia rated only scant mention during the critical days after the change in government. On the afternoon of 18 March, National Security Advisor Henry Kissinger met with Secretary of State William Rogers in an initial discussion about the overthrow of Sihanouk. "I think we should be very careful not to say anything until we know more about it," said Rogers succinctly. To this Kissinger agreed: "All we are saying is that we respect their neutrality and not another word."[2]

On the morning of 19 March, Kissinger called a meeting of the Washington Special Action Group (WSAG).[3] Although this was the first opportunity for key policymakers to discuss the changes in Phnom Penh, their attention was instead focused on the deteriorating situation in neighboring Laos. There, the government base at Long Tieng appeared ready to fall to a PAVN onslaught, and the

CIA—which was running one of the largest covert paramilitary operations in its history—was advocating the risky deployment of an infantry regiment from the Royal Thai Army (RTA) as a stopgap to harden the defenders. Nearly the entire meeting centered on the fate of Long Tieng, the proposed RTA intervention, and what impact this was going to have on the wider war effort in Laos.

Indeed, the only comment about Cambodia during this WSAG tryst came as an aside near the end. The United States should support Cambodia's neutrality, Special Assistant to the Secretary of State Theodore Eliot told others around the table, and not try to force Cambodia "into our camp."[4]

Later that afternoon, in a move that spoke volumes about what topped America's priorities in Indochina, the WSAG convened for a second time. Once again, Long Tieng and the RTA regiment monopolized the agenda; Cambodia never even came up for discussion.[5]

Outside of the WSAG, Kissinger that same afternoon penned a memorandum to President Richard Nixon on the fluid situation in Cambodia. In it, Kissinger lauded Sihanouk's domestic popularity and "tactical brilliance" and did not discount the possibility of the prince returning to Phnom Penh and successfully outflanking his challengers. He further noted that Lon Nol controlled "much of the lucrative smuggling trade with the communists," and though the general might adopt more pro-U.S. and pro-Thai policies he probably would not terminate the smuggling any time soon.[6]

Despite Kissinger's faint praise for Lon Nol, Nixon saw opportunity: "I want [CIA Director Richard] Helms to develop and implement a plan for maximum assistance to pro-U.S. elements in Cambodia," he penned in the margin of the memorandum. Kissinger added his own notation that he was to meet Helms four days hence to discuss Cambodia. Tellingly, Nixon's comments reveal it was he—not his advisers—who took the lead in pushing support for Lon Nol. The memo also betrays a certain lack of urgency on the part of Kissinger, who saw fit to wait an additional four days before he would bring up Nixon's rather unequivocal directive with Helms. Even then, when Kissinger and Helms finally met for the next WSAG meeting on 23 March, it was again the emergency in Laos—not Cambodia—that was the sole agenda item.[7]

Even though Kissinger and Helms had yet to place Cambodia on the front burner, the situation there was deteriorating with dizzying speed. Drawing first blood, the Cambodian military had mobilized against the PAVN enclaves along the eastern border. At the tip of their proverbial spear was the country's paltry air force, which soon registered nearly as many combat sorties as during its entire prior sixteen-year existence. Many of these initial missions were conducted by a small MiG-17 fleet, which delivered bombs and machine-gun fire against PAVN encampments in Svay Rieng province. The Cambodians also benefited from ad-hoc assistance by the Saigon government, which dispatched Douglas A-1 Skyraider aircraft beginning 20 March to support beleaguered Cambodian garrisons along their common frontier.[8]

Although such attacks on PAVN targets might have struck a nationalist chord among many Cambodians, very quickly the Lon Nol regime felt a backlash among pro-Sihanoukists. One week after the fall of the prince, rioting broke out in Kompong Cham. The following day, it was reported, Lon Nol's own brother, a policeman in that province, was disemboweled by a rampaging mob and had his liver eaten. With rumors that thousands of Sihanouk's peasant supporters were planning to converge on Phnom Penh, paratroopers were deployed to block two key bridges leading to the city.

Southeast of Phnom Penh, reinforcements from the Cambodian armed forces—now going by the French initials FANK—cautiously advanced toward Svay Rieng province during the first week of April.[9] Attempting to show some backbone near the border crossing at Bavet village, they resisted for a couple of days before shrinking back toward the capital.[10]

Far worse was to come. During the second week of April, PAVN launched a concerted blitz across the eastern half of the country. As of 17 April, FANK admitted to having lost the provinces of Kratie, Stung Treng, and Mondolkiri in their entirety, as well as eastern Kompong Cham and most of Svay Rieng.[11] PAVN had also cut off two garrison towns in the remote province of Ratanakiri, where the government had stationed a sizable military task force since the previous year.[12] Most disconcerting, a PAVN column on 19 April briefly pushed into the village of Saang, just 29 kilometers from Phnom Penh, causing panic in the capital.

All of this highlighted the glaring lack of preparedness—qualitatively and quantitatively—on the part of Lon Nol's military. True, the general enjoyed an early outpouring of goodwill among the younger masses (including university students), and an initial wave of 70,000 youths had enlisted to join the dozens of infantry brigades created overnight. Also, elementary and secondary schoolteachers were volunteering in droves for highly abbreviated military training, after which they graduated as so-called *assimilé* officers to command FANK's burgeoning ranks.[13]

But FANK's needs required fast, significant foreign help. Intuitively, Washington was a promising source. However, despite Nixon's clear desire expressed on 19 March to back Lon Nol, caution had set in among America's policymaking community. On 9 April, Major Lon Non, Lon Nol's influential younger brother and the head of the gendarmerie in Phnom Penh, met with a U.S. official in the city and made an initial pitch for acquiring American weapons.[14] Just one day later, Lloyd Rives, the U.S. chargé d'affaires that had arrived to head the reopened embassy the previous August, was complaining that no fewer than five persons from five different branches of the Cambodian government had made discrete appeals for aid—but none appeared to have an official stamp of approval from Lon Nol. All of them, lamented Rives, had generic requests for radios and weapons yet lacked any specificity as to the types or quantities required. Frustrated, Rives had urged Foreign Minister Yem Sambaur to first seek assistance from the French—who had maintained a military mission in Phnom Penh since independence—and underscored the reluctance of the United States to get involved, especially in any public manner.[15]

The following day, Assistant Secretary of State for East Asian and Pacific Affairs Marshall Green confirmed in a cable to Phnom Penh that Washington's position largely echoed the sentiment expressed by Rives. The Lon Nol government was emphasizing its continued neutrality, Green noted, and the United States agreed with this approach. American aid could constitute an additional provocation of PAVN, he reasoned, and Washington would still prefer that Cambodians seek military assistance from the French.[16]

But with the situation growing worse by the day, the Pentagon on a parallel track had started to brainstorm possible avenues of military support. Knowing that FANK was largely outfitted with communist small arms, Deputy Secretary of Defense David Packard on 10 April was ordered to discretely determine the amount of captured communist weapons in South Vietnam.[17] Five days later, General Creighton Abrams, commander of the U.S. Military Assistance Command in Vietnam (MACV), was authorized to directly query the South Vietnamese about these stockpiles.

In Washington, meantime, Secretary of State Rogers was still brimming with caution. "We must navigate between giving enough, quickly enough, to the Lon Nol government in order to contribute to its self-confidence as well as its capabilities," he cabled Rives on 15 April, "while on the other hand not doing so much as to embolden Cambodians to take excessively strong military actions against [PAVN] and to abandon attempts to negotiate for a peaceful and, realistically speaking, gradual withdrawal of [PAVN] forces."

Walking a tightrope, Rogers instructed Rives to tell the Cambodian foreign minister that several discrete assistance measures were to be taken over the short term. First, the South Vietnamese were being asked to collect 5,500 AK-47 rifles, along with ammunition, for a covert transfer along the border. Also, the United States would initiate overt medicine deliveries to Phnom Penh. And in addition, the United States would provide spare parts to bring Cambodia's aging fleet of North American T-28 Trojans (converted to prop-bombers) back to flightworthy condition.[18]

Left unstated was a far more significant means of assistance: Khmer Krom troops. As these soldiers have been the subject of conspiracy theories tied to the 18 March change in governments, some background is in order. Through the early 1960s, thousands of Khmer Serei guerrillas loyal to exiled Khmer Krom leader Son Ngoc Thanh had operated from border camps along the Thai and South Vietnamese frontiers. They were tolerated, if not occasionally assisted, by the governments in Saigon and Bangkok, neither of which was on good terms with Sihanouk.[19] There is no compelling evidence that the CIA, or any other part of the U.S. government, provided its own direct paramilitary assistance to the Khmer Serei.

Beginning in 1965, the South Vietnamese wing of the Khmer Serei decided to suspend its covert campaign against Cambodia and instead seek regular employment as paramilitary troops of the Civilian Irregular Defense Group (CIDG) fighting on behalf of the South Vietnamese government. The Thai-based wing of the Khmer Serei, meanwhile, continued to operate from three border bases with tacit approval from the Thai government.[20] But by late 1968, and continuing through early 1970, a steady stream of guerrillas from two of those Thai bases abandoned their cause and rallied to the Cambodian government. Most of those guerrillas were absorbed into the Cambodian army and stationed in the western part of the country. One of the more senior ralliers, Chu Bun Sang, was even commissioned as a major and put in command of an infantry battalion in Battambang province. Despite claims by Sihanouk, there is no evidence any former Khmer Serei guerrillas were in Phnom Penh on 18 March, or that their presence in western Cambodia played a role in swaying the main conspirators in the capital that month.

During late March, after Sihanouk had already been deposed, Khmer Serei guerrillas at Phnom Malai, their third and final base along the Thai border, rallied to the new Cambodian government. They were later grouped at Siem Reap and made the core of the so-called Special Brigade headed by Lek Sam Ouen, a former Khmer Serei leader from Phnom Malai. But by that time Sihanouk was already in exile and they had no impact on the end to the monarchy.[21]

Back in South Vietnam, former Khmer Serei had come to numerically dominate the paramilitary CIDG program in III Corps. Of these, 2,000 of the best were incorporated into the III Corps Mike Force, an elite CIDG formation headquartered at Long Hai that was the strategic reserve strike force for that military region. Except for artillery crews on loan from the South Vietnamese army, the rest of this Mike Force—totaling three regular battalions, two support battalions, a reconnaissance company, and a boat company—consisted entirely of ethnic Khmer Krom. Seventy members of the U.S. Army Special Forces, headed by Major Ola "Lee" Mize, were the cadre for this force.[22]

In the weeks immediately after the fall of Sihanouk, while Mize was operating along the South Vietnamese frontier with two battalions and the reconnaissance company, his Mike Force became the subject of high-level discussions in Phnom Penh and Washington. Back on 23 March, Australian Brigadier General F. P. "Ted" Serong, a counterinsurgency expert serving as a consultant for the Pentagon, had written a classified report brainstorming ways of assisting the Phnom Penh regime. Thinking outside of the box, one of Serong's proposals was to use 3,000 former Khmer Serei troops from South Vietnam to secure Sihanoukville. When Kissinger passed this report to Nixon on 9 April, the president was suitably impressed. "These may be way out ideas," he wrote in the margin to Kissinger, "but they do show some imagination." He then instructed National Security Advisor Kissinger to start collecting recommendations for assistance from the CIA, Department of State, and Pentagon.[23]

Serong's Khmer Serei option soon gained traction. On 18 April, General Abrams broached with General Earle Wheeler, outgoing Chairman of the Joint Chiefs of Staff, the possibility of sending 3,500 Khmer Krom troops to Cambodia. Three days later, a similar recommendation was sent from the Joint Chiefs of Staff to Secretary of Defense Melvin Laird. President Nixon, who by then was expressing fears that Lon Nol might fall any day, on 22 April approved a National Security Council request to send the Khmer Krom as soon as possible.[24]

At that point, Mize received a message in the field to return to Long Hai for an urgent mission: convert the III Corps Mike Force into a brigade prior to them being transferred to the Cambodian army. After returning the South Vietnamese artillery crews who were on loan, he quickly rearranged the rest of the Mike Force into four infantry battalions. Far harder was convincing the Khmer Krom that they would be heading to Cambodia—a country that few had ever visited—without their U.S. cadre. Clearly nervous about their prospects, the troops on 30 April transferred to Bien Hoa airbase and were then flown aboard South Vietnamese C-119 transports to Phnom Penh's Pochentong airbase. Now going by the name

2 Commando Brigade, they were placed in temporary barracks at the city's Olympic Stadium. Their deployment, senior Cambodian officials assured them, would be temporary.

As this was transpiring, the Pentagon had gone into overdrive planning a conventional cross-border assault against the PAVN enclaves inside Cambodia. As early as eight days after the change in governments, MACV had quietly drawn up contingency plans for striking at these PAVN base areas.[25] An initial MACV draft dated 30 March, which outlined a joint U.S.–South Vietnamese cross-border raid, was forwarded to Kissinger and Defense Secretary Laird on 3 April.[26] But it was not until 22 April that Nixon officially authorized planning for U.S. support during a South Vietnamese–led incursion. Under time pressure (the monsoons were starting in two months) and needing to maintain secrecy, all planning was kept from the Lon Nol government. Many U.S. unit commanders, in fact, were notified just two days prior to the onset of operations. On the evening of 30 April, the same day that the Khmer Krom brigade landed in Phnom Penh, Nixon announced the start of the offensive at a televised news conference.[27]

For the next two months, U.S. forces supported the South Vietnamese military during a series of airmobile and ground assaults along the southeastern frontier of Cambodia. Although the South Vietnamese did coordinate some of their efforts with FANK, the United States did not directly interface with the Cambodian military.

There was one exception, however. During the first week of May, MACV became aware of two isolated FANK garrisons—Ba Kev and Labang Siek—in the so-called Green Triangle of Ratanakiri province. Given the assignment of making contact with the garrisons, and determining whether the United States could provide assistance, was MACV's multiservice unconventional warfare organization, the Special Operations Group (MACVSOG).[28] After making initial contact, and determining the Cambodians welcomed help, a composite MACVSOG team under the command of Captain Steve Spoerry was landed at Ba Kev. Their support effort was codenamed Operation Stick.

The two garrisons, the Stick commandos quickly discovered, were in dismal shape. The resident FANK unit, known as Groupement Tactique 2 (Tactical Group 2), consisted of two infantry battalions armed with a mix of World War II–era rifles. In support were two Chinese-made 76mm field guns short of ammunition, some mortars, and a pair of U.S.-made half-tracks, also of World War II vintage. Commander of the group was Lieutenant Colonel Um Savuth, the same officer who until the previous year had coordinated the Hak Ly weapons shipments to PAVN sanctuaries. Still walking with a cane due to his head injury, he now was claiming his military decisions were derived from paranormal premonitions he received during dreams.

Working alongside the FANK troops, the MACVSOG team coordinated defenses around Ba Kev and called in U.S. airstrikes and gunships during frequent PAVN probes. Leading patrols around the garrison, they evacuated on one occasion five emaciated tribesmen from a nearby village that had been pressed into serving as coolies for the communists.[29] In addition, the team directed two nighttime C-123 ammunition drops, supplementing the sporadic supply flights into Ba Kev flown by the Cambodian air force.[30]

In the end, the resupply drops only delayed the inevitable. With American public opinion turning sour toward the Cambodian incursion, and the U.S. Congress threatening legislation to cut off funding for American military personnel in Cambodia, the Pentagon had already scheduled U.S. forces to withdraw from Cambodian soil by 30 June. Although the Green Triangle operation was covert, and could have been creatively exempted from the withdrawal, General Abrams on 2 June declared his opposition to further support after June. The WSAG concurred, and Rives was ordered to break the news to Lon Nol.[31]

The garrison's fate sealed, the MACVSOG team led an evacuation column out of Ba Kev on 23 June toward the South Vietnamese border. With the two half-tracks in the lead and hundreds of refugees in tow (three babies were born en route), they successfully crossed the frontier three days later.[32] Another four days after that, U.S. participation in the Cambodian incursion came to an end.

Sihanouk's rants aside, the one U.S. government entity that had been largely absent from Cambodian issues during the first two quarters of 1970 was the CIA.[33] In fact, the history of CIA involvement in Cambodia during the Sihanouk regime was one rife with setbacks magnified by the prince's wafer-thin skin. This dated back to the so-called Bangkok Plot of early 1959, which involved one of Sihanouk's erstwhile trusted advisers, Sam Sary. Two years before that, Sary had been sent to London as the Cambodian ambassador. But just six months later, he reportedly beat his mistress (ostensibly a domestic servant at the embassy) and sent her sobbing to the police. Recalled to Phnom Penh under a cloud, he rebranded himself as a pro-Western neutralist and announced his intent to enter opposition politics.

For Sihanouk, who had a low threshold for political dissent, Sary's lack of allegiance was intolerable. Compounding matters, at the opening of 1959 diplomats from the Chinese, French, and Soviet embassies all sought audiences with the prince to inform him that Sary was making contact in Bangkok with representatives from the Thai government. There were also indications that perennial dissident Son Ngoc Thanh had offered Sary a lukewarm embrace from South Vietnam. On 13 January, Sihanouk gave a speech exposing the scheme, but by that time Sary had fled to Thai exile.

In hindsight, Sary had made little headway because his liaisons were far from discrete. Like their counterparts from China, France, and the Soviet Union, American diplomats had also gotten wind of his scheming, and documents show they worked behind the scenes to get the South Vietnamese government to back away from whatever extralegislative plans Sary had in mind. But the fact that the U.S. embassy elected not to give forewarning about the plot to Phnom Penh—in contrast to the Chinese, French, and Soviets—had Sihanouk seething.[34]

The very next month, it was the turn of the flamboyant regional commander in Siem Reap province, General Dap Chhuon, to try his hand at rebellion. For years, the gaunt, ailing Dap Chhuon had been prone to treasonous tirades, only to back off with timely reaffirmations of his loyalty to Sihanouk. He was especially distressed by Cambodia's biased nonalignment and openly condemned Sihanouk's leftist foreign policy. Eased out of Phnom Penh to the less visible environs of Siem Reap, the general not only maintained his critical demeanor but also transformed himself into a veritable warlord and enforced brutal street justice among his constituency.[35]

Perhaps inspired by Sam Sary's stillborn plot or perhaps unable to further stomach Sihanouk's lip service to nonalignment, Dap Chhuon began to turn his criticisms into action. He already knew he could count on assistance from the Thai government, which had long been sending him feelers and, as a sign of support, were amenable to increasing the number of Khmer Serei guerrillas on their border fielded by Sihanouk's nemesis, Son Ngoc Thanh. At the same time, the South Vietnamese government, frustrated with Sihanouk's constant baiting and approving of the general's anticommunism, were agreeable to covert help.

In early February 1959, when Sihanouk issued invitations to attend the wedding of his eldest child, Dap Chhuon was the only regional commander to send his regrets. Instead, unmarked planes from South Vietnam arrived at the Siem Reap airfield with two radio transmitters (and two radio technicians) for making propaganda broadcasts and staying in touch with the South Vietnamese authorities. Saigon also turned over 270 kilograms in gold ingots from its treasury, which Dap Chhuon could theoretically use to buy support.[36]

Four days later, the CIA dipped its toes into the fray. Victor Matsui, a thirty-six-year-old case officer of Japanese descent, had already been stationed at the

U.S. embassy in Phnom Penh for two years when he headed to Siem Reap. There he met with Dap Chhuon's half-brother, Slat Peou, who was serving as a Siem Reap provincial legislator.[37] Matsui turned over to him yet another radio, this one for the conspirators to communicate with the CIA station at the U.S. embassy.

Just as with the Sam Sary plot, however, the Dap Chhuon conspiracy leaked like a sieve. Far from concealing the South Vietnamese shipments, the general had arranged welcoming committees composed of civil servants during their arrival. On 16 February, U.S. Ambassador Carl Strom lamented in a cable to Washington that the dispatch of radio equipment and gold bars from Saigon to Siem Reap must be common knowledge among many in Phnom Penh. No doubt sensing impending failure, he urged that the United States put pressure on the South Vietnamese to cease their support for Dap Chhuon.[38]

Hardly reflecting Strom's pessimism, Dap Chhuon edged closer to the brink. On 20 February, he sent a letter to Queen Kossamak saying that he was being forced into rebellion to save the country. For Sihanouk, this was the last straw. The following day, he dispatched infantry and armored cars up the main road to Siem Reap. The town was secured with little fanfare, and Dap Chhuon was later killed while trying to cross into Thailand.

On 26 February, Sihanouk flew to Siem Reap and held a triumphant press conference with many from the diplomatic corps in attendance. Significantly, he had captured the two Vietnamese radio operators as well as Slat Peou. During their subsequent trials (all three went before a public court on 30 September and were sentenced to death), they documented the assistance extended by South Vietnam as well as the CIA.[39] Although Matsui had left the country by then, the skittish Sihanouk was able to highlight the failed CIA hand in his intended ouster.

Three years later, the CIA experienced another Cambodian setback. In mid-1962, the CIA's station chief in Phnom Penh, Robert J. Myers, received a backchannel message from Saigon Station telling him that a South Vietnamese agent would be arriving shortly in the Cambodian capital. The agent in question was a South Vietnamese army sergeant named Le Cong Hoa. Born in Phnom Penh, Hoa spoke fluent Cambodian and French. Although technically out of its jurisdiction, Office 45, the South Vietnamese unit responsible for clandestine agent penetrations into North Vietnam, was given the job of running one source inside the Cambodian capital. On account of his background, Hoa was selected and given the codename Adonis.[40]

When informed of Adonis, Myers protested sharply. A longtime Asia hand with previous postings in China, Indochina, Indonesia, Japan, and Taiwan, he suspected that Office 45 and its parent unconventional warfare and intelligence group, South Vietnam's Presidential Security Office, lacked discretion and it was only a matter of time before the operation came to an embarrassing end. Despite Myers's concern, his superiors in the CIA's Far East Division overrode his reluctance and Adonis was allowed to slip into Phnom Penh.

At that point, Phnom Penh Station compounded the problem with its own gaffe. One of the clandestine projects conducted by Myers and his case officers was the recruitment of ethnic Chinese Cambodians who could visit the PRC as legal travelers (there were regular commercial flights between Phnom Penh and Beijing) and report back on the economic and social situation in the Chinese capital. Safe houses in Phnom Penh were used for meetings with these ethnic Chinese agents and their CIA handlers, but in a display of poor tradecraft they allowed Adonis to share one of those facilities.

As Myers had predicted, it was not long before Adonis was exposed and arrested. Worse, the Cambodian authorities had tracked him to one of the CIA's safe houses. Breaking in during an inopportune moment, they detained Kwang Chu, a CIA officer of Chinese descent who handled some of the legal travelers to Beijing. Chu was held for ten days—during which time his finger nails were pulled out—then expelled.[41]

The prince's reaction, predictably, was deafening. "Sihanouk panicked," recalled Myers, "but he was unsettled quite easily over most things."[42] The Cambodians hounded members of the CIA station for the next three years and began to monitor closely those pro-Taiwanese ethnic Chinese from among whom the CIA had recruited its agents. By the time the U.S. embassy was shuttered in May 1965, what few CIA assets that remained in Cambodia were instructed to post their information to accommodation addresses in Hong Kong.[43]

Without the luxury of a diplomatic post inside the country, CIA efforts in Cambodia were severely challenged for the ensuing four years. This made it especially difficult for the agency to quantify the extent of Cambodia's growing support to PAVN. For Washington policymakers, this was an issue of paramount importance: if PAVN's logistical corridor to South Vietnam primarily meandered down the Ho Chi Minh Trail, as CIA analysts were forcefully arguing, then interdiction efforts needed to remain focused in the Laotian panhandle. But if a significant portion was channeled through Sihanoukville, as some in the Pentagon felt, it put the lie to Sihanouk's neutralist posturing and demanded a greater interdiction effort be focused along the Cambodian frontier.

To shed light on this, the CIA's Directorate of Operations had extended agent networks into Cambodia from neighboring stations. The resultant patchwork of first- and secondhand sources—from Cambodian trucking employees to pur-

U.S. Ambassador to Laos G. McMurtrie Godley reviews the first battalion of Cambodian troops at PS 18, circa September 1970. Left to right: Len Gmirkin (CIA chief of base, Pakse), CIA officer James Dunn, FANK Lieutenant Colonel Lim Sisaath, and Ambassador McMurtrie Godley. (Courtesy James Dunn)

chasing agents for the Cambodian army to French port advisers—offered anecdotal pieces to the puzzle. But those pieces were often contradictory and always incomplete. And in some cases, like when the CIA's Hong Kong Station staged the coerced recruitment of Lon Nol's self-professed business partner, there were lingering doubts about his bona fides.[44]

In the end, even though a multitude of clandestine sources by early 1969 were indicating that Sihanoukville was a major transshipment point for PAVN weaponry, CIA analysts back in Langley, Virginia, found the collective evidence short of convincing. Weapons were flowing through Sihanoukville, the analysts acknowledged, but they incorrectly insisted the Ho Chi Minh Trail was the more important conduit. When asked what could be done to decrease the flow of even its lower estimates, the CIA was vexed. Bribing Cambodian military officers would not work, Helms told Kissinger in March 1969, because the bribes would likely pale in comparison to the profits they were reaping from smuggling.[45]

In theory, the CIA's job of penetrating Cambodia should have been simplified after diplomatic relations were restored in August 1969. But in an unusual move meant to assuage the flighty Sihanouk, the influential Senate majority leader, Mike Mansfield (who enjoyed good rapport with the prince and had visited Phnom Penh that same month), promised that no CIA personnel would be stationed in Cambodia. "Mansfield told Sihanouk that it would not be a 'large' embassy," recalled one CIA officer. "That basically meant no intelligence presence and maintaining a very low profile."[46]

Then in March 1970 Sihanouk was suddenly gone. In an initial memorandum about Cambodia sent five days after the change in governments, CIA Director Helms told Kissinger that he advocated opening a CIA station in Phnom Penh as soon as possible.[47] Bureaucratic foot-dragging ensued, however, leading an impatient Nixon on 31 March to demand the immediate deployment of CIA personnel, especially a communications officer, to the Cambodian capital.[48]

As a stopgap of sorts, the CIA ordered a seasoned officer with prior Phnom Penh experience to quietly slip into Cambodia for a brief fact-finding tour during the second week of April. A summary from the highlight of his trip—a clandestine meeting with a Cambodian government bureaucrat, reportedly the CIA's best-placed agent in the country—was conveyed to Nixon on 15 April. Three days later, the officer returned to Washington and gave a personal briefing to Kissinger; by that time, however, many of the agent's observations had been superseded by events and none came across as especially revealing.[49]

Such limited, tardy insights hardly satiated the White House. Unfortunately, the CIA was still facing bureaucratic hurdles to establish its Phnom Penh Station. On 16 April, Helms told Kissinger that he had already selected a potential station chief and communications officer—but the State Department was balking over the deployment due to a "problem of real estate and room."[50]

By the following day, Nixon's patience had fully worn thin. Exasperated by the CIA's glacial response, and perhaps sensing resistance among the foreign policymaking community to share his enthusiasm for the new Cambodian government, he unleashed at Kissinger over the phone:

> Lon Nol is it and I would urge widespread demonstrations against Sihanouk. . . . Get Helms' radio to broadcast in there that Sihanouk is coming with North Vietnamese liberators. I want a report on my desk at 4:00 with his ideas. . . . I want everyone in this government to know we are supporting the government in power. There is no possibility of our supporting Sihanouk and we are supporting Lon Nol. Tell Helms to have printed one million leaflets with North Vietnam and a picture of Sihanouk saying "Liberate Cambodia." Get my point?[51]

Nixon's pronouncement left little wiggle room. On 18 April, Kissinger sought out the most senior State Department official in town—Deputy Assistant Secretary of State for East Asian and Pacific Affairs Jonathon Moore—and told him to

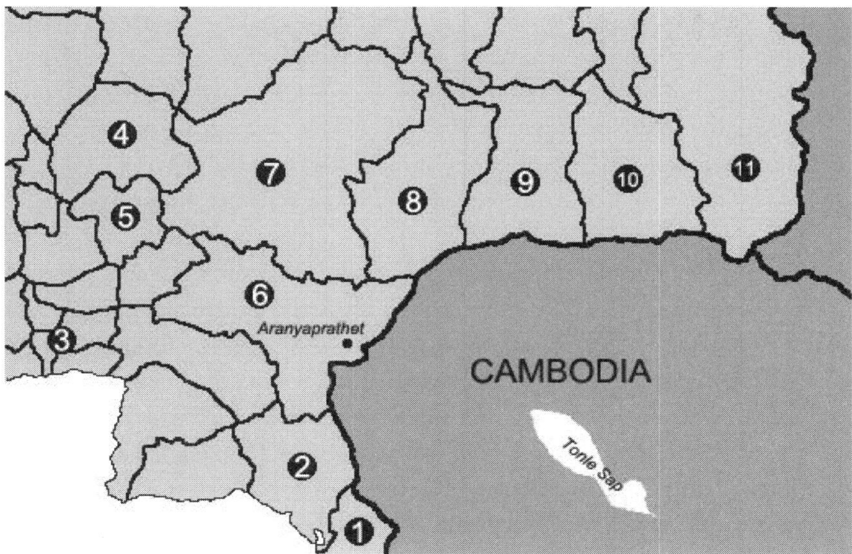

Thai provinces bordering Cambodia: 1. Trat, 2. Chanthaburi, 3. Bangkok, 4. Lopburi, 5. Saraburi, 6. Prachinburi, 7. Nakhon Ratchasima, 8. Buriram, 9. Surin, 10. Sisaket, 11. Ubon Ratchathani.

slash through the red tape and make immediate provisions for the two CIA officers to get to Phnom Penh. For good measure, Kissinger three days later got Secretary of State Rogers on the phone and told him that the CIA would also be secretly handing over $10 million to Lon Nol to bolster the general's hand.[52]

Nixon was not the only one looking to fast-track CIA operations in Cambodia. Across the border to the north, the CIA station in Laos, too, was eyeing a potential role. There the United States supported that kingdom's royalist, ostensibly neutral government in its struggle against communist Pathet Lao insurgents backed by a major PAVN presence. And while the Pentagon underwrote the regular, rather ineffectual Laotian armed forces, the CIA paid for, trained, and advised a parallel, robust guerrilla army that arguably represented the agency's largest paramilitary operation to that time. To manage its guerrilla campaign, Vientiane Station ran five substations (known as units) in Nam Yu, Luang Prabang, Long Tieng, Savannakhet, and Pakse.

The southernmost of these, Pakse Unit, was focused on securing the strategic Bolovens Plateau and, east of that, putting pressure on the Ho Chi Minh Trail.

To do this, the unit fielded a range of road-watching and intelligence-gathering teams and, for offensive operations, Special Guerrilla Unit (SGU) battalions. They staged from a string of remote, hardened outposts that featured their own small airfields, each known as a Pakse Site (PS). One of these camps, PS 18, located 43 kilometers up the Mekong from Pakse, acted as the unit's primary training base with a wide curriculum for team and SGU instruction, as well as communications and medical courses.

As it turned out, the Lao commander of PS 18, Lieutenant Colonel Khamphet Boua, had unique ties to Cambodia. The product of a Cambodian mother and Italian father, he had been born Roland Guzimetazi. With an ear for languages—he was fluent in Lao, Cambodian, English, and French—and sharp intellect, Khamphet's network of contacts across southern Laos extended to the family of Prince Boun Oum Na Champassac, a key powerbroker from the Pakse vicinity.

But it was Khamphet's contacts in Cambodia—he had been raised in the border province of Stung Treng—that held special significance in March 1970. One week after the fall of Sihanouk, Khamphet lobbied Pakse Unit to travel to Phnom Penh on a solo fact-finding junket to see if he could find any well-connected classmates. He received quick approval all the way up to Vientiane Station Chief Larry Devlin, though his trip carried a caveat. "He was under orders not to make any commitments to the Cambodians," recalled CIA officer James Dunn. "But merely to pique their interest."[53]

Taking an Air France flight from Bangkok, Khamphet entered Cambodia and went silent for almost a month. Then one Sunday afternoon in late April, Dunn received a single-sideband radio message from Khong Island on the Cambodian frontier: Khamphet was asking to be picked up, along with some unidentified "friends."

To the surprise of Pakse Unit, Khamphet's friends proved to be a windfall. Heading a twenty-six-man Cambodian delegation to Khong Island was Major Lon Non, the younger brother of Lon Nol, who had been the first person to broach the subject of American military aid to Cambodia back on 9 April. Also present was Tep Khunnah, a dashing businessman and politician who hailed from the same province as Lon Nol.

Whisked to PS 18, Lon Non and his entourage were feted by Prince Boun Oum and the camp's CIA training staff. As Lon Non claimed to have the ear of his brother, the CIA used the opportunity to plant the idea of Cambodian and Laotian troops pooling their efforts against PAVN. Specifically, it was hoped that Cambodia would see Laos as a frontline state and consider the potential for anticommunist military cooperation. With Lon Non's interest suitably

Lieutenant General Robert Cushman, deputy director of the CIA, reviews Cambodian troops at PS 18, circa November 1970. Behind him (in white) is Hugh Tovar, the CIA station chief in Laos. (Courtesy Hugh Tovar)

piqued, the Cambodian delegation left PS 18 in good spirits and returned via Khong Island.

During the last week of April, about the same time Lon Non visited Laos, the CIA at long last opened Phnom Penh Station. Chosen as station chief was John Stein, a thirty-eight-year-old French-speaking, Yale-educated intelligence officer with prior posts in Belgium, the Democratic Republic of the Congo, and Cameroon. He was serving at the CIA training compound in Williamsburg, Virginia, when tapped by Helms for the Cambodian assignment. He recalled the urgency of the mission:

> They wanted someone who had never served in the Far East (especially in Vietnam or Cambodia) and spoke French. I saw Helms at about 1000 when he had just come from the White House. I said I would gladly go to Phnom Penh but had no clothes. Someone called my wife to tell her to pack a trunk of clothes, but she was off making a tourist visit somewhere. The state police found her, gave the message, and she packed the trunk after the police drove her back with sirens blaring. It was flown to Andrews Air Force Base,

> arriving beside Air Force Two about the same time I did. I was airborne in Air Force Two—alone—at about 1400 for Bangkok via Anchorage and Tokyo. I then went commercial to Phnom Penh. Twenty-four hours after my arrival, 1 May, we were on line to Washington, for two communications guys with equipment had been dispatched and arrived the same day I did. As best I know, I was and remain the only fellow deployed as was I.

Given the dynamic situation in Phnom Penh, Stein hit the ground running. One of his earliest tasks was to accurately, albeit belatedly, quantify the amount of arms that had been smuggled through Sihanoukville. Perhaps the best source for this was the senior Cham in the Cambodian military, Lieutenant Colonel Les Kosem. A longtime paratrooper, Kosem had shot to prominence after setting a national freefalling record in 1957.[54] As a captain he became a trusted confidant of Lon Nol, and the two conspired in 1960 to create the Champa Liberation Front, intended to put pressure on the South Vietnamese government. Four years after that the pair lent a clandestine push during the creation of FULRO, and both helped instigate FULRO's September 1964 hilltribe uprising in South Vietnam's Central Highlands.[55]

In 1966, Lon Nol gave his Cham colleague another sensitive assignment. Along with Um Savuth, the two were named cochairmen of the Special Transportation Committee. This secret military unit acted as liaison for the PRC arms delivered at Sihanoukville and warehoused at a special depot in Kompong Speu. They then interfaced with the Hak Ly Trucking Company to run convoys to the PAVN border enclaves.

Much like Savuth, Kosem did not seem to have a problem playing both sides. Wearing a second hat as the commander of the Airborne Half-Brigade in 1969, he sent one of his parachute battalions to Mondolkiri province as part of the initial effort to probe PAVN positions in the northeast quadrant of the kingdom.[56] So on one hand he was a prime mover behind the Sihanoukville logistical pipeline, while on the other his paratroopers were staging some of the earliest clashes with PAVN. In an added layer of duplicity, Kosem's brother-in-law, Hussein Abdul, had made contact with CIA officers in South Vietnam starting in June 1968 and began to feed them anecdotal data about the activities at Sihanoukville.[57]

Once there was the change in government, the CIA directly approached Les Kosem. Ever pragmatic, he proved amenable to cooperate. In early July 1970, Phnom Penh Station conducted an initial debriefing of the lieutenant colonel. Kosem not only provided his personal recollections; in August he granted access to complete files on the Sihanoukville transshipments that he had secretly hoarded at his residence.[58]

What Kosem revealed was shocking. Rather than the trickle claimed by CIA analysts, Sihanoukville had handled 70 percent of the arms funneled to the lower provinces of South Vietnam. This revelation turned on its head the common wisdom about the role played by the Ho Chi Minh Trail corridor, and obviously it called into question U.S. military strategy that centered on disrupting the logistical flow down the Laotian panhandle. When informed of this critical, prolonged misreading, Nixon was livid, and in front of his Foreign Intelligence Advisory Board he called it one of the "worst records ever compiled by the intelligence community."[59]

During this same time frame, other CIA stations were moving forward with paramilitary assistance schemes for Cambodia.[60] One of the plans involved the pool of 800,000 ethnic Cambodians residing in Thailand. Left behind after the borders of the Khmer empire receded generations earlier, these Cambodians lived in an arc along the seven Thai provinces spanning the Cambodian frontier. They even constituted the majority of the population in Buriram and Surin provinces, where most worked as farmers eking out a simple existence in the arid soil. Although renowned as peaceful citizens nominally respectful toward the Thai monarchy, few Thai-Cambodians had integrated into Thai society; most clung to their Cambodian identity and spoke only Cambodian.

Eyeing this diaspora, the WSAG on 12 May 1970 first discussed the idea of recruiting Thai-Cambodians for use in western Cambodia.[61] Their initial plan called for two regiments to be trained in Thailand: one consisting of Cambodians sent from FANK, the other composed entirely of Thai-Cambodians recruited from inside Thailand. The idea was to provide "covert preparation" for the regiments, thereby keeping the U.S. hand in training and financing concealed.[62]

Over the second half of the month, changes to this original proposal ensued. First, the idea of sending one regiment from FANK was dropped; instead, both regiments were now to consist of Thai-Cambodians recruited in the border provinces. Second, with the future looking bleak for the Phnom Penh government as of late May, the United States weighed asking Thailand to make an interim deployment of two existing RTA regiments—much like their rushed dispatch of a regiment to Long Tieng in Laos during March.[63] Third, plans were discussed about shipping two more RTA regiments to its Black Panther Division in

South Vietnam, then using these additional units to make forays into eastern Cambodia.[64]

Very quickly, however, problems began to multiply. Paying for the Thai-Cambodian regiments required some imaginative accounting sleight-of-hand to pass funds between the Pentagon and CIA. Worse, congressional limitations dictated that the United States could not legally pay for any RTA regiments to serve as a stopgap in Cambodia.[65]

In addition, maintaining the covert nature of the Thai-Cambodian regiments became infinitely more difficult on 1 June when Prime Minister Thanom Kittakachorn of Thailand gave a press conference on the subject. The Thai government was committed to send 1,000 Thai-Cambodians to Cambodia, Thanom announced, with their equipment coming courtesy of the United States.[66]

Despite this exposure, some progress was realized over the summer. With the situation in Phnom Penh somewhat stabilizing, it no longer became necessary to consider any emergency deployment of RTA units. For the two Thai-Cambodian regiments, meantime, some 1,000 volunteers had already been gathered by mid-June.[67] In fact, they were Thai-Cambodian in name only: Only half were ethnic Cambodians recruited from Surin and Buriram provinces; the other half was a mix of ethnic Thai veterans from the Korea and Vietnam conflicts. All had been ushered in to a makeshift tent encampment 12 kilometers outside Prachinburi, a provincial capital halfway between Bangkok and the Cambodian border. Acting as their instructor cadre were two teams, one from the RTA Special Forces and one from the U.S. Army Special Forces headed by Major Gene Earlywine.

As training commenced on 1 July, the financing issue was debated for another month. Not until early August was it decided that the Pentagon would transfer funds to the CIA to cover all costs through the first three months of deployment to Cambodia. After that, just like the former Khmer Serei CIDG dispatched from South Vietnam, the Thai-Cambodian regiments would be officially folded into FANK.[68]

Then on 3 September, with deployment just weeks away, Cambodia balked. Apparently unable to move beyond historical animosities and suspicions, the Lon Nol government informed the U.S. embassy that it would not agree to the deployment of any Thai-Cambodian unit on Cambodian soil except in a dire emergency. In a newspaper interview six days later, Thailand's Foreign Minister Thanat Khoman confirmed that no volunteers were heading to Cambodia for the time being.[69]

At Prachinburi, the Thai and American instructors called for the volunteers to assemble. By that time, they had already settled on an unofficial name—the Yellow Tiger Brigade—for the two planned regiments. To that date, however, only two battalions had taken shape: The Thai-Cambodians had been gathered into one battalion, codenamed BP 41; the Korea and Vietnam veterans were grouped into the second, codenamed BP 42.[70] But before any of them had stepped foot in Cambodia, the Yellow Tigers were unceremoniously told to go home pending further notice.[71]

Concurrent with the fits and starts experienced by the Yellow Tigers, a second Cambodian paramilitary program was taking shape in neighboring Laos. The seeds for this had first been planted during Major Lon Non's unscheduled visit to PS 18 in late April. The following month, a camouflaged C-47 from the Royal Lao Air Force landed at Pochentong airbase. Inside was Prince Boun Oum, himself a longtime acquaintance of Lon Nol, who had secretly assembled a delegation from his native south—General Phasouk Somply Rasphakdi, Finance Minister Sisouk Na Champassac, administrative officer Khammay Bounnouvong, and Pakse guerrilla chief Soutchay Vongsavanh—and flown in to discuss potential anticommunist military cooperation.[72] Recounted Soutchay:

> We were taken for an audience with Lon Nol and his brother, Major Lon Non, at the Presidential Palace. All talks were conducted in French, and we were treated to a huge dinner. On our side, we asked for the Cambodian army to station two or three battalions in southern Laos. Our reasoning was that the North Vietnamese would be coming south into Cambodia in increasing numbers, so it would be in Cambodia's interest to fight them while they were still inside Laos. Lon Nol said to us, "*Ils vont se casser*" ("They [PAVN] are going to break"). He rejected our proposal.[73]

Although Boun Oum's appeal for Cambodian battalions had fallen flat, the CIA's Vientiane Station was pressing ahead with its own operation aimed at Cambodia. Part of this effort centered on a clandestine radio station allegedly representing the National United Front of Kampuchea (Front Uni National du Kampuchea, or FUNK), the communist-dominated Cambodian guerrilla coalition proclaimed by Sihanouk on 5 May for the purpose of ousting Lon Nol.[74] When Radio Hanoi that spring announced that the Voice of FUNK would begin broadcasting on 1 August, the CIA took its cue to launch immediately a black station with the same name.

To begin, most of the station's scripts were written in Vientiane, many incorporating disinformation specifically crafted around the historical animosity between Khmer and Vietnamese.[75] Some of the material, for example, contained admissions by Sihanouk that PAVN and the Viet Cong were on Cambodian soil (a fact the real Sihanouk had never admitted to domestic audiences), that PAVN had been responsible for damage to the Angkor Wat temple (a travesty for which Sihanouk allegedly accepted responsibility), and that Sihanouk advocated Khmer girls sleeping with Vietnamese soldiers to abet the revolutionary cause. Other scripts claimed Sihanouk's FUNK was "governed by the thoughts of Chairman Mao" and detailed how the deposed prince had persecuted his current allies, the communist Khmer Rouge, during the late 1960s.

Completed scripts were taken down to Pakse Unit, where a case officer had been specifically stationed at PS 18 to oversee the production of the taped broadcasts. Two Cambodians were dispatched to help. One, a fluent English-speaker named Ven Mom, acted as translator and lead commentator. The second, a man named Sunnary, had a high-pitched voice that was a near-identical copy of Sihanouk's distinctive whine; he doubled on the tapes as the exiled monarch. Cambodian singers and even a seven-man orchestra were periodically flown in from Phnom Penh to add cultural flavor.

Once the tapes were finished, they were sent to a shortwave transmitting station atop a plateau 25 kilometers north of Pakse. From there the fake Voice of FUNK took to the air three times a day. Though exposed as a fraud in August—when the real FUNK radio station based in southern China began broadcasting—the CIA's disinformation channel continued for another year. As a parting shot, the last transmission had Sihanouk admitting he had fallen seriously ill.

Another part of Vientiane Station's efforts were directed toward posting Cambodian troops in Laos. Though Lon Nol seemed coy to the idea when it was raised by Prince Boun Oum, this was because he had already given the nod to a CIA plan to deploy Cambodian SGU battalions to southern Laos. On 27 May, the WSAG signaled its own approval of the project.[76] Though an impatient Kissinger on 10 July lamented that plans still had not ranged beyond the discussion phase,[77] shortly thereafter it received an unexpected boost. Asked to sound out Laos's Prime Minister Souvanna Phouma about the prospect of having Cambodians on Lao soil, U.S. Ambassador G. McMurtrie Godley on 23 July was brimming with enthusiasm: "If more Cambodian SGUs were desired, it could be arranged . . . Souvanna didn't mind; in fact, he would be delighted. Souvanna regarded the Cambodians as 'brown folk,' similar to the Lao, while the South Vietnamese were 'yellow folk.'"[78]

With this racially tinged push from the Laotian prime minister, Washington set aside $4.8 million for four Cambodian SGU battalions in a CIA-managed project codenamed Copper.[79] The plan was to have the battalions positioned on the hotly contested Bolovens Plateau; from there, they would theoretically make eastern forays to slice at the Ho Chi Minh Trail and disrupt PAVN traffic before it arrived in southern battlefields. In doing so, Copper would be the Nixon Doctrine in its purest form: friendly governments—in Laos and Cambodia—taking primary responsibility in providing manpower for their own defense against a communist aggressor, and in this case sharing manpower across borders.

Even factoring out nepotism, it was hard not to take notice of Major Lon Non. Described in a U.S. embassy memo as a "man of unusual energy and initiative in a society in which these qualities are rare," the activist, ever-conspiring younger brother of Lon Nol carried weight and influence well beyond his rank.[80] When the CIA was looking for quick, discrete approval for Project Copper, it came as no surprise that it was to Lon Non that they turned.

As expected, Lon Non lent fast support. Trouble was, the major had no troops of his own to deploy in Laos. As of August 1970, he had been named commander of a new 15 Brigade, but its five battalions had yet to be filled. Not until early the following month had he pooled sufficient manpower to begin fleshing out an initial pair of battalions. Although these included some Khmer Krom who had experience fighting in South Vietnam, most were raw recruits signed up in Phnom Penh.

That September, both battalions were earmarked for Copper and shuttled north aboard Air America C-123 transports (which had their U.S. flags painted out for the occasion, apparently to disguise their U.S. affiliation).[81] Landing at Pakse, the Cambodians were transferred to landing craft and steamed up the Mekong to PS 18, which from that point was devoted exclusively to the Cambodian project.[82]

Upon arrival, the troops found PS 18 awash in construction activity. Its airfield was being lengthened especially for Copper. And because it would not be practical to send the Cambodians back to Cambodia for medical treatment, the CIA was building a hospital complete with surgical room, emergency room, basic laboratory, and X-ray facilities. Meantime, a CIA medical officer had been sent to Manila to recruit surgeons, an anesthetist, and nurses.[83]

Selected by Lon Non to command Copper on the FANK side was Lieutenant Colonel Lim Sisaath. He was an inspired choice on several counts. A native of the crossroads province of Stung Treng (like the commander of PS 18, Khamphet Boua), he spoke excellent Lao and had extended family spanning both sides of the border, including the Pakse mayor. He also hailed from the same academy class as Lon Non and was a trusted associate. A military lawyer in his younger years, Sisaath had joined the paratroopers and became an airborne battalion commander under Sihanouk's reign. In 1969, he had served as chief of operations at the Ministry of National Defense. And after the March 1970 change in governments, he was briefly named commander of the Stung Treng Military Sub-Division before it was overrun by PAVN.

Now the ranking FANK officer for Copper, Sisaath was met at PS 18 by a pair of CIA case officers (a third was assigned in November). One of them, Steve Spence, oversaw the next three months of basic training: "I was assisted by six Khmer Krom instructors who had previously been in the South Vietnamese army. One of them, who had Mike Force experience, had a perfect black accent and would often say, 'Hey baby, move your ass!'"[84]

The training phase for the two raw battalions progressed with little incident. Near the end of their instruction in November, PS 18 was visited by the CIA deputy director, Lieutenant General Robert Cushman. Turning out in formation, the first battalion looked sharp enough. But the recently arrived chief of Pakse Unit, Carl Jenkins, felt reason for pause. "In my experience, there is usually an inverse relationship between gifts and competence," he explained. "When a counterpart comes bearing a lavish gift, it usually is meant to compensate for serious incompetence." The Cambodians, Jenkins noted with concern, had presented him with a magnificent, room-sized bas-relief rubbing from the Angkor Wat.

By year's end, both battalions graduated from PS 18. As yet untested in battle, and with the Lao hard-pressed for reinforcements, it was decided to employ the Cambodians on a live-fire field training exercise on the southeastern Bolovens Plateau. Accordingly, one battalion was loaded into landing craft and steamed back to Pakse. On New Year's Day, an armada of U.S. Air Force CH-53C helicopters lifted all 470 troops to an abandoned outpost known as PS 43. Eight days later, the battalion was shuttled 20 kilometers east, retaking another lost post without resistance.

Two weeks after that, the second Khmer battalion joined them on the Bolovens. The first battalion, meanwhile, had suffered two dead in the course of brief skirmishes and was loudly demanding a return to PS 18. Soon after, PAVN struck at night, inflicting eighty casualties on the second battalion over the next twelve hours. By the following day, all remaining Cambodian troops were retreating on foot to the town of Paksong and from there were lifted back to PS 18.

As if its middling combat performance was not enough, the first battalion was flown back to Phnom Penh for a brief rest—and promptly deserted. Worse, the second battalion decided it had enough of combat and refused to turn out at PS 18; for their mutinous behavior, they were all sent packing back to Phnom Penh.

Taking the fall for the collapse of Project Copper was Lim Sisaath. Rarely venturing into the field, Sisaath was correctly accused of having lost control over his men. Worse, his deputy, the half-Chinese Yu Peng Eang, was caught smuggling heroin from Laos to Cambodia—almost certainly at the insistence of Lon Non. Both were immediately relieved of their Copper assignments.

Looking to restart Copper from scratch, an appeal was made directly to Lon Nol in early February 1971. The general appeared amenable to sending two more battalions, but on 8 February he was temporarily sidelined by a stroke. As the general recuperated, word came back from Phnom Penh on 13 February that the Cambodians were showing little urgency in recruiting the second installment of Copper infantrymen.[85]

Even though Lon Non had fallen short earlier, the CIA once more saw fit to lean on him. By that time he had been promoted to lieutenant colonel and had already brought his 15 Brigade nearly up to strength. Under rather rushed conditions, he selected two trained battalions for a Bolovens assignment during March.[86] Remembers a soldier in one of the battalions:

> 15 Brigade was on a sweep southwest of Phnom Penh when we were recalled to the capital and given three days to prepare for an unspecified operation. We were flown into Pakse aboard C-123s, then by helicopter directly to [the southeastern edge of the Bolovens]. We stayed there a little past the Cambodian New Year in mid-April, when we were treated to a special meal of ox stomach cooked for us in the field. During the entire time [of our deployment], we had some harassing fire, but nobody was killed.[87]

During this same period, the second Cambodian battalion maneuvered between two other Bolovens outposts without encountering serious opposition. There, both battalions remained until late April when Lon Non—itching to get his men home for a planned operation south of the capital—repatriated all of the Cambodian infantrymen and brought Copper to a premature stop.[88]

Not all Cambodians left PS 18, however. Back in September 1970, Lon Non had recruited personnel for Khmer reconnaissance teams slated to be trained in Laos. By year's end, 15 detachments—codenamed Toro Teams—were undergoing instruction at PS 18. According to an initial plan, the Toro Teams would be deployed east of the Bolovens to gather intelligence in support of the Copper infantry battalions. But by the time they graduated in March 1971, the Cambodian presence on the Bolovens was in its final weeks. Shifting focus, a few of the Toro Teams were choppered into Cambodia's Stung Treng and Ratanakiri provinces, where they remained in the field for a month reporting on PAVN trail traffic. In early June, six remaining Toro Teams were repatriated from PS 18 to Phnom Penh for integration into FANK, all but bringing to an end serious military cooperation between Laos and Cambodia.[89]

Despite Lon Non's increasingly spotty track record, the CIA attempted cooperation with him on one other paramilitary venture. In early 1971, while 15 Brigade was still on the Bolovens and the Toro Teams were still being prepared at PS 18, the CIA devised a plan for Lon Non to pick 300 Cambodians to be formed into Commando Raider Teams (CRTs) at Phitsanulok training camp in Thailand. The CRT program, started by Vientiane Station in 1969, had involved intensive sabotage and intelligence training for select Lao teams. Like the Toro Teams, the CIA hoped that the Cambodian CRTs could be employed along the Ho Chi Minh Trail east of the Bolovens. More versatile than the Toros, the Commando Raiders (as their name suggested) would be capable of staging raids rather than only passive reconnaissance.

Training for the Cambodians at Phitsanulok did not start until May 1971. By that late hour, Copper was history and the Toro Teams were facing premature cancellation. Continuing nevertheless, CRT instruction—spanning everything from demolitions to land navigation to small-arms tactics—took place over the next three months.

When it finished, the scales had fallen from the CIA's eyes and they had fully soured toward Lon Non. "He has intense personal ambition restrained neither by good political judgment nor moral scruples," stated one Department of State assessment.[90] "He was an unguided missile," concluded CIA Station Chief John Stein.[91]

Looking to cut its losses, the CIA sent the Phitsanulok contingent packing back to Phnom Penh. Reviewing the group at a ceremony in the Olympic Stadium, Lon Non commissioned them all as lieutenants and merged them into his 15 Brigade.[92] Not surprisingly, none were ever properly utilized in their intended commando role.[93]

3. Finger on the Pulse

Lon Non's shortcomings were many, but they were nothing compared to those of his brother Lon Nol. After squandering the nationalistic euphoria following his March 1970 rise to power, the general by 1971 had left the fickle Cambodian public pondering his idiosyncrasies. What they found did not greatly impress. As U.S. Ambassador John Dean would note a few years later in a scathing appraisal:

> Lon Nol is not intelligent and his prose and conversation betray a disorderly mind. He does not think logically and must be led by the hand through a chain of reasoning. [He] tends to involve himself in details of matters he does not have the time to study and fully understand; consequently, he issues orders on tactical aspects of both the military and civil affairs that often do not square with the realities, thereby causing problems rather than solving them.[1]

Compounding all this was a slavish devotion to mysticism and the occult. By 1972, Lon Nol was reportedly spending $20,000 every month on astrological consultations.[2] Worse, seers reinforced his conviction that it was his destiny to restore the glories of the Khmer empire by fighting nonbelievers from communist Vietnam.[3] Emboldened with such divine authority (in September 1970, the government officially encouraged occult practices to achieve military victory), the general had plunged his country headlong against PAVN in his quest for a Khmer superstate.[4]

As the hardships caused by this quixotic campaign became increasingly apparent, core constituencies fell by the wayside. Some, of course, had never been fully in the general's camp from the start. The overwhelming majority of the peasantry, which in the best of times was largely apolitical, still clung to the reverence afforded god-kings of yesteryear and defaulted in favor of Sihanouk.

Going, too, were middle-class youths. They had been among Lon Nol's most vocal supporters in early 1970, volunteering for the military in droves (even though university students were exempt from military service) and watching with approval when Lon Nol on 9 October 1970 officially proclaimed the Khmer Republic. But they soured when it became apparent the general was paying only lip service to a republic while progressively turning dictatorial. Even after suf-

In Tam, prime minister and presidential contender in the Khmer Republic, later the founder of the ANS. (Courtesy Roland Neveu)

fering a debilitating stroke in February 1971, then attending two months of rehabilitation in Hawaii, he relinquished power for a mere twenty hours on 20 April (during which time he promoted himself from four-star general to marshal) before reclaiming the top slot.

Lon Nol also showed talent for alienating the political elite. Highly suspicious of would-be rivals, he elevated—then summarily dismissed—a string of prime ministers that he used as scapegoats for the Khmer Republic's mounting failures. Topping this list was the scheming yet competent Sirik Matak. The true power behind the March 1970 change in government, Sirik Matak on paper remained second in command to Lon Nol for the first two years of the Republic. But undermined after a series of student demonstrations were staged against him, he abandoned the premiership in March 1972 and was left seething on the sidelines.

The marshal also turned against the popular In Tam. Perhaps the most credible alternative to Lon Nol, In Tam by 1971 had amassed considerable political experience across the top echelon of government. Despite shades of a hair-trigger temper, to his credit he had shunned the trappings of higher office and continued to lead a simple lifestyle. In June 1972, however, he made the mistake of running in a presidential election against Lon Nol. When the latter claimed a 55 percent victory in a count widely viewed as fraudulent (some estimate Lon Nol polled as low as 10 percent), the two became bitter rivals.[5]

Similar shoddy treatment was afforded the influential and popular Khmer Krom leader Son Ngoc Thanh, who the marshal coaxed into the premier's seat in March 1972. But after being targeted in a bomb attack that August (probably planted by the uber-ambitious Lon Non), Thanh was unceremoniously eased out by Lon Nol and elected to return to exile in South Vietnam.

All of this might have been forgiven had the marshal delivered on the military front. This was not even close to being the case. Driven by his vision of recouped Khmer grandeur and surrounded by sycophants, he quickly demonstrated that he was neither a tactician nor a strategist. This was underscored in September 1970 when he initiated Operation Chenla with the intended aim of opening Route 6 between Phnom Penh and the provincial capital of Kompong Thom. A dozen battalions were earmarked for the campaign, as well as artillery, armor, and airpower. Though some fleeting interim gains were made, a PAVN push in November against Kompong Cham forced the government to redirect forces and halt Chenla with inconclusive results.

As FANK's losses had been kept at acceptable levels, Lon Nol walked away from Chenla with an inflated and misplaced sense of confidence. This, plus a desire to showcase a spectacular victory when Sirik Matak met Nixon in the Oval Office on 10 August 1971, led the marshal to launch Operation Chenla 2 with the repeat aim of trying to open Route 6 and take lost territory north of Phnom Penh.[6] This time around, some of FANK's better military commanders—Um Savuth and Dien Del among them—were allowed to wield up to three brigades apiece.

Although Chenla 2 made some incremental gains over its first two months, in late October disaster struck. Biding its time, PAVN dispatched its 9 Division to completely overwhelm the vulnerable, overextended FANK columns. By November, the Cambodians had lost two howitzers, four tanks, five armored personnel carriers, one scout car, ten jeeps, and about two dozen other vehicles. FANK would later claim that the campaign cost them ten infantry battalions and equipment from another ten.

In the wake of Chenla 2, FANK's back was effectively broken. The U.S. embassy spent much of 1972 trying to coax the shell-shocked Cambodian military out of its funk. There was some reason for optimism that September when Major General Sosthene Fernandez was named chief of the General Staff. As a colonel, Sosthene had been secretary of state for national security immediately prior to the March 1970 change of governments. Suspected of being a Sihanouk loyalist, he was briefly detained before being rehabilitated and named a military region commander. Sosthene had performed credibly in that position, and it was hoped that he would add some professionalism when he was placed in charge of the General Staff from the hard-pressed (and physically hobbled) marshal. Such hope proved fleeting, however, as Lon Nol circumvented Sosthene and left the latter little more than a mediator and negotiator, but never a true commander.[7]

There was also some hope in December 1972 when Lon Nol approved a sweeping reorganization aimed at streamlining the confusing array of FANK units above the battalion level. Twenty-nine of the weakest brigades, as well as all autonomous infantry regiments, were dissolved and their men distributed to other units. Then four senior officers were selected to head four infantry divisions to serve as FANK's strategic reserve. Two of them were solid combat commanders—Brigadier General Dien Del and Colonel Un Kauv, both ethnic Khmer Krom—who became the heads of 2 Division and 7 Division, respectively.

Two other division commanders, unfortunately, were selected for reasons other than military competence. Brigadier General Ith Suong, a staunch Lon Nol loyalist blamed as the officer primarily responsible for the Chenla 2 debacle, was put in charge of 1 Division. Lon Nol's own meddling brother, the lowly regarded Brigadier General Lon Non, now commanded 3 Division.[8]

Such nepotism within FANK might have been tolerable had Cambodia not found itself in such a dangerous neighborhood. Unfortunately for the Republican regime, PAVN had been emasculating them not only in larger engagements, like Chenla 2, but also in a series of spectacular surgical strikes that reached within the Phnom Penh municipality.

The first of these took place during the predawn hours of 22 January 1971, when ninety-seven commandos from PAVN's 367 Dac Cong Group approached the perimeter of Pochentong airbase.[9] Dividing into six detachments, they scaled the barbed-wire fence and overwhelmed the resident security battalion (most of which was armed with nothing more than batons). Rushing across the base, they attacked using automatic weapons fire and rocket-propelled grenades.

When the smoke cleared the next morning, thirty-nine people lay dead and another 170 wounded. In addition, the vast majority of the Cambodian air force had been destroyed. This included all of its MiG jets and converted T-28 fighter-bombers.[10] So dramatic was the Pochentong debacle that it was listed as a contributing factor in the stroke that partially disabled Lon Nol the following month.

Later in September, PAVN commandos revisited the capital. This time they destroyed a major fuel depot, cooking off 40 percent of Phnom Penh's civilian fuel stocks.[11] Just more than a year later, on the night of 6–7 October 1972, a battalion from the 367 Sapper Group spread across Phnom Penh, some placing demolitions on the bridge connecting the city to the Chrui Changwar Peninsula, others brazenly taking over a fleet of M-113 armored personnel carriers parked at the Old Municipal Stadium. Those in the former group managed to down the three central spans of the bridge; those in the latter torched four M-113s and drove off in six more toward the Prek Phnou gasoline depot and power plant. Pursuing FANK troops eventually killed or captured all ninety of the Vietnamese commandos, but not before three commandeered vehicles were destroyed.[12]

Sixteen days later, PAVN commandos were again responsible when a 107mm rocket fired from a pushcart nearly hit the FANK headquarters building.[13] And six days after that, a battalion from the 367 Sapper Group lit up the skies southwest of the capital when they set fire to a FANK ammunition depot.[14]

As PAVN picked apart FANK in this fashion, it bought time for Cambodia's homegrown communists to incubate. This was critical, as communism in Cambodia had long been a hard sell. In the immediate aftermath of World War II, communist ideology held virtually no appeal among the (largely satisfied) Cambodian peasantry. Even in 1951, when the Vietnamese communists had helped establish a nascent Cambodian communist party (the Khmer People's Revolutionary Party, or KPRP), it was able to attract only a scant following in the countryside.

Things showed no improvement when the 1954 Geneva Accords were signed to codify France's departure from Indochina. Whereas Vietnamese communists by agreement were able to consolidate within the DRV, and Lao communists were afforded control over two provinces, the accords held no clear benefits for Cambodia's communists. Sensing little opportunity under Sihanouk, a third of all KPRP members and hundreds of supporters—1,015 people in total—elected to take a long march north to Hanoi in order to be held in reserve for future contingencies. What remained of the KPRP's depleted rump in Cambodia was mostly rural, Buddhist, relatively moderate, and pro-Vietnamese. They even naïvely fronted a political party that participated in the rigged 1955 and 1958 elections, but it was predictably trounced and never installed a single legislator.

At decade's end, the KPRP's hard times showed no signs of abating. The party had by that time effectively split along urban and rural lines. The urban faction, which received a modicum of sympathy from the DRV, clung to the hope it could convince Sihanouk to maintain his leftist spin on nonalignment. The rural faction, by contrast, flirted with the idea of revolution, but that goal became ever more remote when a top cadre member defected in 1959 and helped the government run to ground nine out of every ten party adherents in the countryside.

Meantime, a tight-knit band of Cambodian students studying in Paris during the 1950s—mostly the sons of middle-class landowners and civil servants—had been taken in by the allure of communism. One of them, Hou Yuon, wrote his doctoral dissertation about the central role of the peasantry—not urbanization or industrialization—in national development. Arguably the most intellectual of the bunch, Khieu Samphan penned his dissertation on the need for economic self-reliance, blaming the lack of development in the third world on dominance by the industrialized nations. Both of these themes would later color Cambodia's unique strain of communist ideology.

By the early 1960s, these Paris firebrands had made their way back to Phnom Penh to find a party that had atrophied to perhaps 100 members. One of these arrivals, a former Buddhist novice named Saloth Sar—but better known by his alias Pol Pot—wrested control of the party in 1963 and elevated several of his Paris colleagues to senior posts. Together they quickly set about edging out some of the older veterans who were perceived to be too close to their Vietnamese comrades.

Under new leadership, the party still attempted its two-track strategy. A handful of party intellectuals, led by Khieu Samphan, accepted positions in the royalist government and sought to work within the existing system. Others, led by Pol Pot himself, went underground and set up a remote camp in the malarial jungles of Ratanakiri province. From there, Pol Pot in 1965 went on an extended trek to seek backing from the DRV and China.

The results, from his perspective, could only have been seen as disappointing. In Hanoi, he found that the DRV leadership, which was on cordial terms with Sihanouk, could lend nothing more than limp verbal support while counseling

Brigadier General Lon Non, commander of 3 Division, prepares to leave Cambodia for an extended stay in the United States, 30 April 1973. (Author's collection)

against launching any Cambodian revolution.[15] Chinese officials, which only a month earlier had signed a secret treaty with the Sihanouk government to transship weapons via Cambodia, and thus had no intention of jeopardizing ties with Phnom Penh, greeted Pol Pot with many of the same vacuous platitudes.

Returning to the jungles of Cambodia in mid-1966, Pol Pot wasted no time rather than stewing. In September, most impressed by the Maoist emphasis on self-reliance, he secretly changed his party's name to the Communist Party of Kampuchea (CPK) in order to make its nomenclature in line with that of the PRC.[16] He also started preaching that the Cambodian situation was little different from that in South Vietnam and thus equally deserving of support for armed revolution. His patrons in Hanoi and Beijing, both working with Sihanouk, offered deaf ears.[17]

As it turned out, the CPK was upstaged by the Cambodian peasantry in the second quarter of 1967. Over the year prior to that time, the PAVN presence in the eastern Cambodian sanctuaries had created an additional demand for rice, much of which came from the fertile paddyland around Battambang province. Given low official prices for rice, the farmers preferred selling their harvests to

Chinese-Cambodian middlemen, who in turn sold it to the Vietnamese. But after a collapse in rice exports, the government looked to retain more profits for itself via forced rice collection (at a low official price). This enforced collection (which was backed by the military), combined with grievances over a recent land eviction to build a sugar factory, led peasants that April to stage a spontaneous uprising in Battambang's Samlaut district.

The so-called Samlaut Rebellion lasted only four months, during which time hundreds were thought to have been killed in brutal military reprisals. Except for some very minor assistance provided by local CPK cadres acting on their own initiative, the incident had been a peasant phenomenon without any communist underpinnings. This served only to convince CPK stalwarts of the need to prepare a revolutionary army and fast-track their own rebellion.

After half a year of planning, the CPK fired its first shots on 17 January 1968. Farce might be too harsh a description of what followed, but it was nearly so. Would-be communist insurgents raided a handful of rural police posts over the next two months, making off with the occasional antiquated rifle or other bit of ordnance. In Koh Kong province, for example, a youthful CPK member borrowed a hunting rifle from a police acquaintance, then went to the latter's house and demanded bullets and a grenade before fleeing into the jungle with this minimal haul.[18]

In hindsight, the early 1968 uprising had been folly of the highest order. Sihanouk, still smarting from the peasant backlash at Samlaut, gave the military a free hand to go on the offensive through the end of the following year. The prince also coined a name for his new adversary: the Khmer Rouge (or "Red Khmer"). Pursued by the military, shunned by the peasantry, and barely tolerated by its communist brethren in the DRV and PRC, the Khmer Rouge's thin ranks were left to their own devices in the jungle keeping the mosquitoes at bay. The few leftist intellectuals who had taken posts in the government, including Khieu Samphan, were continuously harassed and, facing impending arrest, also took to the bush.

Then came March 1970. Six days after being deposed, a vengeful Sihanouk issued a communiqué from Beijing in which he declared war on Cambodia's new regime and, though unstated, gave an approving nod toward Lon Nol's communist adversaries. Although he was effectively grafting his name to the sputtering revolutionary struggle already being waged by the Khmer Rouge, the wording of his communiqué had been subject to a careful edit from Sihanouk's PRC handlers and Pol Pot (who was also in Beijing at the time) in order to produce an intentionally bland pronouncement bereft of political leanings. This was done to maintain the focus on Sihanouk's name, which still cast a spell over the peasantry.

Behind this pronouncement were multiple marriages of convenience. After all, Sihanouk and the Khmer Rouge had been the bitterest of enemies during the previous two years. But Sihanouk, nursing his overriding desire to enact revenge, was more than willing to act as cheerleader for those seeking to topple Lon Nol. For their part, the Khmer Rouge, having made little headway during the previous years, gladly accepted Sihanouk's fig leaf to win rural recruits and instant credibility on the international stage.[19]

Another set of unlikely partners were the Khmer Rouge and the DRV. As of 1970, the Khmer Rouge leadership was primarily French-educated, increasingly radical, and seethingly anti-Vietnamese. This latter mind-set was due not only to lingering historical animosities but also the (correct) perception that Hanoi had pragmatically shunned the CPK during the previous decade in order to curry favor with Sihanouk's royalist regime.

In this instance, too, differences were quickly papered over. With Sihanouk now part of the revolutionary coalition opposed to Lon Nol, the DRV no longer had any qualms about aiding the Khmer Rouge forces and indeed rushed to them an initial increment of 5,000 rifles. The Khmer Rouge leadership accepted the weapons but made it clear they would not submit to any joint command of communist forces. PAVN offered no argument to this stipulation; they were more than content to unilaterally carry out their 1970 landgrab and inflict crushing body blows against FANK in 1971 while the Khmer Rouge focused on building its thin ranks.

True to this plan, the Khmer Rouge registered sharp growth in quality and quantity during the first year of the Lon Nol regime. There were several reasons for this success. First, and arguably most important, was the immediate veneer of respectability it had won among the peasantry by having Sihanouk anoint its struggle. Just as the largely apolitical rural populations had reflexively lent their support to Sihanouk when he was in power, they were just as quick to approve of any guerrilla coalition he headed—and any coalition partners that that might entail. Whereas they previously gave the CPK a cold shoulder, they now were far more inclined to give them a guarded embrace.

Second, while PAVN was emasculating FANK, the Lon Nol government made the strategic decision to abandon huge swaths of the northern and northeastern countryside in order to defend the more densely populated remainder. Although this might have realistically reflected manpower limitations, it exponentially expanded the Khmer Rouge's unfettered access to potential recruits.[20]

Third, in a foreshadowing of things to come, the Khmer Rouge displayed a propensity for using terror to expand membership and enforce support at the village level. When the carrot of Sihanouk's name did not win over volunteers, the stick of intimidation was readily wielded. Terror tactics also sent refugees by the millions fleeing from the countryside into cities held by the Republican authorities, quickly outstripping the latter's ability to provide adequate food and care.

And fourth, while Khmer Rouge recruitment levels never came close to that of FANK, it was not necessary to match them in terms of quantity or quality. Indeed, in terms of overall numbers, levels of training, and quality of equipment—not to mention aerial and naval support—the Khmer Rouge always paled compared to FANK.[21] But FANK's advantages counted for little against a nimble enemy that could pick the scenes of its encounters and was not encumbered with caring for millions of refugees.[22]

Growing more confident as the war against Lon Nol entered its second year, the Khmer Rouge by 1971 showed hints of being a shifty coalition partner and ungrateful ally. Among the first to feel its wrath was the Khmer Rumdoh (or "Liberation Khmer"), the corps of pro-Sihanouk insurgents recruited and trained by PAVN in eastern Cambodia during the first months after March 1970. Although the Khmer Rumdoh was grouped under the same FUNK resistance umbrella, the Khmer Rouge from the start cast a suspicious eye in its direction because of its close ties to PAVN and also because its ideology lacked a radical Spartan edge. The two groups devolved more into competitors than comrades. When the prince did win some foreign material support for his loyal Khmer Rumdoh—like from North Korea's Kim Il-Sung—the Khmer Rouge elbowed aside the Sihanoukists and claimed the weapons and cash for themselves.[23]

Similarly poor treatment was afforded the Khmer communists who had been held in reserve in Hanoi ever since the Geneva Accords. Of the 1,015 who had marched north to the DRV in 1954, 963 went back to Cambodia beginning in 1970 and set up operations primarily in the east alongside PAVN and the Khmer Rumdoh. But they were soon marginalized by the Khmer Rouge; when a new CPK central committee was selected in September 1971, it included none of the Hanoi returnees. The Khmer Rouge even began staging occasional anti-Vietnamese village rallies by year's end, sending the clear message that their patience was fast wearing thin regarding PAVN's continued presence on Cambodian soil.

Khmer Rouge consolidation continued through 1972, abetted by Hanoi's decision to redeploy PAVN out of Cambodia as it launched a blitzkrieg across South Vietnam that spring. From an estimated 12,000 PAVN troops targeting FANK in February 1972, that number was halved by May as PAVN unleashed its so-called

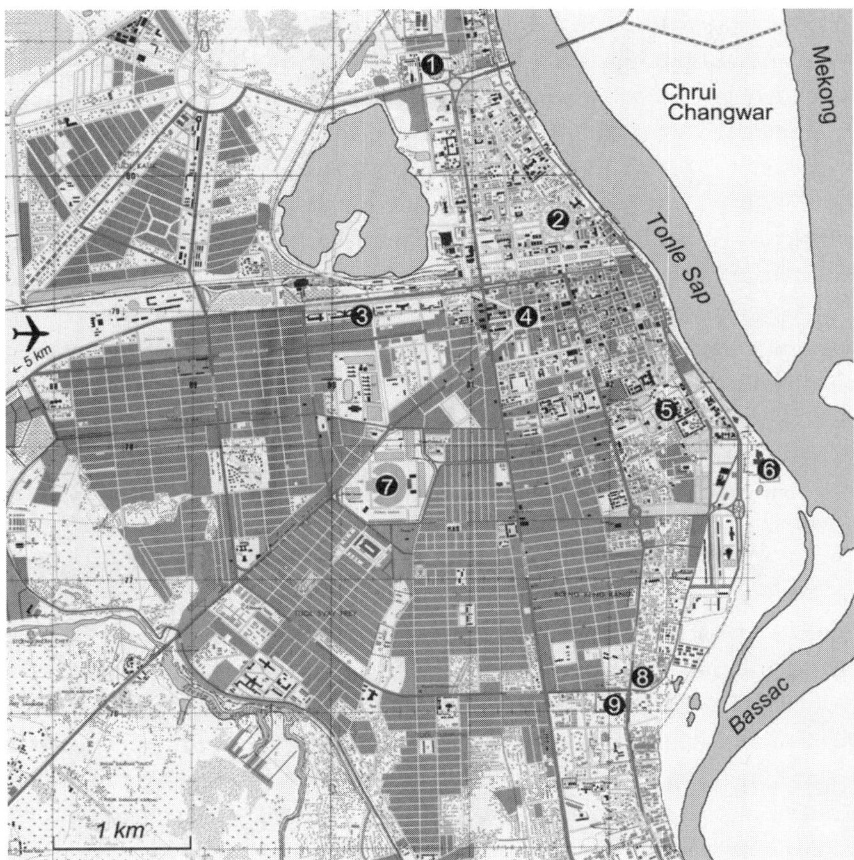

The Phnom Penh capital region as of 1973. Key locations include: 1. Old Municipal Stadium, 2. Wat Phnom, 3. Ministry of Defense, 4. Central Market, 5. Royal Palace, 6. Cambodiana Hotel, 7. Olympic Stadium, 8. U.S. embassy, 9. Presidential Palace.

Easter Offensive against Saigon.[24] In July came an increase in reports of clashes between the Khmer Rouge and its erstwhile Vietnamese allies. Then in November, the U.S. embassy received word that a PAVN regiment had been forced to withdraw from the vicinity of Angkor Wat following a Khmer Rouge demand for Siem Reap to be free of Vietnamese troops.[25]

By early 1973, the Khmer Rouge had also increased the pressure against the Khmer Rumdoh and Hanoi returnees. With the luxury of hindsight, the Khmer Rouge's xenophobic predation on pro-Vietnamese comrades, plus the slippery slope of factionalism and reprisals that it started, are now known and understood. At the time, however, outside analysts were stupefied given the minimal amount of information reaching Phnom Penh.

Among those frustrated was Kissinger. "I don't care who they are loyal to," he announced at a WSAG meeting on 6 February 1973. "I just want to know who is for what in Cambodia." CIA Director James Schlesinger, as well as senior representatives from the Pentagon and the State Department, could not arrive at a coherent answer.[26]

They could agree, however, that the Khmer Rouge—whatever its divisions and rifts—was expanding at an alarming rate. This was a major problem, because Cambodia more than ever was vital to the strategy of U.S. military disengagement from mainland Southeast Asia. Back in October 1972, Kissinger and DRV negotiator Le Duc Tho had been able to achieve a breakthrough in their peace negotiations. This followed the DRV's disappointment with the results of its Easter Offensive in South Vietnam, as well as its fear of being increasingly isolated if Nixon's policy of détente improved relations with both the PRC and the Soviet Union. The resulting Paris Peace Accord, which provided a formula for the United States to withdraw from South Vietnam while leaving behind a sufficiently strong government in Saigon, was signed by the pair on 27 January 1973.

Although pleased to have finalized the document in Paris, Kissinger was more than aware that it was a fragile, flawed agreement. Specifically, it hinged on a viable Khmer Republic that would not let South Vietnam get hit from the flank.[27] This meant that Lon Nol needed to continue his holding game; Phnom Penh could not fall any time over the medium term. It also meant that Kissinger needed his finger on the pulse of events within the Khmer Republic—and he needed to know more about the Khmer Rouge than the collective shrugs of his top advisers.

Kissinger might have wanted better intelligence from the Khmer Republic, but U.S. personnel nevertheless faced stifling congressional restrictions regarding what they could do in Cambodia—and how many could do it. The Cooper-Church Amendment, named after the Republican senator John Cooper from Kentucky and the Democratic senator Frank Church from Idaho, had prohibited U.S. combat troops and military advisers in the Khmer Republic as of January 1971. Although it allowed for defense attachés and a U.S. military team that oversaw equipment deliveries to FANK,[28] a further piece of legislation, the Symington-Case Amendment of February 1972, stated that no more than 200 U.S. officials could be present in the Khmer Rouge at any one time, even including those on temporary duty.[29]

Given such limitations, the CIA was especially hard-pressed to provide any meaningful intelligence from inside Cambodia—let alone the nuanced insights desired by Washington. With the U.S. military taking about half of all personnel slots at the U.S. embassy, and the State Department claiming the bulk of the rest, the CIA's Phnom Penh Station—squeezed into a few small rooms on the embassy's third floor above the ambassador's suite—counted barely enough officers to keep tabs on the Cambodian elite and diplomatic corps in the capital, much less cover the provinces.

Theoretically, there were a few ways to circumvent these personnel limits. One was to base officers just across the border in Thailand. This is exactly what happened in late 1971, when the CIA initiated a paramilitary operation from the spectacular Preah Vihear mountaintop temple. Dating back to the early ninth century, this temple directly straddled the border: To the north, there was a gentle slope down into Thailand; to the south, however, a sheer 525-meter cliff overlooked Cambodia's Preah Vihear province. Both countries had long sparred over control of the site until the International Court of Justice in 1962 awarded jurisdiction to Cambodia.

When the PAVN juggernaut rolled across northeastern Cambodia in April 1970, and Cambodian government posts in the vicinity fell like dominos, those who had been based in Preah Vihear province went in two directions. Most retreated toward Siem Reap, but a handful threaded their way up the Preah Vihear precipice and set up defensive positions around the temple. The outpost was later reinforced with some mortars and machine guns; together with the protection afforded by the cliff, this was more than enough to keep any advancing communists at bay.

Precisely because of the outpost's natural defenses, the CIA saw the cliffside Preah Vihear as the perfect covert launch site. In late 1971, a Thai-based CIA officer named Dave was dispatched to Preah Vihear to discuss such a possibility with the post's ranking FANK officer, Major Kim Sakun. An ethnic Khmer Krom from South Vietnam, Kim Sakun had a backstory with more than its share of intrigue. Prior to 1963, he had been a Khmer Serei member and an occasional informant for Saigon's Central Intelligence Organization. In 1966, however, he apparently had a change of heart and made backchannel contact with Phnom Penh with an unusual offer: He wanted to help broker the surrender of two unruly Saigon-based dissidents—Chau Bory and Chau Mathura—also linked to the Khmer Serei.

Although the trio was given assurances of safe passage, this counted for little with an unforgiving Sihanouk. He immediately had the two dissidents arrested and, in a familiar refrain, publicly executed. Given his ties to the Saigon regime, by all rights Kim Sakun should also have been treated to Sihanouk's tender mercies. But after proving his value by helping lure a third dissident, Sau Ngoy, across the frontier to face capital punishment, Sakun was not only spared but also rewarded with a Cambodian military commission. He then found himself posted to an isolated garrison in Preah Vihear province and, immediately after the 1970 change in governments, withdrew to the temple redoubt and was on hand when Dave came calling.

The CIA's plan, explained Dave, was to take thirty-two men from Preah Vihear and send them to Thailand for training as intelligence teams. This had already been attempted over the previous year in conjunction with Lon Non, with poor results. This time around, however, Dave would maintain direct control from Preah Vihear. Following Kim Sakun's quick consent, the Cambodian contingent was flown to Hua Hin in southern Thailand. There they went to the training base of the Police Aerial Reinforcement Unit (PARU), an elite airborne formation within the Thai Border Patrol Police that had a long, close association with the CIA. Most notably, PARU commandos, acting as covert mobile training teams, had been conducting CIA-sponsored cross-border operations in Laos since 1960.

Under PARU tutelage at Hua Hin, the Cambodians were trained in intelligence collection, communications, and navigation.[30] Three months later, they were sent back to Preah Vihear and, augmented by eight more men, divided into five Special Action Teams. The CIA provided them with radio gear, black uniforms, firearms, and a second salary to augment that already paid by FANK. The CIA also cut an airstrip and built an aircrew mess on the Thai side of the border. Dave, too, was quartered in Thailand—and thus would not be counted against the Symington-Case personnel ceiling.

Once operations commenced in early 1972, helicopters flown by Air America, the CIA's proprietary airline, picked up teams atop Preah Vihear and inserted them into the steaming lowlands below for extended reconnaissance forays. Dressed in black like the Khmer Rouge, the teams on occasion were able to recruit local contacts. This continued for more than a year without any losses among team members. Although such a record might be construed as a success, the operation was concentrated in thick jungles that had never been strongly under Phnom Penh's writ—but these were not areas of heavy Khmer Rouge activity. Indeed, the thin intelligence hauls collected by the teams had little bearing on the pivotal battles being waged near Cambodia's urban centers farther south. Underwhelmed with the results to date, the CIA in late 1973 removed its case officer and turned over administrative control of the operation to FANK.[31]

Another way to circumvent restrictions on U.S. personnel was to use Thai proxies. In fact, the RTA, equally concerned over the Khmer Republic's longevity, since 1970 had established an intelligence-gathering presence in Cambodia. Coordinating this was Tactical Operations Center (TOC) 315, the office headquartered in Bangkok that formulated RTA policy toward Cambodia.[32] Under TOC 315, a smaller group known as Task Force 506 ran clandestine intelligence teams drawn from the RTA Special Forces along the length of the Thai-Cambodian border.[33]

In January 1971, following the steady erosion of the Khmer Republic's control in the countryside, TOC 315 authorized Task Force 506 to deploy intelligence teams within Cambodia. With the concurrence of FANK, ten-man RTA teams were posted to the provincial capitals of Battambang, Koh Kong, Kompong Cham, Phnom Penh, and Siem Reap. Their primary responsibility was to pass intelligence gleaned from their respective posts to the Phnom Penh team, which in turn forwarded reports to Bangkok.[34] From the start, however, the operation had serious limitations. Recalled the commander of the Siem Reap team: "For the first two years, we were supplied with almost no funds. For transportation around Siem Reap, our team was given just a single bicycle. Once a month, I would make my way over to the border, then get on a jeep and drive to Bangkok to give a more detailed report on what little we had learned."[35]

Rather than tapping into this anemic RTA network, the CIA had a different Thai proxy in mind. Specifically, it contemplated taking a page from its Laos playbook, whereby the CIA had long used PARU police commandos to penetrate deep into the Lao countryside, recruit locals as guerrillas, establish intelligence networks, and turn the tables on more conventional communist opponents. Dispatched to gauge the feasibility of using such a PARU-type approach in Cambodia was veteran CIA paramilitary officer William Lair.

Within the CIA's Far East Division Lair was a legend. He had first gone to Thailand in the 1950s and was one of PARU's founders; so close was his association with the Thai establishment that he had even been formally commissioned as an officer in the Border Patrol Police. But more than just helping create PARU, he had been godfather to their operations in Laos. Indeed, in early 1961 he had personally handled the delicate initial negotiations that led to the marriage of PARU advisers and fierce Hmong hilltribesmen in northeastern Laos.

Given this background, few were better qualified than Lair to judge whether the Laos formula could be repeated. At the opening of 1973, he arrived in Phnom Penh to do just that. Accompanying him was Ted Shackley, a senior CIA officer who had served as station chief in Laos through 1968, then station chief in South Vietnam until 1972. From Saigon he had been recalled to Langley and, on account of his strong performances in Southeast Asia, was promoted to head of the Western Hemisphere Division. Though technically no longer affiliated with Southeast Asia, he was tasked with accompanying Lair on account of his networking among senior personalities in the region, as well as the bureaucratic weight he carried.

After five days of meetings in Phnom Penh, Lair emerged pessimistic. He recalled: "Things were already too bad. The countryside was all in enemy hands, which was the opposite of what we found when we first went into Laos. And compared to the corruption of the government, the communist commanders and their soldiers lived the same simple life. You had to grudgingly admit the Khmer Rouge held appeal on this count."[36] Convinced that a Laos-type solution could not be replicated in the hinterlands of the Khmer Republic, Lair and Shackley quietly shelved any thought of using Thai police advisers to extend an unconventional warfare network in Cambodia.

Still in need of a solution to provide Washington with intelligence from the Cambodian countryside, and yet still facing a strict manpower ceiling, the CIA in early March 1973 agreed to the risky proposition of stationing just a handful of U.S. intelligence officers in the provinces. According to an initial proposal, fifteen officers would be in the countryside by June.[37] After further revisions, a more modest plan to augment Phnom Penh Station with just five up-country officers was finalized on 11 April.[38] The up-country augmentation project was given the codename HYTHE, but it was more commonly known within Phnom Penh Station as the Alpha Program.[39]

Playing a key role in turning the Alpha Program into reality was forty-seven-year-old Phnom Penh Station Chief Kinloch Bull. A consummate gentleman of the South, Bull hailed from a prominent family that included the last British governor in South Carolina. As a career CIA officer, he had completed assignments across mainland Southeast Asia over the previous two decades. Though of faltering health (allegedly from a parasite he contracted in Laos during the 1950s), Bull had been given a medical dispensation in August 1972 to take over the station in Cambodia.

When notified of the basic parameters for the Alpha Program, Bull quickly set out three requirements for any up-country candidates. First, he wanted officers who were able to speak passable French. "I did not want a repeat of what I saw in South Vietnam," he explained, "where intelligence officers lost credibility by having to go around with a twenty-two-year-old interpreter in tow."[40] Second, Bull wanted officers who had previous up-country experience, in Laos for example. "I didn't want people who had only been in Paris or Bangkok," he insisted. "That would not have been a recipe for success."[41] Third, he wanted people with foreign intelligence backgrounds. What he did not want were paramilitary officers who were expert in equipping guerrillas but knew nothing about running indigenous agents.[42]

Finally, as Bull and his deputy were stretched thin with assignments, he put in a request for a chief of field operations to separately manage the Alpha Program. Cutting short a Bangkok tour to get this slot was forty-five-year-old Douglas Beed. After arriving at Phnom Penh Station in mid-April, Beed quickly fleshed out what was expected of Alpha:

> The primary mission was intelligence collection on enemy capabilities, intentions, and actions in the up-country areas of Cambodia. This included enhancing the local FANK commanders' intelligence collection through direct support and tradecraft guidance as well as independent collection operations. A small subset of this was targeting data for U.S. air exploitation passed directly and immediately to U.S. military representatives in the embassy.
>
> By proximity and opportunity there was reporting incidental to the main mission, on host (e.g., FANK) capabilities: its will, morale, corruption, readiness, political tendencies, and relationships.[43]

Significantly, the Alpha Program's expansive mandate did not include a paramilitary component. "It was in no way a paramilitary effort," emphasized Beed. "There were to be no heroics or dead heroes."[44]

Arriving along with Beed were the first five up-country officers. As Station Chief Bull had insisted, all spoke French, all had previously served in up-country assignments, and all had experience in foreign intelligence collection. Their initial assignment was to last only three months, in part to test if the up-country program was productive and useful, and in part in recognition of the living conditions that were unusually rigorous and possibly hazardous.[45] Although all of them were declared to, and working in support of, local FANK commanders, in most cases local FANK defenses were porous at best. Moreover, as few foreigners were living in their respective towns, their identities were certain to quickly become known to communist informants.

The first of the five, a case officer named Ed, was a Far East veteran who had once donned a hippie disguise to troll for snippets of intelligence in the Lao capital of Vientiane. He had been serving on a desk job in Langley when he got the Alpha assignment to Kampot town in the southern Cambodian province of the same name. Located just a few kilometers from the Gulf of Thailand, Kampot was renowned in the region for its black pepper and pungent fish sauce. Settling into town, and with generous amounts of Rémy Martin flowing, Ed soon got to work cultivating a local French priest as a good source of hearsay intelligence.

The second, an officer named James, was yanked from a Thai assignment and sent to Kompong Chhnang. Located in the center of the country, Kompong Chhnang served as a port on the Tonle Sap River and hosted a string of floating villages along its bank. It was also the region's historic pottery-making center, with antique shards indicating the trade dated back thousands of years.

The third officer, Mike Magnani, had served with Savannakhet Unit in Laos over the previous three years, helping run a wide range of agents and paramilitary teams along the Ho Chi Minh Trail. In Cambodia he was assigned to Kompong Thom, with additional responsibility for the northern provinces of Siem Reap, Preah Vihear, and Stung Treng.[46] Although it was somewhat unrealistic for a single officer to adequately cover such an expansive swath, Magnani was fortunate to receive strong support from the local military subdivision commander, the able Brigadier General Teap Ben.

The fourth officer, Walt Floyd, had preceded Magnani at Savannakhet Unit. While there in January 1967 he had directed an indigenous team in a raid against a Pathet Lao prison camp near the Ho Chi Minh Trail. Of the eighty-plus Lao and Thai inmates at the jungle camp, fifty-two prisoners (including a Thai crewman for Air America captured in September 1963) were brought back to friendly lines; it stood as the largest successful prison raid during the Second Indochina Conflict. Floyd had most recently been serving at the CIA's Tokyo Station when he was rushed to Cambodia and posted to the country's third largest city, the Mekong-side provincial capital of Kompong Cham.[47]

The last case officer, Richard "Joe" Boys, was a West Pointer who had run intelligence teams along the China frontier from northern Laos, then did a paramilitary assignment with Savannakhet Unit. He volunteered for perhaps the hardest of the hardship posts—the provincial capital of Svay Rieng. Just a few kilometers from the South Vietnamese border, Svay Rieng was under daily pressure from all directions: On good days, they were able to push back the communists to eight kilometers; on bad days, the perimeter shrank to six.[48]

Just a couple of weeks after these initial five settled into their posts, another five Alpha augmentees arrived in May. These included a reports officer, a secretary, a logistics officer, and an air support officer—all of whom would be based at the U.S. embassy in Phnom Penh—as well as a roving up-country officer.

Even with this added cast, the Alpha Program was soon overwhelmed with challenges. Among the biggest problems was recruiting quality intelligence sources. In neighboring South Vietnam, one of the CIA's counterparts—the Special Branch of the National Police—was responsible for penetrating the Viet Cong infrastructure and helped vet potential agents. In Cambodia, however, the CIA had no reliable counterpart that could help locate and vet potential Khmer Rouge penetration agents in the countryside.

In fact, the Khmer Republic had several intelligence organizations. Two of them were small and focused solely within Phnom Penh.[49] For a time there was a third covert intelligence unit, the Comité de Coordination Spéciale (Committee for Special Coordination), but this was tainted by its commander, the notorious Brigadier General Lon Non. Among the many activities undertaken by this committee, it claimed to field 6,000 agents, including some allegedly close to the Khmer Rouge leadership. The U.S. embassy was extremely dubious of such boasts and noted that many of Lon Non's operations relied heavily on political agitation and bordered on terrorism. In any event, the committee was quietly disbanded—and its thousands of claimed agents melted away—when Lon Non was shunted to the United States for an extended visit in late April 1973.[50]

By process of elimination, the CIA was left to cooperate with FANK's Second Bureau, the name given to the military intelligence staffs deployed at the military region and provincial levels. Unfortunately, the Second Bureau ran a haphazard intelligence network that—depending on the province—barely processed prisoner interrogations, let alone more sophisticated information collection from agents.

The Alpha Program faced other early challenges. Mike Magnani, the case officer at Kompong Thom, contracted hepatitis and was evacuated for treatment. He was not immediately replaced, quickly reducing the number of up-country posts to four.

In Kompong Cham, meantime, Walt Floyd was feeling a crushing sense of futility. Two French managers working on rubber plantations to the north and east of the provincial capital occasionally came into town and shared a lunch with the Alpha officer. In a frustrating display of realpolitik, the French were still collecting rubber after having apparently paid off the Khmer Rouge not to interfere with production. They had also come to an accommodation with the Cambodian and U.S. governments not to bomb their plantations. The Khmer Rouge knew this and, as part of a quid pro quo with the French, hid personnel and equipment among the rubber trees with impunity. Floyd reported on their presence, but no airstrikes were flown.[51] "Kompong Cham was not a pleasant experience," Floyd summed up in obvious frustration. After his three months were over, he did not volunteer for a second ninety-day stint.

One month after Floyd left, a morning explosion rocked the riverside road on the southern edge of Kompong Cham city. The street was littered with a single dismembered body, along with the mangled remains of a bystander. An investigation later revealed that a Khmer Rouge terrorist, with a bomb under his jacket, accidentally detonated the device while cycling toward the villa from which Floyd had been operating.[52]

This incident revealed that the communists were, at the very least, aware of the Alpha deployment in Kompong Cham. Shortly thereafter, they would have been aware of the entire program. On 24 July, journalist Tammy Arbuckle reported in the *Washington Star* that the CIA had deployed officers to up-country posts across Cambodia.[53] The following day, during his congressional nomination hearing to become CIA director, William Colby acknowledged that Arbuckle's article reported correctly the gist of the Alpha Program.

For its part, the U.S. Congress was looking to further limit U.S. assistance efforts in Cambodia. The Case-Church Amendment to the Defense Authorization Bill, initially passed on 14 June 1973, required congressional approval for any combat-related expenditures in Indochina. As the law was originally written, U.S. tactical air support for FANK would stop as of 30 June. This prompted U.S. Ambassador Emory Swank to send Washington a hysterical appraisal claiming that the Khmer Republic's demise would come within days, if not hours, after the bombing halt.[54]

After further congressional horse-trading near the close of June, U.S. air support was extended through 15 August. But even with this extension, the U.S. embassy was pessimistic.[55] If the United States was allowed to maintain logistical support to the Khmer Republic via airlifts, Station Chief Bull thought that the impact would be serious but not fatal. If logistical support was also to be prohibited, he grimly predicted FANK would collapse within ten days.[56]

At that point, the communists did the illogical. Although an estimated 3,000 PAVN troops were still focused against the Khmer Republic as of mid-1973, virtually none of them were actively confronting FANK.[57] Instead, the Khmer Rouge, which had started grouping its guerrillas into regiments as of May, felt sufficiently confident in its own abilities to launch an all-out offensive against Phnom Penh late the following month. Its aim, apparently, was to make the Khmer Republic collapse from exhaustion before the height of the rainy season.

In hindsight, Khmer Rouge leaders were being foolhardy for a number of reasons. First, they had never attempted such an ambitious offensive before and had only recently upgraded their command and control structure to the regimental level. Second, friction between the Khmer Rouge and PAVN was taking its toll—with the North Vietnamese apparently dragging their feet on ammunition deliveries to their prickly Cambodian comrades. The situation had gotten so dire that on 9 July Sihanouk gave a speech in Beijing in which he appealed for arms and ammunition from the third world.[58]

Most important was the timing. With U.S. bombing set to cease as of 15 August, the U.S. Air Force was doing all in its power to maximize combat air support for FANK during the final weeks leading up to the halt. "Our objective between now and then," wrote U.S. Navy Admiral Thomas Moorer to Defense Secretary James Schlesinger on 5 July, "is to weaken the enemy as much as possible."[59] With an unprecedented amount of iron raining down on their heads, the Khmer Rouge was slaughtered around Phnom Penh's perimeter. As the U.S. Defense Department's attaché's office later commented: "The offensive ran out of people, supplies, or perhaps will, just one week before the U.S. bombing halt."[60]

As 15 August came and went, it soon became apparent that writing the Khmer Republic's epithet had been premature. Not only had FANK (with a final burst of U.S. airpower) stood strong; in addition, Pentagon lawyers, pouring over the wording of congressional restrictions, had already determined there was wiggle room for ongoing U.S. logistical support. Replacement military equipment (including ammunition), rice, and medicines could be legally airlanded in Phnom Penh, they concluded, and rice and medicines could still be airdropped into beleaguered garrisons.

Even so, there was hardly reason for cheer. Marshal Lon Nol was stubbornly clinging to power, after all, despite growing hints of resentment within his armed forces. Back on 17 March, Captain So Patra, a son-in-law of Sihanouk, boarded a T-28 at Pochentong and headed toward downtown Phnom Penh. After dive-bombing the Presidential Palace, he flew the plane to China's Hainan Island. When the smoke cleared back at the palace, forty-three were dead and another thirty-five wounded. Lon Nol, absent at the time, was livid. He ordered a complete bombing stand-down for three days and fired the air force commander.[61]

Far more serious were the coup rumors tied to top officers in the army, even within Lon Nol's innermost circle. In March, the CIA had established that the marshal's meddlesome sibling, Lon Non, was intending a putsch to replace his invalid brother. When word reached the U.S. State Department, the desk officer for Cambodia, Andrew Antippas, wrote a classified memorandum: "I said if little brother took over he would become 'our bastard' and he wasn't smart enough to be our bastard and run the country. I recommended that Lon Non be removed from Cambodia." General Alexander Haig, until recently Nixon's chief of staff, was assigned the chore of going to Phnom Penh and enticing Lon Non, at least for the time being, into leaving the capital for a tour of the United States.

Another key officer who was eyeing the top slot was General Sosthene Fernandez. During June, Sosthene, who already was chief of the General Staff, was additionally named commander-in-chief of the armed forces. But as before, this proved little more than semantics as Lon Nol remained supreme commander of the armed forces and never ceded any serious decisionmaking power. Now beyond frustration, Sosthene had reached out in early September to Brigadier General Dien Del, the hard-nosed commander of 2 Division, to join forces in their own putsch. The CIA again got wind of their conspiracy, and Station Chief Bull had taken both aside to counsel them against extraconstitutional measures. Still, CIA Director Colby warned Kissinger on 12 September that the generals might still attempt to unseat the marshal.[62]

Compounding matters, the Khmer Rouge—for the second time that quarter—did the illogical. On 16 August, the day after the U.S. bombing halt took effect, an estimated seventeen Khmer Rouge battalions—including three dispatched from Kompong Thom—began a siege on the provincial capital of Kompong Cham. Although this showed some impressive tactical dexterity, again the timing was curious. After all, the Khmer Rouge had just taken staggering losses along the Phnom Penh perimeter. Moreover, mid-August is the height of the rainy season; whereas FANK could use its navy and air force to ferry in men and supplies during torrential downpours, the communist logistical lines would likely remain mired through October.

But the Khmer Rouge held some advantages this time around. At the opening of the month it had overrun a FANK position west of the city and captured eight 105mm howitzers. It had also moved insurgents close enough to the Kompong Cham airbase to frustrate use of the runway. And with U.S. airpower no longer an option, the only tactical air support would be coming from the far less intimidating T-28 fleet out of Phnom Penh.

Very quickly, the battle for Kompong Cham became an epic slugfest. Elements of two FANK infantry brigades arrived by boat and chopper on 18 August. Three days later, half of the elite Airborne Brigade was inserted, as well as an additional 105mm howitzer battery. But even with these considerable reinforcements, the CIA estimated that the government's chances of holding off the Khmer Rouge were dead even.[63]

By the opening of September, the U.S. embassy's only window from inside Kompong Cham was the CIA's Alpha outpost. After Walt Floyd left the program, he had been replaced in the city by Charles "Chuck" Hafner. A former U.S.

Marine, Hafner employed two Cambodian operational assistants. The first was a stout former paratrooper named Nop Prang. The other was a former high-school literature teacher named Kong Thann; assimilated into FANK in 1970 with the rank of captain, Thann had earlier served as an interpreter for the Commando Raider training cycle at Phitsanulok in 1971.

Hafner and his two assistants had recently moved into a palatial villa near the market in the center of Kompong Cham city. Rented from an ethnic Chinese businessman who had retired to Paris, the three-floor villa—with screened verandas and surrounding gardens—might have been an idyllic setting at any other time. But with insurgents lurking, it had been reinforced with fifty guards, a machine-gun emplacement on each corner of the compound, and a bunker in the center with a Honeywell grenade launcher.[64]

At the opening of September, Alpha chief Doug Beed choppered into Kompong Cham to review its defenses. His assessment: Hafner could provisionally stay put, as there appeared to be adequate warning mechanisms if the city was in danger of falling.[65] From a morale standpoint Hafner's presence was deemed critical, not to mention the fact that his outpost was the only direct communications link between the city and the U.S. embassy.

All these considerations were outweighed, however, on the afternoon of 6 September. Bringing forward their captured howitzers, the communists began a sustained bombardment. Sensing that the battle for Kompong Cham was entering its final phase, Beed raced through the embassy to find the highest-ranking diplomat in the building, Deputy Chief of Mission (DCM) Thomas Enders. Recalls Beed:

> The withdrawal from Kompong Cham required a nod from the DCM. There was some resistance at earlier suggestions that an evacuation might be considered. On that day, there was no time for memos or debate. I caught the DCM in the hall. A vivid memory is craning up at close quarters to his 6-foot 8-inch height seeking his oral approval while trying not to appear to plead or convey panic, only straightforward fact, reason, and measured urgency.

Persuaded, Enders offered his consent. A chopper was soon over the roof of the villa, yanking out Hafner while artillery shells continued to rain across the city.

The evacuation proved fortuitous. That same evening, the Khmer Rouge began its final push against the provincial capital from all directions. Its greatest success came from the south, managing to surge halfway across the city in a night of chaotic street fighting. Remaining behind with a handful of guards, Nop Prang continued to radio updates to the U.S. embassy from inside the compound. The Khmer Rouge forces, he reported, were practically at the front iron fence; a block away, FANK infantry were making a spirited stand. Waiting until the last moment, the former paratrooper disabled the radio with a couple of bullets, then, along with most of the guards, made his escape through an alley behind the villa.

As with the Khmer Rouge's abortive push against Phnom Penh the previous month, logistics once again became its undoing. With PAVN filibustering ammunition and the monsoon rains turning resupply trails into ribbons of mud, the forwardmost Khmer Rouge units ran out of bullets while on the verge of overrunning the city.

FANK, meantime, took full advantage of its air force and navy. On 10 September, the 2,000-strong 80 Infantry Brigade steamed up the Mekong from Phnom Penh. Even though the inept use of landing craft led to high losses as boats were exposed to enemy fire on the river for six hours, the brigade did well after it was landed south of the city behind Khmer Rouge lines. Three days later, it expelled the final communist troops and linked up with FANK infantry occupying the north.

Losses on both sides had been astronomical. Some thirty-nine Khmer Rouge battalions had been thrown against Kompong Cham as of early September; as many as 1,500 had been killed by midmonth. Frustrated, Sihanouk—in Beijing—began to rant about Hanoi's duplicity in not keeping the Khmer communists adequately supplied.

On the government side, 70 percent of the city had been razed in the battle. Out of an original population of 200,000, just 30,000 remained as of the close of September. The majority had managed to flee to Phnom Penh, but many thousands had no doubt been killed or marched away to join the Khmer Rouge's attrited ranks.

Among those who escaped was Nop Prang, who made his way to Phnom Penh and held an emotional reunion with Hafner. They later returned to the bullet-riddled villa at month's end and inside found two dead guards. Station Chief Bull also flew in for a visit and stood in awe in front of the battered residence. "It looked like Swiss cheese," he later remarked.[66]

Back in Washington, Kissinger and the rest of the WSAG policymakers were relieved and elated. Although they acknowledged that the rains had been a plus, and PAVN's indifference was a big help, they could not help but shower accolades on FANK. For the first time since Chenla 2, Cambodian troops had not buckled in the face of difficult odds. Optimistic for the first time in months, they grew so bold as to predict that the Khmer Republic would survive the year.[67]

4. Requiem

As predicted, the Khmer Republic did survive to see the opening of 1974. In fact, despite some early pressure on Phnom Penh and continued growth on the part of the Khmer Rouge (which formed its first divisions in January), FANK managed to wrest back the dry-season initiative by early February. "The Khmer Communists are being forced to react, not act," summed up the U.S. Defense Attaché's office with a ring of optimism.[1]

Perhaps predictably, it was not to last. In an unexpected move, on 26 February the Khmer Rouge unleashed a withering heavy weapons assault on the provincial capital of Kampot. The communists then committed one of their new divisions to the fray.

As had been the case in Kompong Cham, an Alpha officer, Chuck Bernard, was the only member of the U.S. embassy remaining overnight in the city to report on Kampot's shrinking perimeter. Going by the alias Monsieur Jacques, Bernard spent most of March with the resident FANK political warfare officer writing propaganda tracts to undermine communist morale.[2] But despite his best efforts, and a massive heliborne lift of infantry reinforcements, the Khmer Rouge managed to seize strategic positions around the city and push FANK to the brink by 2 April.

Meantime, on 18 March—not coincidentally, the fourth anniversary of the fall of Sihanouk—the Khmer Rouge used twenty battalions to launch a surprise attack that overwhelmed the town of Oudong. Located just 40 kilometers northwest of Phnom Penh on Route 5, Oudong held symbolic significance because it had been the country's capital for more than 200 years prior to 1866. The communists then turned their sights on the isolated 1,200-man FANK garrison in the neighboring town of Longvek.

For the Republic's leadership in Phnom Penh, the communist landgrab at Oudong was too much to stomach. Two days later, some 1,000 infantry were shuttled by chopper to the riverbank east of the town. Joining them were twenty M-113 armored personnel carriers, shipped in landing craft up the Tonle Sap River. But even this sizable foothold fell in April, forcing stragglers to link up with the Longvek garrison and together resist the communist onslaught.

Through the close of April, the battles at Kampot and Oudong raged. Like a pair of punch-drunk fighters, each side pummeled the other with artillery and continued to pour in reinforcements. And in both cases, like at Kompong Cham the year before, FANK showed just enough staying power to best the communists. By May, the Khmer Rouge division spearheading the assault on Longvek had been mauled to such a degree that one of its regiments was dissolved. Unwilling to absorb more personnel losses, the communists finally withdrew from the Oudong vicinity two months later, allowing FANK to enter the razed town. Hundreds of butchered corpses were found in the ruins.

At Kampot, too, further FANK reinforcements in April led to a Khmer Rouge withdrawal by early May. Having overextended themselves and underestimated FANK, the Khmer Rouge by June were settling for small-scale attacks ahead of the rainy season. The Republican authorities, meantime, were allowing themselves the luxury of guarded optimism.

By that time, the CIA's up-country program had passed its first anniversary. On 23 April, the CIA sent the National Security Council a report reviewing the first twelve months of HYTHE. In the report's preface, CIA Director Colby assessed that "meaningful progress had been made, but a great deal remains to be done." Kissinger agreed, sending Colby a note of appreciation on 8 June.[3]

To be sure, HYTHE had seen some incremental growth over the preceding year. From an initial spread of five up-country posts (one of which, Kampot, was closed in late March 1974), CIA officers were positioned in seven towns by mid-1974.[4] In several cases, pairs of officers were being deployed to the towns, and many of these new Alpha arrivals were experienced veterans of the war in Laos who had been made superfluous after a 1973 peace accord gutted the CIA's paramilitary program in that kingdom.

Offsetting this minimal growth was a sense of exasperation that had set in among many of the Alpha members. Virtually all of the project officers were excessively tired and/or sick during their tours; Doug Beed himself, who headed the program for the first year, dropped 9 kilograms over the course of his deployment. He noted with hindsight: "I think most of us shared an opinion that the U.S. was not doing enough to really make a difference in Cambodia—only enough so that it would 'go down the drain' more slowly. While we took some pride in our intelligence product, I don't think we were under any illusion it would change the course of events—we only thought it might help policymakers make their decisions."[5]

In May 1974, Beed was succeeded by Colin Thompson. A Laos veteran (he had helped manage Hmong tribal guerrillas during 1964–1966), Thompson had then completed a South Vietnam tour before heading to Manila at the end of the decade. While there, he had developed a unique window into Cambodia. This came about after Long Boret, a highly regarded former finance minister and parliamentarian, had approached a U.S. embassy officer on a trip to Moscow and asked to establish clandestine contact. When Boret was appointed as the Cambodian representative to the Asian Development Bank's Manila headquarters in 1969, Thompson had served as his CIA case officer.

From the outset of his assignment, Thompson was cynical toward Alpha and its unrealistic aims:

> Nobody in Phnom Penh Station cared about the program. No Cambodians in Phnom Penh cared about it. Nobody in Phnom Penh cared, period. This program left one U.S. official in the province, relying on questionable security provided by the Cambodians. These officials had no firm mission. They were supposed to collect intelligence on the plans and intentions of the Khmer Communists, but this was largely impossible. The best they could do was to gather some Khmer Rouge order-of-battle data.[6]

In the provinces, the conditions experienced by the up-country officers Thompson supervised were not getting any easier. None of the posts was arguably more surreal than the provincial capital of Svay Rieng. A parched, battle-scared oasis of Republican control on the South Vietnamese frontier, the town was devoid of public utilities and packed with thousands of refugees that were stretching sparse resources to the breaking point.

Inside the town's cramped perimeter, CIA officer Joe Boys had volunteered to endure the daily pressures of Svay Rieng for a second year with Alpha. Though the accommodations were especially rustic (his office-cum-residence was a simple two-room house with a detached kitchen and toilet), this was somewhat alleviated by his selection of operations assistant: an attractive twenty-one-year-old named Samay Mom. Still, he recalled the overpowering isolation of Svay Rieng: "The locals had not seen Caucasians in a long time, so I was like the Pied Piper—kids followed me everywhere. I also found that there were only a couple of French speakers in town, so I ended up learning rudimentary Khmer pretty fast."[7]

This linguistic foothold helped Boys stay current about the especially potent mix of communist forces confronting Svay Rieng. For its part, the Khmer Rouge launched regular forays against the town's forward defenses. The worst of these, a failed attempt to overrun the town in October 1974, involved elements of six regiments. And owing to its close proximity to the South Vietnamese border, Svay Rieng was still occasionally pressured by PAVN forces long after the North Vietnamese had abandoned the rest of the Cambodian countryside. In August 1974, for example, an attack on the town involved the 275 Regiment of PAVN's 5 Division.

Worst of all, PAVN gunners near Svay Rieng were known to be armed with SA-7 surface-to-air missiles and had already downed one Khmer Air Force plane.[8] Relief flights to Svay Rieng's runway—an improvised portion of Route 1—were thus fraught with danger, yet without a steady stream of such supplies the town would have ceased being viable long before.

Compared to Svay Rieng, the Alpha post at the town of Kompong Speu was more livable. Located only 40 kilometers southwest of Phnom Penh along Route 4, this provincial capital had been a vacation spot established by the French three decades earlier. More recently during the Sihanouk regime, the town had hosted a secret warehouse holding Chinese weapons destined for delivery to PAVN sanctuaries along the border. It had also been the scene of brief but heavy fighting between PAVN and a combined FANK/South Vietnamese task force in June 1970; the latter had retaken the destroyed town after a three-day communist occupation, though in truth there had been little in the quaint town worth razing.

Since that time, an eerie calm had overtaken the environs of Kompong Speu. This was due largely to one man—Norodom Chantarangsey. Born in 1924 in Phnom Penh, Chantarangsey was a Cambodian blue-blood: He hailed from the Norodom royal family and had married Princess Sisowath Samanvoraphong, the daughter of King Sisowath Monivong.

Despite his royal lineage, Chantarangsey from the start had shown himself to be a scrappy fighter more comfortable in a jungle campsite than in the halls of privilege. Just before Japanese capitulation in August 1945, he had joined the Cambodian Volunteer Corps militia that Tokyo had established to fight the returning French colonialists. The following year he transferred to the Khmer Issarak (or "Freedom Khmer"), a network of Thai-supported anti-French guerrilla bands active along the Thai-Cambodian border. He quickly rose within the Issarak ranks, and in August 1946 he was among those that spearheaded a push against the French that briefly overran the town of Siem Reap.[9]

At that point, Chantarangsey came to the attention of the Indochinese Communist Party.[10] In late 1948, internal party documents reveal that its Vietnamese-dominated Politburo felt, due to its more primitive domestic conditions, Cambodia was best suited for a constitutional monarchy along the lines of the Soviet-dominated monarchy in Romania immediately after World War II. But rather than Sihanouk, who had been selected by the French, the communists pre-

Brigadier General Norodom Chantarangsey, Military Region 2 commander, greets a crowd in 1974. (Courtesy Barry Broman)

ferred the dissident guerrilla Chantarangsey. The party went as far as to broach the idea with him—only to have Chantarangsey flatly reject the offer because he did not want to become a Vietnamese puppet. From that point forward, the spurned communists condemned him as a traitorous prince.[11]

Into the ensuing decade, Chantarangsey cemented his reputation as a guerrilla chieftain. The Issarak had by that time already become a spent force due to too many ideologies under its umbrella, as well as growing suspicion toward its Thai patrons. But showing pragmatism, the prince by 1949 has realigned himself with the Khmer Serei. Going from strength to strength, Chantarangsey and his loyal insurgents—numbering 1,000 by 1953—eventually carved out a mini-fiefdom in the jungles of Kompong Speu province.

All of this was rather ironic. For one thing, the Khmer Serei was antimonarchist—which theoretically should have made them shun Chantarangsey due to his royal lineage. For another thing, the Khmer Serei were also anti-French—yet the French saw Chantarangsey as a useful pawn. The French military commander, General Girot de Langlade, minced no words when describing the prince as a true feudal warlord who maintained tight discipline among his men and let them revert to banditry to raise funds—yet this was conveniently overlooked because he kept Kompong Speu free of communist insurgents.[12]

In November 1953, France granted Cambodia its independence. Three months later, Sihanouk enticed his wayward cousin into pledging loyalty to the throne and royal government. In return, all of Chantarangsey's men were granted amnesty and officially accepted into the royal armed forces. The majority—640 out of 1,000—were gathered under the new 3 Mobile Autonomous Battalion (or 3 BAM, based on the French-language designation, 3eme Bataillon Autonome Mobile), while the remainder were accepted as lesser paramilitary auxiliaries.[13]

The marriage was not to last. Angry that only two-thirds of his men were hatted as proper soldiers, Chantarangsey turned a blind eye when his men reorganized as gangs and went back to robbing travelers at night. Sihanouk endured this through December 1955, then dispatched paratroopers to Kompong Speu to forcible dissolve the 3 BAM. Chantarangsey was then shunted off to France to attend a military course for two years.

Returning to Cambodia in 1957, Chantarangsey was hardly repentant. Wasting no time in resuming his criticism of Sihanouk, he was jailed for a year on *lese majeste* charges. He was also stripped of military rank and lived, more or less, as a commoner for most of the 1960s. Toward the end of that decade, however, he seized upon a lucrative profession: running an unlicensed casino out of his Phnom Penh villa. In a brazen move, the guards that ringed the villa were some of his most loyal followers from the Issarak days.[14]

Chantarangsey's illegal gambling den was an open secret among the upper strata of Phnom Penh society. But rather than punishing his cousin, Sihanouk decided to harness the talent and in early 1969 appointed him as the director of the newly opened State Casino. By all accounts, Chantarangsey grew fabulously wealthy over the ensuing year.

Still, there was no love lost between the two princes. When Sihanouk was sacked in March 1970, Chantarangsey was fast to pledge support to Lon Nol. He was rewarded by being reinstated in the army with the rank of lieutenant colonel. In addition, he was given permission to start forming a new 13 Infantry Brigade under his command. He quickly converted his Phnom Penh villa into a recruitment depot and signed up his closest Issarak colleagues to key positions.

When the brigade's three battalions approached full strength, Chantarangsey did the predictable. Bidding farewell to Phnom Penh in late 1970, he trucked his men to Kompong Speu and soon reasserted his grip in the province. Promoted to colonel in 1971, that December he was given a second hat as commander of the entire Military Region 2—a large swath of territory headquartered in Kompong Speu and covering nine military subdivisions. With a range of territorial units now at his disposal, as well as his vanguard 13 Brigade, the prince expanded

Marshal Lon Nol and Lieutenant General Sosthene Fernandez arrive at the first (and only) Armed Forces Day celebration in front of the Phnom Penh railway station, 15 August 1974. The date was chosen to commemorate the Khmer Republic having survived one year after the U.S. bombing halt. The officer on the right is Colonel Thach Reng, commander of the Khmer Special Forces. (Courtesy Barry Broman)

the government writ across the province, even managing to seize back the Kirirom Plateau after three years of communist control.

Back in Phnom Penh, Lon Nol viewed such military flourishes with suspicion and derision. Rather than celebrating the gains, he stewed over Chantarangsey's successes and ordered him to forfeit control of Kirirom. Then in March 1973, after a member of the royal family bombed the palace in a T-28, Lon Nol unleashed on all the extended members of the monarchy and contemplated sending a task force to Kompong Speu to capture the flamboyant Chantarangsey.[15]

Very quickly, however, Lon Nol saw the folly of such a move. Not only was the task force not sent; Chantarangsey was rewarded that month when given a third hat as governor of the newly created Kirirom province, carved out of western Kompong Speu. In return, Chantarangsey took steps to drop the Norodom family name and thus distance himself from royalty.

This was the situation when the first CIA case officer arrived at Chantarangsey's Kompong Speu headquarters in early 1974. Richard Santos was a Laos veteran

Brigadier General Dien Del, commander of 2 Division, acts as Grand Marshal for the Armed Forces Day parade, 15 August 1974. (Courtesy Barry Broman)

who signed up to be one of Alpha's three-month volunteers (dubbed the "Ninety Day Wonders"). He quickly found Chantarangsey to be beloved by his men, but with little patience for the central authorities: "Chantarangsey was good because he was not corrupt. He was independently wealthy and bankrolled himself, and he put his money into the community. His brigade was still supposed to be getting their salaries from Phnom Penh, but a FANK finance major showed up twice with no payroll. He was warned not to come again, but he arrived a third time with no cash. His pressed uniform and bones were sent back to Phnom Penh."[16]

By mid-1974, Santos was replaced at Kompong Speu by a newly arrived pair of Alpha officers. The first, known by callsign "Bear," was a former linebacker at the University of Pennsylvania who had earlier served as an enlisted man with the Army Security Agency (ASA) at Clark Air Force Base in the Philippines. As the U.S. Army's signal intelligence branch in charge of monitoring and interpreting military communications from communist nations, the ASA field stations recruited their enlisted men from among the top scorers on aptitude tests. It was thus no surprise that, in spite of an intimidating frame and famously temperamental attitude, Bear had a sharp intellect and ear for languages: He spoke reasonably fluent Vietnamese and Thai, as well as fair Chinese.

Bear's partner in Kompong Speu was an Italian-American officer with the callsign "Snake." Though a Laos veteran, he had spent his entire tour as the payroll officer posted to the rear support base at Udorn, Thailand. But Snake proved to be a remarkable linguist and, after a crash language course in Udorn, became Alpha's only officer to gain fluency in spoken Khmer. He quickly put this to good use to grow close not only to Chantarangsey but also to his highly regarded intelligence assistant, Colonel Thach Ung. Guerrilla colleagues since the Issarak days, Chantarangsey and Thach Ung formed an inseparable, formidable duo that went far in explaining why Kompong Speu was one of the few bright spots in the Khmer Republic.[17]

Another province that had become synonymous with a dominating military personality was Kompong Thom. Teap Ben, six years younger than Chantarangsey, had enjoyed a rather conventional military career through the early 1960s. As a young officer in 1962, he had sprung to national attention when leading an infantry unit that clashed with the Thai over control of the contested Preah Vihear temple. He had then spent the closing years of that decade serving as the intelligence officer for the military region based out of Siem Reap.

By the time of the change of governments in 1970, Major Teap Ben was on the fast track. First he was ordered to raise a new 12 Brigade in Siem Reap. Early the following year, he was named head of the Kompong Thom Military Sub-Division. Earning a third hat, he was named in 1971 head of the 9 Brigade Group in Siem Reap.[18]

By now a colonel, Teap Ben continued to divide his attention between the neighboring provinces of Siem Reap and Kompong Thom, and in mid-1972 he was placed in charge of Operation Angkor Chey, an attempt to retake the historically symbolic Angkor Wat temple complex from the Khmer Rouge. Although the operation did not succeed, Teap Ben was rewarded that October with his first general's star.

As of late 1973, Teap Ben had settled into Kompong Thom and was still wearing twin hats as both head of 12 Brigade and subdivision commander. His grip over the province was greatly enabled by another of his brigade commanders, the energetic and capable Colonel Khy Hak. Though he had not entered formal schooling until the age of eleven, Khy Hak was a prodigy of sorts and managed to graduate at the top of his military academy class seven years later.[19]

Growing close to this pair was CIA officer William "Chip" Beck. After a brief Laos tour, Beck had been scheduled for deployment to South Vietnam. Instead, he took five months of French-language training and arrived in Phnom Penh in mid-1974. He initially was assigned to Siem Reap but quickly lobbied to reopen the Alpha post in Kompong Thom (which had been closed since Mike Mangnani was evacuated with hepatitis a year earlier).[20]

At Kompong Thom, Beck became enamored with the leadership skills of Teap Ben—so much so that his Alpha colleagues teased him with the nickname "Chip Ben." At times, Beck's attempts to please the general went to extremes. Recalled Phil Runfola, the Alpha support officer in Phnom Penh: "Chip requested an Air America transport plane be sent to Kompong Thom so we could move Teap Ben's herd of water buffalo to a safer environment in Phnom Penh or Thailand. Can you imagine frightened water buffalo banging around and crapping all over the place? So I told him, 'No plane.' He responded by sending in jest some drawings of me with a noose around my neck and knives in the back."[21]

On another occasion, Beck disobeyed the standing order to all Alpha officers and joined Teap Ben on a military operation. The station chief only heard about it when Teap Ben awarded him a FANK medal for killing PAVN soldiers in a firefight. Livid, the station chief threatened to send him home but, in the end, relented.

Yet another province dominated by a single military personality was rice-rich Battambang. There the key FANK officer was the controversial Sek Sam Iet. Toward the end of the Sihanouk regime, Sek had supplemented his military career by being named governor of Koh Kong. Though a sparsely populated backwater along the southwestern border with Thailand, Koh Kong was rich in natural resources; Sek, not surprisingly, grew exceedingly wealthy by taking a cut from fishing, mangrove logging, and the manufacture of charcoal.

Sek had landed the coveted Koh Kong slot by being adept at relationships, and by the late 1960s he had grown especially close to Lon Nol.[22] Reflecting the latter's patronage, in July 1969 Lieutenant Colonel Sek became the commander of Military Region 3 and, shortly thereafter, military governor of Battambang. If anything, these were more lucrative posts than Koh Kong as it allowed him to control the country's most fertile paddyland. Reflecting his clout, Sek was a full colonel by mid-1971, a brigadier general by that December.

Settling into Battambang as the resident Alpha officer was George Kenning. An ASA alum like Kompong Speu's Bear, Kenning had joined the CIA and served a Laos tour at an isolated paramilitary post along the China frontier. Soon after landing in Cambodia, he could not help but be overcome with cynicism: "Our scope of work was open and flexible: advise, train, boost morale, represent the Ambassador, run their intelligence service, file reports nobody read, and do what we could to keep the Mighty Khmer Military Machine working."[23] Very quickly, however, he grew impressed by the abilities of Sek Sam Iet:

> He was by far the best military governor that I dealt with or knew of. The key here is *military governor*, not general or governor. There might have been better Khmer generals (arguable) or better civilian governors (maybe), but as a combination he was the best. Sek Sam Iet had the largest military region and had two main responsibilities: keep the rice harvest from the Khmer Rouge and for the (somewhat corrupt) generals in Phnom Penh and, second, do this without very many troops so that the troops from his area could be sent to defend Phnom Penh. He accomplished this every single year he was in command in Battambang.

And despite whispers in the U.S. embassy that Sek Sam Iet presented a slovenly image unbecoming of a general, and was thus somehow disqualified for his position, Kenning saw beyond the superficial:

> I was with him one day outside of Battambang when we came under a pretty serious attack. The general very calmly told his Huey pilot to shut the engine down. He then told the crowd that was trying to get on the chopper that he would personally shoot them unless they got out of the way and let the seriously wounded be evacuated. After having to shoot one as an example, he actually sent the chopper away full of wounded with instructions to return for him if possible before dark. He stayed on the ground to direct his troops. Generals did not do this very often during those days. We were both out by the end of the day and had a few more VSOPs back in Battambang.

Kenning's sentiments, it turned out, were not shared by others in the U.S. embassy. The U.S. military attachés that made periodic visits to Battambang had soured toward Sek Sam Iet, and their collective feelings eventually colored the opinion of Ambassador John Gunther Dean. Arriving in Phnom Penh in April 1974, Dean by mid-year was in the midst of a quixotic crusade to root out corruption in the Khmer government. He eventually singled out Sek, allegedly because the general was making black-market sales of rice to Thailand (rather than keeping it for the domestic market) and ammunition to the Khmer Rouge.

With Dean convinced Sek had to be removed, Phnom Penh Station as an afterthought asked Kenning for his opinion. The Alpha officer insisted it would be a tragic mistake, but Dean went ahead and urged Lon Nol in the strongest possible terms to select a new military region commander for Battambang. Pressured, the marshal saw little choice other than to sack his loyal friend in the third quarter of 1974.[24] Named in Sek's place was Major General Sar Hor. Though he cut a handsome portrait and was well regarded—he had led the successful defense at Kompong Cham in 1973—Sar had no chemistry with the troops of Military Region 3. Under his watch, the Khmer Rouge immediately surged forward and seized most of that year's rice harvest and, eventually, most of the military region.

Adjacent to Battambang and also under Military Region 3 was Pursat, a province renowned for its top-quality marble.[25] Arriving in early 1974 to open an Alpha post in that provincial capital was Larry Waters, an officer who had earlier run the intelligence teams from the mountaintop post of Preah Vihear. In the third quarter of 1974 Waters was promoted to chief of field operations in Phnom Penh, replacing the departing Colin Thompson. In his place at Pursat came two new Alpha arrivals, Mike Ingham and Robert Baskett.

For Ingham, who had recently completed a harrowing tour managing Thai infantry volunteers in northern Laos, the Alpha mandate was mystifying:

> We were supposed to collect intelligence on the Khmer Rouge, but this was all but impossible and the mission was ridiculous. Phnom Penh Station had a traditional Foreign Intelligence mentality: they focused on recruitments. I developed a good relationship with the deputy province governor, a colonel. He gave me what I wanted. But Phnom Penh [Station] got mad because I did not officially recruit him. I didn't want to insult the colonel, but the Station was grading you like a college professor. They wanted traditional Foreign Intelligence case officers in the middle of a war.[26]

Of even greater concern to Ingham were the security precautions, or lack thereof, being taken to support the up-country officers. Air America was tasked for air support, including possible evacuations, but due to personnel ceilings in Cambodia, the questionable security of facilities at Pochentong, uncertain logistics, and economies of scale, they based their aircraft in neighboring South Vietnam—which would not make for a very rapid reaction in the event of an emergency. "We

A final shipment of supplies for the HYTHE outposts is laid out at the U.S. embassy annex in Phnom Penh, late March 1975. (Courtesy Philip Runfola)

stood out like a sore thumb but there was no cavalry if things went wrong," said Ingham. "I slept in a different bed every night, literally."

Ingham's partner, Robert Baskett, was equally perplexed by their Pursat assignment. Though he made a concerted effort to collect information on the Khmer Rouge, he found an insurmountable divide between the people they had opportunity to meet and those who were tied into the communist leadership. Even worse, when he tried to establish an interrogation center in Pursat, the local military commander gave them a puzzled stare. "He said that he had no prisoners to give us," remembered Baskett, "because they routinely ran them over with armored personnel carriers to save bullets."[27]

Despite the mounting frustrations felt among Alpha officers, the Khmer Republic lived to see a full year after the U.S. bombing halt. To celebrate surviving on

HYTHE officer Chuck Hafner and his fiancée waiting for evacuation from Pochentong, 7 April 1975. (Courtesy Philip Runfola)

its own for twelve months, FANK chose 15 August 1974 as its first Armed Forces Day. At the large open square in front of the Phnom Penh railroad station, military units paraded in crisp formations and the top echelon of the military was lavished with awards.[28]

This anniversary was somewhat tempered by the bad news that followed, however. First, the troublesome Lon Non was back in town. When he had originally gone to the United States at the prompting of General Haig, he had not promised an extended absence. But in an amusing incident that spoke volumes about an underlying belief in the occult, he had decided to prolong his stay outside the country. This came about when his escort, Lieutenant Colonel Alan Armstrong, a U.S. Army officer previously assigned to Phnom Penh, had taken Lon Non on a trip to San Francisco. After a sumptuous Italian meal on Fisherman's Wharf, the Cambodian general had chanced upon an automated fortune-teller stand like those found at traveling carnivals. Plunking in his coin, he pocketed the card bearing his fortune without comment.

A short time after leaving San Francisco, Lon Non belatedly revealed his card to his American escort. Although it stated nothing more than benign generalities—*Go with the flow. Don't make waves*—the words hit Lon Non like a thunderclap: "Alan, I have decided to remain in the United States for further study," he announced gravely. Armstrong was amazed: "Lon Non was a product of French education and prided himself on being a rational thinker. Yet he had acceded to a mindless machine card in making one of the most important decisions of his political-military life. I wondered if the CIA wasn't running that fortune-telling stand. It should set up a bunch of booths around the United Nations."[29] But after languishing in Maryland for more than a year, Lon Non eventually grew impatient and returned to Cambodia in September 1974. Though he no longer held any cabinet or military posts, it was likely only a matter of time before his ambitions resurfaced and his meddling resumed.

In addition, and unlike South Vietnam's President Nguyen Van Thieu, who arguably had grown in stature and ability to fill the demands of his office, Lon Nol had only grown more pathetic and ineffectual over time. In an August 1974 telegram to Washington, Ambassador Dean pulled no punches when unleashing on the marshal. "No one would pick him to lead a modern state," Dean began. After recounting a litany of fatal flaws, the ambassador judged that Lon Nol's only saving grace was that no competent replacement had yet been identified.[30]

Still, not all the news was bad. Although the Khmer Rouge had economically inflicted small but widespread attacks on FANK garrisons during the second half of the year, the communists appeared spent after forfeiting their normal period of rest before the onset of the dry season. This had led the U.S. Defense Attaché's office to optimistically predict in November that the Khmer Rouge might be forced to delay commencement of its annual dry-season offensive, perhaps until after the start of the next year.[31]

As it turned out, hints about the upcoming Khmer Rouge offensive had filtered in from the Alpha post at Kompong Cham. More than any of the other up-country locations, Kompong Cham had been able to gather and process a significant amount of intelligence from refugees, ralliers, and prisoners. This was largely due to personal ties. As with all Alpha outposts, the CIA team at Kompong Cham was heavily reliant on the FANK Second Bureau for its leads. In actuality, they had to deal with two separate FANK Second Bureaus: a Second Bureau covering the military region as a whole, and a provincial-level Second Bureau for the military subdivision.

In Kompong Cham, the Alpha operations assistant, Kong Thann, was close to the heads in both Second Bureaus.[32] Taking advantage of these ties, Chuck

Hafner allocated funds to build a debriefing center in downtown Kompong Cham. Consisting of four debriefing rooms and a small staff of interrogators, the two bureaus assured that it was given a continuous feed of refugees and former guerrillas to query.

Alpha also had timely access to prisoners captured in and around Kompong Cham. The number of detainees had increased sharply after the September 1973 siege on the town, in the wake of which the two Second Bureaus and FANK military police had been mandated to crack down on communist informants and infiltrators.[33]

In a stroke of luck, one of their detainees in October 1974 provided a windfall of information. Chheang Ly, age twenty-seven, had been snatched by the military police for suspected Khmer Rouge ties. The son of an ethnic Chinese owner of a ten-vessel shipping fleet docked at Kompong Cham city, Ly personally captained many of the boats that made a 12-kilometer daily shuttle north to the town of Rumchek. On all these trips, he took salt and medicines north for the Khmer Rouge and, at Rumchek, collected 50 tons of latex a day and carried it back to the provincial capital.

This arrangement was allowed to proceed because the Khmer Rouge got a percent from the rubber proceeds. Republican officials were also getting a cut from the sales, but they had soured—and arrested Ly—after a dispute over their rightful share. When Alpha got word of his arrest, they arranged for his release and promptly obtained agreement from Ly to convey what he heard from his Khmer Rouge contacts at Rumchek.

The daily hearsay picked up by Ly proved informative. He was primarily in touch with Khmer Rouge economic officers, but they had grown close over the preceding months and, out of sympathy, started passing on word of intended Khmer Rouge probes against Kompong Cham.

They also confirmed that the head of the Khmer Rouge East Zone, a rotund revolutionary named So Phim, was active in the vicinity. One of the five founders of the Khmer Communist Party back in 1951, Phim had headed its East Zone since 1960.[34] Due to his proximity to the Vietnamese border, he had grown close to PAVN over the decades and was known for pro-Vietnamese sentiments. Although this did not necessarily put him in good standing with Pol Pot and the other xenophobic party stalwarts, Phim in 1970 had been named deputy commander-in-chief of Khmer Rouge forces. Quick to anger and ruthless in doling out punishments, Phim was nevertheless well liked by his men.

In mid-December 1974, So Phim was apparently planning something big. During his daily Rumchek run, Ly was taken aside by his Khmer Rouge contact and given an unusual order. By 24 December, he was told, the Khmer Rouge needed a large supply of ice, coffee, and sugar, as well as bolts of red cloth. When pressed, the contact alluded to a major meeting planned by the East Zone in the Boeng Ket rubber plantation in order to finalize their participation in the Khmer Rouge's impending dry-season offensive.

Back at Kompong Cham, Hafner and his staff discussed the news from Rumchek. Kong Thann suggested that this was a good opportunity to cripple the East Zone leadership by poisoning the ice. Hafner vetoed the idea, however, as it would expose Chheang Ly's duplicity and close that channel of information. As a result, So Phim held his meeting without incident and the East Zone put the final touches on its dry-season plans.

After almost five years of daily combat, nowhere were the ravages of war more apparent than in Cambodia's beleaguered capital, Phnom Penh. Once called the "Pearl of Asia" for its treelined avenues and blend of colonial structures with delicate Khmer lines, the city had surged from a prewar population of roughly 500,000 to around 2 million due to a deluge of refugees. These helpless masses came with no jobs (unemployment in the country was not even measured anymore), little food (prices were 20 times pre-1970 levels), and no shelter other than shanties erected along the city's boulevards.

Despite this grim picture, calm had descended across the city during the final days of 1974. The Khmer Rouge, apparently succumbing to exhaustion, was thought to have been pushed back an adequate distance from the capital's shaky perimeter. And on the political front, the marshal had retreated to his coastal villa in Kompong Som (formerly known as Sihanoukville) to contemplate yet another cabinet reshuffle.

Taking advantage of the hiatus, many of FANK's top generals and what passed for Republican aristocracy had converged at Ambassador Dean's residence for a New Year's gala. Across town, a far less staid crowd had gathered for a drag party at the British embassy. A pair from the U.S. embassy—including CIA officer Barry Broman—arrived bedecked in sarongs. Somewhat more adventurous, the British guests had opted for a flamboyant selection of skirts and feathers. But the best costume was worn by Colonel Peter D'Arcy, the Australian defense attaché, who was sporting an exquisite bridal gown.

At midnight, the British embassy crowd welcomed 1975 with generous libations. An hour into the new year, however, the atmosphere darkened when repeated thumps resounded from the east. Radios immediately crackled to life with word that attacks by fire were taking place across the northern and eastern perimeters.

Rushing to their vehicles, the partygoers raced toward the Ministry of Foreign Affairs building and adjacent waterfront Cambodiana Hotel. Once intended as the capital's first luxury hotel, the Cambodiana had yet to be inaugurated at the time of Sihanouk's fall. With no tourists to host, its balconies had been walled off and the building instead turned into a makeshift FANK barracks.

From their Mekong-side vantage point, the bizarrely adorned foreigners watched rockets arch from the swamps on the far side of the Mekong. Several rounds had already pounded the edge of Phnom Penh, setting villages afire along the bank. Fearing they might be within range, CIA officer Broman turned to D'Arcy: "How will it look on the front pages of the Australian papers if you get killed in a gown?"[35]

When the smoke cleared the next morning, citizens of the capital went about clearing away the rubble. Though FANK had been taken by surprise, this was hardly the first time the city was pummeled in this fashion. A year earlier on 3 January 1974, sixty rounds of 122mm rockets had impacted around the fringes of Phnom Penh. And in April 1974, artillery and rockets wreaked havoc along the southern periphery.

And much like the failed offensive against Phnom Penh two years earlier, this one began badly for the communists. With clear skies and a full moon illuminating the night, the Khmer Air Force inflicted savage losses for the first week.

It quickly became apparent, however, that the early 1975 offensive came with key differences. For one thing, the Khmer Rouge leaders had conquered the logistical challenges that plagued them since 1973. In particular, they seemed to have an endless supply of Chinese-made 107mm rockets; 100 of these impacted Phnom Penh during the first twelve days of the year alone.[36]

For another thing, the communists had stripped the countryside of enough able-bodied males to vastly increase their numbers. As of early 1975, they counted at least a dozen divisions. Of these, some 100 battalions were being directed by the Khmer Rouge chief of staff, Son Sen, to launch a multifront assault on the capital. Explained Son Sen: "We had been frustrated around Kompong Thom during 1971–1973. We had been frustrated at Kompong Cham and at Kampot. So even though we had poor communications among the Zones, we decided to all go directly against Phnom Penh. In total, there were three divisions hitting from the east, four from the west and southwest, and three from the north."[37]

For its part, FANK was not catching any breaks. First, the Khmer Rouge spent the opening weeks of the year seizing vital real estate along the banks of the

Mekong. In the process, they inflicted unprecedented losses on the Khmer navy. Whereas the navy had lost fifteen vessels during all of 1974, it lost seven ships in January 1975 and eighteen in February. Not surprisingly, the remaining sailors were decidedly reluctant to reinforce key marine outposts along the Mekong corridor.

Second, chronic levels of corruption continued to rot FANK from the inside. Many brigade commanders, for example, were demanding bribes to participate in counterattacks along Phnom Penh's perimeter. And a longtime practice of padding payrolls with phantom troops was now being exposed at the most inopportune time. A battalion commander in Siem Reap, for instance, reportedly turned pale when asked to rush his 400 men to the capital as reinforcements—only to discover he actually had only forty men.[38]

Even in cases where FANK had tried to root out corruption, the results had ironically been counterproductive. In Battambang, for example, the clean but ineffectual Major General Sar Hor had watched idly while the government grip over Military Region 3 slipped away. After losing most of the rice harvest to advancing Khmer Rouge, and then seeing food prices spike, students on 21 February reacted by burning down the Battambang market.

Belatedly realizing it had been a mistake to cave to American pressure, Lon Nol in early March sidelined Sar Hor and reinstated Major General Sek Sam Iet to his Battambang post. "I saw several ranking officers, and numerous enlisted men, kneel down and kiss his feet when he arrived," recalled Alpha's resident officer, George Kenning. "But it was all a bit late."[39]

The loss of Battambang's rice harvest had exacerbated shortages of this staple in Phnom Penh. In fact, the capital was short of all forms of military and nonmilitary supplies—and with the Mekong slowly being constricted by the Khmer Rouge, this had left Pochentong as the city's primary lifeline. Desperate to keep food, fuel, and ammunition flowing, the United States on 16 February initiated a massive airbridge into Phnom Penh. But because of the limits set on U.S. government personnel who could be in Cambodia at any one time, the U.S. Air Force had subcontracted to civilian companies: ten of its C-130 transports were leased to BirdAir, plus an additional five DC-8s went to World Airways of Oakland and Airlift International of Miami.[40]

Based out of Utapao Royal Thai Air Force Base, these airlines for twelve days made daily shuttles of ammunition into Pochentong. After that, BirdAir continued with the ammunition lift from Utapao, while the other airlines—joined by

Trans International, Flying Tiger, and Seaboard World—shifted to Saigon and started daily shuttles of rice and kerosene to the Cambodian capital.

Not surprisingly, the Khmer Rouge zeroed in on the airbridge. On 15 March, the intensity and accuracy of their rocket and howitzer fire on Pochentong dramatically increased. A week later, one C-130 and one DC-8 were damaged, causing a two-day suspension of flights. "We only lost one windshield and one tire," recalled BirdAir owner William Bird with an air of bravado. "When we learned it was rockets—which were very inaccurate—operations resumed."[41]

Although the airbridge was vital for the Republic's survival, it proved a double-edged sword. The subcontracted airlift operation was an expensive venture, after all, and funds for the war in Cambodia were something now in short supply. In December 1974, the U.S. Congress had allocated $452 million for the Khmer Republic, of which $200 million was earmarked for military aid. Given the accelerated tempo of the war, however, this amount had evaporated after mere weeks. In February 1975, the White House returned to Congress with a request for an additional $222 million in emergency aid. Congress, however, was in little mood to accommodate. At month's end, the legislators let it be known that they intended to delay deliberation on the supplemental funds until the first week of April.

All of this had heightened the sense of desperation among American officials. In an estimate prepared by the CIA on 13 February, they pessimistically noted that the airlift would be needed at least until July when the rainy season widened the Mekong and made it harder for the Khmer Rouge to interdict river convoys.[42] On 10 March, CIA Director William Colby was far more somber. In a briefing before the House Foreign Affairs Committee, he summed up the Cambodian situation in one terse sentence: Substantial odds favor a communist takeover in the near future.

So great was the mounting pressure that the U.S. military skirted closer to the congressional prohibition against advising FANK and, in at least one case, blatantly violated it. This took place in mid-March when General William Palmer, the head of the Military Equipment Delivery Team at the embassy, fast-tracked a plan to cobble together a fifty-person Special Operations Force drawn from select Khmer marines and SEAL commandos. The force would be used to interdict the Khmer Rouge along the banks of the Mekong and, theoretically, ease pressure on the riverine supply convoys running the gauntlet to Phnom Penh. In direct violation of the restriction on in-country training, a U.S. Marine lieutenant colonel, John Hopkins, was sent on special assignment to the seaside town of Ream to prepare an instructor cadre during 24–30 March. The remainder of the force was to arrive on 31 March, with plans to continue training until 15 April.[43]

As it turned out, the Special Operations Force never left Ream. During the first half of March, the Khmer Rouge dispatched a regiment to hit Neak Luong. A key ferry crossing at a bend in the Mekong, Neak Luong, was being protected by elements of four FANK brigades. Under relentless heavy weapons fire on 16 March, Brigadier General Lim Sisaath—the same officer who had led the Cambodian battalions for training in Laos five years earlier—was dispatched to steel morale among the defenders. Another two weeks after that, the Khmer Rouge had decimated the perimeter and was on the verge of overrunning Sisaath's command post. Out of options, the general called in a final airstrike on his own position.

The loss of Neak Luong on 1 April made the fall of the Khmer Republic a matter of when, not if. With this critical bend in the Mekong in communist hands, further riverine convoys were out of the question. Phnom Penh's lifeline, as a result, was now reduced to Pochentong. Worse, the Khmer Rouge had captured six 105mm howitzers at Neak Luong, which they immediately began wheeling toward the southern environs of the capital.

By that time, key members of the Republican government were already on their way out. The first to go was the double-hatted FANK commander-in-chief and chief of the General Staff, Sosthene Fernandez. On 12 March, he was toasted in a simple farewell ceremony by Lon Nol before being awarded the Grand Cross. Named a roving ambassador as consolation, he flew to Bangkok the following week on a chartered flight with his wife, seven children, and four elephant tusks.

Replacing Sosthene as chief of the FANK General Staff was the benign Lieutenant General Sak Sutsakhan. With horn-rimmed glasses and foppish hair giving him a decidedly professorial air, Sak had the distinction of rising to the top of a wartime military without having been near a shot fired in anger. Born in 1928 in Battambang, he had attended seven years of French military schools before, at the tender of age of twenty-eight, being named undersecretary of national defense. He held primarily staff positions until 1969, when as a colonel he was selected as head of the army's foray against PAVN positions in Ratanakiri province. Coordinating this operation from Phnom Penh, he never actually stepped foot in the bush.

In March 1970, Colonel Sak briefly showed a scheming side. Early that month, he surreptitiously instigated the mob that torched the Viet Cong and DRV embassies. This cemented his close ties to Lon Nol, who named him deputy chief of staff later that year, then minister of state for national defense in 1972.

At that point Sak fell out with the marshal, apparently over the former's penchant for steering clear of corruption. In 1973, he was named a roving ambassador attached to the Ministry of Foreign Affairs and shunted out of the country. It was not until February 1975 that he was recalled back to Phnom Penh and, as the only lieutenant general with a proper military background, was the sole candidate to inherit the top FANK slot.[44]

On 31 March, Marshal Lon Nol presided over what would be his last cabinet meeting.[45] Tellingly, he used the opportunity to hand out a fourth star to both Sak and Lieutenant General Saukham Khoy. Born in 1914, Saukham had been a bureaucrat in the Ministry of Forestry before being named among the army's first crop of officers. Like Sak, he had risen up the ranks in staff positions, not combat units. During the Republican government, he was sufficiently reliable and nonthreatening to rate a second star and be named to the inconsequential post of FANK inspector general. He then got a third star while holding one of the military's designated seats in the National Assembly.

On 1 April, Lon Nol himself succumbed to the pressure. At midday, twenty-nine of his closest aides and family members filed into an Air Cambodge Caravelle at Pochentong. Half an hour later, the marshal bid farewell to a small crowd at the palace, took a chopper to the airport, then boarded the Caravelle for Utapao. Promoted in his place as Cambodia's new president was the bland Saukham Khoy.

Coming at that late hour, the shake-up in leadership had no appreciable impact. The Sihanouk-led rebel government in Beijing had already announced a list of "supertraitors" (initially seven top Republican personalities, later expanded to twenty-three names), and both Sak and Saukham were among them. The Khmer Rouge clearly were interested in nothing short of unconditional surrender. It was equally clear that they had no intent of giving Sihanouk—who they saw as an "unscrupulous and adroit political operator"—any chance to wield meaningful power once Phnom Penh fell.[46] As of 28 March, Defense Secretary James Schlesinger thought the collapse would come in two weeks. A CIA assessment the following day pegged Phnom Penh's perimeter lasting just "the next week or so."[47]

Predicting the Republic's imminent demise when it was on its deathbed was not especially difficult. Ironically, however, despite the fact that it had a better window into the Cambodian countryside over the previous two years than any other U.S. government agency, the CIA had done a poor job describing the likely aftermath following a Khmer Rouge victory. According to a 30 January forecast issued by Langley, its analysts went only so far as to write that "some, but probably not mass, exemplary executions can be expected."[48]

Foggy Bottom, by contrast, was far more pessimistic and, in hindsight, accurate. On 8 April, Andrew Antippas, the State Department desk officer for Cambodia, was especially prophetic when he wrote:

> How can one believe that the communists will not commit mass murder when one considers that they, the Cambodian communists, number perhaps only 10,000 cadre in all? They are despised and feared by the general populace for their anti-Buddhist, collectivist doctrine, and forced recruitment of all available manpower as cannon fodder to kill other Khmer. The Cambodian communists must, for their own safety, eliminate all possible opposition including civil servants, teachers, village headmen, Buddhist leaders, commissioned and non-commissioned officer, etc. We have been well aware that the Khmer communists, for several years, have made a practice of not taking officers prisoner in order to eliminate possible opposition. . . . They will, in my view, move fast and brutally.[49]

Inside the U.S. embassy, CIA Station Chief David Whipple sifted through the gloomy forecasts. A veteran of Great Britain's Gordon Highlanders infantry regiment during World War II and a confirmed Anglophile, Whipple had joined the CIA and served in such far-flung posts as Elisabethville during the Katanga rebellion and, most recently, Helsinki. Arriving in Phnom Penh during July 1974, his tour eventually devolved into contingency planning for operations in the event of a communist victory.

In February 1975, Phnom Penh Station took the first concrete steps toward these ends. Concurrent with a phased withdrawal of dependents from the U.S. embassy, all of the Cambodians employed at the Alpha outposts were ordered to send their families to houses the CIA had rented in Oddar Meanchey province near the Thai border.[50]

That same month, Whipple approved a belated effort to identify and train stay-behind agents who would function as eyes and ears after a communist takeover. Finding willing agents was a challenge: At least three prospects selected in Phnom Penh turned down the job when pitched.[51] Eventually, however, two suitable candidates—one from Siem Reap, the other from Kompong Cham—were identified by the Alpha officers in those provinces.

The Kompong Cham candidate was none other than Chheang Ly, the boat captain who had been informing Chuck Hafner about maritime trade with the Khmer Rouge. With Kompong Cham operations assistant Kong Thann accompanying him as translator, the two were whisked to Phnom Penh, then shuttled in an Air America transport to Saigon. From there they were taken in a blacked-out van to a CIA safe house a couple of blocks from Independence Palace.

For the next seven days, Ly was drilled by two American instructors. The curriculum focused on radio operations: "I was taught Morse, radio repair, and how to encrypt the Cambodian language using a one-time pad. I wasn't given any special reporting instructions; I was just supposed to radio back general information and observations if the Khmer Rouge took over."[52] Returning to Cambodia in early March, Ly spent two nights in the capital. There he had a hotel room rendezvous with Hafner, who handed over an olive-drab, waterproof box containing a radio and solar cells. This Ly took back to a family-owned house in the city and, while nobody was present, extended the radio's antenna across the ceiling beams and sent out a burst transmission as a test message. Then heading to Kompong Cham, Ly was given a second, identical radio and solar cells by Kong Thann. Like the first, the container was hidden in the attic of a family-owned house.

For the remainder of March, the Alpha officers held ringside seats to witness FANK in its death throes. From Kompong Speu, the program's sole Cambodian linguist, Snake, had been diverted to the coast to assist with the evacuation of foreign nationals—including Danish and Filipina nurses—out of Ream airbase. Others, such as Joe Boys in Svay Reing, nervously watched as FANK depleted its gasoline reserves and cracked open its final crates of bullets and howitzer rounds.

Finally on 7 April, Station Chief Whipple judged the risks to Alpha personnel had fully outweighed any possible benefits from their continued presence. With only two exceptions near the Thai border, all of the up-country officers were ordered to leave the country the following day.

As scheduled, Joe Boys and his attractive operations assistant, Samay Mom, were whisked out of Svay Rieng by chopper and taken to Saigon. It came none too soon, as the resident FANK brigade had exhausted its artillery supply and was on the verge of collapse.[53]

In Phnom Penh, several of the remaining Alpha officers and operations assistants had gathered at a sandbagged bunker on the edge of Pochentong. A BirdAir C-130 came in, dropped its ramp, and they scrambled aboard. All were then shuttled to the marginally more secure Tan Son Nhut airbase in South Vietnam.

Back in Cambodia, most of the Alpha outposts were still being manned by Cambodian employees. On 11 April, Kong Thann boarded an Air America Porter at Tan Son Nhut and headed back across the border with their final salaries. Approaching Pochentong, however, they could see rounds impacting across the runway. In fact, the U.S. airbridge had been suspended the previous day due to the accuracy of incoming fire. Unable to land in the capital, they instead made brief stops at Pursat, Siem Reap, and Oddar Meanchey, dropping off satchels of cash at each location.[54]

The next morning, Ambassador Dean called for Eagle Pull, the codename for the evacuation of the U.S. embassy. A total of eighty-two U.S. citizens were shuttled 2 kilometers to a helicopter landing zone at a soccer field next to the Cambodiana Hotel. They were joined by 159 Cambodians and thirty-five third-country nationals. This included the short-lived president, Saukham Khoy, who in his haste had forgotten to inform the National Assembly of his impending departure. The only other senior Cambodian official to join Eagle Pull was the undersecretary of sports; all others opted out of the exodus.[55]

At 1015, Ambassador Dean arrived at the landing zone and boarded one of the U.S. Marine helicopters dispatched from a naval task force off the Cambodian coast. He was joined by General Palmer and Station Chief Whipple. Adding a touch of the surreal, among the baggage packed for the evacuation were several reels of film. Earlier in the month, Sihanouk had sent President Gerald Ford a plea to save some of the films he directed for posterity; U.S. diplomats, as a result, had scrambled to locate several of these cinematic gems.[56]

At 1059, the final chopper lifted from the landing zone. No shots had been fired throughout the Eagle Pull operation. Cambodian children, seemingly oblivious to the danger massing near the capital's edge, waved at the departing aircraft.

5. Arrested Development

Brigadier General Dien Del glanced skyward as the first trio of U.S. Marine CH-53 choppers passed over Takhmau city on their way toward Phnom Penh, 11 kilometers farther north. Hunkered down in the forward headquarters of his 2 Infantry Division, the forty-two-year-old Del was easily FANK's most battle-hardened senior officer. And like most on FANK's painfully short list of standouts, he was an ethnic Khmer Krom: Born in South Vietnam's Mekong Delta, he had not even stepped foot in Cambodia until a teenager.

From the time he emerged from high school, Del had been a soldier, more often than not near the frontlines. Graduating from Cambodia's nascent military academy just weeks before the kingdom was granted independence in November 1953, he was assigned to an infantry battalion and participated in the country's first postcolonial skirmishes; one especially intense engagement in April 1954 left him with a mortar fragment in his bicep.

Not until late during that decade did Del take leave of the infantry for further schooling. Sent to France for more than a year, he was drilled in legal and administrative subjects. By now a captain, he returned to Phnom Penh and spent a year as a staff assistant for a fellow Khmer Krom, General Lon Nol. Suitably impressing the future marshal, he was retained for another year as the general's aide-de-camp.

In 1965, Del was promoted to major and given command of his own infantry battalion. This particular unit, 24 Infantry Battalion, was part of the army's three-battalion strategic reserve. He saw plenty of action over the next five years, shuttling around the kingdom to quell some of the first flare-ups by the Khmer Rouge. This pace quickened after the March 1970 change in governments, when Del's battalion was first rushed to Kompong Cham to put down a pro-Sihanouk riot, then shifted to Svay Rieng to reinforce that besieged province.

By then, FANK was growing exponentially and Lon Nol did not forget his former aide. Promoted to lieutenant colonel, Del was given command over four battalions, which together constituted the new 2 Infantry Brigade. This brigade saw constant combat over the ensuing year, with Del compiling a record as one of the army's more aggressive officers.

For his success, in mid-1971 Del was given command over two more brigades. Together with his 2 Infantry Brigade, this conglomeration was known as 2 Brigade Group. Now sporting the rank of colonel, Del that August was ordered to take his brigade group up Route 6 toward Kompong Thom in the opening phases of Operation Chenla 2. But smelling a fiasco in the making, he managed to rotate out his brigades after the initial month and arranged to attend a senior command course in South Vietnam. This timely absence placed him out of the country when Chenla 2 was crushed in a decisive PAVN counterattack.

During 1972, as most of FANK had withdrawn into its post–Chenla 2 funk, Del was one of the few brigade group commanders to maintain a good showing. In recognition, that December he was among four brigade group commanders who were selected to lead FANK's four new divisions. Though the divisions were theoretically the army's strategic reserve available for deployment anywhere in the Republic, in practice they were wedded to specific sectors of the Phnom Penh perimeter. For its part, Del's 2 Infantry Division guarded the southern approaches to the capital. Now sporting a general's star, Del was additionally appointed military governor of Kandal province, which also extended across Phnom Penh's southern flank.

Over the next two years, Del and his infantrymen doggedly resisted Khmer Rouge advances. In December 1974, there was even a note of optimism as the division extended its buffer zone slightly southward.

It was not to last, however. Shortly after the opening of 1975, the northern and southwestern perimeters of the capital came under withering pressure. Forced to loan nearly half his men and most of his artillery assets to assist other fronts, Del suddenly found his emasculated 2 Infantry Division hopelessly outmanned and outgunned.

By the opening week of April, Del was barely holding his ground at Takhmau. After enduring years of daily combat, the general was beyond exhaustion. Still, he continued to cajole his men to stand fast against the communist onslaught, relenting only to send his wife and son on 7 April to the coast for easier evacuation. Over the next four days, he was visited at his command post by General Palmer, the ranking U.S. military officer at the embassy. "I last saw him on 11 April," Del recalled. "He gave no indication of wavering."[1]

As the Marine choppers passed overhead, Del felt a brief flash of optimism. He called out for his deputy and asked, "Are the Americans coming to help?"

The deputy, Colonel Sok Pakop, got on the radio and made some calls to the FANK headquarters. His tears spoke volumes. "No," he told his division commander. "They are leaving."

Inside Phnom Penh, the Republican government convened at noon on 12 April to discuss its dwindling options. After ripping into Saukham Khoy for fleeing without handing over power in legal fashion, they agreed to transfer authority to the military. Late that same night, they chose members of a seven-man Supreme Council including General Sak, who represented the army, Rear Admiral Vong Sarendy of the navy, and Brigadier General Ea Chhong of the air force.

The following morning, the Supreme Council duly convened. As their first order of business, they unanimously selected Sak as the Republic's third president. As their next task, they prepared peace overtures to Sihanouk. It was a futile exercise: Sihanouk hardly had the latitude to shape Cambodia's fate, and the Khmer Rouge had long scoffed at a negotiated denouement.

On 14 April, FANK units began to wilt across the city's entire perimeter. In a desperate attempt to keep Pochentong open, paratroopers were rushed to that front. Heading the column was a French mercenary named Dominique Borella. As FANK had no money to pay a foreign volunteer, Borella's motivation as a soldier of fortune in Cambodia was unclear; some speculated he was holding out for spoils in the highly unlikely event of a Republican victory.

In the end, the intervention of Borella and his paratroopers had no appreciable impact. With the Khmer Rouge peppering Pochentong almost at will, the United States that day suspended its airbridge for good.[2] Showing innovation, the Khmer Air Force shifted its T-28 fleet to a road parallel to the Pochentong runway not yet bracketed by communist fire. Taking off, the tiny fighter-bombers would drop their bombs along the city limits and, just minutes later, return for more ordnance. One of the pilots, looking to score points with the advancing Khmer Rouge, that afternoon veered over the city and dropped four bombs near where the Supreme Council was meeting. He then flew north to a communist-held airstrip in Kompong Cham and an unknown fate.

Outside of Phnom Penh, the CIA monitored the Republic's final days from two outposts still manned by American officers. Both were remnants of the Alpha Program and had been exempt from the station chief's evacuation order (and Eagle Pull) due to their proximity to the Thai border. The first was at Samraong—Khmer for "dense jungle"—the backwater capital of Oddar Meanchey province. More of a bloated village than a proper town, Samraong was 40 kilometers from the O'Smach border crossing. It was there that the CIA had rented rooms to house the dependents of its local Alpha employees, as well as several for the employees themselves.

Chaperoning this crowd was Chip Beck, the Alpha officer who had been stationed alongside General Teap Ben in Kompong Thom. Shifting to Samraong on

8 April, he used the time to prepare vehicles for the almost certain evacuation convoy to the border.

Meantime in Battambang, the two-man Alpha team—George Kenning and Brian O'Connor—had ventured to the FANK officer's club on 7 April for a meeting with the city's top brass. O'Connor, who had joined Alpha at the start of the year, was struck by the lack of realism among the crowd:

> George and I had lunch with seven of the most senior military officers in the region, including Sek Sak Iet. Toward the end of the meal, each person at the table commented on what he thought would happen to them. Each one had some reason why they were going to be okay. One guy said he was in logistics so they would leave him alone. Another said his wife was a relative of Sihanouk, so he would be okay. Even one who was a combat commander said the Khmer Rouge would probably put him in prison for a while but his family would be fine. Sek Sam Iet was the only one that did not say anything.[3]

The following day both Alpha officers made a final survey of their office ("there was nothing special to destroy," said Kenning, "aside from a couple of documents") before boarding a chopper to the town of Poipet on the northwest edge of Battambang province.

Like Samraong, Poipet was small and dusty—and just a few kilometers from the Thai border. In the neighboring jungle, General In Tam, the onetime prime minister and presidential candidate, had been living quietly for the past year as a rice farmer. Even though he was high on the Khmer Rouge list of condemned supertraitors, the general exuded a determined, defiant streak. He had surrounded himself with an entourage of 300, a third of which was armed. He continued to give media interviews and vowed to continue fighting—though his bravado was no doubt abetted by his camp being a mere 50 meters from the border.[4]

But apart from In Tam's threatened resistance, there was very little to monitor in Poipet. The pair of CIA officers, as a result, spent much of the next week sitting in front of one of the few stores in town that served cold beers. During one of those late afternoons, a young Caucasian with a backpack came along. Recounted O'Connor: "He looked like a world traveler so we struck up a conversation. It turned out he was an Israeli who had recently finished college and was hitchhiking through Asia. We explained the security situation to him and suggested he might not want to go to points east. He shrugged off our advice and said he was going to push to Phnom Penh. I always wondered what happened to him."[5]

On 15 April, Kenning boarded a chopper to return briefly to Battambang city for a final dinner with Major General Sek Sam Iet. In the midst of their meal, Voice of America reported that the Ford administration, facing an unyielding Congress, had dropped its request for supplemental military aid to Cambodia. Kenning grew nervous yet found the FANK officers resigned to their fates: "They were friendly as possible, almost blasé. It was sort of like, 'Well, that's too bad, see you around some time, George.' And we all went our separate ways."

Back in Poipet, O'Connor was exceedingly uncomfortable. "Up until then, the place had been very friendly," he said. "Once aid was cut off, everyone knew the war was lost and the whole atmosphere changed dramatically."

Driving home the point, the next morning they saw Sek Sam Iet's Mercedes rip through Poipet on the way to the border. It was filled with family members—not the general himself—though the fact he had sent them to Thailand was not a good omen.

Getting on their radio, the CIA officers attempted to contact Cambodian employees still at the Alpha post in Phnom Penh. A female picked up, sobbing uncontrollably.

Seeing no point in staying, the pair sent their few remaining local staff members across the border. As soon as they were inside Thailand, the two CIA officers followed in a jeep. The checkpoint on the Cambodian side was abandoned. On the Thai side, an elderly police officer gave a cursory glance at their passports and sent them speeding on their way toward Bangkok.

Back in Phnom Penh, one of the CIA's stay-behind agents, Chheang Ly, had ventured to the capital from Kompong Cham to attend an ill-timed family wedding. Slipping away to his house, he activated his radio on 15 April and sent his first—and, in hindsight, last—status report. Typing a message that was as brief as it was obvious, he transmitted: THE ENEMY IS CLOSING IN. He then repacked the radio set, placed the container down a dry well on the front lawn, removed the well's spigot, and pulled a concrete slab over the top.[6]

Elsewhere in the city, the Supreme Council was presiding over what was effectively the Republic's funeral. Reports from across the frontline were uniformly negative. That morning, the Khmer Rouge had taken Takhmau city, pushing Dien Del and his 2 Infantry Division into the capital's southern neighborhoods. A separate communist prong had surged across Pochentong. There they captured the mercenary Borella but, showing uncharacteristic restraint, later turned him over to the French embassy.

Six Khmer Air Force UH-1 choppers abandoned at the Olympic Stadium, April 1975. (Author's collection)

With FANK now only holding the city proper, the Supreme Council governed this toehold through 16 April. They spent that day going through the motions of sending negotiation offers to Sihanouk via the United Nations and the Red Cross. With no response forthcoming by nightfall, Sak and the other senior officers convened for the last time near midnight. Out of options, they agreed to abandon the capital and form a bastion of resistance in Oddar Meanchey province along the border. They would flee the capital for their new redoubt in the morning.

That same night, Brigadier General Dien Del left the frontline and made his way downtown to the Khmer Air Force headquarters. Huddling with Brigadier General Ea Chhong, the air force chief advised him in hushed tones to rendezvous at the Olympic Stadium at daybreak. As instructed, Del woke before dawn on 17 April and made the short drive to the sports complex. Capable of seating 60,000, the stadium was framed by 12-meter-tall earthen walls; inside, fourteen UH-1 choppers were lined up along the soccer field.

Wasting no time, Del and Ea Chhong climbed into the rear of the closest Huey. At 0500, their chopper rose out of the stadium, three more ships following in their wake. Curling northwest, Ea Chhong directed the armada toward Kompong Chhnang airbase, where they could refuel and then press on to Oddar Meanchey. What he did not know was that the Kompong Chhnang military region commander, Brigadier General Kem Thy, as well as airbase commander Plok Saphat, had both fled their posts the night before.

As the four choppers settled onto Kompong Chhnang's tarmac, a platoon of airbase security troops materialized around the Hueys, weapons drawn. Their commander, a major, had already worked himself into a frenzy and was gesticulating wildly with a pistol. Petrified about imminent Khmer Rouge reprisals, he announced he was taking possession of the aircraft.

Knowing his rank now counted for little, Ea Chhong tried compromise and reason. One of the choppers could stay at Kompong Chhnang, he granted, if they were allowed to refuel the other three. After several tense minutes, the major relented.

With gas tanks topped, the three choppers slowly lifted back into the morning sky. Shaken by the encounter, Del pressed the pilot, "Do we have enough fuel to get to Thailand?"

Not sure, answered the pilot.

Del was ready to accept the risk. "Just keep going until we cross the border."

Back in Phnom Penh, General Sak had driven through the early-morning streets to Prime Minister Long Boret's residence for a final tryst. They were joined at 0800 by several FANK officers, including the commander of the Khmer Special Forces, Brigadier General Thach Reng.

A proverbial pitbull for Lon Nol, Thach Reng had a colorful history long on scheming and short on actual combat. One of only three legal scholars in the military, he had spent the entire Sihanouk era in the engineering corps. But behind the scenes, by the early 1960s he had worked his way into Lon Nol's inner circle and—under an alias—was named a senior official in the White Scarves liberation movement that was covertly sniping at South Vietnam.[7]

After the change of governments in 1970, Major Thach Reng was briefly placed in charge of an infantry battalion, then a regiment, then a brigade. (Many of the troops under his command were former White Scarves who had been repatriated from South Vietnam.) While these units were active for a time on the Kirirom Plateau, the uncharismatic Reng himself rarely ventured far from the capital.

Rather, Reng was spending more time cementing his reputation as a diehard Lon Nol loyalist. Reflecting this trust, in October 1971 he was placed in command of the newly raised Khmer Special Forces. Like their U.S. Army counterparts, FANK's Special Forces were envisioned as an elite unconventional warfare outfit that would strike deep in the communist rear and empower the rural population to resist the Khmer Rouge.

Reality proved far different. Although Reng was renowned for his personal integrity,[8] he never actually employed the Khmer Special Forces in its intended unconventional warfare role.[9] Rather, they became a sort of palace guard concentrated within municipal Phnom Penh. When Reng got whiffs of another coup being planned by senior FANK officers in late 1974, for example, he had his commandos conspicuously patrol the capital in full battle gear.[10] Only too aware that such dogged loyalty to the marshal gave Reng disproportionate clout, much of the FANK General Staff kept him at a cool distance.

At about that same time, Thach Reng had an eleventh-hour epiphany and agreed at long last to use his Special Forces in a partisan operation. This came about after 1,600 villagers from the lower reaches of the Bassac River announced their intention in November 1974 to evacuate to an area of government control. Of these, the Khmer Special Forces rearmed 100 and helped them reinfiltrate back to their home district to carry on a rear-guard struggle against the Khmer Rouge.[11]

But by then the situation was too far gone in the countryside for the Khmer Special Forces to make any lasting tactical impact, much less a strategic one. A few months later, in March 1975, Reng told Station Chief Whipple of his intention to use his Special Forces to establish a guerrilla staging base along the South Vietnamese border in the mountains of Takeo province. No doubt humoring Reng, who was by then sporting a general's star, Whipple promised to make rice drops to the commandos.[12]

By the time Sak was meeting with Long Boret for their last meeting, Thach Reng's Special Forces were still massed inside Phnom Penh. Reng had beckoned two fellow Khmer Krom officers to the residence: his Special Forces deputy Kim Phong, and Thach Rinh, commander of the 43 Infantry Brigade. Having procrastinated in forming the guerrilla base on the South Vietnamese border, he now instructed both colonels to lead their men out of the capital and rendezvous in Takeo. Both acknowledged the order and left the house; neither was ever seen again.

Reng then turned to Sak and pleaded with the president to leave. Sak relented, though not before one last order of business. Placing a call to the Ministry of Information, he intended to instruct them to announce the Republic's surrender at 0900. Nobody answered; the ministry's staff, it turned out, had fled hours earlier.

At the Olympic Stadium, a heavily armed team from Reng's Special Forces had taken up positions atop the earthen walls to protect the choppers within. Sak's family arrived and, shortly thereafter, so did Long Boret and two other ministers. The prime minister had come with substantial baggage and a sizable entourage—more than two dozen dependents and friends soon massed inside the stadium.

At 0830, Sak and Reng lifted off in one of the Hueys. Three others, brimming with an assortment of FANK officers, followed in their wake. Six more choppers were left inside the stadium for Long Boret and his party, though at least one was no longer in flyable condition. Whether for mechanical reasons or a lack of pilots, those six helicopters never departed; Long Boret, his name prominent on the Khmer Rouge list of supertraitors, was left stranded in the capital.[13]

After reaching flying altitude, the four-ship armada received word from Ea Chhong to avoid Kompong Chhnang airbase. Shifting direction, they vectored north and an hour later reached Kompong Thom. There they met General Teap Ben, the military governor, who still held sway around town. They remained there through noon, at which time they tuned their radio to the Ministry of Information channel and heard General Mey Sichan, the FANK chief of operations, order the military to hoist white flags in surrender.

As the news sunk in, Sak reminded them of their plan to press toward Oddar Meanchey. Assessing the defenses at Kompong Thom to be untenable, Teap Ben joined them as they loaded back into the choppers and headed northwest.

In Phnom Penh, the final Khmer Rouge push was rushed and disorganized. As would later be revealed, the Khmer Rouge senior command had originally planned for the final surge to start on 21 April and last a full ten days. But after the United States evacuated, they had launched a full week earlier on 14 April. While they were able to bring six divisions to bear, and had showered the capital with an ample supply of rockets, coordination among the columns was haphazard at best.

As it turned out, the ad hoc nature to the final communist drive allowed the ambitious Lon Non to hatch one last plot. Ever since returning as ambassador-at-large in the United States the previous year, the marshal's younger brother had been itching to assume a lead political role. Ambassador Dean had managed to frustrate most of these plans, though in late March 1975 Lon Non announced his intention to take over the Social Republican Party (founded by the marshal in 1972 to participate in that year's legislative election).[14]

For their part, the rest of the FANK High Command shunned the meddlesome sibling. When the marshal flew into exile, they deprived Lon Non of any significant position. Even after the United States evacuated on 12 April, and he made no secret he wanted power from Long Boret, his fellow generals continued to keep him at bay.

Frustrated at every turn and running out of time, Lon Non concocted a desperate scheme that, in hindsight, was destined to fail. Conspiring with student leader Hem Keth Dara, whose father was a prominent Lon Nol loyalist who had served in a series of ministerial posts since 1972, they quietly created a so-called National Movement (Mouvement National, or Monatio) that, when the moment was right, would rise up in Phnom Penh and upstage the Khmer Rouge, then presumably call on Lon Non to play an eleventh-hour mediating role with the communists. Dara named himself general in charge of Monatio, and his forty troops were issued smart black fatigues and army weapons. They even fashioned flags featuring a modified cross on a blue and red field.

At 0900 on 17 April, an armed Monatio column made its debut on the streets of Phnom Penh. It was these troops—not actual Khmer Rouge—who intercepted the unwitting General Mey Sichan and brought him to the Ministry of Information. After waiting several hours to get the ministry's radio back in working condition, they flanked the general when he issued his surrender order. With dramatic flair, Dara even had added a short speech of his own calling on senior Republican officials to gather at the ministry.

The scam was not to last, however. By 1230, bona fide Khmer Rouge had reached the radio station and easily sniffed out the imposters. Dara and four of his self-styled lieutenants were led away in chains and later executed.

But believing Dara's order to be real, by 1400 some forty high-ranking military and civilian officials had assembled at the Ministry of Information. Among them was the impeccably dressed Lon Non, who apparently thought that Dara's Monatio would soon be calling on his services. The hardline Khmer Rouge were less than impressed, taking him away and reportedly executing him within hours on the tennis court of the city's once upper-crust sporting club, Cercle Sportif.

From Bangkok Station, the CIA was monitoring radios across Cambodia. In many cases, channels merely went dead. In others, there were emotional final transmissions as towns and cities fell to the Khmer Rouge juggernaut.

One such transmission came from Kompong Speu, where the Military Region 2 commander, Brigadier General Chantarangsey, had suffered a dramatic final week. First, his highly regarded 13 Infantry Brigade had been largely crushed when it was deployed northeast in an unsuccessful attempt to relieve pressure on Pochentong. Next, he had sent his wife, Princess Sisowath Samanvoraphong, and their son to the U.S. embassy to seek help with evacuating—but his CIA contacts were busy in the field and both had been turned back. (Left to their own devices in the capital, the wife and son were killed soon after the Khmer Rouge took over.)

Now huddled in his command post with 2,000 troops and dependents, Chantarangsey took stock of his bleak situation. There was no water supply, no food reserves, local agriculture was ruined, and the communists were advancing on Kompong Speu from all directions. On a personal level, he was accompanied by one consort; another of his minor wives was in Phnom Penh.[15]

Desperate, the former prince decided to return to his guerrilla roots and break through the Khmer Rouge cordon before heading with a core group of loyal troops toward the Kirirom Plateau. Loading aboard a convoy of trucks and M-113 armored vehicles, they were last seen on the afternoon of 17 April kicking up a cloud of red dust as they bore south along Route 4.

Remaining behind in the command post was the Military Region 2 intelligence officer, Colonel Thach Ung. Aside from a brief stint as a teacher, Ung had been a fighting man all his life—and all of it had been at Chantarangsey's side. He had never benefited financially from the war, had never even bothered to upgrade the cramped hovel where he lived with his wife and four children.

Opting not to leave his family at this critical juncture, and knowing all too well his certain fate, Ung got on the radio and raised Bangkok Station. His voice cracked with emotion as he relayed the futility of the situation. The colonel then grew dark and signed off with a flash of anger directed at the Republic's American sponsors: "You people are worse than the French."

The news from Kompong Cham was equally gut-wrenching. There, one of the secretaries employed at the Alpha post, Kon Vorrot, had arrived at the villa on the morning of 17 April. Despite pleas from Chuck Hafner and many of her Cambodian colleagues, the petit Kon had stayed in Kompong Cham because her retired father refused to evacuate.

That afternoon, she raised Bangkok Station on the office's single-sideband. "They are entering the compound," she relayed in quivering English.

Switching to Khmer, she reported a few minutes later, "They are breaking down the door."

A few seconds later, she cried in Khmer, "What should I do?"[16]

The CIA officers monitoring from Bangkok sat in stunned collective silence as the transmission went dead. Chuck Hafner would later describe it as the worst moment of his career.[17]

Slightly better news came out of Battambang. As the Khmer Rouge tightened the noose on that provincial capital, Major General Sek Sam Iet was not alone. As might be expected of an influential military governor in a strategic province along the Thai border, the general had cultivated strong ties among the top brass of the Thai military. Looking to assist him in his hour of need, two senior Thai officers had arrived by helicopter early that morning.[18] Realizing the gravity of the situation, they called in two RTA Hueys at 1400 and whisked Sek Sam Iet across the border.

The rest of the Military Region 3 staff was not as fortunate. As Khmer Rouge reached the city's center, all senior FANK officers were told to report to the governor's office with one small suitcase. Having convinced themselves they would be spared, the officers offered no resistance when they were told to board a convoy of trucks ostensibly for a trip to Phnom Penh. Driven to the city limits, they were ordered off the trucks at gunpoint and summarily shot.[19]

In the early afternoon of 17 April, Sak, Teap Ben, Thach Reng, and their four-ship armada made the short hop to Siem Reap. There they paused long enough to meet with the Military Region 4 commander, Brigadier General Em San, who promised to join them near the border later that day. They then returned to their choppers and flew the final leg to Oddar Meanchey. (Em San waited too long and was captured that night; refugee reports later recounted his grisly execution by having his legs chopped off at the knees.)

Landing at Samraong airfield, they found it packed tight with an assortment of Khmer Air Force planes that had fled there from other parts of the collapsed Republic. They also crossed paths with CIA officer Chip Beck, who was in the final stages of packing his personnel and dependents aboard a convoy before heading to the Thai border.

Over dinner, Sak and the other senior FANK officers discussed their planned resistance. Most of the country was out of radio contact and had presumably fallen, seriously tempering their enthusiasm to continue fighting. Teap Ben observed that Mao Tse-Tung's analogy of guerrillas being the fish and the population being the water did not necessarily apply. The Khmer Rouge would make the water too hot, he reasoned, which meant the fish would not survive.[20]

Worse, a lieutenant slipped Sak a note as they ate. It cautioned that the Oddar Meanchey governor, Colonel King Saman, was extending feelers to the Khmer Rouge. Convinced they needed to leave, Thach Reng contacted Bangkok Station that evening and got clearance to fly to Thailand the next morning.

At 0500, 18 April, Sak and the rest of the senior FANK officers gathered at the Samraong airfield. Packing nearly 100 persons—mostly Khmer Air Force personnel—into a C-123 transport plane, they lifted slowly into the morning sky. Landing heavy at Utapao Royal Thai Air Force Base and taxiing to the apron, they were embraced by General Palmer as they exited the plane.[21]

That same morning, there was a mass exodus of naval craft from Ream base on the coast. Grossly overloaded, they headed for either Malaysia or Thailand. Tea Chamrat, a marine lieutenant at the time, recalled: "I was on P-111, a former U.S. infantry landing ship that was supposed to carry 75 troops, but we had packed in over 200. Along with another two vessels, we were carrying 700 persons, mostly naval personnel and their dependents. We reached Kelatan [state] in Malaysia, but they immediately pushed us back out to sea. The U.S. then sent aircraft to help guide us toward Subic Bay in the Philippines."[22]

With the navy's flight from Ream, the Khmer Rouge was able to consolidate its hold over the country—with one exception. Atop the cliffs of Preah Vihear, the garrison under Major Kim Sakun had refused to relinquish control for a full month after the collapse of Phnom Penh. On 20 May, the Khmer Rouge had tried to snake its way up from the lowlands to the south, only to be shelled and forced back.[23]

Looking for guidance, Kim Sakun raised Bangkok Station over the radio. He managed to reach Larry Waters, the final Alpha chief who had previously served as the case officer atop Preah Vihear. Despite their valiant resistance, Waters told Sakun that the United States had no further funds to support the garrison. Two days later, when the Khmer Rouge attempted another push, they found the FANK troops had already crossed into Thailand.[24]

Inside Phnom Penh, the Khmer Rouge began evacuating residents beginning on 17 April. There is some debate over the reason why Cambodia's communists decided to empty the capital and all other urban centers. Some believe it was part of an effort to totally remake society; others speculate it was primarily to remove Sihanouk's power base. What is not debated is that the decision was premeditated and had been taken months earlier.[25]

Not all of Phnom Penh's occupants initially opposed the idea. Indeed, there was some optimism after the price of rice on that first day dropped from 20,000 riels a bag to 2,000, and Khmer Rouge broadcasts insisted they were seeking vengeance only against their list of supertraitors.[26] And among the 2 million refugees that had been living in the capital as impoverished squatters, leaving behind that fetid city did not seem like a bad thing. So it was with a curious serenity that many took to the streets and filed out toward the countryside.

Very quickly, however, excesses became glaring. At the Preah Ket Mealea hospital, one of the city's largest, some 2,000 casualties—four times its number of beds—had been piled into corridors and storerooms. All of them, no matter the severity of their injuries, were forced on 17 April into the exodus by gun-toting—

mostly underaged—Khmer Rouge cadre.[27] And even though April was the country's hottest month, no water was provided for the columns. Hundreds—seniors, babies, the infirm—died by the time they reached the city limits; their bodies were thrown in common graves on the road to Pochentong.[28]

Not even the handful of remaining embassies was exempt. The French mission, which had been swelled by Western journalists and other foreign nationals seeking sanctuary, was forced to depart for the Thai border in a truck convoy that winded its way for three days through a desolate countryside and empty Battambang. The Soviet embassy was also ordered to leave the country; the ambassador was later awarded the Order of Lenin for keeping Soviet codebooks and other classified materials from falling into the hands of the Khmer Rouge and its Chinese patrons.[29]

Trying to make sense of Cambodia's self-inflicted lobotomy was the U.S. embassy in Bangkok. Down the corridor from the CIA's Bangkok Station, the bulk of officers evacuated from Phnom Penh and the Alpha outposts—and still headed by Dave Whipple—had been given desk space and ordered to form a so-called Shadow Station to handle Cambodian issues.[30] The initial post–17 April information arriving at the Shadow Station, however, only frustrated analysis. Brian O'Connor remembered:

> We were given an overhead satellite photo taken as the Khmer Rouge were evacuating Phnom Penh. The photo showed the streets completely full of people on foot up to a point, and then at the end of the crowd the streets were completely empty of people. It was eerie even to see it in a photo. There were cars scattered at various places in the streets as if they had been abandoned by people not even taking the time to move them to the side of the road. This gave us a pretty good idea of what was happening in a general sense on the ground. What we could not figure out was why the Khmer Rouge were doing it, and what was their plan?[31]

Monitoring Khmer Rouge radio offered some clues. Eavesdropping on internal Khmer Rouge transmissions between 18 and 22 April, it was revealed that the communists were secretly eliminating FANK officers and high-ranking government officials. It also revealed that urban evacuations were being conducted to let the Khmer Rouge become better organized.[32] On a somewhat less serious note, a Phnom Penh radio broadcast on 13 May stated that the Khmer Rouge were intent on purging their society of decadent U.S. influences, including skintight pants with bell bottoms.

Shedding further light were refugee interviews. To gather these, Shadow Station immediately dispatched four of its former Alpha officers—Hafner, O'Connor, Waters, and Snake—to the border to debrief displaced Cambodians gathering at a holding center near Aranyaprathet. They were assisted for the first month by two former operations assistants from Battambang and Kong Thann from Kompong Cham.[33]

For the most part, this debriefing effort was aimed at identifying the CIA's Cambodian employees and dependents who had yet to be evacuated. They also sought to find key indigenous personnel who had assisted the United States over the course of the Khmer Republic's history.

As a secondary function, the debriefings were intended to gather intelligence that would begin to decipher what was happening inside Cambodia. As might be expected, however, much of the refugee information was anecdotal and often dated by several weeks.[34]

By June, the idea of fielding two CIA stations adjacent to each other in the same embassy appeared less than enlightened. "It was like having two cooks in the same kitchen," remarked Phil Runfola, the logistics officer retained from Phnom Penh.[35] Realizing the folly of this, Langley later that month closed Shadow Station. All were sent home, save for five officers transferred to Bangkok Station and extended for a year to continue refugee debriefings.

The three operations assistants went as well. In a brutally honest discussion between Hafner and Kong Thann, the CIA officer confessed, "If I were you, I would go to the U.S. to educate my kids." All three Cambodians were on a flight out of Thailand a week later.[36]

On 5 January 1976, Sihanouk, who had returned to Phnom Penh under close Khmer Rouge supervision, oversaw a cabinet meeting during which time the country was officially renamed Democratic Kampuchea. In line with the modern slave state its leaders were forging, the Khmer Rouge used the opportunity to promulgate a new constitution that granted the right of every citizen to work but—reflecting its secretive nature—made no mention of any communist party or head of state.

From the start, the rulers of Democratic Kampuchea faced resistance. Often it was Khmer Rouge elements themselves who were resisting—not surprising given that the movement since its inception never forged a national army but rather a series of armies with regional loyalties that were not above bloody purges, blatant nepotism, and lip service to egalitarianism that actually favored young, uneducated cadre. The most obvious schism was between the ideological puritans of the Southwest Zone around Takeo and Kampot, versus those of the East Zone under warlord So Phim. For the first couple of years of Democratic Kampuchea, however, Phim kept the ultraconservatives at bay.

Those from the West Zone in Koh Kong province were not as fortunate. The Khmer Rouge in that part of the country had always been well outside the mainstream, a fact grounded in the cultural differences found in that province. For all intents and purposes, many of the inhabitants of Koh Kong were ethnic Thai—they spoke the Thai language, enjoyed extensive cross-border relations with their neighbors, and had familial links spanning the Thai frontier.[37]

Like the population from which it drew recruits, the Khmer Rouge in Koh Kong had operated with much autonomy. Unlike their ideologically strict comrades in the Southwest, who advocated coerced communization and shunned even bartering, those in the West Zone continued a brisk trade in fish with the Thai. And unlike the anti-Vietnamese xenophobes who headed the party, several key communists in Koh Kong had spent time in the DRV and welcomed PAVN advisers after 1970.

All of this had put the West and Southwest on a collision course. In January 1974, the head of Koh Kong region was beckoned for a meeting by the Khmer Rouge central committee; he was never seen again. This was followed by further disappearances, then the dispatch of Southwest troops to effectively sweep the region. Those West cadre members that were able to get their second wind staged a short, sharp rebellion against the Southwest invaders. Outmanned and outgunned, the remnants ultimately fled across the Thai border—revolutionaries expelled for their own revolution.

Over the course of 1976, there were further uprisings by disenchanted Khmer Rouge. This included reported flare-ups in Kratie, Battambang, and Kandal provinces, as well as more skirmishes in Koh Kong. In Siem Reap, rebellious communist cadre allegedly rose up in September 1975, then blew up an ammunition depot in the provincial capital during February 1976.[38] None of these minirebellions were connected, however, and none—as yet—had any significant traction.

It was not just internecine sniping among Khmer Rouge factions that confronted Democratic Kampuchea's leadership. In some cases, it was anticommunist resistance led by former FANK members. Reports of such opposition had started almost as soon as the white flags had been raised in Phnom Penh. The most famous early example, which was probably at least partially apocryphal, involved Brigadier General Norodom Chantarangsey. After breaking out of Kompong Speu city, the general had tried to reach the Kirirom Plateau. Indeed, refugees arriving at the Thai border continued to invoke his name—and credit him with instances of heroic resistance around Kirirom—through 1977. But in hindsight, it is doubtful Chantarangsey lasted through the end of 1975—and more likely met his fate by midyear.[39]

In other instances, resistance by former Republican officers had somewhat more substance. On 19 April 1975, General In Tam, the former prime minister, had sauntered across the border from Poipet with forty-two former FANK soldiers. Among them was his oldest son, Captain In Doondarm. Although they were forced to surrender their weapons when they entered Thailand, the general kept his men together near Aranyaprathet and quickly managed to rearm them in part.[40]

To the south, Major General Moul Khleng, the last commander of Military Region 8 in Kompong Som, had escaped to Thailand aboard a fishing boat on the last day of the war. Although not one of the more high-profile generals during the Republic, Khleng had held a number of senior posts in various military regions. He had also commanded the government's protracted, and ultimately successful, defense of Kampot in 1974. After landing at Thailand's coastal Khlong Yai district, he showed surprising tenacity and immediately began recruiting refugees to take on the Khmer Rouge.

Two other senior FANK officers appeared on the border during the same period. Major General Sek Sam Iet, who was rescued from Battambang aboard an RTA helicopter, divided his time between Bangkok and Aranyaprathet. Meantime, Brigadier General Ith Suong had arrived on Thai soil after a harrowing fifty-four-day trek from Phnom Penh through Kompong Thom, Siem Reap, and Oddar Meanchey. But he found a hostile reception among refugees who—all too aware of his infamous record of military setbacks—assaulted him in one of the border holding camps.[41]

By mid-1975, many of these personalities were talking up ambitious resistance plans. In Tam and Moul Khleng, in particular, had moved to the front of the pack and were claiming support from, among others, former Minister of Justice Danh Sanh, former National Assembly chairman Tan Kim Huon, and fellow General Sek Sam Iet. They also alluded to two Cambodian sources of funds. The first was Ly Yoat Ly, a Sino-Khmer businessman who had run a small airline between Bangkok and Oddar Meanchey and had apparently been able to keep most of his fortune in Thailand for safekeeping. The second was Im Chudett. A former FANK colonel, Chudett had been educated in Thailand and spoke Thai like a native. During the Republican era, he had been named the FANK special representative to the Supreme Command of the Royal Thai Armed Forces. Though he earned poor marks for his performance in this role, he enjoyed especially close ties with the RTA and had amassed a comfortable bank account in Bangkok.[42]

For his part, Moul Khleng also hinted at Thai sources of funding. In July, he claimed to have received a promise of $50,000 from the right-wing Nawapol paramilitary organization. He also claimed assistance from the Venerable Pech, a Khmer monk who was a long-term resident of Bangkok. In fact, these two sources were connected. Bangkok had long been the destination of choice for Cambodian monks seeking to improve their level of Buddhist knowledge. In this case, Pech was a disciple of controversial Thai monk Kittivudho Bhikkhu, who in turn had been a student of the late Cambodian Patriarch Chuon Nath. A devout anticommunist (in a 1976 speech he claimed the killing of communists was not demeritorious), the thirty-nine-year-old Kittivudho not surprisingly had taken a deep interest in Cambodia, especially after hearing reports about the mass defrocking of monks by the Khmer Rouge.[43]

Kittivudho also happened to be closely linked to Nawapol. Created with covert assistance from Thai military intelligence in 1974, Nawapol was a direct reaction to communist gains in Indochina. With the loss of South Vietnam in April 1975, and especially the overthrow of the neighboring Royal Lao government, the Nawapol organization ratcheted up its anticommunist demonstrations and drew aim at Bangkok's left-leaning student population. For Nawapol and Kittivudho, the fledgling Cambodian anticommunist resistance made for a good investment, though there is no evidence that Khleng's promised funds ever actually materialized.

Khleng claimed support from one other critical Thai source. Lieutenant General Chamnian Pongpyrot, a Fort Leavenworth graduate who earlier commanded the RTA regiment assigned to the United Nations in South Korea, was one of Thailand's most experienced military intelligence operatives. Since 1960, he had been working his way up within the Armed Forces Intelligence Operations Center (AFIOC), a secretive unit under the Supreme Command that specialized in covert operations across Thailand's ample borders. As a colonel in 1960, for example, he was assigned by AFIOC to head a small team that lent discrete military assistance to Lao strongman Phoumi Nosovan during his successful push to retake that kingdom's capital.

As of the early 1970s, wearing two stars as deputy director of AFIOC, Chamnian handled covert liaison with, among others, Karen and Shan State rebels in Burma. By 1975, now sporting his third star, the general had taken command of AFIOC with a year to go before retirement.

Given his seniority, and given the plausible deniability afforded AFIOC,

Chamnian had considerable leeway when cutting deals with rebels staging from Thai soil. According to Khleng, the Thai general in July discretely gave him permission to recruit guerrillas from refugee camps that had sprung up in Khlong Yai, Chanthaburi, Surin, and Aranyaprathet. As part of a quid pro quo, the Cambodian guerrillas were to provide Chamnian with intelligence gleaned during their cross-border forays.[44]

But even with such varied assistance, the resistance plans envisioned by In Tam and Moul Khleng smacked of the fanciful. Calling themselves the Khmer Serei Liberation Front, in late July they declared their intent to increase their numbers almost ninefold to 7,000 insurgents.[45] If and when they came to strength, they ambitiously wanted to capture the district capital of Sisophon. They also wanted to contest Cambodia's United Nations seat. They further planned to send Sihanouk a note in Beijing urging him to demand open elections.

Not surprisingly, the Front met none of its objectives. Their numbers never exceeded 800, just a tiny fraction of which had access to weapons. No villages were seized, much less a district capital. And Sihanouk went to the United Nations in the fourth quarter of 1975 as a Khmer Rouge cheerleader, even lauding their decision to evacuate cities.

That this latest incarnation of the Khmer Serei was ineffectual hardly fazed Thailand's leadership. Despite General Chamnian's discrete pledge of support, the Royal Thai government had ample reason to be wary of antagonizing Indochina's communists—especially after the United States appeared incapable of offering sufficient protection.

True, ties between Bangkok and Phnom Penh immediately after the collapse of the Khmer Republic had started off badly. It was especially tense in Trat province, where Thai naval and police reinforcements were dispatched in late April 1975 to prevent Khmer Rouge incursions. The following month, Bangkok publicly stated that its marines in Klong Yai would open fire if the Cambodian communists carried out a threat to shift the border demarcation 1 kilometer to the west.[46]

But reflecting diplomatic pragmatism, there were hints of optimism in late October when Deputy Premier Ieng Sary became the first Khmer Rouge official to visit Bangkok. Although Sary turned down an offer of Thai assistance, and was noncommittal to a proposal to normalize relations, both sides released a surprisingly cordial joint communiqué. Sary was especially pleased with Bangkok's assurance that anticommunist groups would not be allowed to operate with impunity from Thai soil.[47]

Perhaps anticipating Bangkok's desire for détente with Phnom Penh, a frustrated General Moul Khleng in August opted for exile in Paris. As with all displaced Cambodians heading for France, he agreed not to engage in exile politics while on French soil.

Alone, In Tam decided to translate words into deeds. Apparently trying to sabotage closer relations between Thailand and Cambodia, some of his guerrillas during November crossed the border and inflicted several fatalities on a Khmer Rouge patrol. Thai Prime Minister Kukrit Pramoj was not amused and demanded near month's end that In Tam be deported. The Cambodian general managed to stay on, however, and on 12 December his guerrillas instigated another border clash. This time the Thai government sent a car to Aranyaprathet and, on 22 December, escorted him onto a plane bound for France.

With the departure of In Tam, the Cambodian resistance was without a prominent commander on the border. While a number of lesser FANK officers continued to lead pockets of guerrillas along the frontier, most of these officers were motivated by economic incentives rather than any burning opposition to communism. For example, Lieutenant Colonel Keth Reth, whose last post in April 1975 was deputy chief of staff for the Takhmau Military Sub-Division, had assembled a small band of insurgents in Battambang's Malai district. But these troops focused primarily on smuggling tropical hardwoods to Thai merchants—that is, until they were confronted by larger Khmer Rouge numbers in 1976 and forced to flee across the border. Other guerrillas were involved in cattle rustling, and still others were doing a brisk business stealing Cambodian antiquities for the worldwide collector's market.

Not until October 1976 did the fortunes of the Cambodian resistance begin to change. During that month, in a belated reaction to the fall of Indochina, and especially the abolishment of the Lao monarchy, the RTA seized power after a bloody student crackdown (led by the paramilitary Nawapol) on the Thammasat University campus in Bangkok. Thailand's top brass, in turn, installed an ultranationalist, rabid anticommunist as prime minister. Unlike late the previous year, when Bangkok took pains not to antagonize Phnom Penh, such considerations were of far less concern to this new crop of Thai leaders.

At the same time, Democratic Kampuchea did not help its own case. As of March 1976, there were reports that Khmer Rouge patrols were crossing up to 2 kilometers into Thailand's Surin province to plant landmines. Far more dramatic, on 28 January 1977 some 200 Khmer Rouge troops crossed the border in Aranyaprathet district and massacred thirty Thai villagers (allegedly because a Thai middleman had refused to make good on a cattle purchase). Eleven of the victims were female; most had their throats slit.

Between Bangkok's rightist tilt, and the deadly Khmer Rouge cross-border excesses, the Thai military took another look at the Cambodian resistance and saw benefit in boosting their abilities.[48] This time, however, there was a subtle but significant difference in the support that was to be offered. Previously, the channel for assistance had been through Lieutenant General Chamnian's AFIOC, which belonged to the Supreme Command. On paper, the Supreme Command was the pinnacle of the Thai armed forces. All of the services, including the RTA, answered to it.

Reality was far different. The RTA, though beneath the Supreme Command in theory, in fact called the shots in Thailand and was exponentially more influential. With regard to Cambodia, Tactical Operations Center 315—the policy-making body that answered directly to the RTA chief of staff—easily trumped the AFIOC.

And as of early 1977, the new head of TOC 315 was forty-four-year-old Special Colonel Chavalit Yongchaiyud. A signals officer by training, Chavalit had made a good impression early in his career when he was sent to Laos in 1965 to act as an instructor at a CIA-funded command and staff school. Six years later, he was given the sensitive assignment of heading Task Force 506, the intelligence unit under TOC 315. He spent two years in this post, during which time he befriended many of FANK's key personalities.

No stranger to Cambodian affairs as a result, Chavalit was now bringing his hypnotic personality and sharp intellect to bear as he toured the border in early 1977. What he found did not excite. In Surin province to the north was Im Chudett, the poor-performing former FANK colonel with close ties to the RTA, as well as a small camp near the O'Smach border crossing under former FANK Captain Svy Thouen. Keth Reth, who had been run out of Malai district after smuggling tropical hardwoods, was languishing at Aranyaprathet. Nearby, and equally ineffectual, were four would-be guerrilla chieftains: Chea Chhut, a former FANK battalion commander at Thmar Pouk; Prum Vith, who had headed a battalion at Pailin at the end of the war; fighter pilot Toan Chay; and In Sakon, a former teacher.

Toan Chay's backstory was especially poignant. As a young officer in the Khmer Air Force, he had been qualified in the T-28 and was posted to the fighter detachment at Battambang airbase. He was alone there, as his extended family, hailing from a village on the outskirts of Siem Reap's provincial capital, had gone missing during the opening months of the Republic after being forcibly marched by PAVN into the jungle. During that same time frame, North Vietnamese troops had taken control of the Angkor Wat temple complex. Lon Nol was determined to wrest back control of this national symbol but forbid the use of airstrikes or artillery for fear of damaging its façade. Rather, in an attempt to starve out the PAVN occupiers, the Khmer Air Force was tasked with bombing the logistical lines leading to the temple. From Battambang, it was Toan Chay who led multiple sorties that pummeled the Siem Reap countryside around Ankor Wat.

Three months later, Toan Chay got word that one of his relatives had made it back to friendly lines. The two met, and the young pilot pressed his cousin for word about his family. The relative was on the verge of tears. They were all dead, he said, killed during a T-28 strike not far from the Angkor Wat.

Hearing this, Toan Chay had a breakdown. Convinced he had dropped the bombs that wiped out his own family, he vowed never to get in the pilot's seat again. Instead, he became a navigation instructor at the Khmer Air Force flight academy in Battambang.

Fast-forward several years and the Khmer Republic was on its last legs. In an eleventh-hour effort to stave off defeat, a large contingent of air force students was rushed for training at Utapao Royal Thai Air Force Base. Toan Chay went along with the group as a liaison officer. Before they had a chance to graduate, however, Phnom Penh fell. Despite advice to the contrary from their Thai instructors, the students en masse elected to return to their homeland. The Thai reluctantly provided a convoy of trucks, and 162 members of the Khmer Air Force were soon rumbling toward the Poipet border crossing.

The Khmer Rouge had by this time gotten around to manning a small outpost at Poipet, along with a barbed-wire barricade blocking vehicular traffic. As the trucks slowed to allow the barricade to be pulled to one side, Toan Chay had second thoughts. Jumping off the back of his truck, he remained on the Thai side of the border. For the remaining 161 airmen, the Khmer Rouge was not in a forgiving mood. Bound at the hands, they were driven behind the Banteay Chhmar temple and mowed down with machine-gun fire.

Not all of the resistance members Chavalit met were anticommunist. During this same period, a small community of former Khmer Rouge from Koh Kong had exchanged their guns for boats and was working as shrimp fishermen in Trat province. This community traced back to the deadly Khmer Rouge purge of the West Zone in 1974, which had forced the remnants of that zone—most of whom were culturally and linguistically identical to their brethren on the Thai side of the border—to seek sanctuary in Trat.

Chavalit was well aware of the ethnic composition of the Khmer Rouge in Koh Kong and was equally aware that they were a relatively moderate bunch. In 1974,

Chavalit had even approached the Koh Kong border from Trat in order to discretely meet some of these soon-to-be-exiled Khmer Rouge, among them a feisty company commander named Tea Banh.[49]

Over the ensuing three years, Chavalit continued to pay occasional visits to Trat and would enquire about Tea Banh. Now that he was head of TOC 315, Chavalit in early 1977 beckoned him to a discrete meeting at a hotel in Thailand's Chonburi province. Chavalit's proposal was direct: In exchange for weapons, he wanted Tea Banh and his former Koh Kong revolutionaries to trade in their fishing nets and join the resistance at Aranyaprathet. To this, Tea Banh flatly refused. Reasoning that Chavalit would never offer them the weapons they wanted or needed, and no doubt resenting the idea of seeking common cause with FANK veterans, he opted to remain a fisherman in Trat.[50]

The most curious resistance leader during this period was not a former soldier but rather a gem dealer named Ea Nguon. Born to an impoverished ethnic Chinese family in Kompong Cham province, Nguon in his late teens had moved to Battambang's Pailin district along the Thai border to try his hand at mining its famous red and blue rubies. In this, he had considerable talent. By the opening of the Republican era, he had invested the money made from gem discoveries into purchasing a sizable tract of land in Pailin. There he came to employ more than 500 laborers, as well as three full-time doctors.[51]

Not content to be merely a gem dealer, Nguon dabbled in money politics. He made no secret that he turned over bags of cash to General Sosthene, the FANK commander, in order to get a favored colonel named governor when Pailin was elevated to provincial status. Later, he made sizable donations to prevent the sibling of a political rival from taking over that same governor's seat. He was also on close terms with Sek Sam Iet, the Battambang military governor who was no slouch when it came to mixing business and politics.

All of this maneuvering counted for little, however, when the thirty-eight-year-old Nguon had been forced to bury his gem stockpile in April 1975 and cross the border ten days before Phnom Penh fell. Fortunately for him, he had been able to convert a substantial portion of his gem holdings into baht and have it safely deposited in Thailand. But still smarting from having had to abandon his gems in Pailin, Nguon since mid-1975 had been slowly gathering followers to one day cross the border and recover the cache.[52]

By the time Chavalit met him in early 1977, he assessed Nguon to be flighty and prone to conspiracy theories. But there was no denying that the gem merchant had substantial funds, and this automatically gave him credibility along the border.

Coincidentally, two former FANK officers, both of whom had come to the United States as refugees in 1975, elected to visit Thailand at the opening of 1977. The first was Teap Ben, the well-regarded general from Kompong Thom, who was an acquaintance of Chavalit since the latter's Task Force 506 days. The second was Lieutenant Colonel King Men, a former FANK commander in Battambang's Thmar Puok district. Both had been involved in anticommunist activism in California for the past year. Recognizing that they might be able to harness the interests of the overseas Cambodian community (in fact, they claimed to have promises of financial support from an association of Cambodian exiles in Paris), Chavalit granted them nearly unfettered access along the Cambodian border.

Very quickly, the anticommunist resistance began to gain momentum. Chavalit gave Ea Nguon permission to buy limited numbers of older firearms, albeit at inflated prices. Kittivudho Bhikkhu, the right-wing Buddhist monk, then granted them a tract of farmland in Chantaburi's Pong Nam Ran district, opposite Pailin. To forge unity, Chavalit's aide, Captain Wichit Yathip, convinced Nguon to join forces with Major Prum Vith and Lieutenant Toan Chay, both of whom were largely idle at Aranyaprathet. In fact, Nguon hardly needed to be asked twice: As Prum Vith was intimately familiar with Pailin from his FANK days, Nguon harbored hope that the former major would be able to recover his buried gems.

With this critical mass, Nguon in early March was selected head of their burgeoning liberation front. Teap Ben was named his deputy in charge of foreign affairs. True to this role, Teap Ben and King Men on 13 March departed Thailand for a fund-raising tour across the United States and Europe.[53]

Very quickly, word flashed across the Cambodian expatriate community about the revamped resistance. In some cases, this prompted former FANK officers living overseas into action. One of them was forty-nine-year-old Colonel Ea Chuor Kimmeng, the chief of logistics in Battambang immediately before the collapse of the Khmer Republic. He had flown a chopper out of Cambodia on the last day of the war and contemplated joining the resistance through October 1975 before opting for exile life in France.

In April 1977, Kimmeng decided to give the resistance a second chance. Flying back to Bangkok, he briefly stopped at Ea Nguon's residence in the Thai capital. But rather than heading to the primary guerrilla mustering point in Pong Nam Ran, he instead went to Surin and contacted Im Chudett. Loosely aligned with Nguon's united front, Chudett was talking up building his own guerrilla band along the northern Cambodian border.

After remaining at Surin through June, Kimmeng agreed to head for the

United States to seek funds for Chudett. He met with some success in Hawaii: "I visited Lon Nol in Honolulu. He told me that he had requested the Republican government to give him $1 million when he departed the country, but they only gave him $300,000. He was living very modestly in a small house with his wife and five kids. I stayed 23 days as a guest in his house, and at the end of my stay he pledged to give $30,000 to Im Chudett for him to buy 90 rifles."[54]

In August, Moul Khleng, who had abandoned the border in frustration two years earlier, also reappeared in Bangkok. In hindsight, his arrival proved the Front's undoing. Almost immediately, he began to quarrel with the other resistance leaders at Nguon's residence. For the CIA's Snake, who had been reassigned to Bangkok Station as liaison officer with Chavalit's TOC 315, the infighting came as little surprise. "The resistance was more or less destitute on the border," he reasoned, "and now with the possibility of funds flowing in, there was invariably going to be competition and clashes."[55]

But more serious than internal squabbles, Khleng took direct aim at their RTA hosts. Proudly declaring that the Cambodian resistance should be independent of Thai control, he implored his fellow members to keep TOC 315 at arm's length.

Chavalit could accept infighting among the resistance. He could even accept their incompetence in the field. But an independent, ungrateful streak he could not abide. Coupled with this, an October 1977 coup d'état in Bangkok had ushered in General Kriangsak Chomanan as the new Thai prime minister. Unlike the previous administration, which was too anticommunist even for the RTA's liking, Kriangsak from the start sought to pursue a more moderate foreign policy toward China and Vietnam.

All of this led the Thai authorities, for the second time, to crack down on the Cambodian resistance. With uncharacteristic brutality, the RTA rolled up Ea Nguon's entire front. Moul Khleng, Toan Chay, Keth Reth, and translator Ben Vy were arrested on 4 October and spent a month in an Aranyaprathet jail; after that, Khleng was put on a plane to France, never to return.[56] Im Chudett, on account of his close personal friendship with Kriangsak, was allowed to remain at Surin provided he refrained from resistance activities.[57] On a darker note, a dozen resistance members—including two former FANK majors—disappeared from Nguon's Bangkok residence and were presumed killed.[58]

For his part, Ea Nguon bought his way out of detention and opted to leave Thailand. Going back to what he did best, he spent the next six years in Sri Lanka dealing in rubies and sapphires.

6. Trading Places

Although it appeared like TOC 315 was set on dismantling the anticommunist Cambodian resistance in late 1977, in fact the crackdown was selective. Ea Nguon's ungrateful, and largely unmotivated, liberation front was fair game. However, guerrilla bands outside of that front—most of them counting only a few dozen members, and only a fraction of whom were armed—had been largely ignored.

One group had not only been left unchecked; it had received direct paramilitary support from TOC 315. That group was led by Ly Tieng Chek, a former Republican legislator assimilated into FANK as a major. By 1975, Ly had been promoted to lieutenant colonel and named deputy commander of the Oddar Meanchey Military Sub-Division. Given his proximity to the border, he easily escaped when the country fell and had spent the ensuing year in California.

Going against the flow in early 1977, a restless Ly took leave of his new life in America to once more spar with the Khmer Rouge. Returning to Thailand, he headed for a refugee camp that had sprung up in a remote corner of Ubon Ratchathani province. It was a fortuitous decision, as the arc spanning Ubon Ratchathani, Sisaket, and Surin provinces was especially sensitive to the Thai authorities. Ethnic Khmer formed a large percentage of the populations in these provinces; it was estimated that they constituted more than half of Surin and possibly up to a third of Sisaket. Not surprisingly, TOC 315 wanted to closely monitor developments among Cambodian refugees in this vicinity. In March 1977, shortly after Ly began networking in Ubon Ratchathani, the RTA established contact and offered no obstacles as the former legislator scouted the border for potential staging sites.[1]

By October, at the same time the RTA was persecuting Ea Nguon, TOC 315 ratcheted up its coddling of Ly.[2] The reason: Despite the relative pragmatism of the new Kriangsak government, which appeared willing to take a softer line toward Democratic Kampuchea as a sop to China, it did not appear like Phnom Penh was interested in reciprocity. Indeed, as of late 1977 the Thai media was reporting a growing nexus between the Communist Party of Thailand (CPT) and the Khmer Rouge, including creation of a joint force to operate in the heavily ethnic Khmer provinces on the Thai side of the border.[3] This was all the more alarming because hundreds of left-leaning Thai students were thought to have fled to Democratic Kampuchea back in October 1976 to escape a bloody RTA crackdown.

All of these developments had led the head of TOC 315, Special Colonel Chavalit, to issue revised marching orders to Task Force 506, the unit charged with clandestine intelligence operations in Cambodia. The new chief of Task Force 506, Colonel Kasem Thammakul, recalled his priorities: "Our major focus was now against the CPT working with the Khmer Rouge in Surin. Our second focus was the Khmer Rouge themselves. We also began simple cooperation with the Cambodian resistance, especially out of Ubon [Ratchathani]."[4]

As part of that cooperation, Task Force 506 arranged for a training team from the RTA Special Forces to support Ly Tieng Chek. The RTA Special Forces at Lopburi, like its U.S. Army counterparts, was a special warfare outfit assigned everything from long-range reconnaissance to raids to raising guerrillas. Also like the U.S. Army Special Forces, the RTA Special Forces was organized into groups, which were further divided into team-sized operational detachments.[5] For the Task Force 506 assignment, Lopburi dispatched a six-man training team—codenamed Alpha 77—consisting of Captain Wannah Mungkhalee and five sergeants.[6]

Arriving in Ubon Ratchathani province, Captain Wannah found Ly busy recruiting in Nam Yuen district. The southernmost district in the province, Nam Yuen was situated in the mosquito-ridden triborder region where Laos, Cambodia, and Thailand converge. To the south was Choam Khsan district in Cambodia's Preah Vihear province, an area dominated by the eastern extreme of the Dangrek Mountains. Though gently sloping on the Thai side, the southern side of the Dangrek Range featured steep sandstone escarpments overlooking the Cambodian lowlands.

Ly's recruitment effort, Wannah discovered, had been bearing fruit. With funds from Cambodian donors in France, he had signed up eighty men, a mix of FANK veterans, civilians, and Khmer Rouge ralliers. Although some had a modicum of training, none had any weapons. To boost their abilities, Wannah's team gave two months of unconventional warfare instruction at a rudimentary camp near the Chong Bok border pass. Through RTA channels, they acquired several dozen assault rifles and M-79 grenade launchers, as well as some crates of 60mm mortar rounds. No mortar tubes were provided, so the RTA trainers improvised alternatives out of commercial tubing.

The RTA Special Forces team also procured demolition charges, which they used during the group's baptism by fire in December 1977. After hiking for a day across the escarpment, a team of Cambodian guerrillas, augmented by their Thai advisers, penetrated 10 kilometers into Choam Khsan district and successfully set off the charges to take out a bridge.

Although this was an auspicious start, Ly Tieng Chek was not around to relish the victory. Contracting malaria, he passed away at his jungle camp near year's end. Command of his fledgling guerrilla band passed to Keo Chuan, a former village chief from Choam Khsan during the Republic. Under Keo's watch, word of the bridge operation spread quickly among the refugee community. In short order, another ninety able-bodied males flocked to Nam Yuen and volunteered for guerrilla duty.

Before this new influx could be trained, however, Democratic Kampuchea retaliated. On the evening of 9–10 February 1978, a mixed band of Khmer Rouge and CPT insurgents penetrated 7 kilometers into Ubon and descended on the village of Ban Paet Um. At gunpoint, they marched nearly the entire village—300 men, women, and children—across the border into Cambodia.[7]

Such a mass kidnapping was brazen even by Khmer Rouge standards. While the Royal Thai government publicly offered only weak protest, Chavalit sent word to Task Force 506 that it was now a priority for Captain Wannah and his Cambodian guerrillas to rescue the abducted Thai citizens. Stealing across the Dangrek Range, a guerrilla column marched for 20 kilometers before reaching a Khmer Rouge commune where thirty of the prisoners were being held. Safely escorting them back to Thailand, Keo's men were rewarded by Chavalit with a princely 500 baht for each freed captive.[8]

Following this, the border war noticeably heated up in Ubon. Khmer Rouge troops, using Thai communists as guides, began crossing into Thailand with increased frequency. Keo's guerrillas, in turn, started interdicting the Khmer Rouge and Thai communists inside Ubon, as well as staging weekly raids into Democratic Kampuchea. They also used the opportunity to disperse anticommunist leaflets inside Cambodia.

These missions were not without risk. One Alpha 77 sergeant was killed during a Khmer Rouge ambush inside Thailand, and one Cambodian guerrilla died from a booby trap along the frontier. Then in May 1978, a reconnaissance patrol by an RTA infantry unit was attacked along the border; one RTA lieutenant was killed.

This last casualty struck a raw nerve. On 24 June, a twenty-man Cambodian guerrilla team, bolstered by three members of Alpha 77, prepared to enter Democratic Kampuchea to conduct a retaliatory ambush. They had penetrated only 100 meters across the border when Captain Wannah stepped on a mine; the blast took off his right leg. This casualty gave TOC 315 reason for pause, bringing a temporary détente along that stretch of the border.

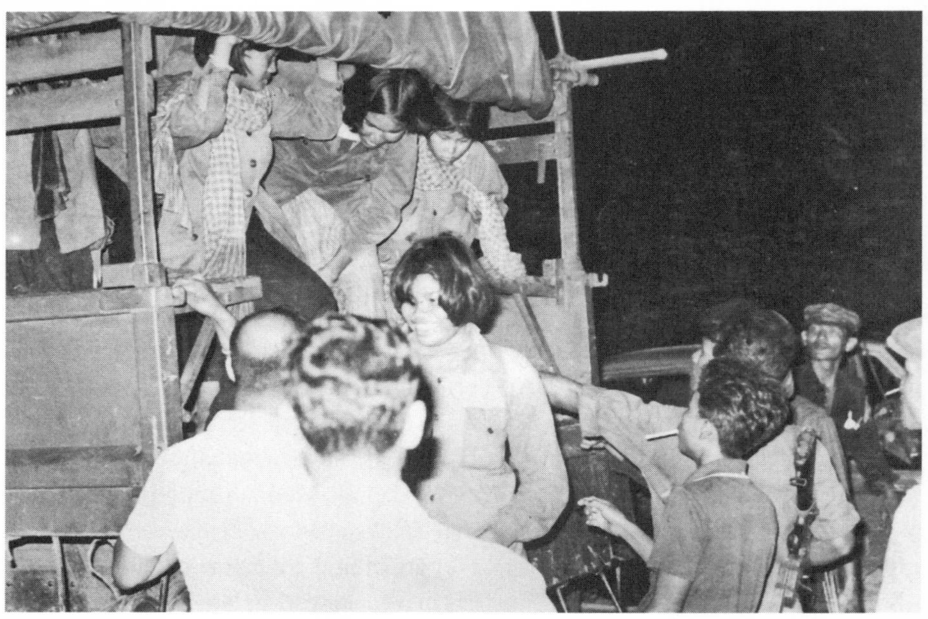

Some of the thirty villagers rescued from Khmer Rouge captivity in Preah Vihear province by anticommunist guerrillas, February 1978. (Courtesy Wannah Mungkhalee)

When put into context, the tit-for-tat raids in Ubon were nothing compared to what was taking place along Cambodia's border with Vietnam. To be sure, the relationship between the Khmer Rouge and Vietnam had always showed signs of strain. But this had been largely papered over during their pre-1975 revolutionary struggle as the Khmer Rouge leadership let their need for PAVN logistical support keep their xenophobia in check.

After Phnom Penh fell in April 1975, however, their restraint wafted away. The very next month, the Khmer Rouge seized control of two contested islands in the Gulf of Thailand, massacring hundreds of Vietnamese civilians for good measure; PAVN responded by butchering the Khmer Rouge occupiers.

Their resultant staredown was exacerbated by the grand rift in the communist world: the Sino-Soviet schism. In the case of the DRV, Hanoi had walked a tightrope during the Vietnam War by accepting assistance from both Moscow and Beijing. But after PAVN marched into Saigon on 30 April 1975, the DRV made no secret it was falling in line with the Soviets.

The Khmer Rouge, by contrast, sided with China. On 20 April, just three days after the fall of the Republican government, a 300-ton Chinese vessel docked at

Kompong Som loaded with an emergency shipment of staples. Three months later, Chinese military experts arrived in Cambodia to survey the country's defense needs. By mid-September, Beijing had exponentially widened its aid spigot to Cambodia—and at the same time abruptly cut the flow to Vietnam.

All of this might still have caused livable levels of friction had the Khmer Rouge social experiment not failed so miserably. But after being evacuated from Cambodia's cities in April 1975, the relocated urban masses were directed to jungle communes and superimposed on an agricultural sector ravaged by war. What little industry that existed was all but dismantled; former Republicans and intellectuals (or even those with the slightest hint of higher education) were hounded and executed; Buddhism was outlawed; traditional social structures were crushed; foreign ties were mostly severed; and a small privileged class of communist idealists—abetted by a network of murderous, primarily adolescent, rubes—enforced Draconian discipline. Predictably, agrarian production collapsed and mass starvation ensued. As their economic policies tanked, the Khmer Rouge authorities in 1976 began internal finger pointing. This quickly gave way to a spasm of ultranationalism and by early 1977 a shifting of blame toward their traditional enemy: Vietnam.

By that time Vietnam was a fully united entity. For a period after April 1975, the PRG had nominally governed the south; in reality, however, PAVN administered the liberated southern territories. In July 1976, the DRV leadership in Hanoi did away with this façade and merged both north and south into the Socialist Republic of Vietnam (SRV) under their control.

So it was against the united SRV that the Khmer Rouge decided to vent in force. The date they chose was 30 April 1977—the second anniversary of the fall of Saigon. Striking across a wide front between Vietnam's Tay Ninh and Kien Giang provinces, Khmer Rouge columns pillaged rice and left behind hundreds of bodies.

Hanoi's response was surprisingly measured. This was largely dictated by their level of preparedness: Vietnam had allowed itself a modest peace dividend over the previous two years and had sought savings by directing many combat divisions to focus on public works projects like laboring on communes and road-building. Most of those divisions were now ordered to revert back into full-fledged combat units. As this process would take time, the SRV tried to mend relations with Democratic Kampuchea through midyear.

Such olive branches, however, were not registering with the Khmer Rouge. On the night of 24 September, elements of a division from the East Zone crossed 10 kilometers into Tay Ninh and left behind some 1,000 casualties, including 300 massacred Khmer Krom. Three months later, having fully run out of patience, a 60,000-man PAVN task force surged into Svay Rieng province. By January 1978, forward PAVN elements had gotten within 38 kilometers of Phnom Penh before withdrawing back to the SRV side of the frontier.

If Hanoi believed Phnom Penh was humbled by this foray, it was sorely mistaken. To be sure, PAVN outnumbered the Khmer Rouge armed forces by more than eight-to-one, as well as outclassing them in every weapons category. Still, the Khmer Rouge were determined to play a psychotic David to PAVN's Goliath. Moreover, as the nimble Khmer Rouge attacked at the location and time of its choosing, it managed to rattle the better-armed and -organized PAVN defenders. The deputy commander of PAVN's Military Region 5 summarized his frustration: "We know the enemy, but we cannot see the enemy, while the enemy can see us, and he sees us very clearly. . . . Pol Pot's people are fighting us the same way we fought the Americans, and we are fighting Pol Pot the same way the Americans fought against us."[9]

Ironically, some of those same East Zone units hitting the SRV were themselves coming under the deadly scrutiny by the Khmer Rouge central authorities. A concerted purge of the East Zone began during the second quarter of 1978, with special attention focused on those comrades who had spent time in Vietnam prior to 1970. It was later determined that of the 963 cadre members who returned from the DRV to Cambodia after March 1970, only 57 survived through 1978; the remainder had largely succumbed to purges.[10] Not even So Phim, the eastern party secretary that ruled like a warlord, escaped Phnom Penh's tender mercies; on the verge of being arrested in May 1978, he opted to put a bullet in his head. His deputy, a cadaverous revolutionary named Heng Samrin, promptly defected to the SRV.

As Democratic Kampuchea continued along its collision course with the SRV, overseas Cambodian communities sensed opportunity. In the United States, where pockets of refugees were dispersed in places like Southern California and northern Virginia, ad hoc anticommunist forums, usually led by former Republican officials, began to pontificate about overthrowing the Khmer Rouge. On the East Coast, its membership included, among others, General Sak and air force chief Ea Chhong. On the West Coast, General Teap Ben topped the roster. But with most members working long hours at menial jobs, they had relatively little time to spare for talking up the resistance.

Not so in Paris. There, the eclectic Cambodian expatriate community—a mix

Carcasses of PAVN tanks destroyed by the Khmer Rouge in Svay Teap district, Svay Rieng province, during 1978. (Author's collection)

of former royalists and Republicans—not only were concentrated in a single city; many had been living in the French capital for the better part of a decade and were financially more secure than their recently resettled American counterparts. And even though they were proscribed by French law from engaging in exile politics, this is exactly what they had started doing almost from the moment Phnom Penh fell.

The first such effort dated to late April 1975, when a group of Cambodian expatriates in Paris formed the Association des Cambodiens à L'Étranger (Association of Overseas Cambodians). Chosen as the association's secretary-general was former Colonel Nguon Pythoureth. The Cambodian military attaché in Paris when Sihanouk was deposed, Nguon had quickly declared loyalty to the prince and was rewarded by being named ambassador to Mauritania (which recognized Sihanouk's government-in-exile). Other prominent members included Colonel Bour Holl, who had led the Royal Guard in Phnom Penh during the Sihanouk era, and Madam Soun Kaset, Sirik Matak's secretary during the Republican government.[11]

Not until more than a year later, in late 1976, did the association begin to gain momentum. This came about when leadership was passed to senior Cambodian statesman Son Sann. Born in October 1911 in Phnom Penh, Son Sann hailed from a Khmer Krom family that had emigrated out of southern Vietnam. An overachiever from an early age, he was the first Cambodian to graduate from École des Hautes Études Commerciales—the School for Advanced Commercial Studies in Paris—then became a deputy governor during his midtwenties and a key economic adviser to Sihanouk by the time he was thirty.

After Cambodia was granted independence, Son Sann founded the National Bank and was its president into the 1960s. But while he ultimately held ministerial posts on seventeen occasions—including an eight-month stint as prime minister beginning in May 1967—Sihanouk never warmed to his devout Buddhism and conservative, austere personal lifestyle. Sihanouk also tended to ignore the advice of his courtly economic adviser, thus assuring the kingdom's economic meltdown. Son Sann belatedly returned the slight, resigning from all government positions (except as head of the Khmer-Soviet Friendship Association) in 1968.[12]

Though he had fallen out of favor with Sihanouk, Son Sann was hardly on good terms with Lon Nol. Immediately after the change of governments in March 1970, a skittish Lon Nol placed him under house arrest for three months. Upon release, Son Sann left for Paris, then Beijing, in a solo attempt to negotiate a fast end to the war. Nobody was in a mood to listen: Still riding on a public high, Lon Nol had visions of persevering against PAVN; still fuming over having been unceremoniously dumped, Sihanouk wanted only revenge. Making no progress, Son Sann sulked back to Paris.

The following year he tried again. First meeting with some of Sihanouk's supporters in Paris, then seeking an audience with Lon Nol in Phnom Penh during July, he sounded them out about an international peace conference. Both sides still gave him the cold shoulder. Frustrated, he cashed in unused tickets for planned peace forays to Moscow, Berne, and Prague.[13]

Two years passed before Son Sann returned to Cambodia for yet another try. In May 1973, he held a series of meetings in Phnom Penh where he (again) urged reconciliation to end the civil war. By that time, however, Sihanouk and the Khmer Rouge sensed momentum and were in no mood for compromise. Son Sann retreated back to Paris, though Sihanouk's government-in-exile continued to snipe at him from afar.

In January 1974, Son Sann attempted one last time to end the war. Burning bridges, he made public a letter in which he asked Lon Nol to step down for the sake of the nation. The marshal, needless to say, ignored the sage advice.

In hindsight, it was perhaps understandable why Son Sann was so consistently rebuffed. Though even-tempered and (rare for a senior Cambodian official) free of corruption, he was not especially trusted by either camp. And prone to soft, flat diction, his oratory skills hardly commanded attention—especially when compared to Sihanouk's soprano delivery and liberal use of hyperbole.

But fast-forward two years, and it was Son Sann's dogged persistence and seniority that were now prized within the émigré community. After accepting leadership of the Paris-based group, one of his first orders of business was to change its name to Association General des Khmer à L'Étranger (General Association of Overseas Khmer). This was more than just semantics. Expanding horizons beyond Paris, Son Sann announced his intent for the group was to act as an umbrella to unite all Khmer associations abroad.

Son Sann also wanted to move toward forming an armed political movement against the Khmer Rouge. As a modest first step in early 1977, his group helped sponsor the trip by Teap Ben and King Men to meet with Ea Nguon's liberation front.[14] But looking to make a more substantial impact, during the second quarter of that year he established a small cabal—known as the Comité de Liaison, or Liaison Committee—that could discretely map out resistance plans.

A key participant in that committee was FANK's most seasoned combat officer, Brigadier General Dien Del. After making his helicopter escape to Thailand on the last day of the war, Del had resettled in a northern Virginia suburb for a year and a half. Bored with his prospects, he jumped at the opportunity when Son Sann beckoned him to Paris in May 1977. Over a series of discussions that month, Son Sann, Del, and three other former Republicans brainstormed the creation of an anticommunist guerrilla army. At the end of all this, Son Sonn asked Del to venture to Thailand to start making their concept a reality. Without any better offers on hand, the general accepted the assignment.[15]

But no sooner had Dien Del signed on for resistance duties when Thailand began cracking down along the border. As word filtered back to Paris about the fate of Ea Nguon's liberation front (and the harsh treatment meted out to fellow Parisian expatriate Moul Khleng), the Liaison Committee judged conditions were not yet ripe.[16] Their malaise would eventually spill over into 1978, with no appreciable progress made through year's end.

While Son Sann and his committee devolved into little more than a talk shop, Democratic Kampuchea was being consumed by ever greater levels of violence. Massing more than a dozen of its twenty-three divisions along the SRV border, the Khmer Rouge continued with cross-border provocations through the first half of 1978. During January and February alone, Hanoi claimed that Cambodia had shelled its territory with long-range 130mm guns on 903 occasions. The next quarter, a bloody Khmer Rouge foray into An Giang province took several thousand lives.

Vietnam, meantime, was biding its time for a response. During June, they eventually launched their own cross-border raid, only to once again pull their punches and withdraw after achieving limited objectives. Behind the scenes, however, preparations were in the offing for something much bigger. For one thing, PAVN was furiously adding to its order of battle, including special operations forces. During the second half of 1978, for example, the Dac Cong Command ordered its elite within an elite, the 1 Sapper Commando Group, to raise two battalions specifically for Cambodian operations. And in November, they established a 120-man company (dubbed the C1 Group) for "special strategic" missions—a euphemism for only the most sensitive of assignments—against the Khmer Rouge.

For another thing, Hanoi on 3 November finished inking a friendship treaty with Moscow. This codified the latter's guardian-angel status, as it guaranteed Soviet aid in the event that the SRV's moves against Democratic Kampuchea prompted Chinese intervention.

By that time, Hanoi's intended maneuvers were shaping into a conventional blitz akin to what the Soviets did to Czechoslovakia in 1968. Already, ten PAVN divisions were poised on the border, plus another three positioned to hook south from Laos. Two divisions had even briefly pushed into Kratie province during early December, testing the waters in a dress rehearsal.

This was to be dwarfed by the main event, however. On 7 December, PAVN's Combat Operations Department received approval from the Politburo in Hanoi for what it termed the General Staff's Combat Readiness Plan for Cambodia. It was to involve eighteen divisions from three corps and three military regions, including 600 armored vehicles, 137 aircraft, and up to 250,000 men. This offensive, intended to decisively defeat the Khmer Rouge, was set to kick off on 4 January 1979 when the terrain was dry and the rice harvest ready.[17]

To wrap their operation in a legal fig leaf, PAVN was adamant that the attack be backed by the "banner of the Cambodian revolution." Put simply, this meant pro-Vietnamese Khmer revolutionaries had to play a public role. As it turned out, PAVN had access to no shortage of Khmer Rouge deserters. As far back as September 1975, early friction among Khmer Rouge factions had led 4,500 disgruntled revolutionaries in Ratanakiri province to flee across the border to Laos and Vietnam. Further waves, especially from the East Zone, began to pick up during the first half of 1977.

That May, PAVN moved to take advantage of this windfall. Fifty-nine young Cambodian men were selected at that time from refugee camps along the Kampuchean border and given basic political indoctrination.[18] A month later, this group began what was intended to be three years of extensive commando training around Ho Chi Minh City (formerly Saigon) under Dac Cong auspices. One of the trainees detailed the regimen of instruction: "They trained us in jungle fighting and urban warfare. We were taught how to kidnap, to raid buildings, to set demolition charges. They taught us about camouflage: how to hide like a frog and make caches near water. We went into the city and learned how to gather intelligence."[19]

This commando training was actually only a small part of what was soon to become a far wider effort. In September 1977, PAVN established a battalion—appropriately called Group 977, in reference to the month and year of its establishment—to offer basic paramilitary instruction to more former Khmer Rouge languishing in the refugee camps. The following May, they declared the first Cambodian company operationally ready.[20] This gave way to a still larger PAVN advisory body—created in July 1978 and known as Group 778—which starting turning out pro-Vietnamese Cambodian troops at a breakneck pace. As of the opening of December 1978, Group 778 had readied twenty-one Cambodian infantry battalions, several support companies, and even a battalion of female troops.[21]

By that time, PAVN was already employing its Cambodian allies across the border. In October 1978, the fifty-nine students undergoing Dac Cong training had their instruction abruptly cut short by two years. Forming ten teams along with their PAVN advisers, their mission was to penetrate deep into Democratic Kampuchea and escort back to the SRV any senior Khmer Rouge cadre seeking to defect. Four of the teams were to target provinces in the northeast quadrant of the country, three were to head for Phnom Penh, and the last three were to focus on Kampot.

The results from these teams was middling at best. One heading for Kompong Cham was told to locate East Zone secretary So Phim—unaware that he had taken his own life five months earlier.[22] One of the teams targeted against Phnom Penh entered from Chau Doc district and promptly disappeared. Another team walking toward Phnom Penh had two members drown while crossing a river. None returned with any high-ranking prospects.

Unfazed, Group 778 on 2 December ushered several hundred of its Cambodian soldiers just over the border to a rubber plantation east of Snuol in Kratie province. Among them was the gaunt Heng Samrin, as well as a twenty-six-year-old with an ill-fitting glass eye named Hun Sen. Acting as witness during their brief speeches was Le Duc Tho, the longtime Vietnamese revolutionary who had been awarded (but turned down) the Nobel Prize with Kissinger in 1973. As these Cambodians formally declared creation of the Kampuchean United Front for National Salvation, Hanoi passed the point of no return.

With a legal fig leaf in place, PAVN had satisfied one of the main preconditions for its general offensive. But even after its grand plan was approved by the Politburo five days later, preparations on the frontline were still far from finished. In particular, one of the corps set to participate was nowhere near its launch positions on the border. PAVN had four strategic corps in its order of battle, all formed during the final years of the Vietnam War. These were directly subordinate to the PAVN High Command in Hanoi and, while each had a traditional base area and was assigned some local security duties, all were considered mobile reserve units that could be sent anywhere in the country. They were not subordinate to any military region headquarters.

For the Cambodian offensive, PAVN planned to use its 2, 3, and 4 Corps. These were normally based, respectively, at Danang, Pleiku, and Ho Chi Minh City. But while 3 and 4 Corps were already maneuvering close to Cambodian border, 2 Corps had earlier been sent to Hue to assist the Pathet Lao across the border during their ongoing consolidation efforts in Laos. Shipping them back south was going to be a major challenge; more than three years after defeating Saigon, the SRV still had a shortage of trucks and had yet to adequately restore its railroad network. Left to its own devices, PAVN simply could not get 2 Corps into position ahead of the 4 January 1979 launch date.

At that point, PAVN benefited from a stroke of luck. By coincidence, a mammoth Soviet transport vessel was berthed at Haiphong and was slowly off-loading a wide range of military equipment for Hanoi. After some quick intervention by the Ministry of Defense, the ship was off-loaded in record time and the Soviet captain convinced to sail down to Danang, pick up the armor, artillery, and vehicles assigned to 2 Corps, and shuttle these to Ho Chi Minh City. Movement started on 19 December, with the entire corps expected to be at the border in twelve days, well before the 4 January launch date.

Before any of this could happen, however, the Khmer Rouge did the unexpected. Perhaps sensing the impending PAVN invasion, on 23 December ten of the nineteen divisions stationed on the frontier launched a preemptive attack across the SRV's southwestern border. As this gave Vietnam a convenient legal excuse to retaliate under international law, PAVN moved up its invasion by ten days. On 25 December, even though 2 Corps had yet to get into position, Hanoi unleashed hell.

Moving generally according to its master plan, 4 Corps first converged on Tay Ninh and began annihilating the Khmer Rouge troops on their side of the frontier. After that, more than a dozen divisions poured across the border and began to systematically pick apart their Khmer Rouge opponents. Ahead of the PAVN infantry columns, airstrikes were conducted by the Vietnam People's Air Force (VPAF). Showing innovation, the VPAF was even using its U.S.-made C-130 transports (acquired when they absorbed the massive South Vietnamese air force in 1975) as tactical bombers. Using wooden racks packed with forty 250-pound bombs that were pushed off their rear ramps, these C-130 bombers were first used on the night of 28–29 December to pummel Stung Treng province.[23]

Although the offensive hinged on overwhelming conventional forces, special operations were to potentially play a decisive role. Specifically, PAVN had conjured a special strategic mission aimed at snatching Sihanouk from Phnom Penh. If PAVN could secure Sihanouk (who had been under palace arrest by the Khmer Rouge since 1976), it was felt they could entice him into throwing his weight behind the united front that Heng Samrin had inaugurated at Snuol. Just as the Khmer Rouge had milked legitimacy from Sihanouk during the war against the Khmer Republic, Hanoi knew that a nod from Sihanouk would win it—and the united front—instant credibility among the rural Cambodian masses.[24]

Tasked with apprehending Sihanouk was a composite team of PAVN's best. This was drawn from the 120-man C1 Sapper Group, a cell from the 861 Naval Sapper Battalion, and intelligence operatives out of the PAVN Second Bureau.[25] They were to quietly make their way toward the Cambodian capital ahead of the main PAVN columns, then steal into Phnom Penh itself just after the new year. There they were to locate Sihanouk, believed being held in a pagoda behind his former palace.[26]

The mission did not go according to plan. Reaching the Chrui Changwar Peninsula opposite Phnom Penh on 2 January 1979, they ran headlong into a swarm of Khmer Rouge defenders. "During a ferocious battle," an official PAVN history dryly notes, "the unit had almost 100 percent casualties."[27]

But even had the PAVN commandos been able to reach Sihanouk's pagoda, they would have found it empty. Panicked by the speed of the Vietnamese advance, Sihanouk's minders on 1 January had bundled the prince into a Mercedes and whisked him westward, passing through a deserted Battambang city before coming to a halt at Sisophon.

Still unaware that Sihanouk was not in town, PAVN made one more kidnapping attempt. On 4 January, a sixteen-man composite team—seven Dac Cong operatives and nine Cambodians from the group that had received commando training since 1977—landed by Chinook chopper at Tonle Bet, a riverside town across the Mekong from the Kompong Cham provincial capital.

From the start, their infiltration was plagued by Murphy's Law. Commandeering a small fishing boat, they made their way south—only to have it run out of fuel en route. Drifting toward shore, they finally found a second vessel but were not able to approach the Chrui Changwar Peninsula until daybreak the following morning. Beaching their vessel after running out of fuel for a second time, they walked south along the peninsula until encountering a Khmer Rouge patrol. While trying to pass themselves off as fellow Khmer Rouge, they were exposed when one of the Dac Cong could not converse in fluent Khmer. The commando team engaged in a short, sharp firefight before scurrying into the bush, abandoning any thoughts of crossing the Tonle Sap and entering the capital.[28]

As this was transpiring, the bulk of the PAVN columns had been ordered to slow their advance and consolidate gains east of the Mekong. With an eerie calm descending over Phnom Penh, the Khmer Rouge deemed the capital sufficiently safe on 5 January to bring back Sihanouk. In an unexpected move, he was taken for an audience with Pol Pot. The two had not seen each other in six years, and on this occasion the Khmer Rouge leader was taking pains to show contrition. Using respectful court language, he stoked Sihanouk's considerable ego and asked him to go to New York and denounce the unfolding PAVN invasion at the United Nations. Sihanouk agreed, provided he could take along his wife and small entourage of retainers. Pol Pot offered his immediate consent, with Sihanouk, along with several dozen Chinese experts (including a band of touring acrobats), scheduled to leave the next morning on the weekly flight by the Chinese Civil Air Administration.

That flight nearly did not take place. Scanning the airwaves, a PAVN signal intelligence unit had intercepted radio chatter about the impending arrival of the Chinese aircraft. This prompted VPAF Chief of Staff Tran Do to draft plans for their squadron of A-37 jets to pockmark the Pochentong runway and render it unusable. But when this was passed to the campaign commanders, they rejected the proposal on account that adequate technical and reconnaissance preparations had not been made.

Sihanouk, as a result, was able to make good his 6 January escape to Beijing. The morning after that, the few remaining Khmer Rouge leaders, as well as a handful of ambassadors, some 600 Chinese technicians, and fifty North Korean advisers, slinked westward out of the capital by convoy and train. After a period of three years, eight months, and twenty days, they left behind a decimated, desiccated husk of a city.[29]

Their departure came none too soon. PAVN infantrymen that same afternoon began to push their way into the capital, mopping up the scant, disorganized resistance Pol Pot left behind. In front of the deserted Central Market they found a massive pyramid of wrecked cars, their tires sliced off to make sandal soles. Trailing behind PAVN came key members of the united front, who on 10 January declared creation of the People's Republic of Kampuchea (PRK). Heng Samrin was named its chief of state.

Looking to deal a death blow to the fleeing Khmer Rouge, PAVN columns barely paused at Phnom Penh. Along the coast, seaborne task forces seized Ream and Kompong Som, then pushed into the coastal reaches of Koh Kong province on 17 January.[30] On 6 February, while much of Vietnam was celebrating the Tet Lunar New Year, its 5 Infantry Division, reinforced by a regiment from 3 Corps, reached the western border and seized control of Cambodia's final town, the gemstone haven of Pailin.[31]

On its face, the PAVN war machine had conducted an efficient, effective campaign for the first six weeks. A closer analysis, however, indicated problems. In particular, Khmer Rouge troops had put up a tenacious fight while withdrawing, inflicting especially high losses on PAVN armored units. Out of a total of 621 tanks and armored personnel carriers mobilized for the invasion, the Vietnamese lost 140 vehicles.[32] One especially bloody engagement took place during the 7–8 January attempt to seize the Kompong Som port, where dogged Khmer Rouge defenders left a PAVN armored battalion with thirty-four dead, twenty missing, and all but two tanks undamaged. And while it was estimated that the Khmer Rouge had lost half of its divisions in the blitz, the other half had managed to reach the sanctuary of the Thai border with their numbers roughly intact.

Worse, from Hanoi's perspective, was Bangkok's pragmatic, seamless diplomatic realignment. Historically, Thailand and Cambodia were rivals, and the Khmer Rouge had been drawing blood along their common border throughout the time it had been in power. But Thailand and Vietnam also had a history of tension, and the ease with which PAVN had advanced across Cambodia—leaving battle-hardened Vietnamese divisions leering from across the border—sent shivers through Bangkok. If forced to choose between an unbalanced, bloodstained Khmer Rouge and a steely, calculating SRV, Thailand saw Vietnam as the greater immediate threat.

There had been a further factor as well. During the second half of the 1970s, guerrillas from the CPT had been able to widen their insurgency and seriously threaten the RTA's grip in some rural, impoverished districts. Since the start of its low-intensity armed struggle in 1965, the CPT's main patron had been China. It had naturally sided with Beijing in the Sino-Soviet split, and Democratic Kampuchea, another Chinese ally, was sympathetic to its cause. Conversely, the pro-Soviet SRV, and to an increasing extent Laos, had little incentive to assist their Thai comrades for as long as they were beholden to Beijing.[33]

But during the final weeks of Democratic Kampuchea, no doubt sensing that Pol Pot was destined for defeat, China made an exceedingly pragmatic decision. On 5 November 1978, Chinese Vice Premier Deng Xiaoping went to Bangkok to give his assurances that the Khmer Rouge would cease and desist from any further frontier violations against Thailand.[34]

Bangkok responded with its own pragmatism. After PAVN surged across Cambodia in early January 1979, most of the Khmer Rouge leadership had withdrawn to the jungle around the border town of Poipet. In a shrewd calculation, the RTA saw merit in ensuring that these revolutionaries could fight another day—or at least provide a robust irritant along the Thai-Cambodian frontier that would inhibit any further westward PAVN advance across mainland Southeast Asia.

Assigned to make sure this happened was Special Colonel Chavalit. Formerly the chief of TOC 315, since the previous year Chavalit had been transferred to head a different tactical operations center, TOC 305, which dealt with overall army operations. Having dealt with Cambodia since 1971, Chavalit arguably knew more about Thailand's Khmer neighbor than any other senior RTA officer. So despite his new assignment with TOC 305, he was given relatively free rein to implement steps to safeguard Thailand's border against further advances by PAVN and its PRK puppet. First, he created a new unit subordinate to TOC 315—codenamed Task Force 838—whose mandate was to manage covert RTA liaison and support for Cambodian forces opposed to PAVN (which for the time being was largely synonymous with the Khmer Rouge).

Chosen as the first head of Task Force 838 was Kasem Thammakul, the articulate colonel who had been heading Task Force 506. With an initial staff of ten men, mostly drawn from the RTA Special Forces, Kasem shifted to the opposite side of Aranyaprathet and set up his office outside the local Royal Thai Border Patrol Police camp.[35]

Second, Chavalit ordered Kasem to offer safe passage to key Khmer Rouge leaders so that they might begin to pull back from the brink. Doing as told, Kasem on the afternoon of 11 January 1979 boarded an RTA Huey and flew across the border to Poipet. There he collected Deputy Prime Minister Ieng Sary and a team of broadcasters who had been running the Khmer Rouge radio station out of Phnom Penh. They were then shuttled to a deserted part of Bangkok's Don Muang Airport. From there, Ieng Sary was escorted to a first-class seat on a commercial flight to Hong Kong after all the other passengers were aboard.[36]

What ensued was a series of whirlwind discussions in Bangkok and Beijing designed to give the Khmer Rouge its second wind. On 15 January, Geng Biao, the secretary-general of the Chinese Communist Party's Central Military Commission, met with Prime Minister Kriangsak in Thailand. Behind closed doors they discussed options for resupplying the Khmer Rouge, including seaborne deliveries off of Koh Kong, parachute drops along the Dangrek Range, or more orthodox shipments through Bangkok's commercial port. Kriangsak preferred the latter and suggested that many supplies could be procured from ethnic Chinese merchants in the Thai capital.[37]

Three days later, Ieng Sary sat down with Deng Xiaoping and other senior Chinese officials in Beijing. He was informed of the agreed supply pipeline via Bangkok and given an initial allocation of $5 million to purchase goods on the Thai market. Deng promised to replenish this fund as needed. Radio contact was also established between Beijing and the Khmer Rouge leadership along the border.

As a clincher to all this, Thailand extracted a key concession from China. In exchange for Thai goodwill in channeling Chinese aid to the Khmer Rouge, Beijing promised to immediately end support to the CPT and ensured that Thai guerrillas would not impede Bangkok's efforts to cope with the threat from Vietnam. Suddenly forsaken, and with little hope of replacing the material and moral support historically given by China, Thailand's communist party wilted with dizzying speed. In early July, its Voice of the People of Thailand, which had been broadcasting from southern China since 1962, announced it would suspend programming. "I take this occasion to bid farewell to listeners," went the last words over the airwaves. "May you enjoy good health and success in your work."[38]

As this was transpiring, Prince Sihanouk had been doing some conspiring of his own. As he had promised Pol Pot during their meeting in Phnom Penh, he had flown from Beijing to New York and on 13 January denounced the PAVN invasion in front of the United Nations Security Council.

But there was more. No longer able to contain himself after being confined to his palace for the previous three years, the prince hurled critical barbs in his trademark falsetto at the Khmer Rouge leadership. His condemnation would no doubt have been far more severe had he known five of his children and fourteen of his nephews and grandchildren had perished at the hands of the Democratic Kampuchean authorities; their dark fates were suspected at the time but as yet unconfirmed.

After venting in this fashion, Sihanouk was genuinely torn. Looking to distance himself from his current options, he stole out of his New York hotel room at night and broached a possible U.S. exile with members of the American delegation to the United Nations. But when Washington's embrace was less warm than he expected, the prince nixed these plans and instead ventured to Paris. There, his prospects were hardly any better. Denied his request for a French passport, he was reminded of French prohibitions regarding exile politics.

As a lifelong Francophile, Sihanouk bristled at the rejection. Deciding to go full circle, he got back on a plane and returned to Beijing. There the Chinese offered him the same comforts extended during his years struggling against the Khmer Republic—and once more with the understanding that he would be supportive of the Khmer Rouge, or at the very least temper his criticisms of Pol Pot and company. Without any better offers, the prince had little choice but to agree.

While Sihanouk had left France stewing over the warning against politicking, in fact the Cambodian émigré population in that country was reaching new levels of activism. Remaining in the forefront was Son Sann, who in December 1978 had taken pains to add more top Cambodian exile personalities, including several former royalists, to his inner circle. This included General Nhiek Tioulong, a lifelong Sihanoukist, and In Tam, the Republican prime minister who was unceremoniously booted from Thailand in late 1975. Gaining critical mass, this broad front, with Son Sann at the helm, initially called themselves the Committee for a Neutral and Peaceful Cambodia.

On 5 January 1979, two days before PAVN entered Phnom Penh, the committee went public. Now calling themselves the Council of Wise Men, they issued a proclamation with numerous demands. Topping the list was the immediate withdrawal of Vietnamese troops from Cambodian soil. Son Sann also began to once more talk up the formation of a noncommunist armed resistance movement and hinted that Sihanouk should play the leading role. But when the prince dashed through Paris at midmonth without offering support, several of the senior royalists around Son Sann lost heart and began to peel away from the council.

Whereas Sihanouk was not biting, Son Sann's call to arms had attracted attention from another quarter. Back in Bangkok, Special Colonel Chavalit had gotten word about the council's proclamation and in the third week of January boarded a commercial flight to France. Making his way to Son Sann's Paris apartment, he huddled with Cambodia's former top banker and General Dien Del to talk about their planned resistance. Though he had never met either man before, the meeting was extremely cordial—their rapport helped after learning he was born on the exact same day and year as Dien Del.

Upon parting, Son Sann promised to dispatch Dien Del to the Thai-Cambodian border to start turning their resistance plans into reality. There was a hitch, however. The French were notoriously fickle about letting Indochinese refugees to whom they had granted asylum travel to Thailand. In addition, Thai immigration officials were routinely blocking entry to Cambodians carrying travel papers short of a full-fledged passport.[39] As Dien Del was carrying only temporary refugee documents, he feared his journey might be prematurely terminated. To circumvent this, Chavalit had an effective solution: Later that week, he delivered a Thai passport bearing Dien Del's photograph but fake biographic details.[40]

On 1 February, Dien Del boarded an Air France flight to the Thai capital. Encountering no delays with his faux passport, he exited Don Muang and was met by a Task Force 838 officer. After little more than a quick shower, he was racing toward the border to begin the daunting task of forging a noncommunist alternative to the lethally efficient Khmer Rouge and a smothering Vietnamese occupation.

7. Fratricide

Escorted by officers from Task Force 838, Dien Del spent a month shuttling the length of the Thai-Cambodian border.[1] What he found were enclaves of guerrilla bands flourishing amid the lawlessness of the frontier. Each pocket of resistance had its own local commander that had risen to the top due to a hint of charisma, some self-taught guerrilla sensibilities, or, most often, a pronounced ruthless streak. Even for the more competent of these mini-warlords, their writ barely extended beyond their camp's perimeter.

At each stop, Dien Del offered a simple proposition. Rather than carrying on an autonomous struggle, the general proposed that they forge a unified movement. As a carrot, he appealed to their nationalist instincts: As a united entity, they had a fleeting chance of better striking back at their historical enemy, the Vietnamese. As a stick, the general made no secret he had backing from the RTA—with the implication that rejection might attract the RTA's ire.

Within a month, five of the commanders embraced Dien Del's offer. In each of these five cases, the guerrilla groups had adopted colorful names—no doubt to compensate for performance shortfalls in the field. In the extreme northeast astride Thailand's Nam Yuen district was Keo Chuan, the former village chieftain who had received RTA Special Forces support the previous year. Plagued by malaria and facing a border festooned with mines, his guerrilla band was now calling itself Baksei Chomkrong, the name of a mythical giant bird that had sheltered a Khmer king under its wings during a siege on Angkor.

Also in the north opposite Thailand's Sisaket province was Im Chudett, the former FANK colonel with especially close ties to the RTA. His small group tucked high in the Dangrek chain was now going by the name Reachasey Chaktomuk, literally "King of Lions of the Four-Faced Mekong." This referred to a legendary beast who dominated the juncture of the Mekong River system in front of the Royal Palace in Phnom Penh.[2]

From the vicinity of Ampil, just inside Battambang's Thmar Pouk district some 69 kilometers northeast of Aranyaprathet, two separate guerrilla factions threw in their lot with Dien Del. The first, commanded by former FANK Captain Prum Saret, had dubbed itself Kok Sar ("White Crane"), a bird known for its patience while stalking its prey. The second, called Nenraung, took its name from a monk of legend. This latter faction was a catch-all group, counting such local guerrilla chieftains as Ta Maing and Ta Luot.[3]

Kong Sileah, the first Moulinaka commander. (Courtesy Hul Sakada)

Finally, just inside Thailand's Chanthaburi province opposite the gem-rich town of Pailin was a group led by Prum Vith. As a former FANK battalion commander at Pailin, fifty-one-year-old Prum Vith was intimately familiar with that district. Ably assisted by Toan Chay, the former T-28 pilot, his guerrillas had taken the moniker Khleang Moeung. This was the name of a mythical fifteenth-century Angkorian general who committed suicide so his ghost could weak havoc on an invading Thai army—a somewhat baffling choice given that Prum Vith's guerrillas were now dependent on Thai hospitality.

Deciding he had reached critical mass with these five groups, Dien Del awaited Son Sann to declare a noncommunist political front. Since he had departed for Thailand, however, a problem had arisen. Several of the prominent royalists within the Council of Wise Men were insistent that Sihanouk alone had sufficient stature to assume command over a resistance front. Not only did this rub Son Sann raw—after all, he had been patiently shepherding the Paris expatriate association for the previous two years—but the moody prince, in the process of shifting to Beijing, was reluctant to take up any offers.

With the issue of political leadership unresolved, Dien Del received permission from Son Sann to go ahead with the pronouncement of a resistance army without any complementary political front. On 5 March in a simple ceremony at Ampil, the general officially proclaimed formation of the Forces Armées

Nationale de Libération du Peuple Khmer (Khmer People's National Liberation Armed Forces, or KPNLAF). Dien Del named himself KPNLAF chief of staff, intentionally leaving open the possibility of a civilian like Son Sann to later become commander-in-chief.[4]

Though Dien Del on paper now had control of approximately 1,600 men, only the smallest fraction of them had access to weapons. Rectifying this would not be easy. After all, the RTA to date had been extremely reluctant to spare its arms. As well, other members of ASEAN had met in January and roundly condemned the PAVN invasion, but none seemed eager to make the provocative leap of offering paramilitary support.[5]

A better option appeared to be China. Beijing was historically the primary supporter of the Khmer Rouge and had taken quick steps to resume military assistance to Democratic Kampuchean elements along the Thai border after Phnom Penh fell.[6] More than that, on 17 February they launched a massive military incursion into the northern SRV in order to "teach Vietnam a lesson." This had forced PAVN to withdraw two of its largest elements from Cambodia—2 Corps and 3 Corps—and rush them to the Sino-Vietnamese border; after a month, tens of thousands of Vietnamese troops lay dead on the battlefield before Beijing declared its lesson taught and withdrew.[7]

As China was obviously intent on continuing to back the Khmer Rouge, and the KPNLAF was avowedly noncommunist, Son Sann saw the possibility of forging common cause with Beijing. After all, the Khmer Rouge was a public-relations nightmare, and a noncommunist resistance group like KPNLAF offered a way of selling opposition to PAVN with a face other than that of Pol Pot. In particular, Chinese support for the KPNLAF would assuage ASEAN by making Chinese involvement in Cambodia appear more palatable than merely backing another power grab by the Khmer Rouge.

In late May, Son Sann flew out to Asia and rendezvoused with Dien Del in Tokyo. From there, the two continued to Beijing. As hoped, they found the Chinese leadership willing to begin funneling weapons to the KPNLAF. But there was a catch: China wanted to part only with dated weapons like the weighty SKS semiautomatic rifle, a poor weapon compared to those they were lavishing upon the Khmer Rouge. Dien Del was especially annoyed by the offer: "I told them that I knew the SKS from my days when they supplied this to my infantry battalion in the mid-1960s. It was heavy and old, and it was already phased out in other armies."[8] Pushed, the Chinese proved malleable. Agreeing to equip 3,000 KPNLAF guerrillas, Beijing promised to include newer Type 56 assault rifles, as well as 60mm and 81mm mortars, and two kinds of machine guns.

Then came the rub: In exchange for weapons, China ushered Son Sann and Dien Del to a government guesthouse and told them to await Ieng Sary. When the Khmer Rouge deputy prime minister arrived, Chinese chaperones implored both sides to agree to a united resistance front against PAVN. To this, Son Sann bristled. Displaying a stubborn streak that was to become his hallmark over the ensuing years, he rejected any call to temper his criticism of the Khmer Rouge. Frustrating his Chinese hosts, he and Dien Del stormed out of Beijing; it would be almost two years before the promised Chinese delivery materialized.

If Son Sann did not get along with the Khmer Rouge, it was more than matched by the bad blood that increasingly characterized the relationship between the KPNLAF and Sihanouk. From Beijing, the prickly royal still harbored an intense hatred for the Khmer Republic's leadership—and thus was seething over the fact that so many FANK veterans were gravitating toward Dien Del's KPNLAF. In addition, despite the fact that it was he who rejected entreaties to head a noncommunist front, he still felt incensed that top Cambodian personalities had gone ahead with forging a resistance organization without his involvement.

No doubt, too, Sihanouk had taken note that at least one guerrilla group on the Thai border had rejected Dien Del and was openly professing its loyalty to the prince. That group, known as the National Movement for the Liberation of Kampuchea (Mouvement pour la Libération Nationale du Kampuchea, or Moulinaka), was led by a former Cambodian naval officer named Kong Sileah.

Hailing from a wealthy family in Svay Rieng province, Kong Sileah had not always displayed royalist leanings. Reflecting his family's clout, he had volunteered for the navy (dominated by sons of the privileged more than any of the other services) and landed the safe, lucrative job as head of naval finances. He had remained in this influential position throughout the Republican era, reaching the equivalent of *captaine de frigate* in the navy's administrative service. His older brother, meanwhile, entered Republican politics and became a national legislator.

Ironically, Dien Del was a family friend of the Sileah clan, vacationing at their palatial villa during holidays while in high school. On a more somber note, Del had entrusted his wife and son to Kong Sileah during the dying days of the Republic, and it was the captain who escorted the pair to the coast and eventually to freedom in Thailand aboard a navy patrol boat.

With lots of money, Kong Sileah and his family barely paused in Thailand before quickly relocating to comfortable exile in France.[9] Two years later, he

Camp Reahou commanders Van Saren and Andre Ouk Thol (alias Norodom Soryavong), September 1979. (Courtesy Roland Neveu)

started shuttling between the United States and France to agitate against the Khmer Rouge. It was not until early 1979, however, that he ventured to Bangkok and, confronted with PAVN's occupation, contemplated heading an anti-Vietnamese resistance effort.[10]

As he discovered, the stretch of the Thai-Cambodian border midway between Aranyaprathet and the KPNLAF headquarters at Ampil had for years harbored an unsavory mix of Khmer resistance fighters, smugglers, and bandits. Among them, a small band of guerrillas opposite the Thai bordertown of Nong Chan were hinting at support for Sihanouk. It was this band that successfully petitioned Kong Sileah to leave Bangkok and head to the border.

Arriving in the jungle near Nong Chan, Kong Sileah found the proverbial cup halfful. While there were only a few dozen pro-Sihanouk guerrillas on hand, two of them showed promise. The first was a former FANK major named Nhem Sophon, who at one time had been Sihanouk's brother-in-law.[11] Although he had been a bureaucrat in the customs bureau prior to 1970, Nhem had shown a natural flair for soldiering after transferring to the army.[12] He had further honed these instincts during several lean years as a guerrilla after 1975. The second was Duong Khem, a longtime paratrooper who had worked his way up from orderly in 1953 to airborne battalion commander in 1974. By then a lieutenant colonel, he spent the final year of the Republic behind a desk at FANK headquarters.

Escaping the capital to find his family, Duong had labored on a Battambang farming commune during the Khmer Rouge reign. He had then made his way toward the border following the PAVN invasion, pausing at the Soeung subdistrict, opposite Nong Chan, after chancing upon Nhem.[13]

Accepting leadership over the group at Soeung, Kong Sileah on 31 August officially proclaimed the establishment of Moulinaka. Though the ceremony was attended by just fifty persons, and the Moulinaka arsenal was strikingly thin, the former navy captain displayed a keen flair for publicity. With his penchant for forgoing footwear and sporting a bush hat atop a moppish hairstyle, there was no denying he cut a roguish figure. But his fluent French, talent for penning romantic poems, and compelling personal tale of forgoing a life of relative privilege for the harsh realities of the Thai border had all combined to make him a darling of the French media.

By that time, Sihanouk had temporarily shifted residences from Beijing to Pyongyang. There, he was lounging in the palace that North Korean dictator Kim Il-Sung had built him in 1974 overlooking scenic Chhang Sou On Lake. Restless despite the creature comforts (the sixty-room palace had its own indoor movie theater), the prince since early August had been flirting with the idea of once again forging a government-in-exile, similar to the GRUNK arrangement he headed against the Khmer Republic. Ideally he wanted to go public with this declaration in Europe. Very quickly, however, France and Belgium—both proposed as venues—let it be known they did not want to play host.[14] The United States and China, too, let slip they were not ready to back Sihanouk's own version of a government-in-exile.

Running out of options, Sihanouk instead called for a lesser gathering in Pyongyang. Rather than declare a government-in-exile, he now had his mind set on crafting yet another league of Cambodian nationalists akin to what had existed in Paris for years. Trouble was, when the tryst finally took place during 25–28 September, many prominent nationalists were apparently inhibited by the problematic logistics of travel to North Korea. Just twenty persons ultimately bothered to make the journey.[15]

What followed was vintage Sihanouk. Perhaps frustrated with the paltry turnout in Pyongyang, the prince began issuing threats, burning bridges, and showing precious little appreciation for geopolitical realities. To begin, in early October he penned a series of five letters to SRV Prime Minister Pham Van Dong in which he demanded that Hanoi agree to settlement talks. But already assuming that he would not get a response, the prince concurrently announced that he would soon form a nationalist army to fight PAVN.

By that time, Moulinaka had already taken shape. But rather than acknowledging Kong Sileah's modest start on the border, Sihanouk displayed flights of fancy when he boldly announced to journalists he intended to appeal to North Korea for arms—and to China for both arms and "military volunteers." On a roll, he further reasoned that because France and Morocco had deployed crack troops to Zaire over the previous two years, he would also be asking those two nations to back him with soldiers. And despite the fact that he had only just conjured this resistance scheme, he took time to gratuitously lash out at the United States for not rushing in to offer weapons or money.[16]

While Sihanouk was intoning from Pyongyang about his resistance plans, Son Sann arrived in Thailand during the last week of September. Arriving, too, was a litany of prominent Cambodians—many of them FANK veterans—from France. Among them was Dien Del, Ea Chuor Kimmeng, Thou Thip, and Chak Bory; the latter three were all former colonels. Coming, too, was Son Sann's wife and two of his sons. Many were carrying only refugee identification and, given French travel restrictions to Thailand, had been forced to route their journeys through third counties.[17]

Since the KPNLAF had been declared back in March, there had been some changes in the field. For one thing, representatives from thirteen provinces had by then made their way to the border and were eager to sign on with Dien Del's noncommunist resistance.[18]

For another thing, one of the five original factions in the KPNLAF—Prum Vith's Khleang Moeung—had run into serious problems around Pailin. This was because a large contingent of Khmer Rouge guerrillas had moved into the area—drawn in part by the lure of gemstones to be mined—and was going out of its way to make life uncomfortable. Compounding matters, by that time Prum Vith had confirmed the Khmer Rouge killed his son—also a FANK officer—and wife. Unable to stomach the company, he elected to work his way south along the border for some 75 kilometers, not stopping until he reached the edge of the Cardamom Mountains just inside Pursat province's Veal Veang district. Although Khmer Rouge encampments were nearby, Prum Vith felt this rugged, forested venue—dubbed Sok Sann—was sufficiently inaccessible to allow him to nurture Khleang Moeung with minimal interference.[19] His deputy, Toan Chay, was less sanguine; in an amicable split, Toan Chay took half of Khleang Moeung and headed north to the border village of O'Ksach opposite Thailand's Buriram province.

Moulinaka guerrillas assemble near Nong Chan, late 1979. On the left is Nhek Bun Chay, later an ANS brigade commander. (Courtesy Roland Neveu)

By the end of the first week of October, Son Sann was finally ready to announce his much-delayed noncommunist political front. As this front would assume control over Dien Del's KPNLAF, the initial plan was for him to slip across the Cambodian frontier and make the declaration at Ampil, where Dien Del had his largest concentration of guerrillas. But the parched flatland around Ampil was relatively exposed, and there were fears that security against a PAVN spoiling attack could not be guaranteed.

Instead, it was decided to stage the announcement at Prum Vith's lush Sok Sann setting. On 9 October, Son Sann, Dien Del, representatives from thirteen provinces, a handful of prominent nationalists from overseas, and leaders from the five original KPNLAF factions ventured there for a ceremony formally establishing the Khmer People's National Liberation Front (Front National de Libération du Peuple Khmer, or KPNLF). Son Sann was unanimously elected as the Front's president. The ailing Chhean Vam, who briefly served as prime minister back in 1948, was chosen as vice-president. Dien Del remained chief of staff of the KPNLAF, as well as commander of its central sector at Ampil. Im Chudett was named head of the KPNLAF's northern sector, and Prum Vith was placed in command of the south.

From the start, the KPNLF was born into controversy. It barely took a day before it was noted that the Front's official proclamation took place on the same date—9 October—that the Khmer Republic had been declared back in 1970.[20] The person highlighting this connection with the loudest voice was In Tam, the former prime minister who had attended Sihanouk's Pyongyang tryst the previous month. During his volatile political career, In Tam had proven to be something of a political chameleon. Initially a royalist, he had become a key conspirator against Sihanouk in 1970, then became a bitter enemy of Lon Nol after the latter blatantly stole the 1972 presidential election. Still, he periodically allowed himself to be wooed back into positions of power for the remainder of the Republic, including a six-month stint as prime minister.

After the fall of Phnom Penh in April 1975, In Tam had remained along the border long enough for his guerrilla antics to get him expelled from Thailand. He then split the next three years between Paris and Salt Lake City, Utah, occasionally contacting Son Sann to flirt about pooling their talents in a resistance effort. But in early 1979 his ego was irreparably bruised when Son Sann assigned Dien Del the task of forging the KPNLAF—a job he felt he deserved. Stewing in Salt Lake City, he had emerged from his depression long enough to visit the prince in Pyongyang to test whether there was room for him to become a royalist once more. As much as anything else, his shrill condemnation of the KPNLF's anniversary date was thus an attempt to shore up his dubious royalist credentials.

In Tam's sniping from Utah was bad, but it amounted to nothing compared to the deadly rivalries brewing among noncommunists along the border. Nowhere was this truer than along the stretch of frontier midway between Ampil and Aranyaprathet. With starvation conditions peaking inside Cambodia, this area had been inundated by tens of thousands of refugees throughout 1979.[21] In their wake, armed Khmer guerrillas also arrived by the hundreds—preying on the refugees and controlling the local black markets funneling scarce commodities into Cambodia. For these guerrillas, resistance against PAVN was barely an afterthought.

At the southern end of this lawless stretch was the Thai border village of Nong Chan. To the immediate east of this village and straddling the Cambodian frontier was a sprawling refugee camp and adjacent guerrilla cantonment. The guerrilla warlord in this vicinity was a balding, bespectacled FANK veteran named Chea Chhut. Despite his unassuming appearance, the thirty-five-year-old Svay Rieng native had been an infantryman at Thmar Puok during the Republic. He remained on the border with a handful of armed loyalists throughout the Khmer

Rouge era, taking a Thai wife and making the occasional cross-border foray. It was not until October 1979, after refugees began massing at Nong Chan, that he opted for profits over resistance and moved in with his 125-strong guerrilla band.

Five kilometers to the northeast was the Thai border village of Nong Samet. Just as with Nong Chan, to the immediate east of Nong Samet along the Cambodian frontier was an expansive refugee camp and adjoining resistance emplacement. Here the resident warlord was In Sakon, the former schoolteacher. Paying lip service to noncommunist resistance activities, he led the so-called Angkor National Liberation Movement (also known as Khmer Angkor). But as with Chea Chhut, In Sakon focused almost exclusively on controlling the local market, with his guerrillas often acting as guards and escorts for smugglers. The Nong Samet vicinity subsequently became known as "Camp 007" due to Sakon's supporting cast of unsavory characters and commercial intrigue.

Midway between Nong Samet and Nong Chan, in a small divot of territory extending into Cambodia, was the Thai village of Non Mak Mun. Just east of the village was a guerrilla camp filled with personalities that, in the constellation of unusual characters along the border, stood in a category all their own. The chief resident warlord was Van Saren, a former elementary school teacher and FANK noncommissioned officer who had earlier headed an illegal logging operation in the Dangrek Mountains. He shared power at Non Mak Mun with a mysterious Cambodian named Andre Ouk Thol. A former student in France, Ouk Thol had earlier alternated his sympathies between Sihanouk and the Republic.[22] Sniffing for guerrilla opportunities, he had made his way to Thailand in early 1979. By the time he arrived at Non Mak Mun, he had undergone a complete transformation in character. Now going by the name Norodom Soryavong—and falsely claiming kinship with Sihanouk—he roamed the camp as a shoeless mystic, regularly holding meditation sessions to pray for food.[23]

On 3 October, Soryavong and Van Saren decided to ratchet up their idiosyncrasies. On that day, Van Saren declared himself prime minister of Cambodia (he would alternately call himself marshal), while Soryavong dubbed himself king. Van Saren then set about penning a new constitution; he also divided his camp into two dozen sectors, each named after a Cambodian province. They both decided to call their border fiefdom "Camp Reahou," after the bisected ogre from Hindu legend.[24]

Very quickly, Camp Reahou became crowded. Aside from the original band of Van Saren loyalists, a second battalion of resistance fighters (half of them Khmer Rouge defectors) had arrived after trekking from Pursat province. Present in the same general vicinity, too, was Kong Sileah's band of pro-Sihanouk Moulinaka guerrillas.[25] All of these groups began to bicker, in part because Van Saren and Soryavong had abrasive personalities. The end result of this was that by late October Kong Sileah decided to lead his guerrillas out of Non Mak Mun and test the climes closer to In Sakon's Camp 007.[26]

This exodus proved ill-timed. On 8 November, following accusations that an RTA soldier had raped a Cambodian woman, resistance fighters—probably from Moulinaka—murdered a Thai private in revenge. Meting out swift border justice, the nearby RTA outpost unleashed a flurry of artillery shells on Kong Sileah's new position, killing dozens of refugees. Fleeing the onslaught, Moulinaka fighters rushed back toward Camp Reahou but were forcibly kept outside the perimeter. Rebuffed at Reahou, they continued southwest until settling on the outskirts of Chea Chhut's Nong Chan camp.

At Nong Chan, Kong Sileah—easily the most educated guerrilla in the vicinity—soon earned high marks from humanitarian organizations that were doling out aid to the destitute masses.[27] It was here that Kong Sileah confirmed his reputation as a media darling, conducting frequent interviews with the French press about the alleged guerrilla exploits of his men.

All of this stoked jealousies among the other warlords in the area. As Moulinaka was helping distribute free rice and other staples courtesy of nongovernmental organizations, its humanitarian activities undercut the lucrative black markets. Seeking an end to this, the guerrillas from Camp Reahou on 30 December, reportedly at the prompting of the RTA, raided Nong Chan. Kong Sileah himself was in the field at the time; as consolation, they ransacked his hut and stole his carbine before retreating back to Non Mak Mun.

Relations among the warlords deteriorated further during the first quarter of 1980. Within Camp Reahou, friction between Van Saren's guerrillas and the Pursat battalion had led the latter to seek temporary sanctuary at Nong Samet. The Pursat guerrillas (many of whom had foresworn haircuts and were sporting flowing locks like Apache warriors) returned on 22 March, violently ousting Van Saren and Soryavong—both of whom disappeared and were apparently murdered.[28]

Meantime, the KPNLF held its first congress at Ampil on 23–25 April.[29] An attempt was made to bring the guerrillas at Nong Samet into the fold, and In Sakon went as far as sending a representative to the congress. But Khmer Angkor was insisting that it be treated as an equal partner to the KPNLF, not subordinated under the Front. This offer was rejected outright, leaving 007 and the two nearby camps—Reahou and Nong Chan—outside of Son Sann's purview.

As it turned out, In Sakon's obstinence was the least of the KNPLF's worries. PAVN had been busy reorganizing its occupation forces over the previous year,

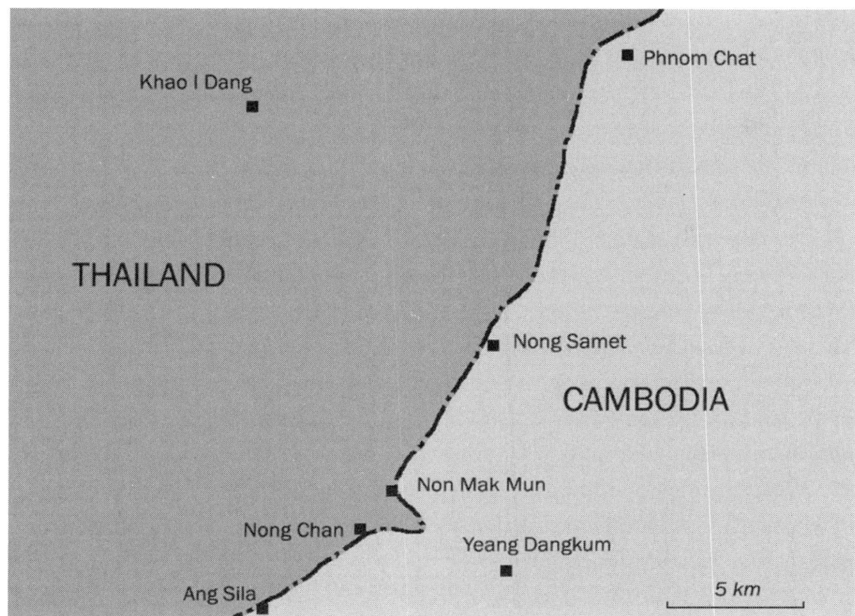

Noncommunist resistance camps on the Battambang border

focusing primarily on consolidating its grip over the interior. The SRV's Military Region 7, which had supplied much of the manpower during the invasion, had its forward headquarters inside Cambodia divided and upgraded. In April 1979, one half, headquartered in Siem Reap and responsible for the northwestern border area, became Front 479.[30] Three months later in July, the other half, headquartered in Kompong Cham and responsible for the five provinces east of Phnom Penh, became Front 779.[31] In both cases, Military Region 7 continued to provide most of the manpower, logistics, and administrative control. For Front 479, two of its three assigned infantry divisions—the 5 and 302—were from Military Region 7; the third, the 309 Infantry Division, was created several months after the invasion.[32] Elements of 4 Corps, like the 7 and 9 Divisions, were occasionally designed as reinforcements but never permanently assigned to the Front 479.

As an operational command-and-control element over the two fronts, Hanoi established a forward headquarters for all of PAVN in Cambodia. Known as Front 719 and located at the former Presidential Palace in Phnom Penh, it was led by Le Duc Anh, an unusually tall and ideologically rigid major-general who was one of the key architects of the invasion.[33]

With this new command arrangement in place, many Cambodia observers had wondered whether Le Duc Anh would wipe out the remainder of the Khmer Rouge (not to mention the noncommunist resistance) when the late 1979 dry season allowed PAVN to move aggressively against the border base camps. Reinforcing this notion, a Soviet diplomat in Bangkok reportedly told an Asian colleague that PAVN hoped to declare complete victory on 7 January 1980, the one-year anniversary of the liberation of Phnom Penh.

The year 1980 opened, however, with a curious amount of inactivity on the part of PAVN. Not until early April did it assign the 341 Infantry Division to strike at the resistance located on the edge of the Cardamom chain in Pursat province.[34] This area, which hosted both Khmer Rouge and Prum Vith's Sok Sann camp, was thought an unlikely target given its hostile topography and thick jungle cover. But in an unexpected move, the PAVN infantrymen negotiated minefields and dense vegetation to assault Sok Sann on 20 April. A day later, they moved into the KPNLF's abandoned bunkers. In true guerrilla fashion, Prum Vith had easily slipped across the Thai frontier; they reoccupied their positions later that month after incurring few losses.[35]

Sok Sann, it turned out, was just a primer. Although the noncommunist resistance around Nong Chan and Nong Samet was little more than an excuse for banditry, PAVN viewed its declared intent to vanquish the PRK—not to mention the media attention garnered by the likes of Kong Sileah—as an affront that could no longer be tolerated. In an attempt to stamp out the guerrillas in this vicinity, as well as to send Bangkok a clear signal about the dangers of harboring insurgents, Front 479, with the approval of Front 719, developed a bold plan to strike across the border.

Spearheading the effort would be 5 Infantry Division, a unit that had been in Cambodia since the invasion. Starting in April 1979, it had been posted to the northwestern border, where its men faced off against several major Khmer Rouge base camps. But by year's end, a mix of Khmer Rouge ambushes, mines, tropical diseases, and a persistent lack of water had taken a tremendous toll on the division. With malaria and edema afflicting an estimated 80 percent of one battalion, desertion rates reportedly were high.

To rectify this, 5 Division was instructed to focus on rebuilding morale over the first five months of 1980. Declared ready by late May, it was assigned with spearheading the cross-border assault—even though logistics would be significantly complicated by seasonal rains. Precipitation notwithstanding, two of the division's regiments marched in mid-June down muddy trails until they arrived at the Cambodian village of Yeang Dangkum, 7 kilometers east of Nong Chan. In a first for the division, and reflecting the importance of the mission, its men were amply supplied with food rations siphoned from United Nations aid sent for starving Cambodian civilians; among this was buckets of butter from Norway, cooking oil from Sweden, and canned meat from the Netherlands.

On 22 June, the division split. Its 4 Regiment quietly approached the refugee camp near Nong Chan, adjacent to which was Kong Sileah's Moulinaka base. The following morning they surged forward, setting afire parts of the refugee camp and inflicting hundreds of casualties. They entered Moulinaka's concrete command bunker, but once more they discovered that Kong Sileah had made a timely exit. The PAVN column soon retreated, carrying everything from pilfered paintings, to foodstuffs, to a cache of Moulinaka camouflage uniforms.[36] They also took along a British doctor and two U.S. journalists; all three were marched deep into the PRK but released four days later.

At the same time, 5 Division's 174 Regiment made an incursion to the north. Reinforced with a Dac Cong battalion, it had slipped into Thai territory and then curled in behind both Camp Reahou and Non Mak Mun village from the rear. Taken by surprise, the Pursat battalion panicked. Afraid of being identified by their trademark long hair, many grabbed knives and sliced off their locks before slipping out of Reahou with relatively few casualties and headed toward Nong Samet for sanctuary; Non Mak Mun was never reoccupied as a guerrilla staging base.[37]

The 174 Regiment, however, did not have time to relish its victory. As it had moved more than a kilometer into Thai territory, and had attacked a Thai village, the RTA unleashed a withering response. Led by 2 Infantry Regiment under Colonel Prajak Sawangjit, and supported by armor and helicopter gunships, it began to inflict heavy casualties on the Vietnamese interlopers. PAVN's Soviet-made 130mm guns started hurling shells from inside Cambodia as a diversion; the RTA responded by moving forward 155mm howitzers and placing accurate fire on the PAVN forward command post at Yeang Dangkum. With shrapnel raining overhead, General Le Duc Anh and the 5 Division commander were sent scrambling eastward.[38]

By the following morning, elements of the 174 Regiment were still pinned down inside Thai territory. Attempting to make a beeline into the PRK, they had encountered a deep antitank ditch the RTA had dug opposite Non Mak Mun. Flooded with rainwater and slick with mud, the ditch was forcing the heavily laden PAVN infantrymen to abandon their equipment while scrambling toward Cambodian territory. As these stragglers were falling prey to Thai airpower, PAVN took the risky move of deploying a seven-man team with an SA-7 missile launcher; they managed to shoot down one L-19 observation plane and an H-34 chopper by noon.[39]

That evening, the RTA held a press conference. It displayed 300 weapons left behind during the PAVN raid. Also on display were a range of food items with United Nations markings, again abandoned by the fleeing Vietnamese. At least seventy-two PAVN corpses were left inside Thailand, although there were bloody traces that dozens more had been lifted back to the PRK. In return, some twenty-two Thai soldiers and airmen died in the exchange.

Over the days and weeks ahead, there were wide-ranging impacts from the attacks on Nong Chan and Non Mak Mun. Surprisingly, repercussions within the SRV were the most pronounced. This was because Vietnamese Communist Party General Secretary Le Duan and Prime Minister Pham Van Dong both happened to be in Moscow at the time, where they were negotiating with Soviet General Secretary Leonid Brezhnev over aid levels—and during which time Brezhnev had expressly counseled the SRV leaders against extending the Cambodian war into Thailand.

Further complicating matters, SRV Minister of Foreign Affairs Nguyen Co Thach was in Bangkok, where he was trying to negotiate for an emergency 50,000-ton shipment of Thai rice to alleviate a shortage in Vietnam. Bangkok, not surprisingly, ignored the request on the heels of PAVN's incursion.

Angered over the twin foreign policy gaffs, the SRV Politburo chided Major General Le Duc Anh against further cross-border forays.[40] Driving home the point, the 5 Division commander was reportedly sacked.

There was another repercussion from the attacks, this one impacting the noncommunist resistance. Showing there was no honor among thieves—or in this case warlords—In Sakon's Khmer Angkor guerrillas had opportunistically attacked the 200-strong Pursat battalion when it arrived from Non Mak Mun seeking sanctuary. Dozens of Pursat combatants were killed or taken prisoner for their weapons before the remainder of the battalion broke contact and fled to a nearby RTA outpost.

For General Dien Del, who had been patiently reorganizing the KPNLAF over the first half of the year, In Sakon's duplicity was of mounting concern. With encouragement from the RTA (which had grown tired of the anarchy around Camp 007), the general dispatched ammunition to the Pursat battalion, plus two battalions of KPNLAF reinforcements from Ampil led by former FANK sergeant Ta Luot. The two reinforcement battalions, significantly, were all sporting SKS rifles; over the preceding months, the RTA had siphoned these off from Chinese aid earmarked for the Khmer Rouge.

On 13 July, this combined force moved against Camp 007, sending In Sakon and a handful of loyalists fleeing south in the direction of Aranyaprathet. The

KPNLF flag was subsequently raised and the camp was rechristened Rithysen, after a Khmer folk hero whose siblings were devoured by a demon.

With the KPNLF consolidating control over Nong Samet, Chea Chhut reconsidered his odds of waging an independent struggle. In a pragmatic move that August, he pledged support to the Front, thus bringing Nong Chan under the expanding KPNLF umbrella.

Dien Del then seized the opportunity to initiate another wave of restructuring. At the time of the KPNLF's creation, the KPNLAF had been divided into zones. Zone 101, formerly the Baksei Chomkrong faction, was at Nam Yuen district in the extreme northeast. Reachasey Chaktomuk, now located in the Dangrek range near the O'Bok pass, was renamed Zone 102. At Ampil, part of the Nenraung faction under Ta Maing became Zone 201, the rest became Zone 202, and the Kok Sar faction became Zone 203. Prum Vith at Sok Sann was now in charge of Zone 401.[41]

Adding to this in the third quarter of 1980, Camp Rithysen under Ta Luot became Zone 204 and Chea Chhut at Nong Chan was put in control of Zone 205.

Each of these zones had both local guerrilla duties as well as the responsibility to care for resident refugee populations. In an attempt to instill some discipline among the camp leaders, the KPNLF in late 1979 set up a political warfare office to teach the necessity of winning support from the civilian populace. Using material adapted from the Republic of China on Taiwan (which had extensively coached FANK on political warfare methods), schools were initially set up at Ampil and O'Bok. In October 1980, another school was established at Zone 205 in Nong Chan.[42]

Next, to provide maneuver elements that could focus on offensive operations inside the PRK, Dien Del in late 1980 began organizing 300-man guerrilla battalions. Continuing with the same numerical sequence as the zones, the first of these, Battalion 206, was the name assigned to one of the battalions that Ta Luot took from Ampil to help seize control over Nong Samet. Three additional guerrilla battalions raised at Ampil became 207, 208, and 209.[43] The Pursat battalion, now camped at Rithysen, became Battalion 212, and another battalion raised at Nong Samet became Battalion 213.[44]

Despite this nominal amount of growth, the KPNLF by late 1980 was experiencing significant growing pains. For one thing, it suffered from chronic weapons shortages. To that point in time, its men were almost exclusively equipped with a diverse array of firearms collected from the interior. In desperation, some members had been reduced to defecting to the Khmer Rouge 519 Division located between Nong Samet and Ampil, waiting around long enough to be issued a new assault rifle courtesy of China, then redefecting back to the KPNLF. Getting wise to the scam, the Khmer Rouge formed a pursuit group to reclaim the appropriated weapons.[45]

For another thing, unity among the KPNLF's zones was lagging. Within Camp Rithysen, for example, members of Battalion 212 were bickering with troops loyal to Zone 204 commander Ta Luot. Intervening before bullets started to fly, Dien Del in January 1981 ordered Battalion 212 to relocate to Ampil. That same month, in an attempt to boost the abilities of its more promising guerrilla recruits, the general opened an officer's school at Ampil; its first class of eighty-two cadets, sixty-eight company commanders, and seventy-six platoon leaders graduated later that year.

As the KPNLF was wrestling with maintaining professionalism, the Khmer Rouge alone was able to retain the discipline and firepower to effectively snipe at PAVN from along the border. The Democratic Kampuchean remnants were sufficiently robust, in fact, that by early 1981 they had easily parried PAVN's second annual dry-season push.

Viewing this, ASEAN was understandably concerned. While they were unanimously opposed to SRV expansionism, the Khmer Rouge was equally unpalatable.[46] As ASEAN's frontline state, Thailand was especially eager for the anti-Vietnamese resistance to be expanded to include cooperation among forces of all political persuasions.

It was a hard sell, however. The KPNLF from the start had billed itself as a Khmer Rouge alternative and rarely lost an opportunity to throw barbs at Pol Pot's movement. In return, the Khmer Rouge, while taking pains to soften its crude image, was in many ways more leery of the KPNLF than of the PAVN occupation forces. Acknowledging its own limited appeal, Khieu Samphan in October 1979 had confided in a sympathetic diplomat that the Vietnamese could never win the hearts of the Khmer people—but the FANK officers joining the noncommunist resistance could. He also feared that Lon Nol and Sihanouk had papered over their differences and were conspiring against the Khmer Rouge.[47]

The RTA had spent all of 1979 trying in vain to change these mind-sets. Attempting to insert himself as middleman in these proceedings was a shadowy Vietnamese figure named Le Quoc Tuy. At one time a junior officer in the South Vietnam Air Force (and the nephew of Prime Minister Tran Van Huu), Tuy had left the military in 1958 and gone to France. Three years later, after receiving French citizenship and getting a degree in chemical engineering, he ventured to

Phnom Penh to work for an international aid organization. Heading back to France in 1967, he began working at a carton factory owned by a former South Vietnamese foreign minister.

Eight years later, with Saigon about to fall to PAVN in April 1975, Tuy quietly returned to the South Vietnamese capital. Joining him was Mai Van Hanh, another former South Vietnamese air force officer who had resettled in France. Although their stated goal was apparently to lay the foundation for an anticommunist resistance, their mission was the height of folly. Both were quickly detained by the victorious PAVN but, owing to their French passports, were allowed to return to Europe in July.

Hardly repentant, Tuy and Hanh continued to nurture their resistance plans from the safety of France. They made some preliminary contact with the Hoa Hao and Cao Dai, both religious sects in the Mekong Delta that had a history of resisting communist inroads. Embellishing this, they staged a Paris press conference in February 1976 where they announced creation of the somewhat verbose United Front of Patriotic Forces for the Liberation of Vietnam.

The reality, of course, was that their front was all but notional. In an attempt to lure some actual members, they began shopping for foreign support. In 1977, they introduced themselves to diplomats at the Chinese embassy in Paris. But while Beijing was a logical source of aid given Sino-Vietnamese animosity, none was yet forthcoming.

Turning instead to the RTA, Tuy began looking for ways to ingratiate himself with the Thai military. His means for doing this was via the Cambodian resistance. As a relatively prosperous businessman, and as a vocal advocate against communism in Indochina, Tuy was already acquaintances with Son Sann and Dien Del. To expand on these ties, in 1979 he paid the airfares for several prominent Cambodians seeking to fly to Thailand for the inauguration of the KPNLF.[48]

Tuy himself soon arrived in Bangkok. There his scheming came to the attention of Major General Chavalit—himself no stranger to plotting and subterfuge. At the time serving as the personal aide to the powerful RTA commander Prem Tinsulanonda, Chavalit—as before—was staying closely engaged in Cambodian issues even though this was outside his official mandate.

In short order, Chavalit and Tuy grew close. In a display of the former's trust in the latter, the Thai general in late December 1979 dispatched Tuy to Ampil with a sensitive message. The RTA was seeking a united Khmer resistance front, Tuy told Dien Del, and if the KPNLF did not comply they risked the Thai authorities cutting off supplies to their camps. The threat, however, fell hollow.

The following month, the RTA tried again. Once more singling out Dien Del, who was judged more pragmatic than the crusty Son Sann, Chavalit beckoned him to his Bangkok residence. Chavalit already enjoyed cordial ties with Dien Del, but there was another dimension at play: Dien Del shared Khmer Krom lineage with Ieng Sary and Son Sen from the Khmer Rouge. In the hope that this ethnic kinship might help soften the stalemate, Chavalit placed all three around the dinner table. Once again, however, the two sides failed to bridge the gaps; no agreement on a unified struggle was reached.[49]

For the remainder of 1980 the sniping persisted. During the same month as the failed dinner at Chavalit's house, Khmer Rouge officials hinted that they intended to take a harder line against Sihanouk and were prepared to tell their allies that the prince was unstable. Two months later, during the first KPNLF congress at Ampil, members of the Front's executive committee rejected military cooperation with the Khmer Rouge as part of a united front.

It was not until the opening of 1981 that hints of a thaw began to emerge. Two factors probably contributed to this. First, in the fourth quarter of 1980 the United Nations General Assembly voted for the second year running—and by a greater margin than the previous year—to award Cambodia's seat to the exiled Democratic Kampuchea government. Second, resistance to the Vietnamese hinged on the Khmer Rouge, whose guerrillas by early 1981 had successfully borne the brunt of PAVN's second annual dry-season push along the border.

Although it was seen as reprehensible, there simply was no denying that the Khmer Rouge remained a linchpin in the Cambodian equation. To discuss this, Le Quoc Tuy once more interjected himself into the proceedings and hosted a dinner on 31 January at his Bangkok house for KPNLF luminaries Son Sann, Dien Del, Im Chudett, and Prum Vith. They then shifted to Chavalit's house, talking into the early morning hours of 1 February.

Their conclusions warmed Chavalit's heart. At long last, the KPNLF resigned itself in principle to coordinating its efforts with the Khmer Rouge. Although Dien Del pushed the envelope somewhat (he wishfully insisted that foreign supporters, presumably China, arm a total of 30,000 KPNLF guerrillas despite the fact that the Front counted no more than 3,000 combatants), he backed plans by Bangkok and Beijing to merge some of their offices with Democratic Kampuchea, but both would continue to field separate militaries. Although Son Sann retained some misgivings about the scheme, these appeared to disappear on 6 February when Khieu Samphan suggested he assume leadership over a united front.

Word of all this quickly spread among the Cambodian diaspora, and it was just days before Sihanouk was briefed on the pending KPNLF–Khmer Rouge nexus. At the time, he was back at his Pyongyang palace and more restless than ever.[50] After all, two years had passed since PAVN marched into Phnom Penh, but Hanoi seemed in no rush to cut a separate deal with him. Also, the noncommunist resistance—both the KPNLF and Moulinaka—were a symbolic presence but were hardly a serious player on the battlefield. If Sihanouk was to entertain any hope of seeing his monarchy restored in Cambodia, he would need to personally get into the resistance game and come to terms with the communists that had butchered his own extended family.[51]

On 8 February, the prince moved in that direction. Writing a memorandum to China, he demanded that Beijing allocate substantial and sustained aid, including weapons, to Moulinaka and other pro-Sihanouk partisans.[52] The next day, Khieu Samphan ventured to North Korea to discuss the prince's joining the proposed Khmer Rouge and KPNLF united front, thus turning it into a tripartite coalition. Although Sihanouk deferred any decision—in fact, he took a swipe at the KPNLF later that month over alleged criticism from Paris-based exiles—a dialogue had been started.

No one was more pleased with these developments than China. To build on this momentum, Beijing in early March dispatched its long-promised shipment of weapons to the KPNLF. Unloaded from a vessel off Trat province, the arms were then divided among a convoy of RTA trucks. Beijing was being especially generous, donating enough arms to equip six new guerrilla battalions—and thus nearly doubling the KPNLF order of battle in a single stroke.[53] Each new battalion would be standardized into companies, platoons, and ten-man sections. Each section was to be outfitted with six SKS rifles, three Type 56 folding-stock assault rifles, and one RPD machine gun. Also provided were two rocket-propelled grenade (RPG-2) launchers per platoon, some 57mm recoilless rifles, and mortars.[54]

At around midnight, the RTA convoy crossed the border and pulled into Ampil. As the crates were broken open to reveal their contents, the KPNLF's Colonel Thou Thip dramatically pointed skyward: "God sends milk," he said in a voice trembling with emotion. "God sends milk."[55]

8. Parity

Although precautions had been taken to keep the Chinese weapons delivery to the KPNLF discrete—like the midnight arrival time—it was not the kind of thing that could be kept secret for long.[1] In a matter of days, word pulsed through the border camps and ultimately to Sihanouk's ear in Pyongyang.

Perhaps more than anybody, the prince fixated on Beijing's largesse to the KPNLF. Over the preceding year, the guerrillas who had pledged loyalty to him—Kong Sileah's Moulinaka—were in a rut. This was largely a factor of personalities. Although Kong Sileah was savvy among international aid organizations and the foreign media, he had stoked jealousy from neighboring warlords and was especially prickly with the RTA. There was also tension within his guerrilla band, with Nhem Sophon and Duong Khem—the former customs official and former paratrooper, respectively—jousting for the deputy commander's slot.[2]

Expelled from site to site, Moulinaka by mid-1980 had settled into a patch of forest just south of Nong Chan. As it was the middle of the rainy season, hordes of mosquitoes plagued this rustic setting. Not surprisingly, Kong Sileah soon contracted cerebral malaria and succumbed to the illness on 16 August, just short of spending a year on the border. In a simple ceremony, his body was consumed on a jungle pyre.[3]

With the passing of its founder, command of Moulinaka went to Nhem Sophon. Under his tutelage, the group continued to languish south of Nong Chan. Sihanouk by that time had taken note of their professed loyalty, but his embrace of Moulinaka—at least through the opening of 1981—was never anything but lukewarm.

Then came the KPNLF weapons delivery in early March. Though always a firm believer in his own indispensability, the prince could not help but realize that the Cambodian equation was evolving without him—to the point where his longtime patron, the Chinese, were now backing rival noncommunists. Instantly reengaging himself, on 21 March he declared from the North Korean capital his intent to form yet another front to counterbalance the Khmer Rouge and Son Sann's KPNLF. As Cambodians appeared to enjoy verbose labels, Sihanouk outdid himself by dubbing his organization the National United Front for an Independent, Neutral, Peaceful, and Cooperative Cambodia (Front Uni National pour un Cambodge Indépendant, Neutre, Pacifique, et Coopératif, or Funcinpec).

More than just a platform for his own pontificating, Sihanouk promised Func-

Nhem Sophon, the second Moulinaka commander, circa 1981. (Courtesy Tony Davis)

inpec would have teeth. Absorbing Moulinaka as its core, the prince stated that the Front's armed adjunct would be known as the Sihanoukist National Army (Armée Nationale Sihanoukienne, or ANS).[4] He appointed former Prime Minister In Tam, who had once more ventured from Salt Lake City to Pyongyang to be present for the declaration, as his personal representative charged with making the ANS a reality.[5] Sihanouk himself would take the slot of Supreme Commander.

Even before In Tam had a chance to make any progress, however, Sihanouk was already racing several steps ahead. During a meeting with an Indonesian diplomat in Pyongyang on 3 April, he declared his willingness to enter a united resistance front—but was insistent that the Chinese offer enough weapons so that the ANS gained parity with the formidable Khmer Rouge. Pushing this theme during a private lunch with Deng Xiaoping on 9 May, Sihanouk received a promise for a maximum of 3,000 weapons, contingent that he not clash with the Khmer Rouge or KPNLF.[6]

Just one day prior to that lunch, In Tam had arrived in Thailand. Now sporting the title of Sihanouk's military envoy, he was partaking in a marriage of convenience long in the making. Ever since the third quarter of 1979, when the KPNLF had rebuffed him in favor of Dien Del, In Tam had pragmatically set aside his earlier distaste for Sihanouk and declared his intention to enter Thailand to organize guerrillas on behalf of the prince. The RTA, however, was still irate over his resistance antics in late 1975, and it was not until 8 May 1981 that In Tam, reinforced with Sihanouk's explicit backing, at long last was granted an entry visa. Even then, he was forced to wait eighteen days in Bangkok before given permission to approach the Cambodian frontier.[7]

Touring the border, In Tam found little reason for cheer. Moulinaka was still tucked away in the forest south of Nong Chan, but they had never managed to grow beyond 600 combatants. Three other armed bands had hinted at support for Sihanouk as well, though none impressed in terms of personnel or armament. In Oddar Meanchey province in the mountains overlooking the O'Smach border crossing was the tiny Northern Liberation Front (Sereikka Odder Tus) led by former FANK deputy battalion commander Svy Thouen. On the edge of the Dangrek escarpment midway between O'Smach and Ampil was Toan Chay of Khleang Moeung, the former T-28 pilot who had split from the KPNLF's Prum Vith and migrated north from Pailin. And near the village of Ang Sila south of Nong Chan were perhaps 160 stragglers from the Khmer Angkor movement led by In Sakon, the former schoolteacher who had been run out of Nong Samet the previous July.[8]

Compounding matters, In Tam was no military tactician, let alone a guerrilla leader. As he outlined needs for assembling classic conventional units operating from the border, a U.S. military attaché wryly commented after a May meeting: "It is envisioned that In Tam (perish the thought) would be Dien Del's equivalent within Moulinaka. His espoused strategy is somewhat sophomoric and does not seem to address the realities of the Cambodian situation."[9]

Despite his suspect military credentials, In Tam forged ahead and on 4 September formally declared the establishment of the ANS. In Tam further decreed that the main ANS base would be at O'Smach, the border crossing that until that time had hosted only Svy Thouen's small Northern Liberation Front.

Despite In Tam's best intentions, the disparate ANS factions barely took note of his proclamation. Even Sihanouk, as the ANS Supreme Commander, was uncharacteristically silent. Apparently harboring second thoughts about In Tam's military expertise, the prince back in August had put out feelers to Long Beach to check on the availability of Teap Ben, the highly regarded FANK general who had last served as the Kompong Thom provincial commander. Largely idle since 1977, Teap Ben jumped at the opportunity to be Sihanouk's military chief of staff. On 7 September, he boarded a Korean Airlines flight from Los Angeles and was in Bangkok the following day.[10]

With both In Tam and Teap Ben rubbing shoulders on the border—like two proverbial cooks in the kitchen—some minor positive changes became apparent. In particular, unlike the frosty ties between In Tam and some of the RTA leadership, Teap Ben enjoyed cordial rapport with the Thai top brass. Relations with Major General Chavalit were especially close, with the two referring to each other as "brother." Still, with overall numbers low and weapons in exceedingly short supply, the ANS had far to go before catching up with its noncommunist rivals in the KPNLF.

In gaining an ally like Chavalit, Teap Ben had made a good choice. Cerebral and ambitious, Chavalit was being promoted within the RTA on nearly an annual basis. He had spent a year as RTA commander Prem's personal aide then, after Prem became prime minister in 1980, was promoted that October to director of army operations. In this key slot, he became one of the authors of the prime-ministerial directives seeking to put the final nails in the coffin of the CPT.[11] As this counterinsurgency campaign was still the RTA's most pressing security concern, Chavalit had gained influence and access well beyond his pay grade. "I had the home telephone numbers of the Five Tigers, the top five officers in the RTA," he would later recount without a hint of modesty. "I could, and did, call them at all times of the day and night."[12]

With much of his time consumed by the CPT counterinsurgency, Chavalit had turned over handling Cambodia on a tactical level to several trusted army allies. One of them, the measured and articulate Special Colonel Kasem, was promoted from head of Task Force 838 to take over TOC 315. Already a longtime Cambodia hand, Kasem had worked closely with the senior ranks of the KPNLF since its inception. He had also gained occasional glimpses inside the secretive Khmer

Rouge: "I went with the Chinese ambassador to meet Pol Pot for the first time along the border in Ubon [Ratchathani] province. He was very calm, no readable emotions. From there, we moved him down to the Khmer Rouge compound along the border of Trat province."[13]

Taking over as head of Task Force 838 was another Chavalit acolyte, Colonel Worawit Phibunsin. Coming off a two-year assignment as deputy commander of Task Force 506, Worawit, too, was no stranger to Cambodia.[14] And as a veteran of the RTA Special Forces, his appointment represented a significant shift toward the Special Forces, which was strongly lobbying behind the scenes to take on a more aggressive role in assisting the Cambodian noncommunist resistance.[15]

On a strategic level, however, Chavalit remained the linchpin on Cambodia. Specifically, he was leading the effort to coordinate a covert ASEAN cabal to support the noncommunist resistance. Two member states, in particular, had assigned their intelligence services to discretely work with Thailand in this regard.[16] The first was Singapore, which since early 1979 had been dispatching the director of its Security and Intelligence Division (SID), its external intelligence agency, to Bangkok for periodic coordination meetings held at Chavalit's residence.[17]

The second was Malaysia. Starting in late 1979, the intelligence representative stationed at the Malaysian embassy in Bangkok, Mohamed Jawhar, attended his first coordination session with Chavalit and SID.[18] With the addition of the Malaysians, the trysts at Chavalit's house became known as sessions of the Executive Coordinating Committee, or simply Exco.

Initially, the Malaysians came to the table with little more than cautious moral support. Said Jawhar: "Malaysia was between the Indonesians on one extreme and the Thai on the other. We backed Thailand, but not too forward. We coined the term 'Third Force' for the noncommunist resistance, as they were the third option after the PRK and Khmer Rouge."[19]

Singapore, by contrast, was more aggressive with its assistance. For the first two years of the KPNLF, SID funneled modest funds to Chavalit to defray the cost of purchasing boots, uniforms, and ammunition for the guerrillas. Beginning in May 1981, however, Singapore's involvement deepened. Early that month, it tried to balance support to the two noncommunist factions by inviting both Son Sann and In Tam to the island republic. In meetings with Lee Kuan Yew, Singapore's prime minister attempted to nudge both factions toward greater unity. It was a hard sell, especially to a leery Son Sann, who was all too aware of Sihanouk's penchant for pitting Cambodians against each other for his own benefit. Lee could not help but reluctantly agree. "Sihanouk is a cracked jar," he privately remarked. "Expect it to leak."[20]

Four months later, Singapore hiked its pressure on the resistance faction leaders. On 2 September, Sihanouk and Son Sann arrived in the republic and held intense discussions at the former's hotel suite. The Khmer Rouge's Khieu Samphan was also in town, allowing tripartite talks to commence on 4 September.

That evening the three signed a document stating their intention to set up an ad hoc committee to study the principles for establishing a coalition resistance government.[21] Encouraged with these roundabout results, Singapore in November edged further into the forefront by dangling a clandestine carrot: If the noncommunist factions took the final step and entered into a coalition, Singapore would provide them with weapons.[22]

Noticably absent from Chavalit's Exco meetings was the United States. Though Washington and Bangkok were treaty partners—with the former theoretically committed by the Manila Pact to defending the latter from communist aggression—the Vietnam Syndrome still very much haunted and limited U.S. policymakers.[23] Even during the early years of Jimmy Carter's presidency, whose moral stamp on foreign policy put an emphasis on human rights, the United States had done little other than to offer verbal condemnation of Khmer Rouge rule.[24]

After the PAVN marched into Phnom Penh in January 1979, Carter was in a quandary. The Khmer Rouge were abhorrent, but Soviet expansionism via their SRV proxy demanded a reaction. Sticking fast to the administration's human rights ideals, Secretary of State Cyrus Vance was inclined to keep the Khmer Rouge at arm's length—and to oppose any attempt by Sihanouk to find common cause with them. Carter, by contrast, held his nose and acquiesced to the prince's Khmer Rouge nexus.

Behind the scenes, Bangkok Station was being kept on a tight leash. Although one officer had liaison with TOC 315 as part of his tasking, the CIA did not entertain any direct contact with the noncommunist resistance through mid-1979.[25] Not until Son Sann was ready to formally establish the KPNLF on 9 October was the CIA slowly allowed to stir.

By that time, Larry Waters, the CIA officer who was the last head of the HYTHE up-country program in Phnom Penh, had been assigned to Bangkok Station with the mandate of following Cambodian developments. Just days before the KPNLF's inauguration, he had placed a phone call to Kong Thann, the former HYTHE operations assistant in Kompong Cham. After leaving the Thai-Cambodian border in the summer of 1975, Thann had spent four months acting as an interpreter at the four camps handling Indochinese refugees in the United States. He had then worked as an interpreter in Washington, D.C., for the Indochina Refugee Task Force run first by the Department of State, later by the Department of Health, Education, and Welfare. In his private time, he had also criss-crossed the United States and France to network among Khmer expatriate forums.

Speaking in vague terms, Waters told Thann of a job opportunity in Thailand. Sensing it was more interesting than helping process refugees from behind a desk in Washington, Thann was on a plane and stepped off the tarmac at Don Muang on 10 October. As he recalled: "I came on a commercial flight but was taken out through the military side of the airport. Larry had rented a place for me near the Royal Palace. My job was to visit the border and meet with the senior officers of the KPNLF—Dien Del, Ea Chuor Kimmeng, those coming from France—and report back to Larry on their activities."

Thann was well suited to the task. Not only was he versed in writing intelligence reports in English from his HYTHE days; he was also on cordial terms with many of the top KPNLF personalities from his time in FANK and networking among expatriate forums in more recent years.

After reporting to Waters on the KPNLF leadership through year's end, Thann's role morphed. With a salary and operational funds from the CIA, Thann permanently shifted from Bangkok to the border. There he was provided with a small house on the outskirts of Aranyaprathet, as well as a car and RTA captain as his driver. Under orders to provide duplicate English-language reporting to both Task Force 506 at Aranyaprathet and Bangkok Station, Thann began making regular trips to the KPNLF headquarters at Ampil.

That Thann was a de facto extension of Bangkok Station was hardly a secret at Ampil. This was hardly a problem for Dien Del, who was more than happy to initiate him into the KPNLF and take advantage of his relative expertise in intelligence topics. During the first quarter of 1980, the general gathered more than a dozen KPNLF members who were high-school graduates—including four females—and turned them over to Thann for an intelligence course focused on interviewing and reporting.

By July 1980, Thann had shifted once more, this time to Nong Samet. By then, the sprawling refugee and guerrilla center at Nong Samet had been brought into the KPNLF fold as Rithysen Camp. With its displaced hordes, Rithysen was a target-rich environment. Thann's job was to sift through the masses and—based on targeting requirements provided by Waters—interview those who might shed light on the political, economic, and social situation in the PRK. There was also a standing order to seek any information on U.S. servicemen missing in action during the Vietnam War.[26] He was further tasked with assembling a team of KPNLF apprentices who could conduct similar interviews and potentially recruit agents who could be sent on collection missions back into the PRK.

All of this was easier said than done. Given the scythe that the Khmer Rouge had taken to the upper half of Cambodian society, most of those seeking sanctuary at Rithysen were simple peasants in search of rice handouts. Still, their collective interviews began to paint a vivid, if depressing, picture of life in the PRK. On an economic level, the Khmer Rouge had left behind no markets and no industry of any substance. Even currency had been abolished; the Cambodian riel had not been reintroduced until March 1980.[27]

The PRK political situation was equally somber. Because those with an education had been disproportionately exterminated (only 15 percent of the country's intelligentsia remained as of January 1979), the initial cast of leaders in the PRK was impossibly young; many, not surprisingly, had negligible communist credentials.[28]

To rectify this, PAVN in mid-1980 had raised nineteen brigade-sized specialist groups and deployed them one per Cambodian province.[29] Each group had a mobile regiment that divided its battalions one per district; these battalions, in turn, dispatched two advisers per village. There, they were to assist—and covertly monitor—Cambodia's freshly promoted cast of village chiefs.

Other PAVN advisers were working feverishly to expand the PRK Armed Forces (PRKAF). From an order of battle of almost two dozen battalions when Phnom Penh was liberated in January 1979, the PRKAF raised its first infantry division—the 196th—during mid-1981.[30] Two more divisions—the 286th and 179th—were inaugurated by year's end, and all three were committed to support PAVN's Front 479 in the northwest.[31]

Monitoring these developments, Kong Thann's network received indications that PAVN was having serious problems in its occupation. For one thing, the personnel assigned to their specialist groups—who rarely had any Khmer language ability and only a rudimentary understanding of political topics—were not well suited to an advisory task. For another thing, the advisers were often poorly equipped, with the Khmer Rouge—thanks to lavish infusions by China—often besting their weapons in terms of quality and quantity.

Even among main force PAVN divisions, challenges were quickly mounting. Tired after a generation of war and provided with insufficient supplies, draftees were deserting in droves. New recruits from southern Vietnam, in particular, would often cross into Thailand and surrender shortly after their arrival at forward units along the border. Task Force 506, the RTA's intelligence unit based at Aranyaprathet, at any given time had a backlog of such deserters to interview.[32]

Not all of those seeking sanctuary in Thailand were as they appeared, however. As early as mid-1980, Task Force 506 had become aware of a twenty-man unit assigned to Front 479 whose task was to dispatch Khmer agents to penetrate the RTA, Khmer Rouge, and noncommunist resistance.

Getting a whiff of PAVN's intent, some of Kong Thann's network at Rithysen was given an added counterintelligence role. Their search, it turned out, was not difficult. Although some of PAVN's penetration agents had been given tradecraft instruction in Ho Chi Minh City, most were rank amateurs that were more than happy to reveal their identities soon after arriving at the KPNLF camp. Most appealed for asylum, including two female agents who reportedly had been dispatched to seduce camp officials. In a couple of cases, they were sent back to the PRK as double agents after having been fed disinformation conjured by Bangkok Station.

Soon after arrival at Nong Samet, Kong Thann had placed written notices around the camp seeking contact with any former agents who had worked for the Khmer Republic. Though admittedly a long shot, it resulted in a windfall. Within a month, Thann was surprised to be contacted by Chheang Ly, the son of the Sino-Khmer boat operator whom he had personally escorted to Saigon for stay-behind training.[33]

The CIA's stay-behind plans, Ly recounted, had not panned out. Stuck in Phnom Penh when the Republic fell in April 1975, he had walked north toward his hometown of Kompong Cham. Though he managed to link up with his parents, wife, and youngest daughter, they were prohibited from entering the provincial capital (and thus unable to retrieve his hidden radio set). Rather, he, his wife, and daughter were directed to a farm and forced to collect animal dung as fertilizer. His father, meanwhile, was put to work in a toolshop; his mother oversaw a children's commune.

For all of them, food was doled out just above the subsistence level. When his wife was reassigned to making fish paste, she tried in desperation to steal some fresh fish to supplement their meals. Exposed by a young cadre, she was beaten to death for the offence. Ly's mother, too, succumbed to the long hours and minimal calories.

In late 1979, after hearing about anticommunists coalescing on the border,

Ly headed toward Thailand with a new wife. He arrived at Rithysen in the third quarter of 1980, just in time to see Kong Thann's posted notice. Thann intuitively knew he had an interesting catch, though he felt compelled to test Ly's bona fides. After giving him some minimal training in Rithysen, and providing both a camera and bike, he sent his former agent back into the PRK to retrieve the radio set hidden in the capital.

Ly's return journey was surprisingly uneventful. After peddling to Sisophon over the course of two days, he took an overnight train to Phnom Penh. After pausing long enough to take photos in front of Wat Phnom, the Central Market, and the Independence Monument, he continued to his old neighborhood. After having been turned into a ghost town during Khmer Rouge rule, Phnom Penh had turned into a squatter's paradise. Though Ly's brother-in-law had managed to take over a house on their old street, the actual residence held by his family for generations was now being occupied by two new families. One set of squatters—the family of a PRKAF soldier—claimed the main building as their own; a second family of squatters had erected a hovel in the rear of the property.

Late on the afternoon of the first day, Ly introduced himself to the family living in the main building. He quizzed them on the status of abandoned family heirlooms—a tiger skin and tiger bones—but was told these possessions were gone by the time the squatters had moved in. Ly managed to glance at the covered well in the front of the property and determined that the concrete block he had left in 1975 appeared undisturbed.

That night, Ly returned to spend time with the second set of squatters in the rear. He drank with them until midnight, then returned to his brother-in-law's house down the street. He repeated this routine the following day, drinking until the early morning hours.

On the third afternoon, Ly arrived for yet another round of drinks. Finding the family in the main house was away on an errand, he instead went straight to the well, slid off the concrete block, and pulled out the waterproof container holding the radio. He immediately went to his brother-in-law's house and placed the radio inside a large plastic can used for carrying viscous palm sugar.

From there, Ly merely retraced his steps westward. Boarding a train to Sisophon, he obtained a bike and pedaled to the border. By the time he crossed to Rithysen, he had been gone almost exactly a week. Triumphantly turning over the radio and camera, he was later given a brick of U.S. dollars as a bonus by Bangkok Station.

The CIA was not the only one satisfied with the rudimentary intelligence network Thann erected out of Rithysen. On 17 October 1980, Dien Del signed a decree formally creating the Khmer Information and Security Agency (KISA) under the KPNLF. With a very modest budget, the agency was to have small subsections for interviewing refugees, running agents, and counterintelligence. Named the KISA director, Thann became the KPNLF's first spymaster.

In the months immediately after KISA was created, the KPNLF was augmented by several significant arrivals from the United States. Senior among them was Sak Sutsakhan, FANK's last chief of the General Staff and the Republic's last president. Aside from being commissioned in 1978 by the U.S. Army Center for Military History to write a history about FANK, Sak had been leading an idle refugee life in California since 1975. Deciding to get reengaged in December 1981, the fifty-three-year-old general made his way to Bangkok and toured the KPNLF's border camps; for the first year, however, he rarely left the Thai capital as Dien Del ceded no significant role to his former FANK commander.[34]

Arriving at the same time was Pann Thai. A colonel in 1975, Pann Thai had had an especially diverse military career. After three years of pilot training in France in the early 1960s, he later became an air force mechanic before transferring to the army and taking over an armored personnel carrier unit in the capital during 1974. In the United States on a training course when the Khmer Rouge took over, he had amassed enough savings by the late 1970s to purchase a donut shop in Southern California.[35]

Leaving the donuts behind, Pann Thai showed up at Ampil and volunteered for duty. Though he had no intelligence background, Dien Del judged him sufficiently competent to name him the new KISA director when Kong Thann opted to return to his family in the United States.

The third arrival, Gaffar Peang-Meth, would give the KPNLF its first—and, in hindsight, only—political scholar. Born into an upper middle-class Cham family, Gaffar had shown early scholastic promise in high school and received an American Field Service scholarship to spend his senior year in Ohio. Returning to Cambodia in 1962, he worked for twelve months as a clerk and interpreter at the U.S. embassy's Military Assistance and Advisory Group before heading back to the United States for college.

This time, his sojourn was far longer. After graduating in 1967 and marrying an American girl, he immediately entered graduate studies at Georgetown University and got his degree in the final months of Sihanouk's reign. By the time Lon Nol took over and Cambodia descended into war, Gaffar—who by now had two sons—opted to remain in the United States and pursue a doctoral degree at

Singapore Deputy Prime Minister Goh Keng Swee makes a fact-finding trip to Aranyaprathet, late 1982. To the left of Goh are KPNLF President Son Sann (with glasses) and Gaffar Peang-Meth. To the right is Major General Chavalit, the director of RTA Operations (with glasses and cap). (Courtesy Gaffar Peang-Meth)

the University of Michigan. But emotionally impacted by the misfortune visited upon his homeland, he found time to write a pro-Republican newsletter titled, appropriately, *The Republic*.

Through this newsletter—which was circulated across North America and Europe—Gaffar came to the attention of the Cambodian embassy in Washington. In 1972, while still a doctoral student, he was invited to be part of the Cambodian delegation attending that year's United Nations General Assembly meeting. The following year, after completing most of his doctoral requirements, Gaffar formally joined the Cambodian embassy as second secretary in charge of press, social, and cultural affairs. As an added assignment in mid-1973, he was designated as the escort for General Lon Non, the Marshal's self-exiled sibling who was marking time as ambassador-at-large in the United States and France.

In April 1975, while still working at the embassy in Washington, Gaffar became stateless. To express his frustration, he again began publishing a newsletter—this one titled *Conscience*—in English and Khmer. In it, he tried to chronicle the emergent details about the horrors of the Khmer Rouge regime; only later would he learn that the communists, who were especially ruthless against the Cham minority, had killed his parents and elder sister.

In 1980, Gaffar's life took several major turns. Completing the last academic hurdles, he received his doctorate in political science from the University of Michigan. Pausing long enough to be sworn in as a U.S. citizen, he flew to Thailand at midyear to successfully search the border refugee camps for his surviving sisters.

At the end of that same year, he made a second trip to Thailand—this time with only a few changes of clothes in a lone suitcase. Showing up at the KPNLF safe house on Soi Maiyarap in Bangkok, he volunteered to assist the Front. But though he added an intellectual depth sorely lacking in the organization, those present were uncertain what to make of their Cham guest.

For the next month, Gaffar waited at the safe house before finally being granted permission to visit Ampil. There, in a surreal initiation rite that ignored his Islamic faith, Gaffar was required to drink sacred Buddhist water and pledge fealty to the KPNLF while guerrillas sprayed bullets into the air.

Although now a full-fledged member of the KPNLF, few responsibilities were initially directed toward Gaffar. Aside from (again) editing a resistance newsletter and occasionally acting as interpreter, he filled his free time taking leave of Bangkok to tour the KPNLF's camps. It was at Sok Sann that he truly became smitten with the Front: "Prum Vith was the epitome of a peasant colonel. His men called him 'grandfather,' and he exuded this disciplined, rugged, romantic image of a guerrilla leader."

By mid-1981, Son Sann at long last came to recognize the value of Gaffar's academic credentials. Now sporting the title of second deputy secretary-general in charge of external affairs, Gaffar was at Son Sann's side for many of the latter's diplomatic forays around the region. He was present, for example, during the September 1981 tripartite meeting in Singapore and, barely hiding his contempt for the Khmer Rouge, counseled Son Sann to forge closer cooperation between the KPNLF and ANS. This made him popular with ASEAN diplomats in general, and Singaporeans in particular, who were urging greater unity among the two noncommunist factions.

Such cooperation was vital, especially after the Khmer Rouge began to shift strategies on the battlefield. Whereas it had been busy consolidating their forces along the border for the first two years after being expelled from power, the Khmer Rouge beginning in 1981 entered a strategic resistance phase whereby it sought to increase infiltrations into the Cambodian interior in order to bog down PAVN in urban centers—a near repeat of what they had done to the Lon Nol regime a decade earlier.

And in a step designed to make themselves more palatable—especially on the international stage—the Khmer Rouge in December 1981 became the first and only communist party to terminate its own existence. Theoretically, from that month forward it became a military organization focused solely on fighting PAVN. The party's standing committee thus became a military directorate; the radio station was renamed Voice of the National Army of Democratic Kampuchea.[36] And while some genuine concessions were made—for example, it

Badge issued to graduates of Malaysian jungle warfare training. This was later adopted as the first beret badge used by the KPNLF Special Forces. (Courtesy Suon Samnang)

ended collective eating and now allowed persons to choose their own marriage partners—few outside the party believed the Khmer Rouge had seriously tempered its hard edge.

Still, PAVN recognized these changes and was rightfully concerned. In late 1981 when Front 719 began planning its latest dry-season offensive for Cambodia, several differences were apparent. First, it attempted to give more of a Cambodian face to its counterinsurgency by making greater use along the border of the PRKAF infantry divisions raised over the previous year. Second, PAVN once more began using transport aircraft—this time their Soviet-made An-26 fleet—as makeshift strategic bombers.[37] Third, for the first time since being disciplined for its cross-border raid in June 1980, Front 479 was once more venturing across the Thai frontier. This time, however, it was launching more precise raids by Dac Cong commandos against guerrilla sanctuaries on the Thai side of the border. The first such attack, conducted by a five-man demolition team on 23 December 1981, targeted a Khmer Rouge rear base. A total of eighteen such forays were conducted over the course of that dry season.

In late February 1982, after being on the offensive for just over a month, Colonel General Le Duc Anh toured the frontlines and expressed satisfaction with the results.[38] A multidivision push against the Khmer Rouge headquarters complex at Phnom Malai had been especially promising, with PAVN taking all but the northwestern corner of the base area. But in reality, this dry-season offensive, like the one a year earlier, had barely given the resistance factions reason for pause.

As PAVN missed another opportunity to seriously cripple its opposition, the resistance factions and their foreign supporters looked to press the advantage. During the last week in February, China sought to restart talks among the three guerrilla factions toward forging a resistance coalition. Though their proposal fell through—due to foot dragging on the part of Son Sann—on 24 February Beijing shipped 3,000 light arms to the ANS in order to fulfill a promise they had made to Sihanouk the previous May.[39]

Three months later, Malaysia had better luck. On 21 June, Sihanouk arrived in Kuala Lumpur from Beijing, while In Tam came aboard a separate flight from Bangkok. The following morning, the prince joined Son Sann and Khieu Samphan at the stately Malaysia House. Witnessed by Malaysian Foreign Minister Tan Sri Ghazali Shafie, the three Cambodian leaders signed their names to a document creating the Coalition Government of Democratic Kampuchea (CGDK). Under this coalition arrangement, Sihanouk was president, Son Sann was prime minister, and Khieu Samphan was foreign minister. From that point forward the CGDK inherited the Cambodian seat at the United Nations, which until then had been occupied by Khmer Rouge delegates.

After the formalities at Malaysia House, Son Sann boarded a plane to return to Bangkok. Sihanouk, by contrast, embarked on an impromptu tour of the ASEAN member states. As both Malaysia and Singapore were especially insistent that the two noncommunist factions unite, a giddy Sihanouk on 29 June announced he was ready to let his ANS merge with the KPNLF.[40]

Four days later, the prince landed at Don Muang. After meeting with Prime Minister Prem and a string of ambassadors, Sihanouk on 7 July made his first visit to the Thai-Cambodian border as head of the resistance coalition. His itinerary reflected the coalition's awkward composition. The prince's first stop was at Ampil, where he met with Son Sann for two hours and later addressed 600 KPNLF guerrillas—reportedly to only mild applause.

From Ampil, Sihanouk ventured to 20 kilometers north of Aranyaprathet to Khao I Dang. Created in November 1979, Khao I Dang was the oldest Khmer refugee camp on the border. Its population was in flux, with many being processed for resettlement in third countries. Unlike the other camps on the border, it was not controlled by any resistance faction; rather, it was officially administered by the Office of the United Nations High Commissioner for Refugees and its residents were thus entitled to relatively better levels of care and nutrition.

Shortly after the ANS had been formed the previous year, Moulinaka had made a point of steering thousands of its civilian sympathizers toward Khao I Dang. Not surprisingly, when Sihanouk addressed these masses he was met with an ecstatic chorus of support. The reaction was equally enthusiastic when he urged all able-bodied males at the camp to volunteer as guerrillas at the ANS headquarters at O'Smach, which hereafter was being renamed New Sihanoukville.[41]

The following day, in a deliberate effort to balance the two previous stops, Sihanouk and his wife, Monique, boarded elephants for a short trek to a Khmer Rouge jungle outpost in Phum Thmei subdistrict, Thmar Puok district. After exchanging pleasantries with Ieng Sary, the two then returned to Bangkok.

There was no denying that Sihanouk's time on the border was a propaganda coup. No doubt in reaction, PAVN on 17 July announced the first of what would become annual claims of troop withdrawals. Though this one, like most of those that followed, were actually troop rotations—and the overall level of the PAVN presence in Cambodia did not drop—it demonstrated that Hanoi felt desperate measures were needed to counteract the positive press being afforded the CGDK.

For the SRV, however, the bad news kept coming. A week later, the KPNLF at long last began to show some signs of guerrilla life. Taking advantage of the rainy season, which tended to bog down the more conventional PAVN, its guerrillas marched 12 kilometers east from Nong Chan and over a two-day period harassed the communist-held village of Phum Soriya. In retaliation, PAVN fired thirty artillery rounds at Nong Chan.[42]

Over the following quarter, the establishment of the CGDK had a pronounced impact on those foreign nations favorably disposed toward assisting the noncommunist resistance.[43] This included the CIA, which at long last was allowed to initiate not one, but two Cambodian projects. The first of these concerned the establishment of an intelligence-gathering post on the border. Rather than relying on the network earlier built by Kong Thann—which in any event had been absorbed into the KPNLF's KISA—Larry Waters moved from Bangkok to a safe house on the outskirts of Aranyaprathet. As it featured such amenities as a volleyball court and swimming pool—which was camouflaged in the construction costs as a "reserve water supply"—the site was nicknamed the "Hilton" in jest.

Within the Hilton compound, Waters oversaw five Khmer working as interpreters and staff. In addition, six more Khmer were put on the payroll at the border camps to conduct initial spot interviews in the search for refugees whose stories were worthy of further scrutiny.[44]

The second CIA operation involved covert assistance to the two noncommunist factions. This was part of a far larger paramilitary campaign to undermine the Soviet Union. Four years before being sworn in as president in January 1981,

Ronald Reagan had bluntly let it be known that he intended to settle for nothing less than the defeat of the Soviets in the Cold War. To do this, Reagan sought to turn the tables on the overextended Soviet empire by providing the means for noncommunist guerrilla movements around the world to better snipe at the communists.

In one case—Afghanistan—CIA covert paramilitary support predated Reagan. There, Operation Cyclone—which was to become the largest paramilitary campaign in CIA history—by 1980 was channeling $30 million a year to the anti-Soviet mujahideen. Closer to home, Reagan in November 1981 approved $19 million in CIA support for the guerrilla groups fighting Nicaragua's Sandinista government. And in Chad, the administration in 1981 funneled about $10 million via the CIA to Hissene Habre in his attempt to overthrow the Libyan-backed Oueddei government. This last operation saw quick success, with Habre's men in June 1982 able to seize control of the Chad capital and set up a provisional government.

But even for a hawk like Reagan, a similar paramilitary effort in Cambodia could not overcome the Vietnam Syndrome. In contrast to the president, CIA Director William Casey insisted on looking beyond the past and as early as 1981 had argued forcefully that the United States should provide weapons to anybody fighting communists—the Cambodian noncommunist resistance included.

Initially rebuked, Casey tried again in mid-1982. This time emboldened by the CIA's paramilitary success in Chad and looking to piggypack on momentum after creation of the CGDK, Casey made a fresh pitch for covert lethal aid. Getting a whiff of Casey's request, the Department of State balked. But Reagan by now saw merit in at least symbolic assistance and in the third quarter of 1982 signed a compromise finding that authorized the CIA to spend $4 million that fiscal year for nonlethal covert aid to the two noncommunist factions. Even though the CIA funds could not be used to buy weapons, it could free up money from other Exco members to purchase military equipment.[45]

By contrast, Malaysia's support to the noncommunist resistance concentrated on training. During the late afternoon of 16 October, twenty KPNLF guerrillas handpicked from across the KPNLF's border bases assembled at Aranyaprathet and loaded into an unmarked bus. Joining them as liaison was Pann Thai, the KISA director who the previous year had left behind his donut shop in Southern California.[46]

On the road all night and into the next afternoon, the driver bypassed Bangkok and worked his way down the Thai panhandle. Approaching the Malaysian border at 1500, he pulled to the side, whereupon the Cambodians were ushered into a convoy of nondescript vans with Thai plates.

Continuing through the border checkpoint in the vans, they continued for just a couple of kilometers before pulling into a clearing well away from the main highway. There they were met by a reception committee from the Malaysian army, before them twenty piles of combat uniforms, jungle hats, and rucksacks. Each of the guerrillas quickly donned the fatigues and packs, then boarded a pair of army trucks and rumbled south. To any casual observer peering into the rear of the trucks, they looked little different than Malaysian military recruits.[47]

By morning, they had reached the highlands of Pahang state. Exiting the main thoroughfare, they weaved their way down a laterite road for another 8 kilometers. Finally, in the vicinity of an elephant conservation center and abandoned tin mines, they came to a stop at a makeshift jungle camp constructed especially for the Cambodians.

This was to be their home for the next three months as a staff of fifteen instructors from the Special Service Group—the Malaysian army's elite commando unit—put the students through a regimen of physical training and guerrilla tactics. The pace was grueling. Recalled one student: "We were completely isolated. No villages. No markets. Just some rubber trees and about a million leeches. The hardest part was a five-day survival exercise where they sent us into the jungle with only a small knife, a fishing hook, and a compass."[48]

After a final cross-country exercise in the neighboring hills, all twenty graduated on 14 January 1983. Each was presented with a set of pale-blue fatigues, a red beret, and insignia featuring a black panther's head, then sent back to the Cambodian border using the same combination of army trucks, vans, and buses.[49]

For Singapore, assistance to the noncommunists took far different forms. During September 1982, it brought fourteen KPNLF students to the island republic for radio and propaganda training. With assistance from the British foreign intelligence service, British technicians and journalists were quietly hired to conduct the classes. By mid-October, the KPNLF propaganda team, using a shortwave radio transmitter initially based in Singapore, was able to start two thirty-minute broadcasts a day combining news, commentary, and music.[50]

One month later in late November, the SID representative at that month's Exco meeting announced that Singapore would be providing its first shipment of lethal aid to the resistance.[51] Considerable thought had been given as to what kind of weaponry was most appropriate. Although the noncommunist guerrillas were hardly standardized, most of their firearms were from the communist bloc. While it thus would have made logistical sense to source weapons of communist origin, Singapore reasoned that the noncommunists might be eager to outfit themselves with U.S. M-16 rifles. This would not only help them distinguish themselves from the hated Khmer Rouge; it would also let them insinuate to the Cambodian populace that they enjoyed Western support.

As it happened, the Singapore Armed Forces in the 1970s had adopted the M-16 as its main service rifle. Due to delays in obtaining these directly from the United States, the Singaporean government instead purchased a license to manufacture the rifle themselves. Produced by Chartered Industries and officially known as the M-16S1, these were virtually identical to the American originals except for the lack of an external bolt assist. As Chartered Industries had overshot its agreed production quota, Singapore happened to have thousands to spare. Thus, with quiet consent from the U.S. State Department (which had to approve any exports), a shipment of 2,600 rifles was discretely sent to Thailand's Sattahip port.[52]

Once the rifles were inside Thailand, Singapore had one more decision to make. Though it was providing balanced diplomatic encouragement to both the KPNLF and Funcinpec, it was felt that the ANS was still too small and faction-ridden to effectively absorb the new weapons. As a result, the entire initial M-16S1 shipment was sent to the KNPLF at Ampil. Predictably, it was only a couple of weeks before word leaked to the media, prompting a livid Sihanouk to denounce Singapore's favoritism toward Son Sann.[53]

Ironically, although both Malaysia and Singapore had seen fit to channel their initial round of paramilitary assistance exclusively to Son Sann's front, it was the KPNLF that was experiencing intense growing pains during the second half of 1982. Dien Del faced two critical issues tearing at the fabric of his guerrilla army. For one thing, he had been coddling the KPNLF's central region—especially around Ampil—while simultaneously neglecting his more unconventional-minded commanders in the northern and southern regions. Not surprisingly, this bred resentment among those who perceived they were getting insufficient attention from headquarters.[54]

For another thing, even within his central region, Dien Del faced near-perpetual insubordination by his camp commanders. Nobody epitomized this more than the wayward head of Camp Rithysen, Ta Luot. Described by Gaffar as a "vulgar, uneducated man," Ta Luot enforced his own crude brand of justice at Nong Samet and had never stopped prioritizing black-market profits over resistance activity by his three resident battalions.

In an attempt to better harness Ta Luot and his other fickle camp commanders, Dien Del had instituted monthly strategy meetings. The venue rotated between Ampil, Nong Samet, and Nong Chan, with the tryst for October 1982 set to take place at Ampil. As scheduled, Ta Luot got behind the wheel of a pickup truck and headed northeast on the morning of 11 October, driving through Thai territory until veering east along the dirt road winding into the KPNLF headquarters. Sitting alongside him was his pregnant thirty-year-old wife, Kim; in the back was his aide-de-camp as well as the commander of Battalion 206.

The strategy meeting hosted by Dien Del, though tense, was otherwise uneventful. But as Ta Luot pulled out of Ampil on his way back to Nong Samet, three guerrillas posing as honor guards stepped in front of his pickup as it crossed the small bridge marking the Thai border. They emptied their magazines into the cabin, instantly killing Ta Luot, his wife, and the Battalion 206 commander.

Ta Luot's aide, wounded, limped back into Cambodia and made his way to Zone 201 on Ampil's northern perimeter. The zone commander, grizzled freedom fighter Ta Maing, was already on poor terms with Dien Del. Recalled one junior officer at the time: "Ta Maing had watched Dien Del and some of the other senior officers regularly get into drunken shouting matches, and was not too impressed. It should have been easy for Dien Del to handle subordinates like Ta Maing, who had been simple farmers and could be very loyal, but he did not have the temperament."[55]

As Ta Luot's aide recounted details of the ambush, Ta Maing fumed. In retaliation, he sent a volley of mortar rounds into the General Staff hut, then another volley into the Battalion 212 encampment on Ampil's southern perimeter. He then moved his two battalions south, where they tensely faced off with Battalion 212 through the following day.

Word of the assassination instantly reverberated across the KPNLF. Within half a day it reached New York, where Son Sann was taking part in the CGDK's debut at a United Nations General Assembly. Taking the call from Thailand was Gaffar, who had been promoted to Son Sann's chief of staff in the latter's capacity as CGDK prime minister. With some hyperbole, those at the KPNLF safe house in Bangkok told him a "coup d'état had taken place on the border." Sensing the urgency of the situation, Son Sann immediately cut short his visit to the United States and rebooked flights to the Thai capital.

Back at Ampil, Dien Del was instantly fingered as the guilty party. The murder had taken place on the outskirts of his headquarters, after all, and it was no secret that the general despised the unruly Rithysen warlord. These suspicions exacerbated a schism between the older generation of freedom fighters who had taken up arms in 1975—like Ta Maing—and the KPNLF's senior leaders—like Dien Del—who had arrived only in 1979.

For his part, Dien Del adamantly denied involvement. He initially blamed the Khmer Rouge though soon became convinced the RTA had conspired to kill Ta Luot over a black-market dispute.[56] Whoever the culprit, Dien Del agreed to take responsibility and tendered his resignation as chief of staff twice before Son Sann reluctantly accepted on 15 October. Dejected, the general headed for an uncertain future in a cold France.[57]

To replace Dien Del, Son Sann immediately appointed a four-man caretaker committee. Senior among them was Sak Sutsakhan, who after almost a year of inactivity in Bangkok was now finally getting his chance to contribute.

Second on the committee was Brigadier General Thach Reng, who had flown from California to Thailand in January 1982 to offer his services to the KPNLF. Though he never lost an opportunity to tout his unconventional warfare credentials as the former head of the Khmer Special Forces (which was debatable given the spotty performance of this mismanaged elite unit), he had spent most of the year grafted to Son Sann's side and was rarely seen on the border. He had also demonstrated pronounced ambitions, stoking Dien Del's insecurity by claiming to be a favorite of Son Sann and (less truthfully) the U.S. State Department.

The third committee member was fifty-year-old Hing Kunthon. A Paris-trained statistical engineer, he had received an additional degree in commercial law and served from 1957 to 1970—for much of that time alongside Son Sann—at Cambodia's national bank. During the five years of the Khmer Republic he shifted to head the Cambodian Commercial Bank. Failing to leave in 1975, he was sent to a Khmer Rouge labor camp and, given his government position and education, should by all rights have been a prime candidate for speedy execution. He avoided identification, however, and emerged as skin and bones but otherwise alive in 1979.

Showing a pragmatic streak, Hing Kunthon then tried to make his peace with the PRK authorities. Given the acute shortage of educated officials, the Phnom Penh government overlooked his complete lack of communist credentials and appointed him a district chief in Kandal province. But the former banker soon bristled under the PAVN occupation and, after a few tense months, made his way to the border and joined the KPNLF. Taking full advantage of his background, he was initially placed in charge of economic affairs on the executive council that advised Son Sann. He was also one of two KPNLF representatives—the other being Colonel Im Chudett—who conducted the Front's first lobbying trip to the United States in March 1981 to raise support among Khmer expatriate groups and on Capital Hill.

The fourth committee member was Nong Chan camp commander Chea

Chhut. He was to represent the interests of the pre-1979 freedom fighters and, hopefully, heal the emergent rift between those freedom fighters and the senior staff.

Within a month, several positive changes were apparent under Sak's watch. First, he and his caretaker committee pledged to give more attention to the northern and southern regions, thereby reversing the benign neglect they felt prior to October. Second, Sak encouraged the KPNLAF to go on the offense in true unconventional fashion—rather than the lower-key border buildup favored by Dien Del.

Near year's end, this new strategy began to pay dividends. Preempting PAVN's own dry-season plans, elements of Chea Chhut's four battalions infiltrated east from Nong Chan on Christmas Eve. After pouring fire into Yeang Dongkum hamlet, they forced the resident PAVN and PRKAF garrison on the morning of 27 December to flee south along Route 5. Some twenty-two Vietnamese bodies were left behind, at the cost of one KPNLF guerrilla.[58]

Farther north, Ta Maing simultaneously unleashed his Zone 201 guerrillas. On 5 January 1983, they had moved 23 kilometers east of Ampil, overrunning a PAVN outpost in the Banteay Chhmar subdistrict. Though they abandoned the post the very next morning, it was enough to garner positive ink in the Thai press.

Perhaps the biggest gain took place at Ampil Lake, the 2-square-kilometer man-made reservoir from the Angkorian era situated 5 kilometers southeast of the KPNLF's headquarters. PAVN outposts dug in along its earthen berms had held off earlier guerrilla advances, but at the turn of the year Colonel Thou Thip used elements of his five-battalion general reserve to overwhelm the Vietnamese defenders. Now taking their places along the berm and training their machine guns eastward, the KPNLF had not only extended the buffer around Ampil but also secured a key source of water and fish.

All of this marked a turning point for the KPNLF. In a first, it had displayed a willingness to engage PAVN in what could generously be called coordinated fashion—albeit in small set-piece skirmishes all within a short sprint back to the border. While none of this posed a major military challenge to PAVN's occupation, it had finally demonstrated that resistance was no longer solely the prerogative of the Khmer Rouge.

9. Pyrrhic Victories

The KPNLF began 1983 with a windfall. After working its way into Yeang Dangkum, it stumbled upon a cache of 107mm rockets in an abandoned PRKAF bunker. The triumphant guerrillas hauled several of the projectiles back to Nong Chan where, reasoning that these could be used to harass PAVN if and when the Vietnamese decided to reclaim lost real estate, they decided to test-fire one using the field-expedient method of propping it against a mound of dirt and hooking up a string of D-cell batteries to the rocket motor. Their technique was wanting, however, as they caused the sympathetic detonation of the motor and warhead in a deafening, unplanned explosion. Two guerrillas died in the blast and no further field tests were conducted.

On the heels of this self-inflicted pain, PAVN added to the woes of the resistance. Pulling fewer punches than normal, Le Duc Anh had conjured what the CIA would later call his best-planned and -executed offensive since the 1979 invasion.[1] To begin, he dispatched tanks and artillery to lead the retake of Yeang Dangkum on 16 January. Five days later, an artillery barrage sent the KPNLF fleeing out of O'Bok in the Dangrek chain.

Nong Chan was next in his sights. Two days before the end of the month, T-54 tanks were in the lead as two regiments from PAVN's 5 Division advanced west from Yeang Dangkum. After softening the base with artillery fire for two days, 4,000 armor-led PAVN infantrymen launched an anticlimatic final assault on 1 February. With no effective antitank weapons at his disposal, local chieftain Chea Chhut, his guerrilla garrison, and nearly 30,000 civilians edged into Thailand, letting the Vietnamese enter and raze the camp against almost no resistance.

Not playing favorites, PAVN waited a month before turning its attention on the ANS. Ever since the Sihanoukist army had been declared in 1981, In Tam had tried to convince the disparate pro-Sihanoukist factions into uniting near the O'Smach border pass. He had been less than successful, with the majority of Moulinaka and Toan Chay's Khleang Moeung reluctant to depart their former roosts. Even after Sihanouk made a surprise visit to O'Smach—renamed New Sihanoukville—in January 1983, and Moulinaka's base near Nong Chan was no longer viable due to PAVN pressure the following month, few heeded the call to gather at O'Smach.

On 13 March, that call became moot. Using a single regiment from the 302

Division, Le Duc Anh had his forces move up to the border and easily overwhelm New Sihanoukville, sending its residents scrambling into Thailand.

On the last day of that month, PAVN finally vectored in on the Khmer Rouge. Once more using a lethal combination of artillery and armor in the lead, it smashed the Khmer Rouge refugee settlements at Phnom Cat and Chamkar Kor, located between the KPNLF bases at Ampil and Nong Samet. Some 22,000 Cambodian civilians fled into Thailand for refuge.

Though the PAVN dry-season offensive on its face had been decisive, in fact it had no lasting impact. Many of the largest resistance bases—including the sprawling Khmer Rouge complex at Phnom Malai—had not been targeted. And in all the cases where bases were overrun, the guerrillas had simply withdrawn a few kilometers into Thailand with negligible casualties. Moreover, of the 170,000 PAVN troops in Cambodia, perhaps no more than 60,000 were deployed against the resistance along the border—a number easily matched by the combined CGDK factions themselves.

By April, with the onset of the rains, the Khmer Rouge was already itching to go on the counteroffensive and retake the minimal territory ceded to PAVN.

The KPNLF, too, was looking to enact gains. On 3 April, it turned back a mild PAVN attempt to overrun its Ampil headquarters. Emboldened, the following month the KPNLF leadership enacted a new strategy of infiltrating guerrillas from the Ampil vicinity up to 25 kilometers into the interior in order to establish caches for a more permanent presence. This sparked an aggressive PAVN campaign of mass arrests, sending the guerrillas sprinting back to the border by midyear. Ironically, however, the PAVN dragnet caused major discontent among the border populations, prompting some 12,000 civilians to flee toward Ampil. This gave the KPNLF a win of sorts, as it suddenly handed Ampil—which until then had been sparsely populated—an ample source of potential recruits.

During this same time frame, the KPNLF's caretaker commission ordered the establishment of a guerrilla warfare school in the Dangrek chain close to the O'Bok Pass. Gathering 1,200 men from Rithysen and Nong Chan (which had since been reoccupied), they were to be trained by the officers who had undergone the first cycle of irregular warfare training in Malaysia. Heading up the school was Pann Thai, who had been the senior officer escorting the first contingent to Malaysia.

Though still a distant quantitative third in the CGDK, the ANS, too, saw come concrete gains by mid-1983. First, the defeated guerrillas at O'Smach shifted 20 kilometers east to a new base tucked high in the Dangrek chain opposite the Thai village of Tatum. In hindsight, the selection of Tatum was an unenlightened choice for several reasons. First, though it enjoyed natural defenses by virtue of being shielded by sheer escarpment from the lowlands to the south, that same escarpment made it exceedingly difficult to infiltrate into the interior. Second, the lowlands immediately below Tatum hosted the thinnest of populations; a guerrilla could walk for days before coming across a sizable village.[2]

On a positive note, however, the shift to Tatum allowed the ANS leadership to insist—successfully this time—that virtually all of its semiautonomous factions assemble at that single location. Once there, a new structure was enacted that reinforced their identity under a unified movement. From that point forward, Moulinaka became known as the ANS's 1 Brigade, Toan Chay's Khleang Moeung was renamed 2 Brigade, and the Northern Liberation Front that had been at O'Smach was now known as 3 Brigade.[3] None of the three, of course, approached the size of a true brigade, but the new nomenclature allowed the ANS commanders to hand out promotions—and thus boost morale and loyalty—in line with these inflated tables of organization.[4]

An even bigger change within the ANS concerned the arrival of two of Sihanouk's sons. The first, thirty-eight-year-old Norodom Chakrapong, had inherited both his father's rotund frame and affable personality.[5] After attending high school in France, Chakrapong had returned to Phnom Penh in his late teens and joined the Royal Cambodian Air Force. Commissioned as the youngest officer in the force—a feat undoubtedly helped by his Norodom pedigree—he eventually qualified as a pilot.

After the 1970 change in governments, however, there was to be no flying as the FANK leadership sidelined all officers with royal familial ties. Assigned to a meaningless desk at the FANK General Staff, Major Chakrapong spent his days reading everything from U.S. Army manuals to tracts by Mao.[6]

This continued for a full three years before Captain So Patra, Chakrapong's air force classmate and brother-in-law, took matters into his own hands. Despite being sidelined like Chakrapong, Patra in March 1973 made his way to the Pochentong apron and was not challenged as he climbed into the cockpit of a T-28. He then proceeded to bomb the Presidential Palace and, once his ordnance was expended, flew to China's Hainan Island and defected.

Although Lon Nol was absent from the palace at the time, three dozen were killed in the attack. Livid, the marshal ordered the mass arrest of the Norodom clan. Chakrapong was caught up in the dragnet and spent six months in detention. Not until that November was he allowed to go to Beijing with his ailing grandmother—and Sihanouk's mother—Queen Kossamak.

Linking up with his father in Beijing, Chakrapong, though still short of thirty years old, was promoted to colonel and named Sihanouk's chief of protocol. He performed this role through early 1975 when, with the Khmer Rouge on the verge of victory and Sihanouk likely to return home, Chakrapong was bundled off to Yugoslavia and enrolled in that country's Air Force Staff College. There he joined So Patra, his mutinous brother-in-law, who had departed China for the same Yugoslavian college the previous year.

By 1976, Chakrapong finished his course in Belgrade. Sihanouk had already gone to Phnom Penh by that time—at which point no further news had been heard. Also, So Patra had returned to Cambodia without further word (and was presumed executed). Not willing to risk his own return, Chakrapong instead went to France and, sharing his father's weakness for rich foods, decided to open a restaurant in Paris.

In 1981, Chakrapong was still serving up dishes when In Tam came calling. On his way to Thailand to forge the ANS, In Tam asked Sihanouk's son to join the effort. Intrigued, Chakrapong made his way to Bangkok and for the next year lent help in the less-than-successful attempt to unite the ANS factions at O'Smach. When the CGDK was declared in June 1982, he was additionally named the coalition's minister of health and social affairs.[7] And when Sihanouk made his surprise visit to O'Smach in January 1983, Chakrapong was placed in charge of a newly recruited company of Royal Guards.[8] Though not especially intellectual, he performed these various roles with a quick smile and (at least initially) likeable demeanor.

Chakrapong's polar opposite in temperament was his half-brother, Norodom Ranariddh. Born a year prior to Chakrapong, Ranariddh had little parental upbringing: His father, Sihanouk, was not close to any of his sizable brood, and his mother, a prima ballerina, was relegated to living outside the palace because she was a commoner. Childhood friends, the two half-brothers had been sent off together to high school in France. After Chakrapong returned to join the air force, Ranariddh elected to remain in France in order to study law in Paris. Though he briefly dropped out in 1961 after failing his exams, he moved south to the small university town of Aix-en-Provence and continued his legal studies. Remaining through the end of the decade, he managed to complete most of his requirements for a doctorate.

In early 1970, Ranariddh returned to Phnom Penh for the birth of his first child. He used the time to collect documents for his doctoral thesis and even considered a run for the National Assembly. These plans were dashed with the change of governments that March. Coming under scrutiny by the new authorities, he was accused of "homicide for political ends" and went before an army tribunal in July 1971. The charges were found to be baseless and he was acquitted after a three-day trial.[9]

Two years later, Ranariddh was caught up in the same dragnet that netted Chakrapong after the bombing of the Presidential Palace. But when the Norodoms were released and Chakrapong joined his father in Beijing, Ranariddh instead went back to France to continue his pursuit of a doctorate. Sihanouk was reportedly livid for being shunned in this manner.[10]

Undeterred, Ranariddh hit the books at Aix-en-Provence. After finally completing his doctorate in 1976, he began teaching at his alma mater. In 1979, he took French citizenship in order to be appointed a full-time lecturer at the university's faculty of law. Settling into his job, the following year he took out a twenty-year mortgage on a three-bedroom apartment.

Sihanouk, however, was set on luring the most intellectual of his children into the resistance business. When the prince founded Funcinpec in 1981, he wrote a letter to Ranariddh inducting him as a founding member.[11] In 1982, he asked Ranariddh to take part in the CGDK, only to be rebuffed.

In mid-1983, Sihanouk tried again. Sending an urgent telegram on 19 May, he instructed Ranariddh to take a leave of absence and come to Bangkok as his personal representative for Asia. Once more, Ranariddh was reticent. Persistent, Sihanouk sent a second telegram on 7 June.[12] Like the Prodigal Son, Ranariddh this time applied for a two-year sabbatical from his university. In July, he headed for Bangkok with his family in tow, renting a house in the fashionable Suanplu section of the city. Several rooms in the back were dedicated for the Funcinpec secretariat.

Thrust upon the regional stage, Ranariddh quickly made an impact. Almost immediately he clashed with In Tam, ostensibly the ANS commander who of late had been largely absent from the border due to faltering health. Whereas In Tam was Sihanouk's personal representative for Cambodia, Ranariddh was the prince's personal representative for Asia; Sihanouk never bothered to clearly define the two seemingly redundant roles. Ranariddh also took steps to sideline half-brother Chakrapong, whom he criticized as ineffectual. Ranariddh went about all this in a detached, deliberate manner, for though he had had inherited his father's shrill inflection, he displayed none of the jocularity or mood swings.

Seeking to funnel assistance to the reinvigorated KPNLF and ANS was the secret Exco cabal of Thailand, Singapore, Malaysia, and the United States. Monthly Exco trysts were still being held at Chavalit's house to map out assistance strategy. By early 1984, additional Exco sessions were being conducted by a lower-ranking set of intelligence and military representatives from most of these same nations in order to discuss methods of implementation. The advent of these second-tier meetings coincided with the selection that January of a new head of Task Force 838, a scrupulously honest RTA colonel named Surayud Chulanont.

Surayud, it turned out, had been soldiering under a shadow.

His father, himself once an RTA lieutenant colonel, had backed Prime Minister Pridi Banyamong, who was deposed in a 1947 army coup and failed in his own comeback coup attempt two years later. Supporting a sacked prime minister might have been a forgivable offense, but then Surayud's father did the unthinkable: In the mid-1960s he joined the CPT and became chief of staff for the communist guerrillas.

By the time Surayud graduated the military academy in 1965, his family's name was blacklisted and he personally was forbidden from assignments to sensitive areas. Although he entered the RTA Special Forces, which saw more than its share of combat, Surayud was relegated to instructor slots through 1978.[13] Only then was he deemed sufficiently rehabilitated from his father's taint to get a pair of infantry assignments over the next four years. Returning to the Special Forces in 1982 as a colonel, he was named commander of 1 Special Forces Regiment at Lopburi.[14] Two years after that, he was concurrently named head of Task Force 838.[15]

Wearing these multiple hats, Surayud personified the changing dynamics of RTA assistance to the Cambodian resistance. Although Lieutenant General Chavalit still wielded considerable influence over Cambodian matters at a strategic level (his acolytes continued to helm TOC 315 in Bangkok), and even though Task Force 838 was still administered on paper by TOC 315, Surayud was the dominant player on a tactical level and answered primarily to the new and powerful Special Warfare Command at Lopburi. This command, created in 1983, included two Special Forces divisions; Surayud's 1 Special Forces Regiment belonged to 1 Special Forces Division, and it was to his division commander that Surayud was most responsive.

Under Surayud's watch, the RTA Special Forces increased its border presence significantly. Drawing personnel from his 1 Special Forces Regiment, he assigned three groups to Task Force 838. Of these, one group (divided into three teams split among Sok Sann, Ampil, and O'Bok) focused on supporting the KPNLF, one company-sized element supported the ANS, and the third group acted as an observer with the more reclusive Khmer Rouge.[16] Still others from 1 Special Forces Regiment were dispatched as intelligence teams under Task Force 506.

Among the other members of the Exco, Malaysia continued to run guerrilla warfare courses for the noncommunist resistance. In March 1983, the second cycle arrived for instruction, this one comprised ten members from the KPNLF and twenty from the ANS. Beginning with the third cycle in late 1983, all the thirty-man classes would be evenly split between members of these two factions.[17]

From Singapore, the SID representative attending the Exco meetings arranged for another dozen KPNLF members to receive radio training from British instructors in 1984. That same year, SID again received British assistance when it covertly acquired 3,000 Czech-made Vz.58 assault rifles and turned over 2,000 to the KPNLF and 1,000 to the ANS.[18]

From the United States, the CIA did not send representatives to the Exco meetings but instead continued to hand over cash on a monthly basis to make nonlethal purchases on behalf of the two noncommunist factions. As of mid-1983, part of the U.S. allocation was also being used for daily stipends given to the noncommunist guerrillas.[19] By late 1984, CIA Director Casey was looking to increase the total amount of nonlethal support to $12 million a year. In comparison, the CIA was handling $250 million in covert aid for the Afghan mujahideen during that fiscal year.

During that same time frame, a senior CIA officer was assigned to Bangkok Station to oversee its Cambodian operations. That officer, fifty-seven-year-old Francis Sherry, had led a diverse, colorful career spanning three continents. Born to French-American parents, Sherry had spent much of his youth in France before attending Harvard University. Returning to France after graduation, he had escaped to Switzerland just hours before the Nazi invasion.[20]

Following World War II, Sherry joined the CIA and, owing to his French background, in 1953 was sent to Indochina as one of two CIA officers embedded with a French-led guerrilla program being extended across the countryside.[21] The following year, with the communists set to formally take over the DRV, he worked with a handful of other CIA operatives to establish secret cache sites in the Hanoi vicinity as part of a rushed stay-behind operation. Not surprisingly, this tardy effort yielded negligible results.

As Vietnam was subsequently bifurcated, Sherry headed south to take up a position in the CIA's newly raised Saigon Station. Through the end of that decade, he was part of the small CIA liaison team at the station working with the Service des Etudes Politiques et Sociales (Social and Political Studies Service, or SEPES), the innocuously titled office in the South Vietnamese government that handled covert intelligence operations in the DRV. It was a vexing assignment, with the SEPES director, Dr. Tran Kim Tuyen, proving to be a master manipulator of his CIA patrons. Recalled Sherry:

> Tuyen claimed to have set up two networks of agents in North Vietnam, but never gave us direct access to them. One of his assets was supposedly a woman who he claimed he sent north to recruit a fisherman she knew; she allegedly had a message written in invisible ink in her underwear. The invisible ink for all the SEPES agents was a special blood-based formula which could only be developed with a chemical we kept at the station. Tuyen also got us to buy him a junk, which he said was going to sail north to Thanh Hoa district, a Catholic area, to raise a network of agents there. Again, we only saw photos of the junk, but never got to actually lay eyes on it.

Perhaps not surprisingly, Tuyen's networks turned out to be notional. Questions were initially raised when the junk earmarked for Thanh Hoa was spotted in Cam Ranh Bay in the south, where enterprising SEPES officers had rented it out to haul sand for a Japanese-owned glass factory. But even more damning was a poor fabrication offered to Saigon Station by the SEPES agent handlers. Explained David Zogbaum, another member of the CIA liaison team:

> SEPES claimed that it had received a report from an agent in their network from the southernmost DRV. They gave us a copy of the report written in invisible ink, which we developed at the station. Although the report was about the area in question, it was signed by the name of an agent they claimed was located much farther north in the DRV. SEPES had obviously written a forged agent report in the invisible ink, but had mixed up the names of the agents and their networks. That was the final straw: we cut off all further liaison with SEPES.[22]

After the better part of a decade in Southeast Asia, Sherry took the SEPES fiasco as his cue to leave the region and shift to Europe. Posted to the bustling Belgian port city of Antwerp in 1960, his mandate over the following three years reflected Washington's preoccupation with the Castro regime in Cuba. One operation involved an unsuccessful attempt to sabotage locomotive parts being shipped to Havana from France. Another was a far more successful effort to corrupt the bright stock—a refined lubricating oil—in tractor engines being exported from Antwerp to Cuba. According to Sherry: "We originally intended

Francis Sherry on the border with Dien Del and Sak Sutsakhan. (Author's collection)

to replace the bright stock with napalm. But then we worked with an oil company to create a contaminant that would eventually make the engines seize up and break. Security was lax at the docks, and we were able to substitute it into the entire shipment of engines."

In 1966, Sherry switched continents and was assigned to Mexico City Station. Mexico at the time was the only nation in Latin America to host a Cuban embassy, and Sherry was placed in charge of a four-man Cuban Operations Section within the station. Some of what they did was psychological in nature, like a black-letter campaign to the Cuban embassy by a person pretending to be a CIA officer offering to help them—but in fact implicating a high-ranking Cuban military leader.[23]

Another operation involved bugging the fortress-like Cuban mission. After painstakingly studying their target from safe houses ringing the embassy, the CIA officers conjured a way of causing interference with the telephone on the ambassador's desk. The embassy eventually called the Mexican phone company for technical assistance, but not before Sherry's team had recruited the telephone repairman and given him a bugged set. The CIA was thus able to listen as the ambassador dictated memos to his secretary—until Phillip Agee, a turncoat CIA officer, later exposed the breach to Cuban intelligence.

Returning to Europe during the 1970s, Sherry eventually went back to Langley in 1980 to head the Cambodia/Laos Desk under the Directorate of Operations'

CIA Deputy Director of Operations Claire George and Francis Sherry receive a briefing from ANS General Teap Ben, late 1984. (Author's collection)

Far East Division. This came about just as satellite photos of a remote jungle camp near Nhommarat in the Lao panhandle were the subject of much discussion in the CIA and Pentagon. According to one photo interpreter (though unsupported by a second), he thought he could see "B 52" stomped in the ground near the camp. Another image showed a man sitting cross-legged near the camp—something normally associated with Westerners rather than the squat preferred by Asians. Taken together, the photo interpreter posited these might be indications that a U.S. aviator from the Vietnam War was imprisoned near Nhommarat and trying to attract attention.

Given the emphasis the Reagan administration placed on resolving the issue of missing-in-action servicemen in Indochina, these pictures caused considerable excitement near the close of 1980. The deputy assistant director of the Defense Intelligence Agency, a rear admiral, was especially bullish about staging a rescue mission, or at the very least sending in a robust reconnaissance party to verify the camp's occupants.

But as word of the camp photos spread among intelligence officials, the military's special operations community, and select congressional members, details eventually leaked. It even reached a motley assortment of U.S. military veterans, who took this as their cue to chaperone a farcical, and inconclusive, reconnaissance foray from Thailand. On a parallel track, Sherry's office in March 1981 oversaw a CIA-sponsored team composed of RTA Special Forces that discretely crossed the Mekong and reached Nhommarat. Outfitted with good cameras and tree-climbing gear, they returned to Thailand with photographs of the camp occupants—none of whom were foreign nationals.

After another two years heading this desk, Sherry packed his bags and went to Bangkok Station to oversee its Cambodian operations. Central to those efforts was the Hilton intelligence base established by Larry Waters at Aranyaprathet in 1982. In the summer of 1984, Waters was replaced as the Hilton base chief by forty-two-year-old James "Mule" Parker. A U.S. Army platoon leader in South Vietnam during the mid-1960s, Parker had been recruited into the CIA as a paramilitary contract officer in 1970. His first assignment was late the following year, when he advised a guerrilla regiment in the hills of northern Laos during brutal fighting against PAVN infantrymen and armor.[24]

When the CIA scaled back its paramilitary presence in Laos during 1973, Parker shifted to South Vietnam's Mekong Delta. There he remained until a day before the U.S. embassy in Saigon evacuated in April 1975, whereupon he led a group of CIA agents and their dependents to a U.S. merchant ship off the coast. He then spent the next two days evacuating others from Vung Tau, after which he became one of the last American officials (other than a fellow CIA officer who had been captured) to depart the Republic of Vietnam.[25]

Following Vietnam, Parker was upgraded from paramilitary officer to intelligence officer and subsequently worked at various posts in Africa and Asia during the ensuing decade. He had been managing the CIA's counternarcotics program in northern Thailand immediately prior to getting the Aranyaprathet assignment.

By the time Parker got to the Hilton, he was joined by a second CIA officer, Gary Fleischer, who had just completed a special assignment in Yemen before being diverted to the Thai base. A few months later, they were augmented by Brian "Doc" Dougherty, a U.S. Air Force technical sergeant who spoke both Thai and Vietnamese. His arrival followed a requirement tendered by the CIA back in 1983 asking the Pentagon to support the Hilton with interrogators. The U.S. Army proposed an unwieldy twenty-man team; the air force said it could do so with one. Dougherty, as a result, landed the job.[26]

Of these three, Dougherty made periodic forays along the Thai-Cambodian border to look for potential sources of information. Fleischer did as well, with an emphasis on covering the ANS at Tatum. They were assisted by five Cambodian staff members and six—later increased to seventeen—spotters, the name given to indigenous assistants who sifted through the new arrivals at the border camps, filling out preliminary debriefing reports to peruse for interesting sources.

Among the best of the Cambodian staff members was a former FANK major named Tepi Ros. An academic standout, Ros had won a USAID scholarship back in 1963 and took engineering courses in Los Angeles. He had worked at the Ministry of Industry on his return, then shifted to FANK's engineering corps in 1970. Four years later, he was assigned to the office of the FANK commander for the final months of the Khmer Republic. On the day that the Khmer Rouge entered Phnom Penh, he changed into civilian clothes and jumped in his sedan: "I was heading toward the Presidential Palace, driving very slow and surrounded by persons on foot. I wanted to go toward my home town in Prey Veng, but an artillery round went off near the Palace and the Khmer Rouge diverted me in a different direction toward Takeo. I was lucky: if I had gotten to Prey Veng I certainly would have been identified and executed as a former officer."[27]

Even with a modicum of anonymity in Takeo, Ros lived on a knife's edge. One of nine newcomers from Phnom Penh in his work detail, they were overseen by three Khmer Rouge cadre. Over time, seven of the newcomers were taken away and executed. Ros survived by feigning enthusiasm for his work assignments, no matter how inane (during the growing season, he worked at a factory that made fertilizer from human excrement). He also lost no opportunity to volunteer his mechanical skills, fixing everything from rice mills to sewing machines.

In late 1978 while toiling in a rice paddy off of Route 1, Ros was startled by the sound of approaching tanks. Two Vietnamese jets roared overhead, sending the laborers into the nearby forest. In the confusion, Ros managed to escape his Khmer Rouge minders, allowing him to slowly make his way toward Phnom Penh.

By the time he arrived in the capital, in January 1979, PAVN had just finished securing the city. It reminded Ros of postapocalyptic science fiction:

> The Khmer Rouge had turned the sides of streets into small farming plots, now all of them overgrown with buffalos grazing. Doors and window frames were missing, burned as firewood. The Khmer Rouge had used various houses as storerooms: one would be filled with car tires, another with suitcases, another with piles of shoes. We needed to stay vigilant. If the patrolling Vietnamese caught us we would be thrown out of the city, so we cautiously moved from block to block.

By June, restrictions on squatters had been relaxed and the new PRK regime was desperate for talent. Once more volunteering his skills sets, Ros was placed in charge of a glassworks factory on the southern outskirts of the city. Not all of his attention was focused on work, however. In the post–Khmer Rouge euphoria, nearly twenty underground political parties had taken shape in the PRK.

These numbered only a few dozen members each, at most, and most of them demanded the withdrawal of PAVN troops as a central party platform.

One of these secret cabals, known simply as the Nationalist Party, had been established by a handful of Lon Nol officers. Heading the party was a former colonel in the FANK transportation directorate. Ros, whose rank was major in 1975, joined the party's Phnom Penh chapter. Meeting occasionally behind closed doors to vent about anticommunist themes, they eluded the attention of PAVN and the PRK through the end of 1979. By early 1980, however, some of its members had heard about the creation of the KPNLF on the border and wanted to dispatch emissaries to discuss possible cooperation.

Ros instinctively thought this was a bad idea. He was outranked, however, by the chairman of the party's Phnom Penh chapter, a former FANK officer named Liv Ne. Claiming to have been a lieutenant colonel in Dien Del's 2 Division, Liv ordered two members—one a former Khmer Krom infantryman, the other working in the Ministry of Commerce—to head for the frontier.

The two emissaries did as told, weaving their way to the border. Delivering their message to KPNLF representatives, they then headed back toward the capital. Once there, the staff member from the Ministry of Commerce belatedly realized that he could not explain away his absence and was out of a job. His wife was furious and demanded that he confess to the police and beg to regain his employment. This is exactly what happened and, predictably, it set off a dragnet in June 1980 for members of the Nationalist Party.

Liv Ne, perhaps anticipating this turn of events, had already voted with his feet and fled to the border. Ros, however, soon found himself in a Phnom Penh prison cell, where he languished for thirty months on sedition charges. Released in 1983, he retained a black mark on his identification papers. But with the PRK still desperate for skilled laborers, he was assigned as a mechanic at a phosphate factory in Battambang. Now closer to the border, he eventually escaped to Rithysen camp in June 1984.

Once at Rithysen, Ros was surprised to find out that the camp commander was none other than his former Nationalist Party boss, Liv Ne. He was also surprised to discover that Liv had somewhat padded his résumé: He had risen only to the rank of captain in FANK, not lieutenant colonel.

Soon after settling into camp life, Ros was approached by one of the spotters working for the Hilton. When Parker learned that he had been schooled in Los Angeles and spoke excellent English, he was offered a job. Twenty days later, Ros was busy in Aranyaprathet translating reports.

For all his hardships, Ros counted himself among the lucky. Surveying the camp populations, U.S. intelligence officers at the Hilton were soon overwhelmed by tales of Khmer Rouge sadism and violence. One recalled:

> I was stunned at the stories of wanton brutality by those young Khmer Rouge soldiers and when I first got to Aranyaprathet I wrote report after report, sort of an after-action assessment on the Pol Pot period. They all got marked "No Dissemination." I would cry to the reports lady [at the U.S. embassy] that the world ought to know what happened. And she agreed, but intelligence reporting is what we do, and what the community wanted in Washington now was how the Vietnamese were consolidating their control over the country. The Pol Pot horror stories weren't intelligence. Those woeful blood-soaked stories never saw the light of day.

The community in Washington also had an insatiable appetite for intelligence about American servicemen missing in action, no matter how outrageous the claim. Recounted one Hilton officer:

> A senior KPNLF official said that his guerrillas had found a U.S. prisoner-of-war living as a gentleman farmer in northwestern Cambodia and wanted support to go back in and get him. This was laughable in hindsight. We had lots of similar claims, but none corroborated by separate reporting. We could get a missing-in-action report and it would go into a database. We would look for other refugees from that area, and we never found that these separate people had the same information.

Helping build the Hilton database was a former PAVN captain named Phong. How he got to the Hilton was a tale in itself. Of exceptional aptitude, Phong as a young PAVN officer had come to the attention of the Soviets and was recruited to attend chemical warfare training at a base just south of Moscow. This was supposed to be six weeks, but he ended up being retained by the Soviets for a couple of years because of his intelligence and personality. With an ear for languages, he grew conversant in Russian and was given the task of teaching Russian to other PAVN officers. As such, he was accorded special treatment like a Soviet officer of equal grade.

When Phong finally returned to Hanoi, however, he was in for a shock. His superiors had judged that his extended absence had not been approved by the PAVN headquarters, and as a penalty his family had their business seized by the government. Pushed over the edge—and reportedly inspired by acts of heroism he had seen in a string of Hollywood movies—Phong made his way to the Thai border. At a refugee camp, he was picked up in an interview by one of the Hilton runners. In just a few weeks, he was speaking passable English and, recruited as one of the Hilton's local staff, was exacting his own personal revenge on PAVN.[28]

Ironically, neither Phong nor the rest of the Hilton team was allowed to deal with any members of the many anticommunist Vietnamese resistance groups that had sprung up along the Thai-Cambodian border. One of the larger among them, the so-called National United Front for the Liberation of Vietnam, was headquartered in San Jose, California, and led by former South Vietnamese Rear Admiral Hoang Co Minh. Formed in 1980, this group was best known for slick leaflets they distributed in the United States and propaganda they spouted from a small Thai-based radio transmitter beginning in late 1983. They also claimed to have assembled armed guerrillas along the Cambodian frontier as of 1982; this resistance did painfully little resisting, however, and was largely written off as a fund-raising scam.[29]

Another group located along the Thai-Cambodian border was the grandly titled Vietnam Liberation Armed Forces headed by former South Vietnamese Brigadier General Nguyen Van Chuc.[30] Assisted by eleven other South Vietnamese veterans, Chuc's 400-man group formed what he called Yankee Teams; unlike some of their rivals, these teams actually did conduct the occasional reconnaissance foray into western Cambodia. They also planned to secretly infiltrate into Vietnam to carry out a campaign called "Flowers Blossoming Inside the Enemy's Area," though there was never any evidence they got around to it.[31]

A third Vietnamese resistance group—the United Front of Patriotic Forces for the Liberation of Vietnam—was perhaps the most aggressive. This was the same movement led by former air force officer Le Quoc Tuy, who in 1979 had acted as the intermediary between General Chavalit and the KPNLF. Having convinced the Thai authorities that he was worthy of paramilitary assistance, he was authorized in October 1980 to recruit 200 Vietnamese refugees in Thailand and send them for guerrilla training under RTA Special Forces auspices at Phitsanulok. He also worked his way into the good graces of the Chinese, visiting Beijing seven times and winning ample supplies of weapons and cash (including a large amount of counterfeit SRV currency).

During the opening of 1981, the United Front's first team, with the help of the RTA and Khmer Rouge, was escorted across southern Cambodia and into the SRV's An Giang province.[32] On 12 May, a second team of eleven guerrillas boarded a vessel off of Thailand's Trat province and headed to the waters near Vietnam's

Nong Chan camp commander Chea Chhut (left) and KPNLF Special Forces commander Pann Thai, July 1984. (Courtesy Tony Davis)

Ca Mau province. Two guerrillas were killed en route when they balked at completing the journey.

Even before making landfall at Ca Mau, the team's radio signal drew the attention of PAVN counterintelligence. The Vietnamese authorities located the team within a day after infiltration, killing one and capturing the remaining eight. They then doubled the radio operator and coerced him into sending back a message to Thailand on 22 May.

What happened next was a near repeat of the radio play that netted dozens of CIA-sponsored commandos infiltrated into the DRV during the Vietnam War.[33] Beckoned by the doubled radio operator, the United Front between September 1981 and September 1984 launched eighteen supply trips by boat from Trat to Ca Mau. As they were secretly in control of the radio traffic with the United Front, PAVN was easily able to apprehend all of the resistance members shortly after they made landfall, including Le Quoc Tuy's own younger brother.[34] Hanoi finally exposed the charade in December 1984 when they put 21 resistance members on trial (out of 148 they had captured); among them, 3 were executed by firing squad the following month.[35]

Though it had acted decisively against Vietnamese anticommunist resistance groups like the United Front, PAVN was proving far less effective against the CGDK. As of December 1983, it had mobilized troops and armor in western Cambodia and was apparently preparing for another dry-season offensive. Instead, nothing happened as of the opening of 1984.

This was just as well for the KPNLF, which of late had taken a couple of missteps. For one thing, the caretaker commission heading the Front had not been able to heal the rift with the older generation of freedom fighters. Ta Maing, still sour toward Dien Del, had voted with his feet by moving his Zone 201 to a new camp 4 kilometers north of Ampil. Though he remained loyal to the KPNLF on paper, he made no secret about extending feelers to Toan Chay and seeking a closer alignment with the ANS.

For another thing, the guerrilla warfare school established 40 kilometers north of Ampil in the Dangrek chain had proven a bust. The original idea had been to use the Malaysia-trained officers to train 1,200 recruits at this site as six-man teams equipped with new rifles and uniforms. But when the students arrived in May 1983 they were shocked to find that construction of the camp had not even started. No new weapons had arrived either, leading the troops to practice with old rifles in the raw, malarial jungle. When Pann Thai made a brief return to the United States in November, 800 students used this as their cue to desert back to Ampil.[36] The remainder, divided into two battalions, was dubbed the KPNLAF's Special Forces and, donning red berets to denote their elite status, shifted in early 1984 to the frontline at Nong Chan.

During this same time frame, the KPNLAF military leadership had been in flux. Back in April 1983, after a six-month absence, Dien Del had successful petitioned Son Sann to let him return to the border without a portfolio. Later in June, he had been named to a new nine-member military council that was supposed to provide ideas to the KPNLF's Executive Committee (which was somewhat redundant as the council and committee had almost identical membership).

On 28 January 1984, a new KPNLAF military structure was unveiled. Gone was the caretaker commission. In its place, General Sak was now officially named chief of the General Staff—the same position previously held by Dien Del before his brief exile. Sak's deputies now included Prum Vith from the southern front, put in charge of tactical military matters, and Hing Kunthon, the former banker, overseeing civilian and support matters.[37]

With this slightly revised lineup, the KPNLF faced a belated PAVN dry-season push in March 1984. The Vietnamese effort was initially focused near the marshy area just west of the Tonle Sap, where a 100-man contingent from Rithysen camp had infiltrated since the opening of the year. Notable about this encounter was PAVN's first use of Mi-8 helicopter gunships equipped with machine guns and rocket pods. The debut of this aircraft to the Cambodian theater was devastating, with only about a third of the guerrillas able to retreat back to the border.

Also in March, PAVN dispatched elements of its 330 Division to once again attack the KPNLF camp at Sok Sann in the south. This elicited another vintage performance from Prum Vith, who briefly eased west into Thailand with negligible losses and just as quickly reclaimed his base.

Next on the PAVN hitlist was the KPNLF complex at Ampil. By that time, however, the KPNLF had already grown supremely confident in its ability to defend its headquarters. Ampil, in fact, had started to resemble a proper town. To support a civilian population that now stood around 32,000, it featured a thatched-roof hospital, several primary schools, a secondary school, and a cultural center that ran shows by a ballet and orchestra. And in support of the KPNLAF, it hosted a military academy and political education facilities.

Overseeing its defenses was General Dien Del. Though he no longer commanded on paper, and still was prone to heavy drinking, there was no denying his bravery as demonstrated by his insistence on remaining at the front. When not touring the trenches, he could be found indulging his love of horticulture by patiently tending roses and orchids around his Ampil residence.

But as it turned out, Dien Del and the rest of his men had been woefully derelict in spotting signs of imminent danger on the horizon. Instead, they had focused on the Khmer New Year, a three-day annual marathon of festivities starting around 14 April when farmers traditionally enjoy the fruits of their harvest before the start of the rains. With liberal amounts of alcohol flowing during raucous celebrations, the KPNLF guerrillas were on less than vigilant footing shortly after midnight on 15 April when a team of Dac Cong commandos slipped undetected through their outer defenses near Ampil Lake.

At daybreak, the Dac Cong struck. Taken by complete surprise, the KNPLF defenders wilted and offered almost no resistance as they retreated toward the camp proper. By noon, PAVN had maneuvered more of its task force across the scrub-covered terrain toward the lake. Fortunately for the KPNLF, the PAVN task force was extremely limited in size: just an estimated three infantry companies from the 5 Division, supported by a dozen field artillery pieces (including two 130mm guns and two 155mm howitzers) and the division's own organic mortars and recoilless rifles.

Over the ensuing day, fighting devolved into a heavy weapons duel. PAVN sent a volley of shells into Ampil, destroying forty huts and sending much of the civilian population fleeing into Thailand. The KPNLF, in turn, brought forward 82mm mortars and B-40 rockets supplied by China. On 17 April, PAVN attempted a half-hearted infantry advance toward Ampil, but they barely progressed past the lake.

Forty-eight hours later, it was the KPNLF's turn to initiate a counterattack. Reinforced with a battalion on loan from Nong Samet, it managed to reach the western edge of the reservoir. At that point, PAVN belatedly called upon the PRKAF to join the fray with elements of its 286 Division. This accomplished little apart from getting a PAVN senior colonel—an adviser to the division's political commissar—killed when he tripped a mine.[38]

Concurrent to all this, PAVN began light shelling of Nong Chan and Nong Samet. Other than forcing resident civilians to seek temporary sanctuary on the Thai side of the frontier, neither base was seriously threatened.

At that point, heavy seasonal rains began to inundate the border. With the ground getting too soft for artillery (much less armor), PAVN on 22 April brought an end to its tardy offensive. After having kept the Vietnamese at bay for a week, the KPNLF spun its defense of Ampil into a resounding political victory. In retrospect, however, it was hardly its finest hour. PAVN, after all, had managed to wrest back control around most of Ampil Lake—and had done so with a minimal commitment of troops.

On a strategic level, in fact, PAVN was laying the groundwork for an endgame to its occupation. As SRV party stalwart Le Duc Tho had noted during a January 1984 political seminar in Phnom Penh, there was an "imperative need for a definitive solution to eliminate the Khmer resistance movements." A big part of this involved handing greater responsibility to the PRK regime. Accordingly, in March 1984 the PRK Council of State ratified a conscription law that required all citizens between ages eighteen and twenty-five to serve two years in the military.[39] Along with this influx of fresh recruits, the PRKAF that year organized four military regions, each corresponding to a PAVN front. Within these military regions, the PRKAF was given responsibility for defending cities, provincial capitals, and district capitals. The most sensitive of these was Military Region 4 headquartered in Siem Reap, which corresponded to Front 479.[40]

A second part of PAVN's endgame involved a multilayered barrier to be erected along the Thai frontier in order to prevent the infiltration of CGDK guerrillas. Approved by the PRK government in July, the so-called K5 Plan was to consist of a cleared buffer zone 10 kilometers inside the border.[41] Along this buffer would be minefields, fences, cleared terrain, and fortified outposts at regular intervals. Manpower quotas to build the barrier were distributed to provinces and districts in late September; during the last two months of the year, some 50,000 civilian laborers had already started slaving to meet K5's ambitious goals.[42]

For its part, the CGDK had seen its struggle advance in fits and starts. On a positive note, its two noncommunist partners had forged closer cooperation during 1984.

At the opening of the year, for example, it had started broadcasting a joint noncommunist radio station, Voice of the Khmer.[43] It had also opened joint information offices in Brussels, Canberra, Stuttgart, and Tokyo.

On the military side, the KPNLAF and ANS in May 1984 initiated the Permanent Military Committee for Cooperation (abbreviated as Permico) featuring equal representation from both factions.[44] With General Sak as its chairman and General Teap Ben as vice chairman, Permico was envisioned as the structure under which the two noncommunist factions could synchronize their planning, operations, and logistics. The Thai military rented a separate safe house for Permico in Bangkok, which they envisioned would be used to coordinate assistance provided by the Exco.[45]

There was negative news, however. Sihanouk was more than living up to his mercurial reputation while head of the CGDK. Back in the first quarter of 1983, for example, he had whined to the media that he was "gravely insulted" that a meeting of CGDK military officials had taken place on 18 March—the date he was deposed in 1970. Son Sann fired back in the media that the date of the meeting was actually 19 March.[46] In the months and years after that, similar slights, both real and imagined, prompted Sihanouk to threaten with disturbing regularity to leave the CGDK.

Of equal concern to the CGDK was the fact that the Khmer Rouge—by far the strongest of the three factions—had turned in an uncharacteristically uninspired performance in 1984. In March and April, PAVN had dispatched a robust task force—supported by helicopter gunships and An-26 bombers—to attack a pair of its jungle bases in the northeast. One of these, a Dangrek position known as Hill 547, had been impervious to four previous Vietnamese assaults. This time PAVN not only overran the terrain; the Khmer Rouge had disappointed its Chinese patrons by lackadaisically withdrawing into Thailand and abandoning vast stores of ammunition and food.[47]

Rather than taking the fight to PAVN, the Khmer Rouge instead had instigated a series of clashes with its noncommunist CGDK partners. During a pair of confrontations with the ANS 2 Brigade in June and July, for example, more than twenty Sihanoukist guerrillas had been killed. General Teap Ben sought an audience with Khmer Rouge officials to protest the incidents, but this devolved into a shouting match. Somewhat more diplomatic in his approach, Ranariddh delivered a démarche to the Khmer Rouge's Son Sen in a secret August dinner meeting.[48]

This was the situation as the skies cleared at the opening of November and the CGDK awaited PAVN's dry-season plans. Impressed by its defensive acumen during the April staredown at Ampil (as well as their ability to retain control at Sok Sann, Nong Chan, and Nong Samet), the KPNLF—more than any of the other CGDK partners—exuded a misplaced sense of security. But by abandoning any guerrilla pretenses at Ampil, and thus presenting an exceedingly ripe target for Le Duc Tho's "definitive solution," the victories of 1984 were almost destined to be Pyrrhic.

10. Event Horizon

For movements that purported to be engaged in a guerrilla struggle, there was always an overriding conventional air to the KPNLF and ANS. For its part, the former took guilty pleasure in flaunting its model camp at Ampil. Its uppermost echelon, stuffed with former FANK officers, not surprisingly looked little different than a streamlined copy of the Republican-era General Staff. At the insistence of Dien Del, who was a great proponent of training programs, there was even a small but surprisingly complete military academy at Ampil turning out classes of officer cadets.

The ANS, meantime, had overplayed its own model camp at Tatum. From there it oversaw a robust, and hardly unconventional, order of battle topped by five brigades (two more had been added in late 1984), each consisting on paper of three battalions apiece.[1] And in another nod toward conventionality, the Sihanoukists had announced a round of promotions near year's end, adding to the list of general-grade officers.

The Exco members had tried to nudge the noncommunists back toward a more partisan path. The Malaysian training program, for instance, was an effort to instill guerrilla principles in the best junior leaders from both factions. But the lessons learned in Malaysia were never properly exploited; the KPNLF guerrilla warfare school, which used Malaysian-trained officers as instructors, had folded almost as soon as it was created. After that, Pann Thai's vaunted Special Forces, infused with many of those same instructors, had done little to differentiate itself from the KPNLF mainstream.

There was one other attempt during that period to coach the noncommunists in things unconventional, but this originated from outside the Exco. British Prime Minister Margaret Thatcher, who entered office in 1979, had come to closely align her foreign policy vis-à-vis the communist threat with that of Ronald Reagan. Part of this involved joining the CIA in supporting some of the noncommunist guerrilla movements that were sniping at the Soviet Union and its proxies, such as covert British paramilitary support for mujahideen groups in Afghanistan.

In the second half of 1984, the British looked to extend similar support to the noncommunist portion of the CGDK. Already, British nationals had been quietly hired by Singapore as instructors in radio broadcasting, but that was in a private capacity. Now, in a deal brokered with the royal Thai authorities, the Thatcher government sought to secretly dispatch a military training team to Thailand from their army's elite commando unit, the 22 Special Air Service (SAS) Regiment. Because the deployment was covert, logistical support from the British embassy in Bangkok was handled by the station chief from their Secret Intelligence Service, commonly known as MI6.

As originally conceived, the SAS training assistance was to be indirect. British instructors, went the plan, would give a course in guerrilla tactics to a select group from the RTA Special Forces, following which the Thai commandos would run classes for candidates from the KPNLF and ANS. But belatedly judging this arrangement to be too diffuse, the first class was divided in half: Twenty were drawn from the RTA Special Forces and twenty more from the KPNLF. To keep the trainers far from prying eyes around Bangkok, a thirteen-man SAS team, led by a Major Roberts, opened the course at the RTA Special Forces training base in distant Phitsanulok.

This compromise arrangement, however, also proved unsatisfactory. The KPNLF candidates, in particular, appeared to be peasants without any particular mental or physical aptitude. Driven beyond frustration after two weeks, Major Roberts declared all of the Cambodians were washouts. They were unceremoniously sent back to Ampil with the request that subsequent candidates be of better quality. For the remainder of the initial 10-week program, twenty more RTA Special Forces members—for a total of forty—participated in the SAS guerrilla primer.

At the same time the KPNLF went packing to the border, PAVN came knocking. It did not take a veteran Cambodia-watcher to surmise that Front 719 could ill afford a repeat of the symbolic setbacks it suffered the previous dry season. During the third week of November 1984, Le Duc Anh did not disappoint. Taking a page out of his 1983 playbook, he had assembled an exceedingly robust task force to first focus on the KPNLF camp at Nong Chan. Drawn largely from the 9 Division, the force also included a contingent from 7 Division, elements of two tank battalions, thirteen guns from the artillery command, and part of the PRKAF 179 Division. Perhaps anticipating the need to cross the border, and thus become vulnerable to airstrikes by the Royal Thai Air Force, they were also allocated a team with four SA-7 antiaircraft missile launchers.

On 12 November, most of this PAVN contingent had assembled at Sisophon. Five days later, it slowly rolled toward the border. Elements of an engineer regiment were in the lead, discretely clearing paths through the extensive minefield forward of the KPNLF lines.[2]

At Nong Chan, local warlord Chea Chhut anticipated the PAVN onslaught. Though controversial—for his constant dabbling in black-market activities, as well as the human rights lapses against the civilians in the seven village clusters under his purview—there was no denying that his 2,500 guerrillas were among the more aggressive in the KPNLF's roster. More than any of the other camps, they made regular forays into Cambodia; earlier that same month, for example, they had staged raids near the Sophi train station.

True to form, when PAVN struck at 0600 on 18 November, Chea Chhut once more proved himself a wily guerrilla operator. Though hopelessly outnumbered, his men put up a spirited defense and clung to portions of their base for a full six days before retreating into Thailand. They gave as good as they got, with the 9 Division's 1 Regiment incurring serious losses from Claymore ambushes.

The following month, on 12 December, the Vietnamese staged what was becoming an annual stab toward Sok Sann in the south. In a familiar refrain, the grandfatherly Prum Vith took leave of his mountain redoubt and chaperoned his guerrillas and civilian followers west across the Thai frontier. Both sides went through the motions with a wink and a nod, with minimal casualties inflicted or sustained.

A few more jabs against the KPNLF ensued. The 9 Division, coming off its success at Nong Chan, shifted its attention just north and easily overwhelmed Rithysen Camp at Nong Samet on Christmas. That same day, the PRKAF's 286 Division used 122mm artillery to good effect during a pummeling of O'Bok camp; Im Chudett ushered the 1,400 civilians under his care into Thailand the following week.[3]

Not playing favorites, PAVN also staged a Christmas assault against the Khmer Rouge border encampment at Phnom Chat, halfway between Nong Samet and Ampil. Spearheaded by a regiment from 5 Division, the attack was supported by a generous amount of field artillery and eleven T-54 tanks. The resident Khmer Rouge 519 Division resisted for an afternoon, then slipped into Thailand to fight another day.

Having moved in a methodical northern sweep from Nong Chan to Nong Samet to Phnom Chat, next on the PAVN hitlist was Ampil. Here the mission was once again handed to 5 Division, reinforced by a regiment from 302 Division, a regiment from the PRKAF 286 Division, five tanks, and more than two dozen artillery pieces. Anticipating fierce resistance, they had also prepared their first combined military-civilian surgical complex 25 kilometers behind the frontlines; the resident medical staff was quietly told to prepare for at least 300 casualties.

PAVN had good reason for pessimism. The KPNLF complex at Ampil included combatants from Zones 202 and 203, as well as General Reserve units—making for a critical mass of some 5,000 guerrillas. Moreover, KPNLF press releases since the start of the year indicated it was braced for an impending PAVN push.

For its part, Task force 838 did not like Ampil's odds. On the evening of 6 January 1985, Colonel Surayud, the 838 commander, visited the KPNLF headquarters. As usual, Dien Del was the senior officer present; his considerably younger second wife, whom he had wed on the border in 1982, was fixed by his side. (The rest of the KPNLF top brass had moved to a small compound established in Aranyaprathet.) While lauding Dien Del's tenacity, Surayud urged him to send his spouse to the safety of Aranyaprathet. But motioning toward a Chinese mortar and heavy machine gun set up next to a bunker he had dug near his house, Dien Del—and his wife—voiced their determination to take on whatever PAVN had to offer.

The next morning at 0630, they had a chance to prove their mettle. Zeroing in with their 130mm field guns, the Vietnamese blasted Ampil with a forty-five-minute barrage. One of the first shells landed squarely on Dien Del's bungalow, smashing it and his beloved rose garden. Hunkered down in a partially collapsed bunker, Dien Del stood his ground.

At 0715, PAVN next unleashed an infantry and armor assault from Ampil Lake to the southeast. There the KPNLF's 212 Battalion was ready, training a line of Chinese-made recoilless rifles across the flat scrub. The first volley twice found their mark, leaving two T-54 tanks burning on the battlefield.

This was just a feint, however. The main PAVN thrust, again supported by armor, came from the north. The 5 Division then committed its reserve regiment to the south, catching Ampil in a pincer. They methodically closed the gap through the afternoon, sending streams of KPNLF guerrillas into Thailand.[4]

That night, only a small core of resisters remained inside Cambodian territory. Realizing the futility of further struggle, and the imminent danger of capture, Dien Del and his wife walked the 50 meters from their smoldering house to the stream that delineated the border. Surayud was waiting on the opposite bank to greet them. "It will be a blessing," the general promised. "We will be forced to become real guerrillas."[5]

PAVN continued mop-up operations through the following morning, though resistance had ceased hours before.[6] The battle had been so lopsided that the surgical hospital, set to receive 300 casualties, treated only 7.

The Ampil operation had been big. The 5 Division's official history would later describe it as only its second combined arms battle at the divisional level, the first being the 1972 Easter Offensive in South Vietnam. Still, it paled to what PAVN was preparing for the Khmer Rouge. In a pair of simultaneous multidivision attacks, the Vietnamese were looking to smash a Khmer Rouge stronghold in the triborder area to the northeast, as well as the massive Phnom Malai headquarters complex along the western border.

The triborder operation kicked off first. Back in December 1984, elements of PAVN's 307 Division had already moved into the vicinity and easily overran the KPNLF outpost near Nam Yuen, then seeded mines along the escape routes into Thailand. Three days before year's end, PAVN began shelling the nearby Khmer Rouge 801 Division base camp. On the morning of 4 January, two Vietnamese divisions, approaching from opposite directions, penetrated 13 kilometers into Thailand and unexpectedly attacked from the north. Catching the Khmer Rouge by surprise, they overwhelmed the entire camp by the following noon.[7]

PAVN did not have it so easy at Phnom Malai. This was understandable, as Phnom Malai was a hive of base camps peppered throughout 180 square kilometers of virgin jungle and rugged mountains. So hostile was the topography and flora (only one single-lane road meandered from north to south through the vicinity) that the Khmer Rouge had not even bothered to erect fortified defenses. The Vietnamese were aware of these challenges after having made a concerted effort to overrun the vicinity during the 1981–1982 dry season, only to be denied victory after incessant guerrilla harassing attacks and chronic malaria forced them to withdraw.

On 9 January 1985, PAVN tried again. Using 9 Division—fresh off its victories at Nong Chan and Nong Samet—and thirteen field guns, it spent the remainder of the month wresting control of three strategic hill positions on the Phnom Malai periphery. Using these as springboards, beginning on 31 January it pushed its way into a bivouac area for the Khmer Rouge 320 Division.

All of this was leading up to a major showdown on 13 February. Using two full divisions and elements of three others, as well as a tank regiment, more than three dozen field guns, and six BM-14 multiple rocket launchers, PAVN bulldozed Pol Pot's men back toward the border. Several Khmer Rouge pockets put up fierce resistance; a PAVN field hospital established 30 kilometers behind the frontlines treated 732 casualties during the first 36 days of the push. But in the main the Khmer Rouge was unwilling to sacrifice men for territory; most merely faded away rather than engage the Vietnamese in pitched battles.

Then, with most of PAVN's aims met, the border fell silent in late February. The KPNLF, for one, had been all but decimated. And the Khmer Rouge—though it still held a sizable base area centered along the northern border near Anlong

Veng—had lost many of its camps, including the symbolic seat of the CGDK government at Phnom Malai.

But what PAVN had not targeted was what was most puzzling. The ANS headquarters at Tatum had been completely unmolested. Also, a single KPNLF base camp—Zone 201 under Ta Maing—had been spared. Tellingly, although Ta Maing was still listed on the KPNLF roster, he had gone out of his way to forge close ties with the ANS. This left Cambodia-watchers pondering whether Hanoi was attempting to divide and conquer the CGDK, selectively pummeling part of the resistance but overlooking Sihanouk loyalists. Given Sihanouk's past diplomatic pragmatism, one would have been forgiven for speculating whether the prince had cut a deal with the PRK.

As it turned out, Hanoi's strategy was not that nuanced. On 5 March, PAVN's 5 Division—rested after its January romp at Ampil—spearheaded a thrust just to the north against Ta Maing's Zone 201. It was a bit of overkill, with more than two dozen artillery pieces, six BM-14 multiple rocket launchers, and a generous supply of tanks, in addition to the infantrymen, slicing through the KPNLF base area over the course of a day.

Then came Tatum. More than perhaps any of the other targets during that dry-season offensive, Tatum promised to be a daunting challenge. Eleven kilometers long and 6 kilometers wide, the northern side had a gentle slope toward Thailand. To the southern flank, however, was a sheer rock cliff; to the east and west were equally craggy walls overgrown with jungle. Only a single trail wove up the escarpment, and the ANS had already taken pains to liberally seed it with mines. The Sihanoukists had grouped their five brigades in the immediate vicinity, giving them a critical mass of perhaps 10,000 troops and 30,000 civilians. They also had mortars and recoilless rifles trained down the cliffs, not to mention several RTA fire bases on the Thai side of the frontier capable of long-range artillery support.

PAVN took this into account when planning its attack. Since the start of the year, it had been sending reconnaissance teams to nose along the escarpment—and presumably around the rear of the base from Thai soil. It had also allocated a sizable amount of firepower for the operation, including two composite artillery battalions, a tank battalion, and 107mm rocket launchers. On 20 February, immediately after Lunar New Year celebrations, hundreds of Cambodian coolies were sequestered to begin hauling these heavy weapons toward the front. They also carried in thousands of U.S.-made howitzer rounds left over from the Vietnam War.

Later that same week, the main force assigned with the attack—the 302 Division—began seven days of intensive military and political training to prepare for a vital, but as yet unstated, assignment. Not until 3 March were the division's

Prince Sihanouk presides over King Men's funeral at Surin, 13 March 1985. CIA officer Gary Fleischer (with sunglasses) is in the rear. (Author's collection)

officers gathered around a sand table (a map etched into the ground) and formally briefed about their target.

The plan of attack, the officers learned, mixed overwhelming firepower and guile. One of its regiments—the 271st—was to climb the eastern cliffs and attack toward the west. Another regiment—the 88th—would be augmented by a regiment of PRKAF troops; supported by direct fire from tanks, they would scale the western cliffs and move east.

The key to the plan was the 429 Regiment, which was to circle deep within Thailand and attack from the northeast. As it would be vulnerable to Thai airstrikes, it would be carrying SA-7 missile launchers.

With the farthest distance to travel, elements of the 429th loaded up with supplies at noon on 4 March and quietly penetrated 8 kilometers into Thai territory. Each man carried 400 AK-47 rounds, grenades, and two mortar rounds apiece. Moving westward parallel to the border, most of this column reached their assembly point by 0400 on 5 March. Two battalions had strayed off course in the dark, however, forcing the frontline commander to briefly delay the onset of the attack.

Not until 0510, almost one hour after the planned start, did the artillery crews south of the escarpment open fire with the first of three barrages. The mountain at that hour was shrouded in fog and mist, making direct artillery observation all but impossible. Still, the flurry of rounds sent the ANS troops into a panic. Surging forward, the 429th was able to secure a foothold near the camp's rear perimeter after three hours.

At that point, luck began to wane for the Vietnamese. Thai airstrikes hit the 429th and forced it to disperse under the jungle canopy, leaving several bodies behind on Thai soil. And with the ANS firing heavy weapons from behind the crags at the top of the cliff, it kept both the 88th and 271st at bay in the lowlands below.

With the battle stalemated on 6 March, PAVN began to rush reinforcements toward the front. An entire regiment—the 55th—was contributed by the 310 Division, with most of these men directed around the rear to bolster the 429th pinned down along the frontier.

With these infantry reinforcements having little impact, the battle devolved into an artillery duel by 7 March. From the south, PAVN peppered volleys across the mountaintop. The odd round invariably fell north of the border, each time prompting the RTA to respond with counterbattery fire from its 155mm howitzers. The Thai artillery crews were for the first time using base-bleed ammunition, a system to reduce drag on artillery shells and thus increase their range by about a third.

As of the morning of Friday, 8 March, the stalemate continued. In a precautionary move, the ANS had loaded most of its supplies aboard trucks during the previous two days and moved them just north of the border to Thai-based warehouses. The civilian population, too, had joined the northern exodus out of harm's way.

Meantime, making an unexpected appearance was Sihanouk, who arrived in Thailand flanked by a bevy of North Korean bodyguards courtesy of Kim Il-Sung. He quickly took up residence in a rustic guesthouse the Thai had constructed for him in the Surin provincial capital. Although the prince urged his guerrillas not to make a costly final stand at Tatum, many of his loyalists felt compelled to stiffen their resistance following his arrival.[8]

This had put Task Force 838 in a quandary. Operating from the backwater town of Ban Phleung in Surin province, task force commander Surayud had assigned Lieutenant Colonel Sonthi Boonyaratglin to head liaison duties with the ANS at Tatum. A soft-spoken officer, Sonthi traced his family back to Thailand's first Islamic spiritual leader. Graduating from the military academy in

1969, he had gone to South Vietnam as part of the RTA's Black Panther Division. He then spent more than a decade in the RTA Special Forces and was serving as a battalion commander in Surayud's 1 Special Forces Regiment when he got the 838 assignment.

From Ban Phleung, Sonthi was allocated an eighty-man company—most of them fellow Special Forces members—to discretely assist the ANS. Of these, ten had ventured to Tatum at daybreak on 8 March to review the situation. The senior among them, a Special Forces major named Jong Buranasompob, had gone straight to the ANS command bunker. Joining him was Captain Phrom Anusornrum, an RTA officer from Surin who spoke fluent Khmer, and Master Sergeant Manit Nasangiem, a radioman.[9]

Inside the command bunker they found Lieutenant General Teap Ben, the ANS chief of staff, and forty-four-year-old Major General King Men, the ANS deputy chief of staff for operations. This was the same pair of former FANK officers who had visited the border together in 1977. After that, Teap Ben had returned in 1981 for the formation of the ANS and stayed, while King Men had joined the ANS in 1982 as a deputy for tactics.[10] His wife, Tith Kanha, an attractive thirty-two-year-old Eurasian and aspiring actress, had accompanied him to Thailand but was thoroughly opposed to her husband's resistance activities; she had even implored members of Bangkok Station to pressure him into returning to his five children in the United States. The station was hardly in a position to do so—especially since King Men was rated as one of the more effective ANS leaders—and had quietly paid for the wife to take acting lessons in order to alleviate the stress she felt from her husband's vocation.[11]

At 0900, the Thai advisers had huddled briefly with Teap Ben and King Men to discuss tactical deployments. After three artillery rounds landed nearby, Teap Ben had wandered a few meters away toward a bunker at the now deserted ANS Guerrilla Training School. The move saved his life. Seconds later, a PAVN 155mm round soared upward from the lowlands and found its mark. Tipped with a delayed fuse, it sliced deep into the command bunker's earthen roof before detonation. Standing just outside the bunker, Jong and Manit were dismembered by the shrapnel and concussion.[12] Inside, little remained of King Men and Phrom. Lieutenant Colonel Nhek Bun Chay, the deputy commander of 1 Brigade, worked his way into the collapsed bunker later that day and managed to scoop 15 kilograms of human flesh into a poncho for later burial.[13]

Despite the loss of its chief of operations, the ANS was still able to cling to the mountaintop over the ensuing two days. During the predawn hours of 11 March, however, PAVN launched a concerted artillery barrage followed by a massive infantry assault from all directions. Most of the ANS garrison by that time had made a quiet retreat into Thailand, offering only minimal resistance as the Vietnamese pushed their way across the summit through noon. In a last great act of defiance the Sihanoukists drew final blood, firing a rocket-propelled grenade that took off the entire lower jaw of a battalion commander from the 429 Regiment.

The guerrilla base, PAVN found, was awash in death. Numerous Vietnamese bodies, killed during the opening skirmishes on 5 March, could finally be retrieved from the base of the cliffs. In a macabre scene, the elephant grass where some of the corpses lay had withered and turned black due to leaking bodily fluids, leaving an exact outline of the bodies.

Picking among the ANS bunkers, the Vietnamese looked for spoils. Most of the base's supplies had already been evacuated to Thailand, though they were able to find two 75mm recoilless rifles and thirteen mortars, plus a large stock of Funcinpec propaganda magazines and a container of French-made medical plaster used for fixing broken bones. After hearing a BBC News report that King Men had been killed earlier on 8 March, they attempted to dig through his destroyed bunker—only to be driven off by the stench of decomposing flesh.

Not until the afternoon of 14 March did PAVN withdraw from the Tatum vicinity. Its victory had been costly. The surgical unit dedicated to the battle had treated 469 casualties; official accounts placed the number of dead at a suspiciously low 125. More than a decade later, the commander of 302 Division reportedly told a delegation of visiting Cambodian officers that some 2,000 PAVN soldiers were casualties in the battle.[14]

For the ANS, its defeat at Tatum was spun into a win. After all, it had held off the Vietnamese juggernaut for an entire week. Its losses, too, had been relatively light: just over 150 killed and 200 wounded. Undoubtedly its biggest blow had been the death of King Men, whose funeral at Surin on 13 March was overseen by Sihanouk himself. During the solemn cremation ceremony, King Men's widow, barefoot and dressed in white, led the procession as his body was placed atop a pyre. The CIA's Francis Sherry and Gary Fleischer, the Hilton officer who had forged ties with many of the ANS leaders, quietly took in the ceremony from the back of the crowd. For Fleischer, the event was especially poignant: He had been getting updates on the radio from an ANS operator in a neighboring bunker when the fateful round hit.[15]

With the fall of their base camps, both of the noncommunist resistance factions were in a daze. The KPNLF faced particular dire straits, with an estimated one-

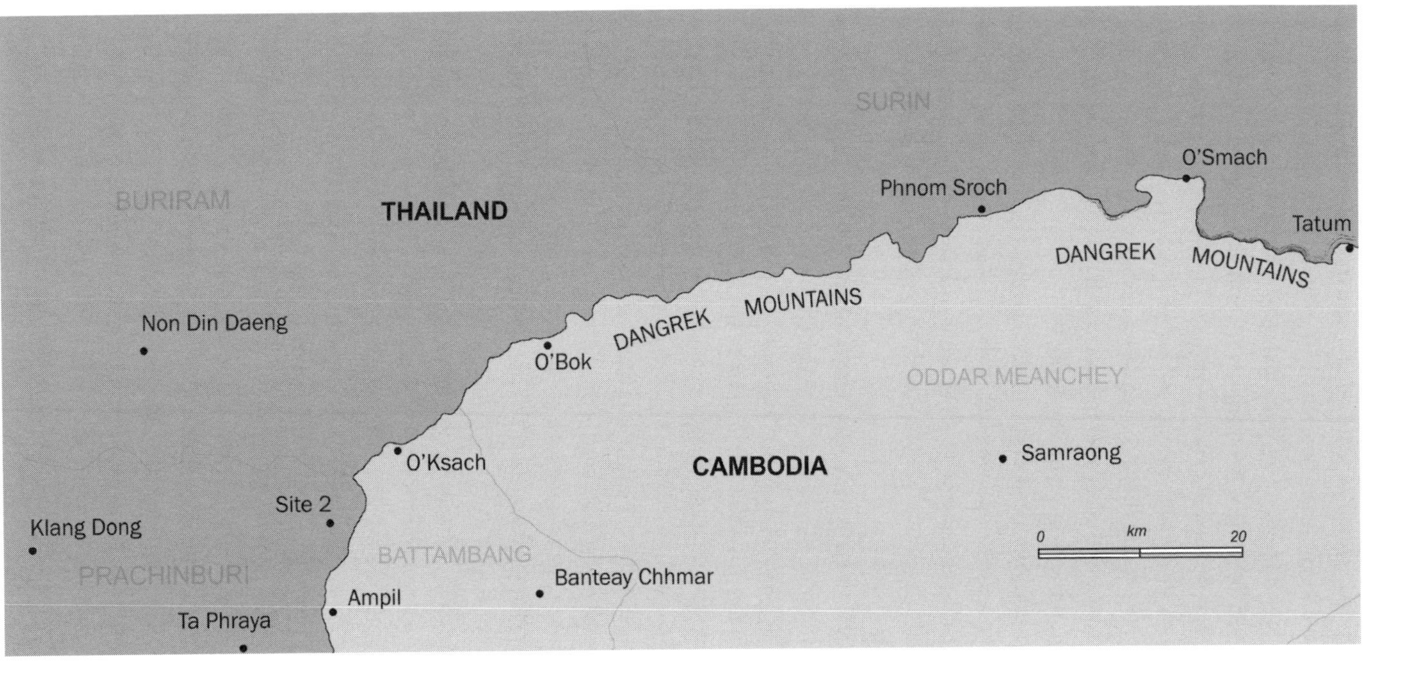

The northwest quadrant of Cambodia

third of its 15,000 guerrillas lost due to death or desertions. The remainder had been dispersed in small pockets inside the Thai border, out of communication with their leadership. Most of them instinctively headed north toward the Dangrek chain. Srey Sangha, a young guerrilla recruit at the time, recalls: "We kept walking north; it seemed like we were in Thai territory but we weren't sure. There were nine in my group with no radios and no food. We came across a baby leopard, still alive, in a poacher's snare. We were afraid of attracting attention by shooting it, so we tied a bayonet to a stick and stabbed it to death. Then we ate it on the spot, no seasoning or anything."[16]

In time, several hundred of the KPNLF stragglers reached the northwestern corner of the Dangrek escarpment. Dien Del was among them, establishing a temporary headquarters near the O'Bok Pass.[17] In the south, Prum Vith alone had been able to slip back into his old Sok Sann base with his guerrilla roster largely intact.

For the ANS, the situation was hardly better. Shifting 20 kilometers west of the O'Smach border crossing, it established a new base straddling the border at Phnom Sroch. With part of its compound extending inside Thai territory, this locale offered the possibility of licking its wounds in relative peace.[18]

There also remained the question of what to do with the hundreds of thousands of CGDK civilian dependents forced into Thailand. As their previous camps had been razed and were in no condition to be reoccupied, it quickly became apparent that their Thai sojourn would extend well into the medium term. The Thai authorities thus made provisions for these civilians to be gathered in new camps inside Thai territory—safe from the tender mercies of PAVN but still under the nominal control of the various CGDK factions.

In the case of the Khmer Rouge, it was given authority over dozens of Thai-based civilian camps. Of these, the three largest—known as O'Trao, Site 8, and Site K—had a combined population of 62,000 people.[19] For the ANS, its 56,000 displaced civilians were pooled for a two-hour walk across the border from the demolished Tatum base at a camp known as Site B.

For the KPNLF, some 8,000 civilians were still under the care of Prum Vith at Sok Sann. For the nearly 150,000 others, the Thai decided in March to establish a megacamp known as Site 2. Located 70 kilometers north of Aranyaprathet and 2 kilometers inside Thai territory near the district capital of Ta Phraya, Site 2 was actually an umbrella for seven subcamps. In the northern part of the complex were subcamps containing the populations formerly at Ampil, Ta Maing's Zone 201, the failed guerrilla warfare school in the Dangrek Range, Nam Yuen, and

Nong Chan. In the south were subcamps for displaced persons from Nong Samet and O'Bok.

From the start, there was a surreal quality to Site 2. Inside its confines, entrepreneurial refugees opened businesses ranging from restaurants serving lobster and beer, to tailors and jewelers, to shops peddling antiquities smuggled in from Cambodia. For the most part, the subcamps retained the same KPNLF administrators from their old locations; now forced into close proximity, they squabbled endlessly among themselves and often handed down harsh justice.

All of this was exacerbated by the questionable Thai security arrangement ringing Site 2. Since 1980, a paramilitary organization that was the brainchild of General Chavalit had been helping guard the various Khmer refugee camps. Officially known as Thahan Phran ("Hunter Soldiers") but more commonly called Rangers, they were a locally recruited home guard considered a cheap first line of defense along the border. Given minimal training, it came as no surprise that they often showed lapses in discipline, especially when charged with overseeing tens of thousands of destitute refugees. When the number of displaced persons inside Thailand increased exponentially after the first quarter of 1985, there was a corresponding spike in the number of human rights excesses tied to the Rangers.[20]

All of this proved a tipping point for Representative Stephen Solarz of New York. A member of the House since 1975, Solarz had first shown interest in Cambodia two years later when serving on the Subcommittee on International Organizations in the House International Affairs Committee. In May 1977, that subcommittee had heard four witnesses analyze the chaotic, apparently bloody situation unfolding in Democratic Kampuchea. Two of the witnesses were former Foreign Service officers; one of them, David Chandler, pinned the blame on past U.S. military action for bringing the Khmer Rouge to power. Another witness, the academic Gareth Porter, went as far as defending the Khmer Rouge decision to evacuate cities. Only John Barron, an editor at *Reader's Digest* who had recently written an expose on Khmer Rouge excesses, supported strong public condemnation of the Phnom Penh regime.

The testimony appalled Solarz. Though he was no fan of the past U.S. bombing, he felt what was happening in Cambodia was one of the most contemptible crimes in the history of humanity. His view ultimately helped edge the Carter administration in April 1978 into issuing a stinging rebuke of the Khmer Rouge as the world's worst extant violator of human rights.[21]

The following year, Solarz again weighed in on Cambodia. In March 1979, shortly after the PAVN invasion, Assistant Secretary of State for East Asian and

Pacific Affairs Richard Holbrooke made a public call for the withdrawal of Vietnamese troops. Solarz did not oppose this move but pointed out that it might be nice to brainstorm some kind of plan to prevent the Khmer Rouge from slipping back into power.[22]

By 1981, Solarz had enough seniority to be able to claim chairmanship of the House Subcommittee on Asian and Pacific Affairs. Now with an ability to shape the subcommittee's schedule, this gave him and his staff considerable influence over the House foreign policy debate. The next year, following the formation of the CGDK, he was able to wield this influence regarding the Cambodian situation. Specifically, he had come to see the Cambodian noncommunist resistance, which was getting only a lukewarm embrace by Washington, as an inconsistency in Reagan's foreign policy. Said Solarz:

> The fault line was over the best way to stop the Khmer Rouge. Some thought that the U.S. government should deal with the PRK. They did not like the CGDK because it included the Khmer Rouge. They did not realize it was a coalition in name only, created for the practical matter of the United Nations problem. They could not grasp the logic that helping the noncommunist resistance was a means of preventing the return of the Khmer Rouge. They did not want the Khmer Rouge to return, but they did not address the need for an independent, democratic Cambodia.[23]

By early 1985, with the CGDK factions getting pummeled on the border, Solarz decided to turn proactive. At about that same time, a fellow Democrat, Charlie Wilson from Texas, had emerged as a leading proponent of expanded paramilitary support for the Afghan mujahideen. Taking to the House floor, the flamboyant Wilson in late 1984 had taken it upon himself to source millions of dollars in extra funds for the mujahideen, foisting this money upon the CIA for additional covert assistance.

Far more sober (both literally and figuratively) than Wilson, Solarz sought to take on a similar role as congressional cheerleader for the noncommunist portion of the CGDK. Without bothering to schedule hearings, he convinced his subcommittee colleagues to support legislation to extend $5 million in overt paramilitary aid to the Cambodian guerrillas. This soon became the subject of much debate in the full House Foreign Affairs Committee, where it faced objections not only from liberal Democrats but also from the Reagan administration. The former opposed out of dovish proclivities against possibly expanding the war. The latter was against congressionally mandated overt aid because it argued the resistance was already getting enough support from ASEAN and China. Behind the scenes, it might have opposed the overt aid because it did not want to draw attention to the covert CIA assistance—by then about $12 million a year—that had been flowing under the public radar since 1982.[24]

In the end, Solarz's argument that the Cambodians were worthy of assistance was persuasive. On 3 April, the full House Foreign Affairs Committee voted 24-9 to authorize $5 million in military aid to the noncommunists.[25] The following month, the Senate similarly approved lethal aid by a voice vote. The debate then moved back to the House, where the Solarz aid package in July won by a convincing 288–122 margin. Reagan signed the bill on 8 August. Though his administration had now been brow-beaten by the legislative branch into extending overt aid to the noncommunist resistance, it was given the option of using the money for either lethal or nonlethal purchases.

While the Solarz aid was still being debated back in April, Ranariddh had visited Foggy Bottom and paid a courtesy call on Secretary of State George Schulz. His junket came at a time of significant flux in the ANS leadership. After King Men was killed, Prince Chakrapong lobbied hard, and successfully, to be appointed his successor as deputy chief of staff for operations. This might have been a welcome move during earlier years, but by that time Chakrapong had fully fallen foul of Bangkok Station. Francis Sherry, the head of the station's Cambodian effort, was especially sour toward the prince, accusing him of rampant womanizing and padding his 5 Brigade's payroll with phantom troops.[26] In addition, he had reportedly misappropriated his guerrillas to repeatedly liberate the Andong Bor vicinity in Thmar Puok district; not coincidentally, this area had attracted gold prospectors since the French era.[27]

Despite his tarnished reputation, Chakrapong added another title in March. That month, In Tam, the founder and (ostensibly) commander-in-chief of the ANS, resigned from all of his positions in the ANS and Funcinpec via an open letter to the Agence France-Presse. In the letter, he was sharply critical of support from Thailand and Singapore. His real differences, however, were with Ranariddh, who had effectively circumvented and sidelined In Tam for the past two years.

In stepping down, In Tam left several shoes to fill. As defense minister assigned to the CGDK, this largely symbolic title was conferred upon Chakrapong. The role of first vice-president of Funcinpec went to Sihanouk's wife, Monique. As for ANS commander-in-chief, this slot seemingly should have gone to the ANS chief of staff, Teap Ben. However, it was Ranariddh who was instead named temporary commander. For good measure, Ranariddh also added for himself the title of ANS inspector general and personal representative of the Supreme Commander of the ANS, Sihanouk.

Having increasingly consolidated power, Ranariddh in late June ventured to Phnom Sroch and instituted another wave of promotions to motivate his top officers. Still, he had to contend with the fact that his ANS—and the KPNLF, for that matter—had been all but stripped of any presence inside Cambodia.

Ranariddh also had to contend with his own father. In a vintage Sihanouk moment, the head of the CGDK in July predicted that Cambodia was destined to become a Vietnamese province. For good measure Sihanouk again threatened to quit the resistance, this time after he accused the Khmer Rouge of killing thirty-eight ANS guerrillas during the first half of the year.[28]

The Exco, for its part, was trying hard to get the noncommunists out of their rut and back into the interior. During midyear, the RTA initiated a one-month command and staff course at the Special Warfare School in Lopburi for twenty high-ranking KPNLF and ANS officers. Chakrapong was named chairman of the class; Pann Thai was the vice-chairman.[29] In a similar move, Malaysia in April began a 10-week senior commander course for many of the KPNLF and ANS guerrillas that had attended the earlier unconventional warfare classes.[30]

Some of the best assistance came from the British, who in March restarted the SAS training at Phitsanulok after the abortive effort the previous year. This time forty-eight ANS candidates were accepted into the three-month program. According to one course graduate, the Cambodians took well to the material: "The SAS gave better map, weapons, and demolition training than the Malaysians. They were able to teach land navigation to some of the students who were completely illiterate. They also spent a full month on weapons training. Many of the guerrillas could not hit a target at first—they were closing the wrong eye. Very quickly, they had everybody zeroed in on their target."[31]

Of acceptable aptitude this time around, the class graduated at midyear. The SAS had broken them into a dozen teams of four apiece: a commander, medic, radioman, and demolitions expert. In early August, three of the teams—totaling a dozen commandos—infiltrated into Siem Reap and successfully set off demolitions at a former college being used as a PRKAF ammunition dump. Belgian journalist Jacques Berkaert, writing a weekly column for the *Bangkok Post*, alluded to SAS training for the Siem Reap attackers—but the scoop went largely unnoticed and the Phitsanulok program continued in relative secrecy.[32]

For its part, the CIA in mid-1985 contented itself largely with monitoring the Cambodian situation from Aranyaprathet. At the Hilton base, a sense of close camaraderie had taken hold among its diverse staff. This was apparent around their communal dinner table during most evenings. Said one CIA officer: "Meals were a big deal. Our cook would take everyone's suggestions for favorite foods into consideration. After the evening meal, conversation went on for hours and covered everything. Between the Americans, Thai, Cambodians, Khmer Krom and Vietnamese, we had every major religion represented around the table: Mormon, Jew, Muslim, Buddhist, Christian, animist, Hindu."

Also represented at the Hilton was a growing roster of pets. Initially this was limited to a German shepherd and a civet cat. Then a Cambodian runner came back one day with a pair of leopard kittens; their mother, he said, was killed by a hunter. Taking pity on the felines, the CIA officers built a large cage on the premises. Though still small in size, the kittens could, and did, use their fangs and claws to inflict some serious cuts on the U.S. officers. They also ate the civet cat after it inadvertently ran into their cage.

On nearly a weekly basis, the spotters also began bringing back primates sold around the refugee camps. The staff built another large cage to house two macaques and a rhesus monkey; base chief Jim Parker ordered that a dozen others be released into the nearby jungle and issued a moratorium on further additions to the simian collection.

Rounding out the makeshift zoo was a variety of birds. Recalled one of those present: "We got some peacocks but they died. Finally, in a stroke of complete insanity, we got some geese . . . as guard animals. Someone had heard that they always give the alarm in case of dead-of-night intruders, but I tell you what, they shit a ton. Pretty soon all the grassy areas of the compound were covered with goose shit."

On hand to view these animals, as well as get briefings from the Hilton's CIA staff, were a seemingly endless stream of congressional delegations and other high-ranking visitors from Washington. Among the former was Orrin Hatch, the Republican from Utah on the Senate Select Committee on Intelligence. In a memorable moment before heading back to Bangkok, Hatch turned to the CIA staff and, apparently recalling some sage advice more applicable to World War II, intoned them to "watch the railroads."

Another visitor was a White House envoy wielding the title of Special Representative for Undeclared Wars. Staying for dinner, the envoy was on hand when one of the female macaques escaped from its enclosure and leapt to the lamp chain above the table. She hit the hot metal shade and immediately fell into a big bowl of spaghetti sauce. CIA officer Gary Fleischer grabbed the primate, cleaned her off, and placed her back in the cage. The special representative was appalled, however, when the base personnel continued ladling out sauce on their pasta. "Doesn't monkey add flavor?" queried Fleischer.

The Hilton officials hosted equally senior visitors from their own agency. Clair George, the deputy director of operations and third-ranking in the CIA hierarchy, passed through in 1984. But none were more senior than CIA Director William Casey himself, who arrived in his unmarked C-141 Starlifter on the military side of Don Muang airbase in May 1985, then was whisked out to the border in a helicopter with the TOC 315 chief, General Kasem.

Despite a propensity to mumble, Casey immediately won over the CIA staff. Turning to base chief Parker on the ride from the helipad to the Hilton, he recalled numerous details of their meeting the previous year in Chieng Mai. Then upon meeting Fleischer, he asked, "What are you doing here? I thought I sent you to Yemen!"

Both officers were left wondering whether Casey had a phenomenal memory, or if he had taken the time to memorize details about them before arrival. In either case, both were flattered he had made the effort to personalize his meetings with comparatively low-ranking officers.

Once at the Hilton, Casey was introduced to a selection of Cambodian employees. One was a female ANS radio operator. She had been in an adjoining bunker when King Men was killed and was on line with Fleischer when the fateful 155mm round hit.

Another was one of the Hilton's runners. When asked by Casey what he did before the Khmer Rouge took over, the runner said he was an engineer.

"What kind?" asked Casey. "Civil, mechanical?"

"Choo-choo," responded the runner. Casey broke into a wide grin.

After a briefing from Parker, a round of questions, and lunch, Casey prepared for the trip back to Bangkok. Turning to the base chief he said, "What we need now in the history of the CIA is a good success story." With strong eye contact, a smile, and a sincere wish that things go well, he headed to the helipad.

Since the opening of the year, Cambodia had been teetering on the edge of a black hole. With the Cambodian occupation in its seventh year, the CGDK resistance groups had experienced unparalleled reverses in the field. Despite all this, Casey's visit had been uplifting. At least for those CIA officers sequestered at the Hilton, a hint of optimism—for the moment—prevailed.

11. Dry Rot

A key topic of discussion during Willam Casey's May visit to Aranyaprathet had been the sad state of affairs within the CGDK following PAVN's latest dry-season offensive. To help get the anti-Vietnamese coalition back on its feet, China that same month had extended one of its largest aid shipments to date. The lion's share went to their Khmer Rouge proxies, but the ANS had also been given an assortment of 1,500 rifles, grenade launchers, and antitank rockets.[1]

For the KPNLF, the faction that had arguably taken the biggest proportional hit in the number of combatants, even a generous infusion of Chinese aid could not reverse its fortunes. As it turned out, PAVN was only partly to blame for their sorry condition; many of their problems were self-inflicted and, in hindsight, years in the making.

At the core of the KPNLF's woes was its obstinate, courtly patriarch, Son Sann. Not one to brook criticism, or even abide a critical sounding board, Son Sann was often less than supportive of the democratic ideals that the Front theoretically espoused. He had even stifled junior officers who showed a whiff of potential; when Dr. Gaffar Peang-Meth grew popular on the ASEAN diplomatic circuit, for example, he quickly began dropping hints that Gaffar might want to leave Southeast Asia and take up the inconsequential post as CGDK ambassador in Egypt.[2]

For the military leaders in the KPNLAF, the Front's military wing, Son Sann's chokehold on power was tolerable during the period when their border base camp strategy prospered. But once they were run off the border, and the concept of cohosting guerrillas with tens of thousands of civilian dependents was exposed as folly, the KPNLAF's top brass realized the need to thoroughly revamp their liberation strategy. As part of that, General Sak sought to address the messy leadership structure by formally becoming the KPNLAF commander-in-chief, a title previously held by Son Sann. At the same time Dien Del would once more be elevated to chief of staff, replacing Sak.

Not wishing to appear obstructionist in the wake of the setbacks along the border, Son Sann acquiesced to Sak's formalized promotion. But later that same month, when Sak sought to forge greater unity with his ANS coalition partners, Son Sann dug in his heels. The push for synergy between the KPNLF and ANS, in fact, was nothing new. Way back in 1982, in a tryst with Son Sann shortly after the formation of the CGDK, an exuberant Sihanouk had advocated merging the two noncommunist guerrilla armies. Eavesdropping on the meeting, Gaffar recalled: "Sihanouk said he was happy with the name 'KPNLF' and the Front's flag. Since we had the same objectives, he saw no problem merging them into one movement. Son Sann, however, said nothing in return."[3]

Son Sann's silence, in fact, reflected his deepseated, and barely veiled, suspicion toward Sihanouk, Funcinpec, and the ANS. Such suspicion could be pinned in large part on Sihanouk's character flaws, which made him a quirky, often unreliable ally at best. Also, Son Sann no doubt realized that a merged noncommunist effort would be thoroughly dominated by the prince, effectively relegating himself to a distant second seat despite his pioneering efforts to establish the Front.

But personalities like Sak and Gaffar did not necessarily see it that same way. Concerned with tactical expediencies on the battlefield, many of the KPNLF leaders—strongly encouraged by the Exco—supported greater unity with the ANS in their logistical and planning efforts. This had led to the creation of Permico in May 1984, along with the separate Bangkok safe house at Soi Saisin.

More than anything, it was the establishment of the Permico safe house that enraged Son Sann. In reality, Permico had never lived up to expectations. Though its officers sat around Soi Saisin talking up plans about implementing a "crab claw" pincer strategy whereby their two factions would simultaneously push from the north and southwest in order to liberate the region around the Tonle Sap as a noncommunist bastion, nothing even remotely like that had taken place in the field. Even so, Son Sann had seen the safe house as a grave affront to his full control over the Front, especially now that Permico representatives could deal directly with the Exco.

Seething, Son Sann began to lean on those KPNLF members who saw merit in Permico. Seeking to avoid confrontation, those same procooperation members elected to spend more of their time at Soi Saisin—which only served to cast further doubt on their loyalty in Son Sann's eyes.

One year on, in late May 1985, the Permico advocates—led by Sak and Gaffar—looked to upgrade noncommunist cooperation into a more formalized merger. Over discussions that lasted nearly a month, they laid out plans for an evenly divided Joint Military Command (JMC) in which Sak would be the overall commander, Teap Ben the deputy commander, Toan Chay the chief of staff, and Gaffar the deputy chief of staff. Privy to these talks, the joint noncommunist radio station, Voice of the Khmer, announced the merger in early June as a fait accompli. And in late June, Gaffar and Toh Lah, an ANS political counselor, were publicly named JMC spokesmen. Seeking Sihanouk's formal approval, Teap Ben was given a draft of the JMC structure and sent off to Beijing to get the prince's signature.[4]

Pending Sihanouk's blessing, the two guerrilla armies were doing what they could to reenter the Cambodian interior. The KPNLAF still had its temporary headquarters in the Dangrek Range, though small numbers of its combatants (minus civilian dependents) had moved back into staging locations near the razed camps at Nong Chan and Nong Samet. Although it claimed that nearly 5,000 troops had managed to infiltrate into the PRK by early June, this number was likely wildly exaggerated.[5]

The ANS, meantime, still had the bulk of its combatants clustered around new headquarters at Phnom Sroch. In a bold attempt to motivate them, Ranariddh in late July embarked on a shallow, four-day foray into Odday Meanchey province. Escorted by Chakrapong, Toan Chay, a handful of Western journalists, and forty ANS guerrillas, he visited three border villages during what was his first combat patrol inside the PRK.[6] The following month, Ranariddh claimed that his men were opening the so-called Sihanouk Trail to infiltrate supplies from the border to the interior.[7]

For his part, Son Sann had been driven past the breaking point by talk of the JMC. In August, he sent an emissary to the Soi Saisin safe house with an ultimatum: Gaffar and Hing Kunthon, two civilian members of the KPNLF's leadership board who had been most outspoken in their support for closer cooperation with the ANS, were told to report across town to the Soi Maiyarap safe house to face a disciplinary hearing. When the pair refused to present themselves, Son Sann summarily dismissed them from the board, then, taking a page from the Sihanouk playbook, threatened to resign if the Front was not reorganized.[8]

Though Son Sann did not make good on his resignation threat, relations between the two safe houses festered into the fourth quarter. Things got so bad that General Chavalit—once the RTA's Cambodia czar—saw fit to enter the fray in an attempt to mend fences within KPNLF. With his career going from strength to strength, Chavalit in recent years had been hard-pressed to devote himself to Cambodian matters. In October 1983, he was promoted to lieutenant general and named RTA deputy chief of staff. And recently, in September 1985, he had mobilized anticoup forces when fellow officers had tried to stage a putsch. The very next month he was given his fourth star and promoted to RTA chief of staff. This now placed him among the Five Tigers—the five most powerful men in the RTA.

Only a month at his new post, Chavalit in November ventured to the Soi Maiyarap safe house to attempt his mediation effort. On one side of the room was Son Sann and several key loyalists. Among them were four KPNLF elders from France, as well as Colonel Im Chudett, General Thach Reng, and Delopez Sanguar.[9] The last figure, Sanguar, had been the air force chief of operations during the final months of the Lon Nol regime; the U.S. embassy at the time had rated him as "uneven in performance."[10] Moving to a Virginia suburb outside Washington, D.C., he had operated the KPNLF's U.S. information bureau from his house.

Among these Son Sann loyalists Thach Reng was by far the most controversial. Ever since joining the Front, he had stoked paranoia among his fellow generals—first Dien Del, later Sak—by hinting that he had Son Sann's blessing to take their jobs. He was also vocally dismissive of close cooperation with the ANS. Though this endeared him with Son Sann, it irritated the Exco. The previous year, when his rants undercut the cooperative spirit at Permico, the Thai authorities had firmly ordered him to leave the border.[11]

Leaving Thailand, Thach Reng spent most of his time touring Khmer communities in the United States. Rumors among the expatriate community claimed that he planned to recruit a new army responsive to Son Sann, not Sak. Now back in Bangkok, he was once more dropping hints that he might take over the KPNLAF's top slot.

On the other side of the room were Generals Sak and Dien Del. Joining them was former Major General Pok Sam An. A graduate of the first class at Cambodia's military academy, Pok Sam An had initially been an armor officer. By the time the Khmer Republic was born, he was rated one of the country's more competent generals and eventually worked his way up to assistant chief of staff in charge of training. He then made the political miscalculation of launching the upstart Republican Party to contest the 1972 presidential election. Although the party went nowhere, Lon Nol did not appreciate the token competition and directed Pok Sam An out of the country as ambassador to South Vietnam. He had stayed there for the remainder of the war, and he had been living a quiet existence in the United States before Sak beckoned him to join the KPNLAF as his adviser earlier that month.

Both Gaffar and Hing Kunthon, who had come to personify the rift, had found this an opportune time to temporarily take leave of town.

With Chavalit acting as a neutral referee, the two sides tried to hammer out a compromise. In this, they failed miserably. If anything, Son Sann exited the meeting with a hardened heart, and in early December he took the extra step of expelling Gaffar and Hing Kunthon from the KPNLF entirely.[12]

Following this, it was Sak's turn to reach his breaking point. On 17 December, he formed the Provisional Central Committee of Salvation (PCCS) to replace the KPNLF's existing leadership committee dominated by Son Sann loyalists.

A meeting of the JMC, 1986. At the head of the table is General Teap Ben, RTA Colonel Surayud Chulanont (commander of Task Force 838), and General Dien Del. Gaffar Peang-Meth is third from right. (Courtesy Gaffar Peang-Meth)

Besides Sak, the eight-man PCCS included Dien Del, Gaffar, Hing Kunthon, Colonel Thou Thip (who had headed the General Reserve at Ampil), Special Forces commander Pann Thai, Liv Ne (the former member of the Nationalist Party in Phnom Penh, and previously in charge of Camp Rithysen), and logistician Chak Bory.[13]

Declaration of the PCCS, of course, opened the KPNLF to full-blown internal conflict. On 30 December, the camp administrators at Site 2 let it be known that Son Sann was no longer welcome on the border. The next day Sak announced to reporters that 1986 would be the year of victory not over PAVN—but over Son Sann.[14]

The following month, the feud grew messier. On 7 January 1986, Representative Solarz, the biggest fan of the noncommunist resistance on Capitol Hill, visited Bangkok. Reflecting the split, Son Sann met the U.S. legislator in the morning, followed by a separate meeting with Sak and Gaffar. It is doubtful that the musical chairs instilled confidence in Solarz.

Ten days later, Son Sann finally received permission to enter Site 2. This set in motion a round of stiff competition to gain the loyalties of the KPNLAF's senior commanders. Although several ultimately declared sympathy for Son Sann—including Chea Chhut, Liv Ne, and Prum Vith—they pragmatically kept feet in both camps and went on to regularly meet with Sak. Many of the senior officers, in fact, wanted to put the internal conflict on ice and, on 28 January, pledged to focus solely on the liberation struggle.[15]

Sensing there were even more bridges to be cut, however, Son Sann on 15 February issued a new set of directives. This time around, Sak and Dien Del were both officially fired. In their place he promoted Prum Vith to head a four-member command committee.[16] The rift, it seemed, would not soon be ended.

Not to be outdone, the ANS had embarked on its own figurative fratricide during early 1986. By that time, Ranariddh had grown into his role as de facto ANS commander. As Teap Ben was increasingly superfluous (his royalist credentials were always suspect), the general was unceremoniously sacked in late January in a decree penned by Sihanouk in Beijing. Teap Ben, according to the order, was removed because he was allegedly brutal to subordinates, embezzled refugee funds, and displayed disloyalty. Few believed this laundry list of wrongdoings, but it provided sufficient cover for Ranariddh to be formally elevated to both ANS commander and chief of staff.[17]

As consolation of sorts, Teap Ben was allowed to retain the title of JMC deputy commander. Back on 12 December 1985, Sihanouk had signed the directive that theoretically merged the commands of the KPNLAF and ANS. According to this document, the JMC would formulate strategic and tactical concepts for both armed forces, coordinate and direct all operations, and plan and develop the growth of both through recruitment and training. It was to have six departments: planning under Gaffar, operations under Toan Chay, and intelligence under Kong Thann, as well as logistics, information, and psychological warfare. The former Permico office on Soi Saisin was transformed into a JMC safe house; in addition, they were given considerable space at the KPNLF compound in Aranyaprathet.[18]

Though Teap Ben's title of JMC deputy commander might have looked good on paper, it was largely hollow.[19] Shortly after the JMC was formally inaugurated on 4 January 1986, it was declared inactive—ostensibly due to the KPNLF infighting—after holding its first working meeting in March with the Exco.

There was another factor at play that undercut the JMC even before it had a chance to prove itself. As explained its intelligence chief, Kong Thann: "Ranariddh and Teap Ben were not getting along, so Teap Ben had been 'exiled' to the JMC. But Ranariddh didn't want Teap Ben to be successful, so he never wanted the JMC to work. The only ones that were really motivated were Toan Chay and Gaffar; they tried to issue joint military orders, but their bosses didn't share their enthusiasm."[20]

For his part, Kong Thann tried to nudge his joint intelligence department to produce some meaningful results. And though some useful nuggets from refugee sources began to filter in, most of them concerned mundane smuggling and black-market activities. One early 1986 report, for example, claimed that enterprising KPNLF cattle rustlers were fitting Bata boots to the feet of appropriated bovines so as not to leave telltale hoof prints leading across the border. Another report indicated that stolen pigs were being forced to drink beer and then stuffed into sacks so that the inebriated animals would be silent when being smuggled over the frontier.[21]

There were some isolated instances of joint resistance operations during the first two quarters of 1986, yet they were not the kind envisioned by the JMC or condoned by the Exco. On 19 January, two ANS battalions for the first time linked up with Khmer Rouge elements and attacked a PAVN company in Battambang province. The next day, two companies from the ANS 2 Brigade joined with the Khmer Rouge in attacking another PAVN position in the same province.[22] Showing little appreciation for the taint conferred by Pol Pot's troops, the noncommunist Voice of the Khmer radio station announced on 28 March that the KPNLF's 234 Battalion had staged a joint operation with the Khmer Rouge. The next month, ANS guerrillas operated alongside the Khmer Rouge while attacking PAVN in Siem Reap province.[23]

Such joint operations with the Khmer Rouge might have made tactical sense on the battlefield, but cooperation between the noncommunists and the Khmer Rouge could be seen only as a public relations gaff. Not only did it allow PRK propagandists to discredit the noncommunists by association; it was the kind of negative publicity that could easily allow congressional opponents of the Solarz aid initiative to derail that effort.

As it turned out, those opponents were being handed more proverbial ammunition from within the KPNLF itself. Historically, the Front's border camps—bloated with desperate refugees, magnets for black marketeers, and surrounded by unruly Thai paramilitary guards—had been plagued by human rights abuses. Arguably none had been worse than Nong Chan and Camp Rithysen and, by association, their resident warlords Chea Chhut and Liv Ne.[24] Chea Chhut's rapsheet included everything from extortion to murder; on one occasion, he directed his brother-in-law, who was also one of his battalion commanders, to execute a refugee for the unforgivable offense of touching his daughter's hand. In the case of Liv Ne, many of his excesses were in fact traced to his wife, who was said to run local black-market activities and relentlessly henpecked her husband in public. Accusing Liv Ne of infidelity, she reportedly had her thugs apprehend the alleged mistress and had a crude penis tattooed across the girl's face.

Brian "Doc" Dougherty (left) and Harold James Nicholson at the Hilton, 1985. Given his later betrayal, Nicholson's choice of shirts is prophetic. (Author's collection)

After Nong Chan and Rithysen had been razed, guerrillas and refugees slowly began to repopulate these sites over the course of 1986. Both of the controversial commanders soon returned to their previous positions of power—and resumed their track record of ethical breaches. In the fourth quarter of 1986, their excesses had belatedly come to the attention of Capitol Hill after being highlighted in a critical report submitted to Congress by journalist Al Santoli.[25]

There was a problem, however. In his report to Congress, Santoli had ladled blame on the Sak faction, alleging that the PCCS had rebelled because it opposed Son Sann's efforts to bring an end to the human rights miscarriages. Not only was this a gross misreading of the background to the rift; in fact, the two warlords most closely identified with border brutality—Chea Chhut and Liv Ne—had publicly declared loyalty to Son Sann. Unwilling to alienate any of the chieftains supporting his faction, Son Sann had made no attempt to rein in their behavior.[26]

For his part, Sak was trying desperately to reinvigorate his General Staff. Back in July an exhausted, demoralized Dien Del had suddenly opted for introspection. Shaving his head at Site 2, he entered the monkhood for what turned out to be a three-month stint. With Dien Del temporarily gone from the lineup, Sak toyed with changes to the KPNLAF leadership during the second half of 1986. Concurrently, word of the congressional criticism had reached the border, and he was taking the brunt of the blame. Pretending to address the problem, Sak on 19 November released a communiqué claiming he had dissolved two battalions

Target practice at Aranyaprathet, 1986: Harold James Nicholson, Jim Parker (kneeling), and unidentified communications officer. (Author's collection)

for human rights abuses and that their commanders had fled to the interior. But the announcement was without specifics, and in reality no such disbandment had taken place. On 24 December, in yet another attempt to show a civil face, the general sat down with Son Sann to brainstorm a solution to the rift. Neither was in a giving mood, however, and the talks went nowhere. It was a fitting end to a dismal year.[27]

As the noncommunist portion of the CGDK floundered, PAVN saw reason for cheer. Seeing it appropriate to start thinking about final victory, PAVN in June 1985 held a conference at Tan Son Nhat airbase during which time the director of the Combat Operations Department outlined a five-year, two-phase plan to hand over full responsibility to the PRK and remove all Vietnamese troops from Cambodia. During the first phase, covering 1986–1987, they would withdraw up to two-thirds of their soldiers.[28]

By late 1985, however, this schedule was looking a bit too optimistic. The Vietnamese, in fact, faced some serious underlying issues, part of which could be pinned on Mother Nature: Cambodia had suffered a severe drought during the peak of the 1984 growing period, followed by torrential rains that devastated harvests in 1985.[29]

But many more of their troubles were self-inflicted. For one thing, there was the PRK's highly unpopular conscription law that targeted males between seventeen and twenty-five, as well as some unmarried females. Back in 1984, the Vietnamese estimated that 2,000 PRK soldiers per month were defecting along the border, even though PAVN was doing most of the fighting.[30]

For another thing, the K5 border defense network was taking a massive economic toll. In early 1985, the government prepared certificates of appreciation for nearly 400,000 civilians, militia, and state workers forced to participate in its construction. Of this number, a whopping 90 percent had succumbed to tropical diseases—and possibly as many as 10 percent died from malaria and accidents.[31]

Making matters worse, the K5 border plan almost from the start proved to be a flawed strategy. It was conceived as a tropical version of the Maginot Line, but it was exceedingly porous in practice; black-market smugglers, not to mention CGDK guerrillas, soon weaved paths through the minefields and other border obstacles. Moreover, PAVN units were concentrated along the border to assist with the construction of the K5 barrier through the second half of 1985, leaving large swaths of the countryside denuded of troops. This allowed CGDK troops—primarily Khmer Rouge—to congregate with virtual impunity in the interior.

It was not until early 1986 that PAVN realized this glaring shortcoming. In February 1986, it introduced Mi-24 helicopter gunships—the menacing, wasp-like airborne tanks made infamous in Afghanistan—against Khmer Rouge pockets near the Tonle Sap Lake. Extensive use of armed choppers and An-26 bombers continued around the Tonle Sap through midyear.[32] Still, the Khmer Rouge was ready for a fight and in many cases more than held its own. During two separate instances near Battambang's Mongol Borei district during the fourth quarter of 1986, it decimated entire PAVN companies.[33]

With the Khmer Rouge by far the most aggressive element within the CGDK, the Exco redoubled efforts in 1986 to enhance the performance of the noncommunist resistance. For their part, the Malaysians were still taking mixed classes of thirty KPNLF and ANS students for guerrilla training; in a nod toward the JMC, the Malaysians instituted a buddy system whereby the factions were coached in mixed pairs. Meantime, the Singaporeans in 1986 restarted domestic production of the M-16S1 rifle. Some 10,000 were produced in this batch and split evenly between the KPNLF and ANS.[34]

Outside of the Exco, the British SAS was still busy at Phitsanulok. Beginning in the second quarter of 1986, it began offering an advanced commando course to mixed classes of twenty-four ANS and twenty-four KPNLF members.[35] Focusing on command and control, the SAS added a deputy commander and an additional demolitions expert to each team, making for a total of six guerrillas.

As with earlier cycles, the Cambodians bonded well with the British instructors. Although the Thai authorities were doing a good job of keeping this program shielded from the media, there was one major lapse in security at Phitsanulok. During a morning jogging session, the Cambodians passed a second group of Asian students in the midst of a commando course. The Cambodians eventually learned that they were Lao anticommunist guerrillas being trained by the RTA Special Forces; the RTA, apparently, wanted an effective Lao guerrilla proxy in the event that border skirmishes, which had flared in 1984, reoccurred.

Also outside of the Exco, China had started training members of the noncommunist resistance. Not surprisingly, hundreds of Khmer Rouge had already cycled through China, mostly for armor and artillery courses. In a trial program, five members from the two noncommunist factors were sent in 1985 to Guangzhou for nine months of medical training. The next year, another seventeen members drawn from these two factions departed for the same course.[36]

As for the CIA, several of its Cambodia programs were ratcheted up slightly during the course of 1986. At Aranyaprathet, Jim Parker had finished his tour at midyear, leaving the base temporarily in the hands of thirty-six-year-old Harold "Jim" Nicholson. Adopted by a Mormon family as a preteen, Nicholson had a rather conservative upbringing. Enrolling at Oregon State University, he attended ROTC and earned a Ranger tab. This he advertised with a crude "RANGER" tattoo across one forearm; colleagues were convinced he had etched the word into his own skin.

After college Nicholson entered the U.S. Army. He had risen to captain in the 101st Airborne Division before switching to the CIA in October 1980. After two years of training as an intelligence officer, his first posting was to Manila, where he was focused against Soviet diplomats. In mid-1985, he moved to Aranyaprathet as the second-ranking officer under Parker.

At the base, Nicholson impressed his fellow CIA officers. "He had a natural talent for espionage," one would later comment. Much of his time was spent in downtown Aranyaprathet, where he rented a room ostensibly in order to cultivate contacts among aid workers in nongovernment organizations.[37] Aranyaprathet, in fact, was fast becoming crowded with agents looking to peddle kernels of intelligence to a growing roster of resident spies and attachés. With a finite number of vetted sources and an insatiable appetite for information from inside the PRK, sharing inevitably occurred: The CIA might interview a promising agent in the morning, then a Singaporean intelligence officer would sit down with the same agent that afternoon.

Nicholson's term as interim chief lasted only a couple of months before the arrival of Parker's replacement, Steve Almy. The younger brother of Dean Almy—a highly regarded chief of station who had served at prominent posts in Asia and Europe—Steve faced a litany of administrative issues while settling into Aranyaprathet.[38] For one thing, the Hilton still maintained its diverse collection of animals and had added several over the past year. Even when the officers tried to trim the menagerie by letting several go—including a pair of monitor lizards and a fox named Twentieth Century—the animals continued to linger on the outskirts of the compound to beg for food.

For another thing, the Thai national hired to manage the compound was found to have embezzled thousands of dollars. His replacement, who had earlier managed a local brothel, turned out to be more honest and efficient.

As before, numerous personalities from Washington continued to file through the Hilton for briefings. Among the highest ranking from the CIA was Robert Gates, who had recently been promoted to deputy director. The director himself, William Casey, was scheduled to make an encore appearance, but he died of a brain tumor in May 1987.

But apart from these visits, Almy saw work at the Hilton as an endless series of refugee and defector debriefings of little consequence. "We were the post that was physically closest to Vietnam," recalled Almy. "But in hindsight, nothing happened."[39]

By contrast, the CIA's involvement with the noncommunist resistance had grown far more dynamic. This coincided with the arrival of a new chief at Bangkok Station, Harry Slifer. A longtime Asia hand, Slifer was no stranger to Cambodia: He had served at Phnom Penh Station in the late 1950s, then was the second intelligence officer assigned to the reopened station during the Khmer Republic from September 1970 through mid-1971.

In 1977, Slifer had gone to Indonesia as chief of Jakarta Station. It was under his watch that the CIA struck gold, recruiting Vladimir Mikhaylovich Piguzov as a defector-in-place. Although listed as a first secretary at the Soviet embassy, Piguzov was actually a KGB colonel. Not only was he intimately aware about the operations of his fellow KGB officers in Southeast Asia; he had driven the car and performed countersurveillance when former CIA officer David Henry Barnett came to Jakarta with an offer to sell secrets to the Soviets.[40]

For Piguzov, the 1968 Warsaw Pact invasion of Czechoslovakia had been a pivotal event. Coming to see the Soviet empire as a glass half-empty, he agreed in the second half of 1978 to a pitch from Jakarta Station. Said one CIA officer familiar with the case: "He was a determined man, a real pro as an operations officer, and prolific. He liked the money, of course. But he also liked the recognition and the sincere thanks he always got from his handlers."[41] In November 1979, Piguzov returned to Moscow and was assigned to the KGB's elite training academy as the communist party representative and adviser. For five years, he knew the names and evaluation of all graduates of the academy—and passed this to the CIA.[42]

Given the untold value of Piguzov's information, Slifer was lauded for his part in handling this case while in Jakarta. Upon return to Langley, this helped propel him to chief of the Far East Division. Peaking at this position, Slifer then voluntarily stepped down a notch to become chief of Bangkok Station for his final few years until retirement.

Very quickly after arriving in Thailand, Slifer made his impact on aid to the Cambodian resistance. Since 1984, two sets of meetings among the foreign supporters of the resistance were being held. High-ranking intelligence and military officials from Malaysia, Singapore, and Thailand gathered for the monthly Exco sessions to plot the direction and tempo of assistance.[43] Below this, focusing on implementation, were meetings by less senior representatives from the same nations; chaired by the RTA's assistant chief of staff for operations, these meetings included intelligence officers from the embassies of Singapore and Malaysia, as well as members of Thailand's National Intelligence Agency and the myriad of covert RTA units linked to Cambodia.[44]

Slifer's predecessor as chief of Bangkok Station, known to his colleagues as Ted, was on extremely close terms with General Chavalit and had limited his involvement in Cambodian affairs to handing over bundles of cash to the RTA officers serving on the Exco.[45] Even Francis Sherry, the station's Indochina chief who was closing out his tour, had not been a fixture at these sessions. Slifer, by contrast, began to regularly show up at the Exco gatherings.[46]

Slifer's presence at the Exco came at a time when U.S. support for the noncommunist resistance was on a slow rise. CIA covert assistance, which started back in 1982, was up to an estimated $12 million as of 1986; plans called for this to possibly double by the next year. At the same time, the congressionally mandated $5 million in overt support began in 1986. In the case of the former, the CIA had opted to limit itself to nonlethal forms of assistance. With regard to the latter, Congress gave the Reagan administration the latitude of deciding whether assistance was to be lethal or not; as with the CIA money, it elected to dedicate the funds to nonlethal support.

To critics of such assistance, the debate over lethal versus nonlethal assistance was laughable. It was little more than a shell game, they said, with the money easily used to reimburse ASEAN members like Thailand, which then doled out lethal support from its own stocks. Even Solarz once remarked that the line was blurred, a "distinction without a difference."[47]

This was true in a sense, at least for the CIA's covert support. This cash ended up at what the RTA termed Project 328, the logistics office that pooled funds from the CIA and some ASEAN members, then used this money to purchase and distribute nonlethal aid—everything from rice to canned beef to cooking oil to camouflage uniforms—for the KPNLAF and ANS. CIA money was also used to build one field hospital each for the KPNLF and Funcinpec.[48] From the start, General Chavalit ensured that a small group of his most trusted RTA officers staffed this project.

For overt congressional support, a different pipeline was used. Beginning in 1986, much of that aid was turned over to the U.S. Agency for International Development (USAID), the U.S. federal agency primarily responsible for administering civilian foreign aid. During that year, USAID used the cash to fund the training of 440 members from KPNLF and Funcinpec in such subjects as landmine detection, food technology, printing, nursing, and local government.[49]

The remainder of overt congressional aid was given to a new RTA office codenamed Project 287. This office was headed by the urbane Special Colonel Ayupoon Karnasuta. A graduate of Pennsylvania Military College, Ayupoon came from a wealthy family with close ties to Field Marshal Praphat Charusathian, Thailand's powerful codictator during the early 1970s. Between his family's gilded connections and Praphat's push, Ayupoon's career initially flourished as he landed a string of choice assignments in the RTA Special Forces and military intelligence.

Once Praphat was ousted, however, Ayupoon's career trajectory wavered. After a tour as attaché in Singapore from 1982 to 1985, he returned to Bangkok to find that he was being overlooked and the best jobs were going to graduates of the RTA military academy. In 1986, aimlessly roaming the proverbial halls, he bumped into Lieutenant General Suchinda Kraprayoon, who had just been promoted to RTA deputy chief of staff. At Suchinda's suggestion, and with few other options, Ayupoon took the job as the first head of Project 287.[50]

In many respects, Ayupoon was an enlightened choice. Hailing from a family that was already fabulously wealthy, he had little incentive to siphon Project 287 funds into his own pockets. And fluent in English with considerable overseas experience, he moved easily among the Exco crowd.

As head of Project 287, Ayupoon found its mandate little different from that of its sister program, Project 328. He, too, was charged with purchasing such innocuous items as uniforms, agricultural supplies, foodstuffs, and propaganda equipment like radios and cameras. These were to be provided to both the noncommunist guerrillas and their civilian dependents, including those inside the PRK. The only difference was that he was required to keep scrupulous financial records that were audited by USAID personnel.

At times, the oversight was stifling. "They once asked for transport receipts from KPNLF guerrillas along the border," Ayupoon recalled. "It amounted to pennies."

On another occasion, the USAID representative quibbled over tobacco purchases. The noncommunist guerrillas saw this as a necessity on par with other food staples. USAID, however, insisted that tobacco was a luxury and thus not eligible for U.S. funding. This sparked a protest from the highest levels of the resistance factions; eventually the RTA was forced to divert funds from its own coffers to cover the bill.

By contrast, Ayupoon got whiffs of far less immaculate bookkeeping at Project 328. There were indications, for example, that camouflage uniforms were being grossly marked up by Project 328 officers. Francis Sherry, in his final months before retirement, had received the same information and cornered Chavalit during a meeting. "What are your uniforms made out of," he chided, "gold thread?"

Harry Slifer was especially concerned over such procurement improprieties, especially with plans afoot to hike the amount of covert CIA aid to the resistance. In order to add accountability, he brought in a CIA officer who would provide logistical assistance for the Exco. Receiving that assignment was Thomas Fosmire. Within the Far East Division of the Directorate of Operations, Fosmire had been one of its most experienced paramilitary operators for a quarter of a century. Beginning with an assignment to Thailand in the early 1950s to establish the elite PARU police airborne unit, he had gone on to advise Indonesian rebels in 1958, train Tibetan tribesmen in the early 1960s, then work with Lao guerrillas for most of the remainder of that decade. During the final months of the Vietnam War in 1975, he had been assigned as a deputy base chief in the Mekong Delta, from where he helped evacuate key indigenous personnel when Saigon fell.[51]

Two years later, Fosmire, like literally hundreds of fellow intelligence officers, fell victim to the so-called Halloween Massacre when the Carter administration ordered the CIA to gut its covert ranks. The CIA director at the time, Stansfield Turner, would later claim that 820 intelligence officers were sacked as part of an effort to shift the agency's focus away from clandestine action and toward analysis; some CIA insiders, however, put the number closer to 2,800. Undisputed was the fact that the CIA's roster of paramilitary officers was practically eliminated.

Four years later, with the Reagan Doctrine demanding covert support for a growing number of anticommunist guerrilla movements, the CIA found itself hard-pressed to provide paramilitary experts. Fosmire and dozens of former colleagues were suddenly hired back on contracts and dispatched to hotspots around the globe. Fosmire himself was soon shuttling between Pakistan and Honduras to offer his expertise on supporting the mujahideen and the Contras.

In 1986, at age fifty-five, Fosmire added Thailand to his itinerary. Reporting to Bangkok Station on a quarterly basis, he was assigned with examining the Exco's logistical arrangements for the noncommunist factions. As a first step, he visited the warehouses that had been built in Aranyaprathet near the KPNLF compound.

He was appalled with what he saw: At the building housing lethal aid, weaponry was stored in a haphazard fashion and explosives were leaking on the shelves. The storeroom for nonlethal equipment was little better, and it was obvious that no proper inventory had been performed in years. He quickly implemented several remedial measures: "I began marking U.S.-funded equipment with the unit's name and keeping records. Then when a guerrilla unit was ready to go on a mission, I took photos of the men with their equipment, noting if anything was missing. Medical kits and radios were checked, even the crystals were counted."[52]

It quickly became apparent that this would be a full-time task. To double the coverage, a second contract officer, Jerry Kilburn, was assigned to the project. A former major in the U.S. Army Special Forces during the Vietnam War, Kilburn had then gone to work for the Vinnel Corporation training the Saudi Arabian National Guard. After three tours he got tired of the desert and went back to the U.S. government to instruct guards at atomic energy plants. But this, too, was hardly to his liking, so he jumped at the chance to shift to the CIA for the Thai assignment.

As Fosmire and Kilburn roamed the border crossing points, they soon were dubbed *The Tom and Jerry Show*, after the cartoon about the long-suffering feline. As CIA aid had been used to buy a shipment of camcorders, they instructed the guerrillas to use these to film their incursions so that they could better corroborate their exploits—and document their use of radios and other U.S.-funded items for the duration of their forays.

But when even this failed, Fosmire and Kilburn took to touring Aranyaprathet's central market to look for items sold by the guerrillas. "Invariably we turned up the odd piece of marked gear," said Fosmire. "We would bring these back to the Cambodian commanders, wave a finger at them, and give them the sternest warning we could muster."

12. Détente

As Tom Fosmire and Jerry Kilburn roamed the border to document guerrillas and their gear, the reality was that relatively few noncommunist combatants were heading into the interior. In the case of the ANS, part of the problem might have been attributed to the heavy workload foisted upon Ranariddh. Triple-hatted, Prince Ranariddh had tried to foist off the chief of staff post to General Toan Chay in May 1986, but Sihanouk insisted on keeping the army a family affair and would not certify the appointment.

Another part of ANS's problem was a shortage of weapons. As of mid-1985, it claimed to have 11,093 men, of whom 8,536 were armed. By the close of 1986 it had recruited almost 2,000 additional fighters—but was able to put less than 100 of these new guerrillas under arms.

The noncommunists were also complaining that Task Force 838 was micromanaging their struggle. The KPNLF found this especially grating: Unlike the free hand given to the Khmer Rouge, they accused the RTA of demanding that it approve all of their tactical plans before implementation. The KPNLF additionally accused the Thai of rationing ammunition and supplies so that only short forays were possible. These criticisms had reached all the way to Singaporean Prime Minister Lee Kuan Yew. Making a secret trip to Aranyaprathet for an 838 briefing, Lee made a pitch for fewer restrictions on the noncommunists. "Treat them like the Boy Scouts," he implored Chavalit in extremely simplistic terms. "Let them run around, explore, and learn."[1]

But much more than smothering RTA oversight, the KPNLF had only itself to blame for the full-blown paralysis that had set in within the Front. As of the opening of 1987 its leadership feud was as shrill as ever, due in large part to the fact that Son Sann and Sak each thought he had the upper hand. In the case of Son Sann, he took strength in his grass-roots popularity among the civilian masses at Site 2. Such popularity was understandable among a displaced population craving for role models. Compared to the corrupt chieftains who had long dominated the border, Son Sann was renowned for his frugal lifestyle. And among his guerrilla peers who took multiple wives and too often were abusive alcoholics, Son Sann shunned womanizing and was a teetotaler.[2]

But as much as Son Sann had a solid following among the refugees, Sak dominated the military ranks. Tied to this, Son Sann was starting to feel the pinch as money from foreign donors was increasingly channeled to underwrite Sak. Back in March 1983, the Exco had turned over 1,227,684 baht to the KPNLF's executive committee for monthly expenses; from this, Son Sann retained most and parceled out a relatively small share to his military. By July 1986, this division had been reversed: Son Sann's executive committee got only 505,922 baht; the rest of the KPNLF's monthly allowance was handed straight to Sak.

Even at Son Sann's power base—Site 2—Sak was making inroads. On 14 January 1987, the general initiated a reorganization within this three-square-kilometer camp. A new deputy chief of staff for civilian affairs was now placed in charge, overseeing a council of pro-Sak sector chiefs.

With his war chest fast dwindling and Site 2 under new management, Son Sann blinked first. On 16 February, he ventured north of Aranyaprathet to the new KPNLAF headquarters at a remote site nicknamed "Klang Dong." Located in the Ta Phraya district of Pranchinburi province, the location had been chosen by the RTA because it was situated in virgin forest bracketed by imposing mountains, thereby lessening the chance of the Cambodian guerrillas coming into contact with Thai villagers.[3] And unlike the original KPNLAF headquarters at Ampil, which was always vulnerable to PAVN attack, Klang Dong was located some 25 kilometers inside Thai territory and unlikely to fall victim to a cross-border raid.[4]

Offering an olive branch of sorts, Son Sann stayed at Klang Dong long enough to present Sak with the KPNLAF command flag at the latter's new General Staff compound. The move was ripe with symbolism, as it confirmed that Son Sann once more officially recognized Sak as commander-in-chief of the KPNLF's military.

With this formality out of the way, Sak on 4 March announced a major overhaul in leadership. Dien Del, his hair having grown back after his sabbatical as a monk, was named to the new position of deputy commander-in-chief. Sak also placed Dien Del in charge of a campaign to root out black-market activities and corruption within the KPNLF ranks.[5] This move was deemed especially necessary after the U.S.-based Lawyers Committee for Human Rights, a nonprofit human rights group that supported refugee rights around the world, issued a highly critical report in February that once again highlighted the excesses of the chieftains Chea Chhut and Liv Ne.

On that same day, Sak elevated sixty-five-year-old General Pok Sam An as chief of staff. Pok had been without a formal portfolio for more than a year, but he had been profitably spending that time brainstorming various ways to revamp the KPNLF. One of his ideas was implemented the following day, the KPNLAF anniversary, when Sak presided at Klang Dong over their first formal promotion ceremony. Seven officers were presented with the stars of major general: Thou

Thip,[6] who had earlier commanded the General Reserve troops at Ampil; Keo Chuon, who had headed Nam Yuan base in the northeast; Pann Thai, the Special Forces commander; Prum Vith, who still held the southern base at Sok Sann; the problematic Liv Ne, who had moved back into the Rithysen vicinity at Nong Samet; and the equally problematic Chea Chutt, who once again was holding court at Nong Chan. Two others were named brigadier generals: Sopheak Rachana, a former Khmer language teacher; and Chum Cheang, a former economics student during the Lon Nol regime.

To accommodate assignment of these new generals, Pok divided among them nine military regions covering the entire country. But the effort was largely a farce, as the KPNLF had only the narrowest of toeholds at a couple borderpoints. In only a couple of cases did the region commanders have even a fleeting presence within their designated zone. For instance, Major General Prum Vith, whose writ barely went beyond Sok Sann in the south, now commanded Military Region 4 extending across Koh Kong and Kompong Som. Most of the other military regions were complete works of fiction that existed only on paper. For example, Major General Pann Thai, operating from an isolated Dangrek outpost in the northwest, now ostensibly was in charge of Military Region 9 covering Siem Reap, Kompong Thom, Kratie, and Mondolkiri.[7]

Sak and Pok, of course, knew their military regions were a notional exercise. However, the exercise served another purpose: As six of the nine new generals (all except Thou Thip, Pann Thai, and Sopheak Rachana) had publicly professed sympathies toward Son Sann, their promotions were part of the healing process between the factions.[8]

Bringing a halt to the KPNLF's rift was all the more critical as its fighters, tired of internecine squabbles, were starting to vote with their feet. A growing number were either opting for civilian life or, in an indictment of the abuse at Site 2 and Sok Sann, taking the dramatic step of shifting to camps controlled by Khmer Rouge. And in January, some 300 KPNLF combatants under the leadership of Men Pheng marched to Site B and announced their intent to join the ANS.[9]

This defection to Site B, more than anything, was a firm indicator that the JMC partnership between the noncommunist factions was effectively dead. Rather than trying to promote cooperation with the ANS, Sak, Pok, and the rest of the KPNLAF's leadership were increasingly looking inward to shore up their own weakened organization. This became apparent especially in the intelligence: The JMC's intelligence department under Kong Thann was more or less stillborn. At the same time, the KPNLF's original intelligence unit, KISA, had atrophied in

Scarf worn by APPCO members, 1987. (Courtesy Gaffar Peang-Meth)

recent years and was now focused solely on counterespionage at Site 2.[10] Seeing the need to fill a strategic intelligence niche, Sak on 14 January signed a decree establishing a new KPNLF unit: the Bureau of Intelligence, Research, and Documentation (BIRD).

Building BIRD from scratch was a familiar face: Kim Sakun, who commanded the final Republican outpost atop Preah Vihear back in 1975. He had been living a quiet life in the U.S. Pacific Northwest before getting a visit from two CIA officers in 1985. Urged to return to the border and offer his services to Sak, he accepted the challenge—only to spend the next two years without a clear portfolio. Although not the original choice to lead BIRD, Kim was quickly elevated to the top slot within weeks after Sak issued the original decree.[11]

To map out BIRD's structure, Kim was given a small office close to Sak's residence at the KPNLF compound in Aranyaprathet. On paper, the bureau was to have a support office, an analysis wing, and an operations section. Although BIRD was eventually able to fill these with 101 staff members split between Aranyaprathet, Klang Dong, Site 2, and the various border crossing points, it was beset from the start by crippling problems. Funding, for one thing, was never adequate. At the time of its establishment, Task Force 838 conservatively estimated that BIRD would require a budget of about $10,000 each month. In reality, the Exco never provided more than $1,000 in any month, and it often handed over as little as $350—not even enough to cover administrative costs let alone fund any significant agent operations into the PRK.

For another thing, there was endless bickering among the overlapping intelligence bodies run by the noncommunists. Kong Thann, who headed the JMC's intelligence office, did not get along with the chief of KISA; for good measure, he also clashed with Kim Sakun. Further complicating matters, KISA was angry that BIRD had pilfered some of its best officers.[12]

Despite all this, BIRD claimed the occasional success. Not only did it allege to have recruited informants in the PRK bureaucracy; although technically forbidden from spying on its CGDK partners, it also purloined documents from the Khmer Rouge. Copies of these reports were provided to both Task Force 868 and the CIA's Hilton base. Years later, BIRD veterans would boast they had been able to do so in complete secrecy, evidenced by the fact that the PRK government never once exposed BIRD officers in any propaganda. One wonders, however, if this oversight was due to BIRD's laudable discretion—or whether the Phnom Penh authorities saw BIRD and its leaders as too benign to merit greater mention.

As much as the 1987 reorganization within the KPNLF bore the fingerprints of Pok Sam An, it was equally the result of input from Gaffar Peang-Meth. In addition to his role in the JMC, Gaffar had been acting as Sak's cabinet secretary—*directeur de cabinet du commandant-en-chef*—for the preceding year. In May 1987, he received a third hat when Sak announced slots for four deputy chiefs of staff and a string of new departments for military aid, planning, popular alliances and coordination, and military justice.[13] The most important of these, the Department of Planning and Analysis (PLANA), was given to Gaffar. Not only did PLANA include an intelligence oversight role; Gaffar was now officially tasked with conjuring new ways of jolting the KPNLF out of its daze.

To do this, Gaffar had unprecedented support from Task Force 838. Back in October 1986, Special Colonel Surayud had been promoted up and out of the task force, getting stars for major general and being named an aide to Prime Minister Prem. Replacing him at the top of 838 was his deputy, Special Colonel Boonrod Somthat. Known along the border by his callsign "Norasing," the quiet, competent Boonrod was a French-educated Special Forces officer who had also taken over command of Surayud's elite regiment at Lopburi.[14]

Named the new 838 deputy commander was Colonel Nikorn Hamcumpai. The

RTA Colonel Nikorn meets with APPCO guerrillas prior to their first deployment, November 1987. (Courtesy Gaffar Peang-Meth)

first RTA cadet to graduate from the Royal Military College in Australia, Nikorn had entered the RTA Special Forces in 1975 and never left. In 1985, following heightened border tensions with Laos, he had briefly helmed the training of Lao anticommunist guerrillas at Phitsanulok. Switching to the Cambodian theater and using the callsign "Pisanu," Nikorn had grown especially close to Gaffar, and between them they attempted to chart the KPNLF's medium-term future.[15]

In theory, the KPNLF should already have been experiencing gains. Its new base at Klang Dong, after all, featured three training centers that could turn out a total of 1,200 guerrillas each month. The officer academy, formerly at Ampil, had also been relocated to Klang Dong; this institution ultimately graduated ten classes of cadets, more than any other CGDK faction. In addition, Task Force 838 had established a training center for both the KPNLF and ANS inside the RTA base at Pakchong district, Nakhon Ratchasima province. Staffed by RTA instructors, this base offered instruction to noncommunist company commanders and gave specialized courses in skills like sniping.

But this still was not translating into more guerrillas crossing the frontier, much less establishing a meaningful presence inside the PRK. Back on 11 January 1987, Nikorn had ventured to Klang Dong to meet with the KPNLAF General Staff and deliver what amounted to a peptalk. The Soviets and Chinese were secretly meeting to cut a deal on Cambodia, he warned the guerrilla leaders, and the KPNLF was not going to factor into a settlement if their performance did not improve. He admitted that Task Force 838 had been conspiring with the KPN-LAF top brass to publicly—and falsely—proclaim the Front was making progress. In reality, said Nikorn, top Thai officials, not to mention foreign representatives at the Exco, were increasingly irate with 838 for not squeezing gains out of the KPNLF.

"Cambodia is your country. Liberation is your business," he implored. "We are here to help."[16]

Thinking creatively to enact such gains, Gaffar began to pass Nikorn a stream of requests to take up with the Exco. Some showed innovation. For example, could KPNLF guerrillas be provided with special grease to coat railroad tracks in the PRK and bring its train network to a slippery halt? Or could their guerrillas be outfitted with crossbows to assist with silent assassinations? (Neither was provided.)

Some ideas were more fanciful. Could the Exco get the KPNLF remote-controlled boats and planes that could be loaded with explosives and rammed into PAVN positions? After hearing this Nikorn chided Gaffar, "What books have you been reading?"

Eventually Gaffar settled on the theme of psychological warfare, where mental shrapnel replaced real bullets with steel jackets. Already, the KPNLF had armed propaganda teams in its roster that, as their name suggested, handed out leaflets and gave lectures at select villages in the PRK. They also prepared brochures and cassettes in the Vietnamese language, though none of the teams were sufficiently confident (or foolhardy enough) to directly deliver their message to a PAVN outpost.

What Gaffar had in mind, however, were teams with far better training that could not only expound on psychological themes and recruit sympathizers but also be skilled in demolitions and sabotage.[17] After instilling a nationalist, non-communist spirit among the rural populace, these operatives could then attempt to transform public dissent—especially against the K5 border defense plan—into an armed insurrection. To jumpstart this "people's war," the teams would also be able to set off demolitions and conduct other acts of sabotage against government targets. Left unstated was the fact that the vast mandate given these teams would demand of them polar opposites: To build a network of sympathizers they needed to act in the shadows, but by setting off explosives and conducting sabotage they would attract attention and court a crackdown from the authorities.

Regardless, the Exco liked what it heard and offered fast support. So did the KPNLAF General Staff, with General Pok lending official approval on 22 July to a pilot program that was being called Armed Political, Psychological, and Clandestine Operations (APPCO).

Perhaps realizing that the APPCO mission was too diverse, the concept morphed during its early weeks. By late July, it called for twelve-man teams to be specialized in one of three areas: sixteen teams would focus on sabotage, thirty would be experts in psychological and political indoctrination, while others would be "administrative focus groups." A total of fifty-nine teams—some 708 men—would enter the PRK together and support each other for months on end. Infiltration initially was set for the August rainy season.

Already, Gaffar had chosen ninety-six initial APPCO recruits. All were young and untrained. One especially cherubic candidate, claiming to be sixteen, was more interested in playing at a nearby stream. "I caught him with his pockets filled with frogs," recalled Gaffar. "He was probably not a day over thirteen."

For this first wave, the KPNLAF General Staff had created the Office for Psychological Operations at Site 2. The cadre from this office drilled the APPCO inductees through early August, after which they endured a second phase of training in basic military skills at Klang Dong. Only then did each candidate receive more specialized training, such as demolitions or sniping. Meantime, a second wave of ninety-six recruits began the psychological operations course at Site 2.

By late August, the original launch date, the two APPCO contingents had been whittled down to thirteen teams totaling 156 men. Revised plans now called for them to be spread over much of the interior—three teams to Siem Reap, two to Kompong Thom, two to Kompong Cham, two to Pursat, two to Kompong Chhnang, and two to Battambang—where they would link up with KPNLF agents already in place. They were then to cause turmoil in towns and cities before and during the United Nations General Assembly session in late September.

Bureaucratic delays ensued, however, and the September launch date slipped to October, then November. Equipment for the APPCO program had already been stockpiled by that time, including cameras, tape recorders, loudspeakers, and wooden mimeograph machines. All members were to be issued a Chinese-made Type 56 assault rifle and a new camouflage uniform with a blue scarf featuring an Angkorian archer. Each team was also provided with two rocket-propelled grenade launchers.

By mid-November, attrition had once again cut into the APPCO roster. Just ninety-seven men remained in the program; from an initial plan of fifty-nine teams, they were now down to eight. But as much as they had shrunk in numbers, mission creep was expanding their mandate. According to their final operational order, six men would guard a hidden weapons cache while the remainder would stage a hit-and-run attack on the Thmar Puok district office. After that, they would head toward Siem Reap and engage in such activities as making leaflets, burning houses, blowing up vehicles, and mining roads. They were to kidnap lone soldiers and train a local militia if possible. There were even plans for them to push on farther to Kompong Cham and make contact with Cham Muslim dissidents. They would have been lucky, of course, to realize just a small fraction of this.

On the evening of 25 November, equipment was issued to the APPCO members. Colonel Nikorn, who had taken an intense interest in the pilot program, showed up with a surprise: solar-powered Morse radios for each of the teams. At 0300, they took trucks from Klang Dong to the border. There they were given a speech by Gaffar and another by Dien Del. Nikorn then shook the hand of each guerrilla as he crossed the frontier. If all went well, they were not expected back to Thailand for another six months.

Despite having patiently nursed the APPCO program over the second half of 1987, Gaffar hardly had time to monitor progress inside the PRK. During the same week they had crossed into the interior, there was an unexpected shake-up in the KPNLAF leadership. Though both Sak and Pok were longtime colleagues, the two had been consistently bickering behind the scenes. Sak had finally lost patience in late November, handing Pok a one-way plane ticket to California. Shaking with emotion, Pok had stormed out of Thailand without bidding a formal farewell.

With the chief of staff position vacant, Nikorn began to champion the idea of Gaffar getting the promotion. He had even gone camp to camp to sound out the regional commanders, only to face stiff resistance from several. This was due to the simple fact that Gaffar was a Cham—not a Khmer, and not a Buddhist. As a seemingly simple solution, one of the Singaporean officers attending the Exco meetings urged Gaffar to make himself more palatable by temporarily entering the monkhood like Dien Del. Gaffar, proud of his ethnic and religious heritage, did not dignify this with a response.[18]

Gaffar probably also counted himself out of the running for another reason. As of late 1987, he had started penning contingency plans not only to focus on the struggle against the PRK but also to redirect part of the KNPLF against its coalition pariahs, the Khmer Rouge. To his way of thinking, if the KPNLF were to stage some pinpoint attacks against the Khmer Rouge, it would make the Front a far more attractive alternative to the average peasant in the PRK. At the same time, he felt that a strike by the KPNLF might incite foot soldiers in the Khmer Rouge to revolt against their officers and widen fissures within Pol Pot's organization.[19] Gaffar believed this needed to be done in order to hobble the Khmer Rouge ahead of any potential peace settlement.

Of course, such considerations, even in whispered tones, were diplomatic poison. Although some ASEAN members, notably Singapore, were intrigued, the Thai wanted no part in any scheming that ran counter to unity in the CGDK. Even Sak emitted nothing but nervous laughter when the topic was raised by Gaffar during an ASEAN tour.

Sak, in fact, was under more pressure than perhaps at any time to date. In addition to the sacking of Pok and conspiring by Gaffar, he had to contend with the fact that the KPNLAF had barely been able to infiltrate any combatants during 1987 other than the modest APPCO contingent.

Compounding matters, the détente with Son Sann at the start of the year had not even lasted the quarter. Back in March, Sak had tried to show a brave face to the media by claiming the Front fielded 20,000 men. Effectively calling the general a liar, Son Sann released a 5 May communiqué placing the actual troop total at a paltry 8,000.[20] Four months later, the renewed infighting again took a toll when 400 KPNLF troops under Su Kin Soon marched to Site B and pledged loyalty to the ANS.[21]

At the BIRD office in Aranyaprathet one afternoon near year's end, the general finally reached his breaking point. While discussing the Son Sann feud with an officer from Task Force 838, tears began to roll down Sak's cheeks. "Don't take me wrong," he said, "but I would rather be in my own home in my own bed in California."[22]

While KPNLF guerrillas were not entering the PRK, others in the CGDK were. Over the course of 1987, the PRK government grudgingly admitted that 21,000 enemies—their byword for the CGDK—were operating inside the country. Even if this was underreported, it was a significant increase over three years earlier when they admitted to only 15,300.[23] The vast majority of this figure consisted of Khmer Rouge, who again were active in Battambang and Siem Reap, and especially along the shores of the Tonle Sap.

In response to this threat in the west, the new head of Front 719, General Doan Khue, had launched an extended offensive in February codenamed T6.[24] Once again, this campaign was noteworthy for some innovative use of airpower. In early October, this included the first use of An-2 biplanes to drop clusters of mortars around the Tonle Sap. That same month, they also used armed Mi-8 helicopters northeast of the Siem Reap provincial capital. Though some caches were reportedly seized, no significant losses were inflicted on the CGDK's most formidable faction.[25]

The Khmer Rouge were not the only coalition guerrillas making inroads. The ANS, too, had enjoyed a relatively substantive year. While their forward headquarters remained at Phnom Sroch, the ANS had been allowed to build a more complete headquarters and training center in Non Din Daeng district in Thailand's Buriram province.[26] Located just across the Sankamphaeng Range from the KPNLAF's Klang Dong camp, it, too, had been chosen because its remote location was far removed from Thai villages.[27] It was not completely desolate, however: "When we were clearing away the jungle, we sometimes encountered communist guerrillas. Some were CPT, some Lao, some said they were Khmer Rouge who had come to attack Thailand prior to 1979 but stayed. They were all hiding, not trying to attract any attention. One group gave us a wild fowl as a peace offering, and they implored us not to reveal their location to the Thai army."[28]

Between refresher training at Non Din Daeng, as well as courses given by the RTA at Pakchong, the ranks of the ANS grew. While its core still consisted of five brigades, Ranariddh had also sanctioned the establishment of a string of autonomous regiments. These were regiments in name only—most consisted of just 300 men—but they served the purpose of rewarding a new crop of younger officers with their own commands. Moreover, in a testament to the allure of Sihanouk's name, one of the new regiments consisted of PRK defectors, while another was built around a company that switched sides from the Khmer Rouge.[29]

Despite losing these men to the ANS, the Khmer Rouge was not publicly bearing any grudges against the Sihanoukists. During February, in fact, it had ratcheted up cooperation with the ANS in the field. This rapprochement enabled ANS guerrillas to penetrate into areas of the interior previously unthinkable. Spearheading this effort had been Chakrapong's 5 Brigade, elements of which had reached Kompong Thom province by the second quarter of the year. It returned to the border in September, but not before establishing the beginnings of a resupply network to support subsequent waves of ANS troops.[30]

Ironically, despite the fact that the ANS was on better terms with the Khmer Rouge than ever before, Sihanouk threw one of his annual tantrums that May—allegedly because the Khmer Rouge had killed two of his men. The Khmer Rouge denied the charge, but not before Sihanouk carried out his threat to take a one-year sabbatical from the CGDK presidency. Ranariddh, in Bangkok at the time, was completely taken by surprise.

In hindsight, Sihanouk most likely had taken his leave of absence for reasons other than the claimed internal CGDK strife. He had no doubt sensed that the international mood was changing with regard to Cambodia. For one thing, the Vietnamese had held their Sixth Party Congress in December 1986. Using the opportunity to enact significant economic changes—not unlike the radical perestroika reforms pushed by Soviet leader Mikhail Gorbachev earlier that year—it appeared as if Hanoi very much wanted to rejoin the international community. As this could not be achieved while still occupying Cambodia, the Vietnamese had added incentive to show flexibility toward a resolution.

For another thing, the PRK was also showing greater flexibility and diplomatic tact. During a meeting in June 1987, their Politburo, chaired by Hun Sen (who now held both the posts of prime minister and foreign minister), decided to go on a charm offensive and proclaim its focus was national reconciliation.

Most were rightly skeptical about Phnom Penh's sincerity. "We have to provide the enemy with sticks so they can fight each other," read one document from the meeting that became public. "We will provide Sihanouk with a stick to beat the Chinese and the Americans," added Hun Sen.[31]

In using Sihanouk as a lever to sow dissent within the resistance coalition, the PRK had picked a good target. Sihanouk, conveniently, had already distanced himself from the CGDK the previous month and was thereby free to pursue his own private efforts at a settlement. Discrete notes were passed to the prince, urging him to consider a meeting with Hun Sen. Appealing to his vanity, the PRK, SRV, and most socialist countries immediately stopped calling him *monsieur*, and instead reverted to his honorific title of *samdech*.

All of this had the desired effect. On 3 December in the northern French village of Fère-en-Tardenois, Sihanouk, flanked by his wife, Monique, and son Ranariddh, sat down for the first time with Hun Sen. Expectations were set unreasonably high and, predictably, no breakthroughs were achieved. Still, the impact was substantial. Perhaps as the PRK had hoped, Sihanouk's erstwhile CGDK partners, all too aware of the prince's history as an unreliable ally, were suspicious of his solo efforts. Son Sann, for one, felt compelled to issue a wordy communiqué that stopped just short of condemning the tryst.

But beyond sparking dissent among the resistance partners, the meeting was important for other reason. Hun Sen, long derided as a Vietnamese puppet, had met Sihanouk on more or less equal terms, significantly enhancing his stature for future negotiations. Just as important, the latest dry-season offensive had kicked off in Cambodia—and for the first time the PRKAF was playing the lead role at the frontline. PAVN, while still very much present, was there in a lesser support capacity.[32]

With 1987 coming to a close, the PRK thus found itself with a strengthened hand. By comparison, the CGDK had one hopelessly crippled noncommunist partner and their diplomatic ace—Sihanouk—preoccupied with his individual initiatives. If this Cold War chapter in Cambodia was slowly heading toward an end game, the outcome was more unpredictable than ever.

13. Limelight

The year 1988 began with a housecleaning inside the KPNLF. It was long overdue. For more than a year, some of its border commanders had been roundly condemned by international human rights activists in the shrillest possible terms. Dien Del had been given the mandate to clean up such excesses but had made little headway over the preceding year.

Impatient, Task Force 838 decided to take matters in its own hands. In early February, Colonel Nikorn beckoned both Chea Chhut and Liv Ne—the two greatest offenders, both from the Son Sann faction—to Aranyaprathet. So as not to appear to be taking sides in the rift, he also called Dien Del and another Sak loyalist, Hing Kunthon. On the pretext of attending a weeklong seminar, all four were bundled into a chopper and ferried to the RTA Special Warfare Center at Lopburi.

One week later, the two pro–Son Sann chieftains were dropped off at the Soi Maiyarap safe house, while the two from Sak's faction were sent to the Soi Saisin safe house. All four were effectively placed under house arrest in Bangkok and expressly forbidden from returning to the border.

Coincidentally, that same month guerrilla stalwart Ta Maing died of natural causes while on a cross-border foray into Siem Reap province. With three military region commanders now gone, Sak used that as an opportunity to once again restructure the KPNLAF. In late February, he consolidated the nine military regions into seven, with three newly promoted brigadier generals taking over the slots left vacant by Chea Chhut, Liv Ne, and Ta Maing.[1] Then in April for reasons not readily apparent, Sak replaced the term "military region" with "operational military zone" (OMZ). Aside from the new nomenclature, each OMZ kept its same number and commander.[2]

The OMZ commanders also inherited the same troops—or lack thereof—that had been under the military regions.[3] In the case of OMZ 4 under Prum Vith, he controlled two 300-man battalions at Sok Sann. Others were somewhat larger, like OMZ 6 at Nong Chan that marshaled four guerrilla battalions. At that point, allowing for the same creative inflation in their order of battle that let the ANS claim it wielded brigades, the OMZ commanders were ordered to redesignate their battalions as regiments. This expansion was largely a paper exercise, of course, with the regiments never controlling more than 500 men apiece.[4]

There was also the issue over what turf the operational military zones actually held. In theory, they still extended across the country. OMZ 1, for instance, supposedly had jurisdiction for Kompong Cham, Prey Veng, Svay Rieng, and Kandal provinces. In reality, the KPNLAF stayed wedded to the smallest of pockets along the western border; during the rare instances they ventured inland, it was usually to protect smuggling routes.

The one major exception during 1987 had been the infiltration of the APPCO contingent. According to plan, the bulk of this group—minus a handful that had gone missing—returned to the Thai border in April 1988. The results of the extended foray were mixed. Though it had reached Kompong Thom as instructed, it had done little to incur the wrath of the PRK authorities. Suspiciously, every team had lost its solar-powered radios; Gaffar speculated they sold them on the black market for easy cash.[5]

But even in this middling performance, the KPNLF saw reason for cheer. Recruitment immediately commenced for a second APPCO cycle, with deployment tentatively set for year's end.

For the rest of the KPNLF's guerrilla roster, meanwhile, results remained decidedly underwhelming. To help turn this around, the Exco in March 1988 opened its checkbook and pledged to General Sak 2 million baht per month for his army, nearly double the previous monthly allotment. With more cash in hand, the KPNLF in June arrived at a novel solution for incentivizing its troops: a menu of rewards for hardware destruction. For every enemy rifle a guerrilla could verifiably destroy, he would receive a bonus of 300 baht. For PAVN or PRKAF artillery pieces, the bonus rose sharply to 5,000 baht. Destroyed tanks earned a whopping 15,000 baht. Assuming this might prompt more guerrillas to seek action, a social fund was also established to pay out 2,500 baht for light injuries, double that for more serious wounds.

As anticipated, several KPNLF guerrillas responded to the bonuses. More than a few went straight for the brass ring, looking to collect for a tank kill. But without effective antiarmor weapons in their inventory the confrontations were invariably lopsided: No tanks were destroyed, and the would-be tank-killers were almost always removed from the gene pool.

In the ANS, somewhat better gains were seen during 1988 without having to resort to cash inducements. By year's end, it was conservatively estimated that the total strength of the Sihanoukists was fast approaching 21,000. Of this number, almost 15,000 were armed and inside the PRK; the remainder straddled the border.[6]

Of those inside Cambodia, roving ANS bands were now regularly making extended forays into provinces like Kompong Thom and Siem Reap. One 120-man unit from 6 Brigade had even clashed with PAVN in Kampot, nearly on the SRV border.[7]

In many cases, the key to success was infiltrating in tandem with the Khmer Rouge. Though Sihanouk was still issuing the occasional rant that his guerrillas were being victimized by Pol Pot's troops, the fact was that the Khmer Rouge protective umbrella was often the only thing enabling the ANS to make serious inroads. This caused confusion in the minds of the peasantry, who in many cases failed to see the difference between the typical ANS and Khmer Rouge guerrilla—especially as both were armed with identical Chinese weaponry.

The noncommunists recognized this dilemma and very much wanted to differentiate themselves from the Khmer Rouge in both appearance and philosophy. On a purely visual level, one way they sought to do this was by outfitting their guerrillas with Western weapons. And of all the Western weapons, none was more identifiable than the M-16. Problem was, the CIA was providing nonlethal aid only and had no intention of refitting the noncommunist guerrillas with American-made assault rifles.

Back in 1982, the Singaporeans had somewhat addressed this issue by turning over a single shipment of their locally produced M-16 rifles to the KPNLF. But by early 1988, ANS and KPNLF leaders began leaning on the Exco to provide non-Chinese weapons in more substantial numbers. In April, Ranariddh had even made a public pronouncement urging his foreign donors to help the noncommunists transition to Western weapons.[8]

For whatever reason, the Exco was reluctant to significantly alter the noncommunist arsenal. China, by contrast, was—and it had the perfect firearm in mind. Back at the start of the decade, the state-owned China North Industries Corporation—abbreviated as Norinco—had manufactured a near-perfect clone of the M-16 rifle. Known as the Norinco CQ, this copy was sold to the anti-Soviet mujahideen in Afghanistan, apparently because China thought (incorrectly, in hindsight) that the United States would be providing large amounts of 5.56mm ammunition to those guerrillas.

During the second half of 1988, as part of one of its occasional infusions of military aid, China shipped 10,000 Norinco CQ rifles to the noncommunist Cambodians. This number was split evenly between the ANS and KPNLF. The irony of it all was staggering. The noncommunists had been seeking to demonstrate support from the West, only to have a communist nation—China—supply them with a copy of a Western weapon.[9]

Elsewhere along the Thai-Cambodian border, 1988 had seen other instances of housecleaning. Stung by foreign criticism of human rights abuses at the refugee camps, Thailand had taken several steps to make improvements. In late 1987, Thai merchants first began to enter the sprawling Site 2 camp. Then in March 1988, a framework for legal markets was established at the camp, thereby helping curtail the corruption tied to black marketeering.

The next month, the organization that had been providing security around the refugee camps, Task Force 80, was summarily disbanded. This task force had faced a steady stream of condemnation from human rights groups in recent years, largely because it employed paramilitary Thai rangers that too often preyed on those they were mandated to protect.

In its place, the Supreme Command of the Royal Thai Armed Forces established the aptly titled Displaced Persons Protection Unit (DPPU). Unlike their predecessors in Task Force 80, the seven companies recruited by the RTA for the DPPU were to be funded by the United Nations. Supplemental aid, such as the provision of uniforms, was to be handled by the U.S. State Department.[10]

Significantly, the DPPU was to be largely unarmed and limited to camp perimeters. Within the camps themselves, the United Nations turned over security to Khmer police forces that were to be raised by the CGDK faction that held jurisdiction over that particular camp. For example, a KPNLF police force would patrol within Site 2, while a Khmer Rouge police force would be responsible for Site 8.

To assist with the formation of these police forces, the United Nations formed a Special Liaison Team. This team, deployed along the border by late 1988, consisted of two members of the Australian Federal Police, a British cop, a Finnish officer, and a U.S. Army colonel. The U.S. member of the team, Charles "Denny" Lane, had served multiple tours in Thailand and was fluent in both French and Thai. Now wearing a blue cap while seconded to the United Nations, Lane found himself in the unusual position of working with all of the CGDK members while they attempted to write a legal code for Cambodian policemen operating on Thai soil. He was especially struck by the Khmer Rouge, whose camp officials regularly outshined their noncommunist counterparts. Explained Lane: "The Khmer Rouge camp leaders were elected and knew the problems in their respective camps. Those in the KPNLF and ANS were appointed and, for the most part, could have cared less about the people under their patronage. When traveling along the border, I often encountered Cambodian hitchhikers. They were often Khmer Rouge, and would insist on going back to their own camps."[11]

Hilton members in 1988. From left to right: Davis Knowlton, Charlie Bulner, Brian Dougherty, and Dennis Elmore. (Author's collection)

The dubious ethics of KPNLF camp commanders was highlighted near year's end, when the four guerrilla leaders under house arrest in Bangkok unilaterally decided to return to the border. Both Dien Del and Hing Kunthon resumed their former roles without fanfare, while Liv Ne decided he had enough of soldiering and retired to Site 2. In the case of Chea Chhut, however, he tried to wrest back control over his stronghold at Nong Chan. To his credit, Sak wasted no time issuing an arrest order. This prompted Chea Chhut to recruit thirty followers and announce he was going inside the PRK to carve out a liberated zone near the Tonle Sap. But the logistics for this proved daunting, so the unrepentant warlord instead marched north and, like several others before him, swapped shoulder insignia and joined the ANS.

A housecleaning of sorts was also being experienced at the Hilton in Aranyaprathet. This coincided with the arrival in 1988 of Davis Knowlton as the new base chief. Born into military royalty, he was a direct descendent of the founder of Knowlton's Rangers, America's first special forces unit formed during the Revolutionary War. More recently, his father William had commanded a division in Vietnam and ended his illustrious career with four stars. With this lineage, Davis Knowlton by all rights should have enjoyed a prosperous career in the army. But after serving a tour with a reconnaissance company in the 101st Airborne Division in Vietnam, he left the service, let his hair grow past his shoulders, and took up with a motorcycle gang in Florida.

Several family interventions later, Knowlton joined the CIA in 1976 to get cleaned up. The agency's operations directorate was being gutted by the Carter administration at the time, with plans being discussed to retain its dwindling number of paramilitary experts as a reserve cadre of sorts. Given his military background, Knowlton initially was headed in that direction. On his initial overseas deployment, he was assigned to Saudi Arabia to work on a joint paramilitary program directed against North Yemen. But switching to more traditional foreign intelligence work, a string of South Asia postings followed, including India and Bangladesh tours, then two more years in Saudi Arabia.

Upon arrival at Aranyaprathet for a two-year assignment, Knowlton was not impressed by most of what he found. For one thing, he rated most of the Cambodian staff to be of suspect quality. Several were polygraphed; one turned out to be passing information to the Khmer Rouge. Knowlton ended up firing the majority.

For another thing, the Hilton was far too open to be a debriefing operation for a denied area. He immediately put an end to the frequent visits by members of the U.S. Defense Attaché's office. He even placed the base off limits to other members of Bangkok Station who were working with Task Force 838 and the noncommunist resistance. "I did not want to be yanked down if and when they fell afoul of the Royal Thai government," he reasoned.[12]

Which is exactly what happened. For years, in fact, all had not been well with regard to U.S. aid extended to the noncommunists. On the overt side, things were stable enough. Staying under the proverbial radar, Congress continued to approve roughly $5 million in nonlethal Solarz aid on an annual basis. This largely went into the Economic Support Fund overseen by USAID, which, thinking ahead to give the noncommunists viable skill sets during peacetime, was almost fully used on border courses for KPNLF and ANS members. Some 1,114 Khmer had been trained during 1988, with new classes added in various medical topics.[13]

Added to this, USAID began to handle sporadic infusions of so-called McCollum aid. This was named after the Florida Republican, Representative Bill McCollum, who had championed an amendment to the Pentagon's 1985 authorization bill that called on the U.S. Air Force to collect excess nonlethal military supplies at American military bases around the world and deliver it to Pakistan for the mujahideen.[14] During Fiscal Year 1988, McCollum's legislative director, a Vietnamese-American with more than a passing interest in Southeast Asia, arranged for $3 million to fund airlifts of excess gear to Thailand for distribution to the KPNLF and ANS. For Fiscal Year 1989, the amount of funds for airlifts had been raised to $13 million. Both the McCollum and Solarz aid initiatives were coordinated through Project 287 under Special Colonel Ayupoon; with USAID accountants constantly peering over his shoulder, Ayupoon's ledgers, not surprisingly, were meticulous.

On the covert side, however, there had long been whispers about abuses of CIA funds. This was set against the heavily politicized backdrop of the RTA's top leadership, specifically the rise of General Chavalit and his entourage. Back in October 1985, Chavalit had been promoted to RTA chief of staff, and it was widely expected he would be named army commander when the incumbent, General Arthit Kamlang-ek, retired in September 1986. But Arthit frequently clashed with the powerful Prime Minister Prem and had even lobbied to have his term extended into 1987 in order to outlast Prem's stint as prime minister.

Faced with such insolence, Prem had enough. In a shocking announcement without precedent, Prem on 27 May 1986 abruptly fired Arthit and elevated Chavalit to the top of the RTA. (Arthit retained the largely symbolic post of Supreme Commander of the Armed Forces, which Chavalit also inherited when Arthit retired in September.)

Chavalit soon proved to be a different kind of army commander. He was the first to reach this position after graduating under the Thai military academy's West Point–style curriculum. He was also a full six years younger than Arthit. The fact that he had been able to rise from an obscure signal corps staff officer to army chief in such a short period spoke volumes about his close personal relationship with Prem.

But Chavalit's meteoric rise was also due to his longtime control of Thai-Cambodian border policy. This allowed him not only to make himself known among the foreign diplomatic and security community but also to utilize whatever resources might be available to an officer in charge of a sensitive border—and in pursuit of political gains.[15]

To be sure, Chavalit had been the godfather of the Cambodian resistance since its inception. As he was promoted to bigger and better things, he had ensured that his acolytes controlled most of the programs in support of the guerrillas. Chief among them was Lieutenant General Wanchai Ruangtrakul, Chavalit's academy classmate, who began chairing the Exco meetings after being promoted to deputy army chief of staff in September 1985.

At the same time, Chavalit also retained tight control over Project 514, a covert antinarcotics program done in concert with the CIA out of the northern city of Chiang Mai. At the core of this project, the CIA paid for nine companies of Chavalit's paramilitary Rangers for use during cross-border raids against drug warlords in Burma.

Combined, these programs gave Chavalit and his inner circle access to tens of millions of dollars in U.S. funds. As with many such covert programs where tight financial oversight was not always possible, some inefficiencies in spending were to be expected. Even when rumors began to reach Bangkok Station that the losses might be considerable, the status quo persisted for years.

But by 1987, several factors conspired to focus unprecedented light on the situation. First, Station Chief Harry Slifer had fully settled into what was to be his sunset tour. Already a regular at the Exco gatherings, he had taken considerable interest as to how CIA money was being spent. Contract officers Tom Fosmire and Jerry Kilburn were still making occasional visits to the border, but they were focused on inventories and distribution—not purchasing, which was Slifer's main reason for pause. And because he did not have to fret about a career trajectory after Bangkok, Slifer could pursue these concerns with little worry about stepping on toes.

Second, Slifer shifted his capable deputy, Joe Murray, down the hall and placed him in charge of Cambodian operations.[16] A seasoned Asia hand, Murray had started his CIA career in Laos during 1965, spending a year at an isolated guerrilla base just across the border from the infamous valley of Dien Bien Phu. He had been lucky to survive the tour: His Pilatus Porter on one occasion was riddled by machine-gun fire when checking on a remote outpost; the pilot had been barely able to limp back to friendly territory.

After taking time off for schooling in Taiwan and Singapore through the late 1960s, Murray had shifted to South Asia for a string of tours extending more than a decade. He had most recently finished a stint as station chief in wartorn Kabul, where he spent his time dodging stifling KGB coverage while meeting the handful of communist emissaries left on Afghanistan's lean diplomatic circuit.

In 1986, Murray took leave of decrepit Kabul for bustling Bangkok. After a year as Slifer's deputy, he elected to become—as his colleagues dubbed him in jest—"Mister Cambodia." Like the nickname implied, from that point forward he was the station's point man for its various programs targeting Cambodia. Almost immediately, problems were apparent. He recalled:

RTA Special Colonel Ayupoon and CIA officer Joe Murray (center) during a Working Group dinner, 1989. (Author's collection)

> Reports were accumulating over time, and I could see something was amiss. The guerrillas were going across the border with almost nothing. In one case, a team went in wearing little more than their underwear, and they were supposed to stay for more than sixty days. When U.S. aid was a couple of million, perhaps it was meant to be only a political gesture. But when the aid levels went up, and the reputation of the U.S. government was on the line, and lives were involved, it got my attention.[17]

There was a third factor at play as well. During the September 1987 reshuffle of top RTA officers, Suchinda Kraprayoon entered the Five Tigers when he got his fourth star and was named assistant army commander. Not as outwardly ambitious as Chavalit, Suchinda was nevertheless astute and easygoing. But more than that, he was the leader of the especially large and influential Class 5 of academy graduates, many of whom gained divisional commands in the reshuffle. Although Class 5 a year earlier had been supportive of their seniors in Class 1—including Chavalit and Wanchai—the 1987 round of promotions made them a power in their own right.

With this enhanced clout, Suchinda in late 1987 elbowed his way into control of the RTA's Cambodia programs and began chairing the Exco. He was closely assisted by Special Colonel Ayupoon, whom he had personally placed in charge of coordinating overt U.S. aid the previous year. Like Murray, this pair could immediately sense that all was not right on the accounting side. Scratching the surface, in fact, they found indications of massive overcharging in Project 328, which included nonlethal supplies covertly funded by the CIA. For example, the CIA was apparently being charged more than three times the going rate for locally produced camouflage uniforms. Prices for vegetable oil were almost doubled; salt and salted fish were higher still. And while the CIA was paying for good quality rice, the resistance was getting kernels rated as animal feed. The bottom line: Of the $12 million covertly funneled by the United States in 1987, more than a quarter was being lost due to corruption.[18]

Outside of Project 328, Suchinda also identified pilfering of Chinese aid to the Khmer Rouge. If anything, this was on an even larger scale. By 1987, as much as 40 million baht per month was being handed over by the Chinese embassy to the RTA in order to purchase staple foods for the Khmer Rouge. Of this, up to half was being siphoned into personal coffers.

By the opening of 1988, Suchinda had a sufficiently good grasp of the problem to begin remedial action. Two senior officers helming Project 328 were removed, though both—backed by Chavalit—continued to interfere from the sidelines. In addition, some of the initial findings were shared with Joe Murray, whose own inquiries were leading to similar conclusions.

Simultaneously, Station Chief Slifer had started a probe into Project 514 at Chiang Mai. When he tried to eyeball the nine Ranger companies ostensibly being funded by the CIA, only four could be produced. As well, some of the personnel were collecting double CIA salaries: one as guards, another as Rangers.

This was the last straw. Slifer immediately took steps to halt further funding for Project 514. With regard to the Cambodian resistance, he and Murray drew up a blacklist of suppliers most guilty of markups. For a time, local tailors were shunned and camouflage uniforms were sourced out of South Korea. Slifer then prepared a new budget for future covert nonlethal funding. To signal the RTA of his displeasure, Slifer slashed the amount requested for Fiscal Year 1989 by a quarter, from $12 million down to $8 million. This was probably not as dire as it sounded: Theft had accounted for almost a fourth of the earlier figure; if Suchinda could reduce markups, the resistance would still be getting nearly the same amount as before.

After Slifer and Murray finished cleaning up the books in Thailand, they reported their progress to Langley at the end of the first quarter of 1988. The CIA's liaison team on Capitol Hill then briefed the House and Senate intelligence oversight committees—which promptly threw a fit after the fact. In mid-1988, a stream of staffers from both committees filed through Bangkok to pour over the CIA's records. "I had excellent ties with all of them," said Murray, "but by that time everything was already accountable."

The staffers agreed. On 12 July, they issued a report to the members of the Senate Select Committee on Intelligence detailing $3.5 million in losses over the previous fiscal year but noting that adequate auditing measures appeared to be in place.

Coincidentally, just two weeks prior to issuance of this report a tragedy had taken place with direct implications to the scandal. On the afternoon of 28 June, Colonel Supachai Rodpothong had boarded an RTA Huey chopper in Bangkok and headed for the Cambodian border. A combat engineer by training, he was a trusted Chavalit loyalist and had played a lead role in Project 328 until falling afoul of Suchinda during efforts to root out corruption. But shielded by Chavalit, Supachai continued to interject himself into 328 and was scheduled that day to tour resistance training sites. His chopper flight, however, was reportedly delayed so that he could catch the televised broadcast of Mike Tyson's much-hyped heavyweight bout with Michael Spinks in Atlantic City.[19]

It would prove a fateful decision. Getting to the border later than planned, Supachai did not reboard the chopper until midafternoon for the flight back to Bangkok. The weather had turned foul by that time and, flying into dark skies, the pilot hit high-voltage wires on the outskirts of the capital. All six passengers and crew died in the wreck.

Supachai's funeral was attended by several senior members of the noncommunist resistance. Though posthumously promoted to general for his good service, his untimely death had provided a convenient scapegoat for the corruption scandal. Supachai, went the whispers, had been tied to the missing funds and carried any secrets to the grave. Those farther up the food chain could thus maintain their innocence.

The U.S. ambassador to Thailand, William Brown, was not so easily satiated. In one of his last acts before finishing his tour, he, along with Station Chief Slifer, met with Prime Minister Prem for thirty minutes in mid-July and outlined their concerns over the theft. Though Prem was more focused on legislative elections slated for 24 July, he realized the necessity of implementing reforms to Washington's satisfaction. Some oversight had been exerted by the Exco, but that forum was meeting at most twice a month and most of its members—like Slifer—had much more on their plates than just Cambodia. Though the Exco would continue to provide high-end policy guidance, Prem authorized creation of a new, more focused forum—called, simply, the Working Group—that would provide oversight on a daily basis.

For its part, the RTA assigned to the Working Group some of its best and brightest. Named chairman was Major General Surayud, the highly principled former 838 commander who had been serving as Prem's aide for the past year. Special Colonel Boonrod, the French-trained officer who had also served a stint as 838 commander, would oversee training programs for the noncommunist resistance. Special Colonel Ayupoon, already in charge of Project 287, now had oversight for all logistics and funding to the noncommunists. Special Colonel Teerawat Putamanonda, a graduate of Virginia Military Institute who had just finished a tour as attaché in Australia, was named politico-military liaison with the Ministry of Foreign Affairs. Finally, Special Colonel Nareunart Kampanartsaenyakorn, a Sandhurst graduate, was named an adviser for public relations. They all operated from an upscale residential compound off of Soi Chereonporn in the Phayonyotin section of the capital.[20]

From the CIA, Joe Murray was named the U.S. representative to the Working Group. Several highly competent intelligence officers and military men from Singapore and Malaysia were also assigned. As they were all dedicated solely to the Cambodian project, they huddled at Soi Chereonporn several times a week; in the case of Murray, he had daily interaction with the "brutally honest" Ayupoon.

The impact of the Working Group was almost immediate. During an audit by U.S. Senate staffers in mid-September, they found solid evidence that the Working Group's monitoring procedures were effective. Because of this, most of the CIA's Fiscal Year 1989 funds were being frontloaded for distribution during the last quarter of 1988.

To that time, both the funding scandal and the subsequent reforms had been handled in private. Chavalit, who on 1 October had been extended as both army commander and supreme commander of the armed forces, had his loyalists largely removed from the Cambodian equation—but on a personal level he had been allowed to emerge with his reputation barely tinged.

At the end of that month, however, the Cambodian scandal very much entered the public realm. On 30 October, the *Washington Post* ran an investigative piece titled "How Scandal Almost Sank Our Secret Cambodian War." In it, the two authors generously ladled out details of the scam, the CIA probe, and the Senate audits. It noted that when the Senate oversight committee found out $3.5 million had been skimmed, some congressional members wanted to kill the program outright.

The scoop had an immediate impact in Washington. The White House panicked and reflexively pointed the finger at Democrats in the Senate, accusing them of the media leak. The State Department also panicked, with Morton Abramowitz, the deputy secretary for intelligence and research, calling in one *Washington Post* editor to convey Foggy Bottom's concerns.[21]

The fallout in Bangkok was equally sharp. The RTA top brass went into denial mode, unconvincingly claiming to have no knowledge of the markups. Losing the most face was Chavalit, who lashed out at the *Washington Post* and told its unnamed sources to "go to hell."[22] His sentiments were echoed by a band of protesters calling themselves the Thai People's Interest Protection Group, whose twenty members burned an effigy of the *Post*'s editor outside the U.S. embassy.[23]

Behind the scenes, the once exceedingly close ties between the CIA and RTA grew strained. In particular, bad blood for a time coursed between Slifer and Chavalit. The Thai daily *Naew Na* claimed that Chavalit unsuccessfully demanded that Slifer be expelled from the county. "It did not enhance our careers," concluded Joe Murray. "But maybe in the longer run it led to a more mature relationship."

It also led to a new round of brainstorming within Bangkok Station to see how the Cambodian support program might be made more efficient. It was at that point that Bill Lair, the legendary paramilitary operator who had managed the CIA's shadow war in Laos, reentered the scene. Lair had retired back in 1978, having spent all but two years of his CIA career in Thailand. Heading to the United States while his children attended college, he had settled in his native Texas. But it was hard to get Thailand out of his blood and in late 1988 he returned to the kingdom on vacation. Wandering through his old haunts in the U.S. embassy, he chanced upon Murray and was brought up to speed on the trial and tribulations of supporting the noncommunist Cambodian resistance.

Offering to think outside the box, Lair was put on a six-month contract to formulate ways of stretching the CIA's limited covert aid to the guerrillas. This was the second time Lair had been asked to work his magic in Cambodia. The first time, in 1973, he had suggested that his allies in the Thai Border Patrol Police, whose elite paratroopers had performed magnificently in Laos, be allowed to take over covert assignments in the Khmer Republic. The idea fell flat.

Though more than a decade had passed, Lair's suggestions this time around were not all that different. Touring the Khmer border camps with the Border Patrol Police commander, he came back to Bangkok and wrote up a report stating that the police were ready and willing to take over the duties of Task Force 838.[24] The reality, of course, was that the all-powerful RTA saw support of the Cambodian resistance as its turf. To think that it would concede its monopoly to

Major Powpong from Task Force 838 poses with a KPNLF team, circa 1988. The team's heaviest weapon is the 82mm mortar. (Author's collection)

the police in any meaningful way was sheer folly. Not surprisingly, Lair's policy recommendation went nowhere.

Beyond missing CIA funds, Surayud's Working Group from the start faced a myriad of challenges. In particular, there was growing realization among its members that the clock was ticking and that the war in Cambodia was approaching the endgame sooner rather than later. The deciding factor, of course, was Vietnam's occupation force. Ever since 1982, PAVN had made annual claims that it was slowly withdrawing its men from Cambodia. Through at least 1986, however, these were little more than troop rotations and the overall size of its Cambodia contingent barely wavered.

In 1987, however, things began to change. That year, PAVN saw far more troops heading east into the SRV rather than the other direction—with the size of its contingent perhaps being reduced by as much as 20,000 men.

In late June 1988, PAVN claimed its latest drawdown. This time an estimated 12,000 crossed the eastern frontier, still leaving another 120,000 inside the PRK. Hanoi was promising to withdraw this sizable remainder by no later than December 1990.

Prince Chakrapong (center), commander of 5 Brigade, and Duong Khem (right), commander of 1 Brigade, circa 1988. (Courtesy Nhek Bun Chay)

There were some reasons to believe this promise might not be all bluff. For one thing, Hanoi remained eager to reenter the international economy in a meaningful way and had no chance of doing this for as long as its troops occupied Cambodia. This meshed well with the new Royal Thai government—led by Chatichai Choonhavan, the kingdom's first elected prime minister in a very long time—which made no secret it wanted to transform Indochina into a marketplace and was throwing hints it wanted to soften its hardline approach toward the SRV.[25]

For another thing, the PRK was arguably showing steady gains in competence. This was largely due to the deluge of skilled students returning from scholarship in the SRV, Soviet Union, and other communist nations toward the end of the 1980s. Its military, too, had certainly benefited from the steady provision of overseas training and equipment. Augmenting them was a parallel formation of combatants raised by the PRK Ministry of the Interior—so-called A3 troops, which were spread one battalion per province, plus a five-battalion reserve.[26]

PAVN troops, of course, were still present in a support role and taking losses. In a surprisingly candid press conference in Ho Chi Minh City on 30 June, Lieutenant General Le Kha Phieu, the deputy commander of Vietnamese troops in Cambodia, had for the first time quantified their casualties. From 1979 through the end of 1981, he revealed that 15,000 PAVN troops had died on Cambodian soil. From 1982 through mid-1988, they had suffered another 10,000 fatalities. Though this number was high (by comparison, only 15,000 Soviet troops had died in Afghanistan during the same time frame), Hanoi could take some comfort in the fact that the average monthly number of fatalities had fallen to about a quarter of the pre-1981 rate.[27]

Given Hanoi's litany of half-truths in the past, members of the Working Group were hardly ready to take PAVN's 1990 withdrawal pledge as gospel. Still, they intuitively felt the time was right to ratchet up efforts to expand the sizes of the noncommunist armies so as to give them a chance at approaching their rivals in the PRK, not to mention the Khmer Rouge. Even taking into account the reduced level of covert CIA funding, they hoped to boost the KPNLAF and ANS at an ambitious monthly pace of 1,000 new guerrillas apiece beginning in the final quarter of 1988.

In the case of the ANS, this target was not seen as unreasonable. For the KPNLAF, however, there were problems. In an 11 December letter to the Working Group, Sak detailed efforts by the Son Sann faction to derail his recruitment efforts. Back in August, wrote Sak, Son Sann claimed he was assembling a rival force of 5,000 troops for a postsettlement peacekeeping force, plus another 6,000 for refugee camp defense. Dredging up a name from the past, it was alleged that General Thach Reng would lead these troops. Son Sann vowed he would provide salaries and good weapons for the entire number, even though he clearly lacked sufficient funding. These same hollow claims were repeated by his senior aides in October, then again in leaflets distributed in the refugee camps during early December. The KPNLF feud, quite obviously, was alive and well.

Then there were issues between the KPNLAF and ANS. Over the course of 1988, an effort had been made to resuscitate the dormant JMC. This had culminated with an official relaunching of the JMC on 12 October, then, two weeks later, with preparation of the top secret "Operational Plan for the Non-Communist Resistance for 1989." The plan, which was presented to the Working Group, called for creation of a mixed tactical staff and ambitious funding in 1989 for a defector program targeting PRK troops.[28] But with seemingly no political will in either camp to push for any true merger, the JMC officers ended up using it as little more than a talking shop to enact the most basic levels of coordination.

Sihanouk himself was hardly helping matters. Back in April, he had penned an editorial for Funcinpec's official bulletin in which he publicly harangued his KPNLF coalition partners for opposing "Sihanoukism" and sabotaging his efforts to resolve the conflict.[29] Then in July he abruptly left the presidency of the CGDK, the second time in as many years.[30] From Sihanouk on down, the noncommunist leadership was proving its own worst enemy.

Somewhat better news came from Phitsanulok, where British SAS instructors continued to turn out semiannual commando classes. The only minor snag was the increasingly cramped quarters at Phitsanulok: Aside from Burmese and Vietnamese partisans being trained there by the RTA Special Forces, yet another contingent of Lao guerrillas arrived in early 1988 after a brief, bloody border war with Laos led the RTA to contemplate using them for behind-the-lines raids.[31] Because the presence of the SAS instructors—and the Cambodians—was supposed to be secret, the decision was made for them to transfer to a more discrete location. Shifting south, an isolated stretch of jungle was cleared in Saraburi province, close to the RTA Special Forces headquarters at Lopburi.[32]

The move to Saraburi, it turned out, was less than auspicious. A good part of the difficulty could be pinned on the RTA Special Forces team assigned to administer that jungle site. The head of that team, Major Powpong Ponglaokam, was no stranger to Cambodian affairs. He had served with Task Force 838 since its inception, and he was the only member of the task force to grow fluent in Khmer. He was especially close to the KPNLF and was lauded by their top officers.[33]

But at Saraburi, Powpong proved an uncompromising disciplinarian. Very quickly, the forty-eight Cambodian students began to rebel, first complaining about the poor food being served, then—bristling at the slight to their nationalism—refusing to stand when the RTA began playing the Thai anthem during morning reveille. A mutiny nearly ensued, with the Cambodians and Thai, both armed, staring each other down.

Taking on the role of diplomat, the head of the SAS team, Major Chris Banks, worked overtime to bring about reconciliation. In the end, Powpong ratcheted down his discipline a notch, the Cambodians agreed to be less vocal about their complaints, and the commando training continued on schedule.

During the same time frame that tempers were flaring in Saraburi, the Task Force 838 leadership was increasingly irate over the heat they were taking for the nonperformance of the noncommunists. Though true that the ANS was getting inside Cambodia, more often than not they were spreading leaflets rather than initiating any attacks. Out of frustration, the task force in early 1988 had come to the conclusion that the KPNLAF and ANS needed RTA members not only to train them and review tactical plans but also to actually integrate themselves into the noncommunist ranks and join them across the border on missions. "We needed to inspire them," said Colonel Nikorn, the 838 deputy commander. "To steel them in battle."

This line of reasoning led to the establishment of Task Force 909, a new secret unit composed of ninety-eight members of the RTA Special Forces. Led by Nikorn himself, he numbered his task force in honor of King Bhumibol Adulyadej, the ninth monarch in the Chakri Dynasty. Six-man teams from 909 were to be assigned to each of the ANS brigades, as well as several of the KPNLAF regiments.

As might be expected, Task Force 909 started off slowly. On its initial cross-border foray, fifteen RTA commandos tagged along as Prince Chakrapong's 5 Brigade made its way toward Kompong Thom province. In hindsight, the imbedded Special Forces advisers had no discernible impact. "We couldn't get them to be more aggressive," admitted Nikon. "So we ended up just taking lots of pictures."[34]

Task Force 909 escorted several additional ANS missions over the course of 1988. Most accomplished little apart from some minor psychological warfare efforts. During the first quarter of 1989, Nikorn switched the task force's focus to the KPNLF. Given the Front's three-year stupor, he would have been forgiven for setting his expectations exceedingly low. What happened next, however, changed the course of the war.

14. Phnom Penh Spring

As 1989 opened, Son Sann figured it was a good time to dust off a tired refrain from years past and reiterate his status as KPNLF commander-in-chief.[1] On a roll, he had another of his loyal generals, Keth Reth, start peddling around Bangkok a wishlist of weapons he deemed necessary for the KPNLAF. The list was heavy on U.S.-made equipment, including 200 FIM-43 Redeye surface-to-air missiles and 3,600 M72 antitank rockets. Given that Washington had been reluctant to provide any lethal aid, much less relatively sophisticated rockets and missiles traceable to the United States, and especially in such quantities, it showed precious little appreciation for geopolitical realities.

The Working Group, of course, was hearing none of this. It continued to coordinate with Sak on all things military. It even insisted that the KPNLF's portion of Solarz aid—largely used for training—be directed exclusively to the Sak faction.[2]

For his part, Sak continued to soldier on despite the brickbats being thrown by his intraparty rivals. To recognize sacrifices among his men, he oversaw a 20 January presentation ceremony during which eighty-four medals for bravery were handed out. Then on 5 March, the KPNLAF anniversary, he conducted another mass promotion to boost morale, elevating 5 more officers to general, another 5 to colonel, and 128 to midranking officers.

As it turned out, these promotions had the opposite of their desired effect—or at least with a scrappy colonel named Khuon Roeun. A decade earlier, Roeun had started his military career as a midlevel Khmer Rouge officer in Pursat province, only to pragmatically abandon that cause in early 1979 and lead more than 100 Khmer Rouge defectors toward the border. There he ultimately merged them with the KPNLF, where they became known as Battalion 212. Appropriately, he was named the battalion commander.

In this position, Roeun never strayed far from the action. He was in the forefront when PAVN hit Non Mak Mun in 1980. Two years later, some of his men were fingered for assassinating camp commander Ta Luot. And it was his battalion that shouldered some of the heaviest fighting around Ampil through 1985.

But while Roeun more than held his own among his KPNLF peers on the battlefield, he had been less than successful when it came to currying favor among the Front's leadership. This was apparent during the first round of KPNLF promotions in 1987, when Roeun was elevated only to colonel while some of his less accomplished colleagues landed general's stars. Denied a slot as an OMZ commander, he was instead placed in charge of a regiment.

To be fair, Khuon Roeun was not given control over any ordinary regiment. As part of the 1987 reorganization, a Special OMZ had been established directly under the General Staff. This OMZ handled two special regiments—numbered 801 and 806—which were designated as the KPNLAF's elite intervention units. Roeun commanded the first of these—Special Regiment 801—which was actually little more than his old Battalion 212 augmented by a few hundred recruits.[3]

Special regiment or not, Roeun was left stewing at his lesser appointment. Complaints to Sak elicited some words of sympathy but no change in his rank. Worse, he was again overlooked during the 5 March 1989 mass promotion. Spurned for a second time, Khuon Roeun's temper edged toward the boiling point.

Meantime, those 5 March promotions had been intended by the KPNLAF General Staff as an inducement prior to a series of cross-border stabs to take place later that month. Ambitiously titled Operation Liberation One, these were to take advantage of intelligence that PAVN had fully withdrawn 30 kilometers from the border, leaving behind only scattered PRKAF border outposts. This operation was to be the KPNLF's grand reentry into the guerrilla business, snapping several years of preciously little paramilitary activity inside the PRK apart from some benign propaganda forays.[4]

Khuon Roeun, however, was impatient. Taking to the bottle on the night of 5 March, he decided that he would flaunt his mettle by jump-starting Operation Liberation One on his own. Shortly before the following dawn, he and his men of Special Regiment 801 surged across the frontier and pushed toward Ampil Lake. This was familiar territory to him, as his old battalion had skirmished around that body of water for years.

This time, there were changes. PAVN was indeed gone from the lake vicinity, but the PRKAF had brought forward four 76.2mm field guns, establishing a firebase with a sizable stock of ammunition near its embankments. These did little to deter the seething Roeun, however, who led his men through the bush and quickly raced around the lake's perimeter. Taken fully by surprise and showing little appetite for conflict, the PRKAF defenders sprinted inland.

When Roeun radioed back that he was in control of Ampil Lake—and that he had captured the KPNLF's first artillery pieces—there was ample shock among his compatriots. That same afternoon, several truckloads of senior officers—as well as a delegation from Task Force 838—rushed across the border to congratulate the wiry colonel and raise the KPNLF flag over the fallen PRKAF base.

The Task Force 838 representatives, speaking on behalf of the Working Group, were in an especially generous mood. Looking to promote the KPNLF's newfound spirit of aggression, they announced that the participating guerrillas would get monetary rewards. For leading the attack, Roeun was handed the keys to a Toyota pickup truck.

Roeun almost didn't live to live to enjoy this largesse. Piling into the cab of his new truck with eight bodyguards in the rear, they barreled down the dirt road leading back toward the Thai border. Swerving a meter off the lane to avoid an approaching vehicle shuttling in more RTA delegates, they triggered an antitank mine. The blast threw Roeun through the windshield and flung his guards across the bush. All survived, the colonel after a two-week stint in an Aranyaprathet hospital. His pickup, gifted just hours earlier, was left a twisted heap of scrap.[5]

While Roeun remained temporarily out of the game, the remainder of the KPNLAF rushed to join Operation Liberation One. Over the next five days, more than 10,000 of the Front's guerrillas hit a dozen border targets.[6] A few, like Yeang Dangkum, were familiar KPNLF haunts from previous years. On some of their deeper penetrations they placed mines, one of which was detonated by a vehicle carrying the PRKAF military region commander in Battambang.[7]

None of these gains were lasting, however. On 12 March, the PRKAF scrounged up enough reinforcements to head back to the border in force. Its advance was unopposed: The KPNLF had already withdrawn into Thailand, hauling along the four 76.2mm artillery pieces. Still, Operation Liberation One had been like an epiphany for the Front. It had confirmed that PAVN had indeed vacated the border region and that, toe-to-toe, they could outmaneuver and even outmatch the PRKAF in modest set-piece skirmishes.

What's more, its aggression had proven lucrative. Eager to reinforce success, the Working Group lavished the guerrillas with cash. A total of 169,000 baht was distributed as rewards for Liberation One, along with eight Toyota trucks (one of which had already been destroyed). The bulk went to the vanguard Special Regiment 801: Roeun's whiskey-stoked bravado earned his men a princely sum of 108,000 baht.

For very different reasons, Liberation One had also been an epiphany for the Phnom Penh regime. Back in December 1988, the Vietnamese had conducted their seventh partial troop withdrawal from the PRK. Though Hanoi's claims always left room for healthy skepticism, it was estimated that their overall troop strength in Cambodia was indeed down and had probably dipped below 100,000 men.

But it did not stop there. On 7 January 1989 during a ceremony to celebrate the tenth year since Phnom Penh was liberated from the Khmer Rouge, the SRV's communist party boss, Nguyen Van Linh, announced that Vietnam would withdraw all of its remaining troops by that September. Earlier they had spoken of a late 1990 deadline; the fact that Hanoi had brought this forward by more than a year made clear their mounting desire for an accelerated exit.

For the PRK regime, this underscored the impending reality that it would soon be facing the CGDK with little or no PAVN crutch. Its immediate response to all this was to dangle an olive branch toward Thailand, no doubt in an effort to appeal to the probusiness mind-set of Prime Minister Chatichai. On 25 January, Hun Sen paid a private visit to Bangkok at Chatichai's invitation. Shortly thereafter, the PRK Council of Ministers formed the Committee for Cambodian-Thai Cooperation.

Three months later, Hun Sen launched what came to be known as the Phnom Penh Spring. After dropping hints over the first quarter about impending reforms, the PRK on 30 April promulgated a new constitution and renamed itself the State of Cambodia (SOC). This entailed a series of cosmetic changes: a new SOC flag and new SOC anthem, for example. But some of the changes were far more substantial. For instance, Buddhism once again became the state religion. In addition, private property was recognized and a market economy theoretically established. Shortly after midyear, foreign investment was officially welcomed.[8]

If the SOC intended its Phnom Penh Spring as a means of chipping away at its economic and diplomatic isolation, Washington was not listening. In a telling visit one month before the new constitution was promulgated, Stephen Solarz—the godfather in Congress of the noncommunist resistance—had ventured to the Cambodian capital in an effort to determine whether the reform pledges—and the PAVN withdrawal—were genuine. He departed the country unconvinced.

Indeed, Operation Liberation One had left Washington policymakers with newfound enthusiasm for hiking assistance to the SOC's noncommunist opponents. At almost the same time Solarz was in Phnom Penh, Prince Ranariddh was on a lobbying junket in the U.S. capital.[9] The highlight of this was a ten-minute unscheduled meeting with a supportive President George H.W. Bush. Hints were also dropped that the United States might provide weapons to the noncommunist resistance, provided it could guarantee the Khmer Rouge did not come back to power. The Bush administration, in fact, had suddenly taken a very aggressive

KPNLF guerrillas demonstrate a Chinese-made 120mm mortar on the border, 1988. (Courtesy Dennis Elmore)

stand in support of Cambodia's guerrillas. The U.S. ambassador in Bangkok, Daniel O'Donohue, was somewhat confused by this hawkish turn:

> During the Bush administration in the United States, there was a drive to "unleash" the noncommunist Khmer resistance. In other words, this was a combination of the views of Congressman Steve Solarz and some analysts of various backgrounds, all saying that we should arm the noncommunist resistance and "unleash" them. . . . Here I was, having to spend much of my time holding these entities together and "keeping them alive." Then, all of a sudden, we were under pressure to arm them, which meant that the U.S. would arm them. The view of some was that, once they were armed, they would have the strength to "turn on the Khmer Rouge" and defeat them. In my mind, this was utterly unreal.[10]

This issue of U.S. lethal aid to the resistance—*covert* lethal aid—soon became a surprisingly public topic in Washington. In late April, just as the PRK was formally rebranded as the SOC, Bush administration officials leaked to the press word about a possible shipment of 12,000 rifles and other light arms to the resistance. Early the next month, Vice President Dan Quayle was dispatched to Bangkok to discuss the issue with Thai officials.

Until that time, the CIA had voluntarily limited its covert aid to nonlethal purchases so as not to court undue congressional scrutiny. The Bush administration, apparently, was confident that it could make the switch while still staying below the radar and free of controversy.

Such calculations were to prove overly optimistic. In late May, the administration informed Congress of its intended shift from nonlethal to lethal aid. But the Senate Select Committee on Intelligence, which until that time had been extending annual consent with almost no reservation, now demanded that the issue be subject to debate. Thus began a shockingly public discussion in Congress over what was theoretically still a covert operation. In the end, the Senate ended up approving lethal aid in principle during July by a surprisingly wide 59–39 margin. When it came before the Senate Appropriations Committee, however, Robert Byrd, the long-serving West Virginia Democrat and committee chairman, stonewalled any funding for arms. Unwilling to expend more political capital on the tough cross-aisle tussle that would have been required, the Bush administration never again seriously entertained the notion of giving weapons to the noncommunists.[11]

Back in Thailand, meantime, the CIA felt relatively little heartburn over the congressional rebuff. The push for lethal aid had been championed by the executive branch, after all; it was not a request that had percolated upward from Bangkok Station. Moreover, the timing of it all was poor: The administration's sudden fixation on unleashing the noncommunist resistance against the Khmer Rouge was not only a death wish for the former—given the massive disparity in their military abilities—but also something that would have dashed the diplomatic network supporting the CGDK at a time when the SOC was certainly weakened but its defeat was far from assured.

At the Working Group level, Joe Murray continued to direct CIA funds toward nonlethal purchases, secure in the knowledge that the noncommunists were already adequately supplied with weapons and lethal training from a growing number of patrons.[12] From among the Working Group members, this included guerrilla classes in Malaysia, as well as a range of combat courses run by the RTA.[13]

Singapore, in particular, was filling many gaps. In addition to rifles, ammunition, and grenades, it started providing the M-203 grenade launchers by 2008.[14] And the following June, after the noncommunists complained about being harassed by helicopter gunships around the Tonle Sap, Singapore's SID used its close ties with Mossad (Israeli intelligence) to source twenty captured Egyptian SA-7 surface-to-air missiles. An initial increment of several dozen ANS students were gathered in Surin and spent one month training with Thai instructors on this new weapon. In the end, however, it was never turned over; ANS commanders speculated that the RTA feared the noncommunists might inadvertently shoot down a Bangkok Airways commercial plane, which had just started twice-weekly flights to Phnom Penh.[15]

There was also significant support coming from outside the Working Group. Topping this list was China. In fact, Beijing by far had donated more military hardware to the three CGDK factions than any other nation. To be fair, the noncommunists received only about one-tenth of the weapons China gave to the Khmer Rouge.[16] Still, some of the largest weapons in their arsenal came courtesy of China; as of mid-1989 this included 120mm mortars as well as a handful of Type 51 antitank rockets.[17]

China was also ramping up its training assistance. As of 1987, it had put two dozen students from both noncommunist factions through a medical course at Guangzhou. On 1 July 1989, thirty ANS students were sent to the outskirts of Beijing for instruction at the Armored Force Institute of the Chinese People's Liberation Army. Though the resistance had no armor in its inventory, China apparently wanted to prepare them for future contingencies. In this, the Cambodians did well: Their Chinese instructors later told them that they mastered in three months what fellow students from Tanzania took two years to grasp.[18]

On a lesser level, training and hardware was also being extended by North Korea. Pyongyang had a long and unusual connection with Cambodia dating back to the especially close rapport Sihanouk had established with North Korean dictator Kim Il-Sung during the 1960s. Though lacking Kim's murderous edge, Sihanouk had many of the same character traits: "They shared similar egos and absurdly grand designs of the superiority of their race and culture, that they had the best answer, aggrieved by every country and major power. They were the two, in their minds, great Asian leaders who were victims of the plots and actions of their enemies and humiliated by the surrounding and great powers. They were truly best friends."[19] The bond they shared had endured through the 1970s. During the first half of that decade, Pyongyang reflexively threw its support behind the anti–Lon Nol resistance coalition ostensibly helmed by Sihanouk but in reality controlled by the Khmer Rouge.

During the second half of the 1970s, however, Kim Il-Sung had a slightly more difficult choice to make. Kim's Democratic People's Republic had always been more of a Confucian religious cult–cum–monarchy than a more conventional Maoist or Stalinist dictatorship—and he had always cut his own unique path through the socialist world. At the outset of the Sino-Soviet split Kim had leaned toward the Chinese, thus irritating the Soviets. Then after China's 1968 Cultural Revolution, he had broken with Mao and sided with the Soviets. Pyongyang had grown economically dependent on Moscow by the 1970s, with more than half of its trade consisting of raw materials and oil provided by the Soviets at concessional prices. Clearly there could be a reasonable expectation that Pyongyang would lean toward Moscow (and, by extension, Hanoi) when tensions began to heat up between the pro-Soviet SRV and pro-Chinese Democratic Kampuchea.

But perhaps predictably, North Korea hardly let Soviet economic support color its foreign policy. In October 1977, Pol Pot ventured to Pyongyang in an effort to shore up support in his quixotic campaign against the SRV. Kim Il-Sung proved happy to oblige, denouncing the Hanoi government as "expansionist."[20] The Soviets, who were keeping the North Korean economy afloat, could only marvel at the lack of gratitude.

By the time the CGDK was formed, Kim Il-Sung remained cordial with the Khmer Rouge and continued to coddle Sihanouk. The prince's palace in Pyongyang was lavish by any world standard, but the contrast was especially stark in the dank North Korean capital. West African and East European diplomats, deprived of ample shopping and entertainment venues, flocked to the compound in order to partake of its posh sitting rooms and movie theater; Indonesian diplomats were constantly on hand to use the palace's badminton courts. Whenever he was in town, Sihanouk flitted among his guests, surrounded by a bevy of family members and retainers, a company of North Korean bodyguards, and two Chinese doctors.

Not until mid-1988 did Kim Il-Sung's brotherly nexus with Sihanouk translate into some modest assistance for the ANS. An initial arms shipment, which the Chinese carried aboard one of their regular seaborne deliveries to the Khmer Rouge, included 7.62mm pistols and some North Korean copies of the Chinese Type 69 rocket launcher.[21]

During July of that year, North Korean aid shifted toward training. Prince Ranariddh, an avid soccer fan, had recently built a soccer field at the Non Din Daeng training base and founded a small Funcinpec league. When he informed his father that the fledgling league was short of qualified sportsmen, North Korea quickly agreed to train two ANS officers in both coaching and refereeing. On 1 August, the designated pair arrived in Pyongyang via Beijing. In the resource-poor North Korean capital, the two were initially afforded meager rations and an antiquated car. This was soon to change, however: "Sihanouk took us for an audience with Kim Il-Sung. At that time Sihanouk directly asked Kim to take care of us. This was like magic. When we exited the meeting, our old car had already been exchanged for a new sedan. Our food rations were doubled for the remainder of our time in the country."[22]

While these changes made their stay relatively more livable, Pyongyang still smacked of the surreal. One night every quarter, the capital would stage an air raid drill: Residential electricity was cut, spotlights were trained across the sky, and artillery pieces were wheeled out from camouflaged caves on the outskirts of the city. On one occasion, the Cambodians attended a massive patriotic rally. Like something out of a James Bond movie, the street near the stadium opened and Kim Il-Sung's limousine rose out of the ground on a hydraulic platform; the beaming dictator was then shuttled only a few hundred meters to his reviewing stand.

In March 1989, as the two coaches were approaching the final phase of their soccer course, they were joined by an additional six ANS officers. Led by a lieutenant colonel, this new contingent was given forty-five days of artillery training on the periphery of the North Korean capital. Just as the Chinese were doing with tanks, the North Koreans were prepping the ANS to handle weaponry they did not yet possess. On 24 April, all eight concluded their instruction and departed Pyongyang for the Thai-Cambodian border.[23]

Ironically, North Korea had an impact on the assistance provided by another donor nation: Great Britain. During 1988, Sihanouk had twice met with British Prime Minister Thatcher. The first occasion had been at the Site B refugee camp on the Thai border; two months later, Sihanouk had ventured to London for the second meeting. On that first occasion, Thatcher could not help but notice that Sihanouk was surrounded by a ring of intimidating North Korean bodyguards.

Sihanouk, in fact, never went to Thailand without his contingent of North Koreans. Totaling forty men, all were unmarried martial-arts experts who had been trained for the role since their early teens. Each had been specially selected and dispatched by Kim Il-Sung himself, a perk North Korea extended to no other foreign dignitary.

Sihanouk took well to this kind of pomp, but the British figured they could do better. Specifically, they conjured the idea of forming a detachment of well-trained ANS bodyguards that would make the North Koreans superfluous. Coincidentally, in early 1989 the SAS had finished coaching the latest cycle of ANS and KPNLAF students in commando tactics at the jungle site near Lopburi. When that SAS team rotated home, it was replaced in July by eight British military instructors who were specialists in training Britain's own Royal Guardsmen.

On the last day of that month, the instructors were met by ninety-one ANS recruits. Leading the group was an especially learned colonel named Hun Phoeung. A medical student during the Sihanouk era, Phoeung was like thousands of his college peers who flocked to join FANK at the outset of the Lon Nol regime. Entering the paratroopers, he saw more than his share of bloodshed on the frontline for two years. He then dropped out to resume his medical studies, where he remained through the end of the Republic. After surviving the Khmer Rouge period, he stayed after their ouster and, with qualified medical personnel in chronically short supply, was named head of the newly reopened hospital at Kompong Som. But two years into the PRK he could no longer tolerate the smothering PAVN presence, so he walked to the border and joined Moulinaka. He had remained with the ANS since its inception, being named the deputy commander of Chakrapong's 5 Brigade.[24]

The ninety recruits under Phoeung had been carefully chosen from across the ANS brigades. Aside from a headquarters staff, thirty-six from this contingent were grouped into three close personal protection teams. Another twenty-four were designated a quick reaction force that included snipers and a 60mm mortar crew. Fourteen more were to be drivers.

In mid-September, training concluded and the newly minted ANS Royal Guard awaited the arrival of Sihanouk.[25] It was also to prove the conclusion to British paramilitary assistance after *Jane's Defense Weekly* on 30 September ran a scoop that accurately reported SAS support to the noncommunist resistance had been taking place since 1985. Other journalists with political agendas leaped on the story, falsely claiming that the SAS had even provided training to the Khmer Rouge. Suddenly in the limelight, the covert project was halted due to the exposure.[26]

As it turned out, the Royal Guard was to have a short, unfulfilling history. In March 1990, it was mobilized for the first time when Sihanouk landed in Thailand and was ushered out to the border to meet delegations from the United States and China. But years of being on the receiving end of conspiracies both real and imagined had left Sihanouk leery of placing his safety in the hands of fellow Cambodians, even those from his own ANS. As a result, his North Korean bodyguards maintained their presence in the inner ring, while the British-trained ANS contingent was kept at a healthy distance. Rejected in their intended role, the Royal Guard was instead turned over to Ranariddh and placed in charge of his compound security. But adding insult to injury, Ranariddh later in 1990 opted to handpick his own twelve-man bodyguard team and sent it out of the country for training—in North Korea.[27]

Curiously, one of the most secretive patrons of the noncommunist resistance was France. This secrecy was probably because France was trying to play all sides: keeping the Francophile Sihanouk placated, while still claiming neutrality toward Phnom Penh and Hanoi—no doubt in part to give Paris a leg up on Western competitors in the emergent Indochina market. Perceived neutrality also allowed Paris to claim impartiality when it had hosted informal meetings among the warring parties.

All this had not stopped key ANS officers from making frequent requests for paramilitary support over the years, most of them directed toward the French embassy in Bangkok. Beginning in 1988, the French had responded with vague promises of arms, but nothing had ever been forthcoming, nor was anything really expected.

In the first week of April 1989, however, that changed when the French intelligence representative assigned to their Bangkok mission arrived at Ranariddh's residence in the Thai capital. From his truck, he turned over crates that included 120 radios, 120 FAMAS assault rifles, and 300 Luchaire rifle grenades.[28]

But the pièce de résistance was a promise to provide the LRAC F1 89mm antitank rocket launcher. With an accurate range of 400 meters, each F1 launcher could fire up to 130 rockets before the fiberglass tube was burned out. Better still, each launcher weighed in at a mere 5 kilograms—perfect for smaller Asian guerrillas hauling it through the bush.

There was understandably some speculation about the timing of the French delivery. Just days earlier, Sihanouk had formally asked France to organize an international peace conference on Cambodia. Were the arms meant to show determined French political support for the prince just ahead of this critical phase of negotiating?[29]

If so, it raised more questions than answers. After all, French neutrality on Cambodia was now more important than ever given that they were being asked to host the conference. And if they wanted to boost Sihanouk's hand at this pivotal juncture, why had they sworn Ranariddh's staff to secrecy about the shipment and not even coordinated it through the Working Group?

Stranger still, if the French wanted the shipment to remain secret, why had they only provided arms that were directly traceable to France? The FAMAS rifle, Luchaire rifle grenades, and LRAC F1 rocket launcher were manufactured only in France and were in service only with a handful of countries, most of them former African colonies. Were any to be captured on the battlefield, or even seen in the hands of guerrillas at their training bases, the French would have little plausible deniability.

But it never even got that far. In mid-April, just a week after the first weapons were turned over, journalist Jacques Berkaert, who had excellent ties with the upper echelon of the ANS, printed the scoop.

The French, predictably, were not amused. The LRAC rocket launchers, which were still in the pipeline, were held in abeyance. And afraid of incurring even greater French wrath, Ranariddh discretely shipped the rifles and grenades out to his compound in Surin—but kept them firmly under lock and key. The FAMAS rifle, with its distinctive bullpup configuration, never saw the light of day on the Cambodian battlefield.[30]

Had the French weapons been distributed as originally planned, they might have given a boost disproportionate to their modest quantities. This was because as of mid-1989 the ANS had found itself in the midst of a rare but pronounced crisis of confidence. One of its top generals, Toan Chay, had spoken candidly about his concerns in August to a U.S. officer on the border. The Khmer Rouge, not surprisingly, was a main source of angst. "The Khmer Rouge do not eat rice," the general explained. "They eat ideology."[31]

In theory, the relationship between the noncommunists and the Khmer Rouge should have shown some improvement. Back in March at the insistence of the Chinese, the CGDK factions had established the Higher Council of National Defense to foster cooperation among the three.[32]

But that same month, the Khmer Rouge had broken a three-month hiatus and once again started initiating fatal clashes with their noncommunist partners.[33] The Higher Council, meant to lead to a unified command structure, had instead devolved into a monthly forum for the noncommunists to air complaints about Khmer Rouge misconduct.

Moreover, despite Toan Chay's hyperbole about the Khmer Rouge subsisting on ideology, generous funding from the Chinese tipped the balance. Pol Pot's men were entering the SOC interior, Toan Chay claimed, with thick stacks of $100 bills to purchase supplies and win support from the peasantry. The noncommunists were not even close to matching such buying power.

Toan Chay had been disheartened by the gains displayed by the KPNLAF even more so than the Khmer Rouge. He could not deny that Sak's armed forces had made strides over the previous year and, as demonstrated in the Liberation One blitz, were at that point more militarily effective than was the ANS. Though it was true that Funcinpec had a better political organization, the ANS had grown soft after years of relying so heavily on Sihanouk's name.

Worse, even Sihanouk's explicit backing was no longer a given. On 30 July, the Paris Peace Conference on Cambodia, with delegations from seventeen nations, had opened. Set to last a month, the conference's ultimate goal was to hammer out the terms of a comprehensive peace treaty. Given the number of delegates and amount of time on hand, expectations for success were relatively high.

But as the weeks wore on, and the parties could not agree on a division of power during a transition period, those expectations started wafting away. It was at that point, just three days before the conference was to conclude, that Sihanouk threw a timely fit and resigned as chairman of Funcinpec.

Like many of Sihanouk's moves, there was some question as to his motivation to abandon Funcinpec. He claimed it was because some Paris-based Cambodian royalists had voiced opposition to Ranariddh as commander of the ANS. More likely, he was looking beyond the Paris conference and resigned in order to burnish his political neutrality during any future peace negotiations. Sihanouk's vacuum in Funcinpec was ostensibly filled by his wife, Monique, and former General Nhiek Tioulong. Just one year away from being an octogenarian, Tioulong was a bit long in the tooth, but his slavish devotion to Sihanouk was beyond question. Neither of them, of course, had anywhere near Sihanouk's pull or prestige.

The Paris conference adjourned on 30 August before reaching any major agreements. Back on the border, meantime, the war had been raging without pause. There was the added dimension of an imminent PAVN withdrawal, with Hanoi sticking to its pledge to pull out all of its remaining combat forces by the end of the following month. This had contributed to a palpable sense of urgency among the Working Group, which speculated that the noncommunists were about to face a window of unprecedented SOC demoralization and thus vulnerability.

Also, the Working Group could not help but notice the Afghan precedent. Back in May 1988, Soviet combat troops had started a slow withdrawal from Afghanistan. This was completed on 15 February 1989, when the last Soviet general walked back into Soviet territory over the Afghan-Uzbek Bridge. Although the puppet Afghan regime they left behind was still clinging to power in urban centers, mujahideen resistance groups were advancing across much of the countryside.

Now it looked as if history would be repeated a quarter of a world away in Cambodia. Anecdotal evidence picked up by the Hilton's intelligence networks indicated that much of the peasantry was not optimistic about the future of the Phnom Penh regime, with reports that ethnic Vietnamese were fleeing the SOC in droves for fear of a CGDK (read: Khmer Rouge) offensive after September.

The Khmer Rouge, determined the Working Group, would not be alone. Both noncommunist factions were given the green light for a major coordinated offensive timed to start just as the last PAVN troops crossed east over the SRV border. For the KPNLAF, in particular, Sak saw this as a golden moment to win the respect the Front had long been denied. Even during the Paris conference, his faction of the KPNLF had not been afforded a seat. Eager to prove that Liberation One had been no fluke, he and his men began counting down the days before they were to unleash hell.

15. White Pigeon

A quarter of world away within the Hindu Kush, the Cold War in Afghanistan had, until very recently, been white-hot. For the first half of the 1980s, the mujahideen had been especially brutalized by Soviet air tactics. The craggy, open terrain over much of that country had been conducive to such operations, ranging from commando air assaults to interdiction by aircraft and, more infamously, armed helicopters. Indeed, nothing was more iconic of that war than images of the wasplike, seemingly invulnerable Mi-24 chopper.

For just as long, the mujahideen's foreign patrons—especially the CIA—had wrestled with ways of countering the Soviets in the air. As the United States initially tried to mask direct involvement, deniable weapons had been sourced by the agency. Among the first of these were SA-7 missiles captured by the Israelis during their various wars against Soviet proxies in the Middle East. But as these were mostly older and less accurate models of that missile, few hits were registered.

Then in 1984, the CIA had arranged delivery of forty Swiss-made Oerlikon 20mm cannons, a weapon foisted upon them by the top mujahideen supporter in Congress, Charlie Wilson. Weighing in at nearly 550 kilograms each, not including ammunition, these had been wholly inappropriate for transport to the Afghan interior. Indeed, no losses were ever attributed to these hefty, pricey cannons.

Sampling other options, the CIA in 1984 gained approval to send fifty U.S.-made FIM-43 Redeye missiles to the Afghan guerrillas. As a first-generation weapon susceptible to countermeasures, the results from these were less than impressive. The next year, it arranged for delivery of an improved version of the SAM-7, and Britain's MI-6 sent a small number of Blowpipe missiles. None, however, had much of an impact.

Then came the shoulder-fired FIM-92 Stinger. This was the most accurate man-portable surface-to-air missile of its day, forcing the Reagan administration to weigh whether introducing such a sophisticated, nondeniable weapon to Afghanistan was too much of a provocation. In the end it decided it was worth the risk, and in mid-1986 the CIA was given permission to send a handful of these launchers to select mujahideen. On 26 September, the first guerrilla unit outfitted with Stingers approached the Soviet airbase near the Afghan town of Jalalabad just as a formation of eight Mi-24 helicopters was returning to base. After one missile went wide, three more found their marks and sent a trio of choppers tumbling out of the sky in flames.

From that point forward, the Stinger became a game-changer in Afghanistan. The mujahideen now had their magic bullet, sowing fear and reportedly forcing the Soviets to significantly curb their air tactics until the final withdrawal in February 1989. "It was the most significant battlefield development," concluded the CIA station chief in neighboring Pakistan.[1]

Cambodia, of course, had been a far different war. In particular, PAVN's approach to counterinsurgency never had a heavy aerial component. For one thing, air assault tactics were never utilized, despite the urgings of Soviet advisers.[2] For another thing, while PAVN conducted some interdiction operations with armed helicopters and makeshift tactical bombers, CGDK guerrillas more often than not were able to use the country's tropical cover to their advantage.[3] Even in the flat scrub found along parts of the western border, PAVN and SOC aircraft posed not even a fraction of the pre-Stinger threat faced by the mujahideen in Afghanistan.[4]

But that same flat scrub was conducive for tanks. As much as aircraft had been the scourge of the mujahideen, armor was the bane of the CGDK. Ever since 1983, in fact, the PAVN's seasonal offensives had been spearheaded by tanks. Although the actual encounters between PAVN armor and CGDK guerrillas had been few, they had instilled a level of fear disproportionate to those small numbers. And not surprisingly, much like the mujahideen had sought to neutralize the Soviet aerial threat, Cambodia's guerrillas had been searching for a magic bullet against Vietnamese tanks. China (and, later, North Korea) had turned over RPG launchers, but these required the guerrillas be unrealistically close to the target in order to score a kill. China had also provided the 90mm Type 51 rocket, a copy of the Korean War–era U.S.-made Super Bazooka. Though an improvement over the RPG, these were heavy to haul through the jungle and in short supply.

The Working Group had listened to the antiarmor lament from the noncommunists for years. For just as long, however, they had refrained from sourcing any suitable countermeasures. By mid-1989, however, the stakes were different: With PAVN seemingly on the way out, the SOC was about to face the CGDK on its own. Of late the SOC had been provided with a liberal amount of armor to stiffen its ranks, and these tanks might be all that kept the Phnom Penh regime from teetering over the edge. Judging the potential gains from such an escalation, the Working Group decided the time was right to give the noncommunist Cambodians the antitank equivalent of a Stinger.

Exactly which weapon they would receive was now the subject of debate. An

Senior PAVN and SOC officers bid farewell to PAVN units in the Siem Reap provincial capital, September 1989. General Khieu Anh Lan (second from left) was the last commander of Front 479. General Phung Dinh Am (third from left) was a former deputy commander of Front 479 and a senior adviser to the SOC armed forces. General Pol Saroeun, the chief of staff for the SOC armed forces, is fourth from left. General Nov Sam, the Siem Reap governor, is second from right. (Author's collection)

obvious choice was the U.S. M72 Light Anti-Armor Weapon, or LAW. A one-shot, disposable 66mm antitank system, the LAW was light (2.5 kilograms) and had a proven track record for lethality. But it was of U.S. origin, meaning that, even if it was sourced from the stocks provided to the RTA, Capitol Hill watchdogs would understandably suspect it was CIA lethal aid that had been dispersed without congressional funding approval.

As it turned out, Singapore had a solution—in fact, two solutions. A tiny city-state surrounded by far larger, often intimidating neighbors, Singapore had always seen fit to keep its military well supplied with antitank rockets. Its army had long used the 84mm M2 Carl Gustav from Sweden; in 1983, the government-linked Chartered Industries had even started manufacturing Carl Gustav rockets under license. Though effectively a two-man system—one for carrying the launcher, the other for hauling the ammunition and loading it—the Carl Gustav packed a wicked punch but was still deemed sufficiently light for use by Asian guerrillas.

In 1988, Chartered Industries had also purchased production rights for a sec-

M-113 personnel carriers file past the Royal Palace during what PAVN claimed was its final withdrawal ceremony, 26 September 1989. (Author's collection)

ond antitank rocket, the West German–made 67mm Armbrust ("Crossbow"). Like the LAW, an Armbrust tube was used once and then disposed. Its design was rather unique, with a mass of shredded plastic ejected out the rear when fired. This countershot system allowed it to be safely discharged within buildings without causing damage usually inflicted by backblast.

In both of these cases, the Singapore government was obliged to seek permission from the country of origin before rockets could be exported to third-party users. For Swedish weapons, its export restrictions were among the strictest in the world: No arms could be sent to a country embroiled in armed conflict, or to a country in an ongoing conflict that might lead to open warfare, or to a country in which internal armed disturbances were taking place. Whereas Singapore fit this profile—and was a good Swedish customer—Cambodia certainly did not.

But Singapore, it turned out, had a history of occasionally skirting Swedish rules. In October 1985, Sweden had slapped a two-month ban on Singapore after it was learned the city-state reexported Swedish antiaircraft missiles to Dubai and Bahrain without permission. Then in September 1988, the media reported Carl Gustav rockets were sent from Singapore to the blacklisted regime in Burma.

Several of these rockets were captured by insurgents three months later when Burmese forces raided a rebel encampment near the Thai border.[5]

In the case of Cambodia, the Singaporeans in late August informed the Working Group that they were prepared to once more turn a blind eye to export regulations and would provide antitank weapons to the noncommunist resistance. Rather than let these pass through the normal RTA-supervised logistical channel, the Singaporeans insisted they dispatch an army team to take the rockets to the border and directly hand them over to the resistance. With the RTA providing its consent, a dozen Armbrusts were discretely given to each noncommunist faction in mid-September, along with a similar amount of Carl Gustav launchers and several hundred rounds apiece.

As this was taking place, PAVN on 26 September staged with pomp and ceremony what it claimed to be its final withdrawal from the SOC. Putting the best face on the retreat, a PAVN battalion commander was overheard waxing optimistic. The Khmer Rouge only had a few weeks to take advantage of the rainy season, he reasoned. After that, the incoming dry season would enable the SOC to use heavy artillery to its advantage.[6]

Tellingly, the PAVN battalion commander had made no reference to any threat posed by the noncommunists. Such an oversight was understandable given the relative performances of the CGDK factions to date. But emboldened by the Ampil Lake victory earlier in March, the KPNLF was determined to dispel the noncommunist stereotype and go for broke immediately after the PAVN pullout.

As the top echelon of the KPNLF commenced marathon planning sessions in mid-September, General Sak found time to—yet again—restructure his senior staff. Familiar faces like Dien Del and Gaffar remained. Joining them was Penn Thola, who was now in charge of the so-called Department of Population Alliance.[7] This department was charged with ginning up public support in the event Sak one day converted his faction into a political party, which either showed prescience or extreme wishful thinking on his part.

Perhaps the biggest change was the promotion of General Pann Thai to chief of staff. To that time, Pann Thai had never really gained a strong following among the KPNLF rank-and-file. His earliest claim to fame had been helming the Special Forces, but that unit had never done much beyond posture in their trademark red berets. Still, even though derided as miserly and plodding by many of his peers, he had proven adept at winning favor with Sak and, now sporting a third star, was the third-ranking military man in the Front.

With this revamped cast, planning took place at the JMC compound at Aranyaprathet. Ever since the JMC was relaunched the previous year, there had been hopes that the two noncommunist factions would at long last seriously focus on pooling their military efforts. This proved fleeting: The ANS, still in a funk, dispatched no officers to the compound, and planning for the post-PAVN offensive remained an all-KPNLF affair.

The focus of the campaign was to be in what was now called Banteay Meanchey province. Khmer for "Fortress of Victory," Banteay Meanchey was a direct result of the K5 border plan. When K5 construction had been in full swing in 1986, much of that effort was concentrated in the northern part of Battambang province. Because Battambang was deemed too large to give sufficient attention to the maintenance and supervision of the K5 system, the PRK government decided to carve off the five northern districts, along with a sliver of Oddar Meanchey, and form Banteay Meanchey. With its provincial capital in Sisophon, this newest province had been officially inaugurated in January 1988.

As the province had been born out of the K5 plan, it came as no surprise that the western edge of Banteay Meanchey—which bordered Thailand—was heavily laced with minefields. But from almost the moment these had been laid, Khmer smugglers—and guerrillas—had cleared paths through the fields, rendering the K5 a most porous barrier. The KPNLF planned for its guerrillas to infiltrate along these paths by the thousands, then simultaneously hit a trio of targets in the northeastern quadrant of Banteay Meanchey.

The uppermost target was a commune of fourteen villages known as Banteay Chhmar 20 kilometers from the border. Although these villages in themselves were rather insignificant, Banteay Chhmar held symbolic value due to the sprawling Angkor-era temple complex in the neighboring forest. Due to their proximity to the border, these historic structures had long been a magnet for antique smugglers, who had chiseled off many of the bas-reliefs for international collectors.

Fifteen kilometers to the south was the second target, the district capital of Thmar Puok. Though this on its face appeared to be an atypical, impoverished Cambodian town—indeed, its name meant "Crumbled Stone"—looks were deceptive: The Working Group had informed the KPNLF that an entire SOC regiment was in residence. In addition, a major SOC firebase was located at the village of Kandaol, 5 kilometers to the northwest.

Another 20 kilometers south of Thmar Puok was the third target, the district capital of Svay Chek. The two towns were connected by a north-south dirt road, which on maps was dignified with the lofty title of Route 69. Though now

An SOC T-54 at Banteay Chhmar with its turret blown off by a Carl Gustav rocket, 30 September 1989. (Courtesy Gaffar Peang-Meth)

reduced to a slippery ribbon of mud by the incessant rains, Route 69 was the only viable means of bringing in reinforcements from Sisophon, another 20 kilometers farther south.

If its guerrillas could take these targets in short order, went the KPNLF plan, it might be able to build enough momentum to seriously bear down on Sisophon. With luck, it harbored hopes of marching into Sisophon by 9 October, thus liberating its first provincial capital on the anniversary of the KPNLAF.

Once plans were finalized, the Working Group offered its blessing. Support from Thailand was deemed especially important, as the noncommunists in the past had accused the RTA of slowly doling out arms to keep them on a tight logistical leash. No such limitations were apparent this time around, with bullets, rifles, and even Chinese-made 107mm rockets dished out in ample quantities.

On 28 September, two days after the PAVN withdrawal, General Pann Thai established a forward tactical headquarters at the old Rithysen camp. The next day, columns of KPNLF guerrillas quietly began their infiltration into the SOC.[8] The northernmost column comprised the bulk of OMZ 3 under General Kho Chhien. By 0400 hours on 30 September, he and his men had closed in on Banteay Chhmar. When small-arms fire broke the still of the morning, the resident SOC commander dispatched three T-54 tanks from the center of the commune.

As the first vehicle clanked down the road, its 100mm gun and 99mm armor would normally have sent the guerrillas fleeing. This time, a team of insurgents came abreast and leveled a Carl Gustav launcher. The first round sliced into the tank's side, detonating near the magazine. The resultant explosion blew off the turret and set it down neatly on the shoulder of the road. Dazed by the concussion, the guerrillas quickly recovered and began to celebrate near the smoldering hull; several were later injured as bullets cooked off throughout the morning from inside the wreck.

A few hundred meters down the same road, another Carl Gustav team closed in on the second tank. Before it had time to fire, the tank strayed off the road and hit a mine, snapping a link in one of the caterpillar tracks. Knowing he was hit, the tank driver attempted to flee. As the track stripped off one side, however, he got only fifty meters before the bare wheels lost traction. The crew quickly leaped from the crippled vehicle and made good their escape into the bush.

Two hundred meters farther on, the KPNLF again did not need to bring rockets into play. In the poor light, the third tank driver had failed to maneuver around a gaping pothole and hopelessly wedged his vehicle. Finding themselves surrounded by guerrillas, the crew pragmatically defected.[9]

Over the course of the afternoon and at the cost of six guerrillas, OMZ 3 consolidated its grip on Banteay Chhmar. KPNLF flags were soon fluttering over the temple complex, and dignitaries from the Front started shuttling in to congratulate Kho Chhien. Smugglers were also on hand, prying off some of the remaining bas-reliefs for the overseas antiquities market.

That same morning, a second column of guerrillas drawn from OMZ 3 and OMZ 7 approached the district capital of Thmar Puok. Forward elements had Carl Gustavs and Armbrusts at the ready, but these proved unnecessary: The rumored regiment of SOC defenders was nowhere to be found. Even the district headquarters was abandoned; it had been housed in the only concrete building in town, on the side of which was painted "Long Live the Communist Party of Vietnam" in Vietnamese. Though somewhat anticlimactic, a victory was a victory—and the KPNLF had liberated its first district capital of the conflict.

Documenting the advance of the KPNLF was American journalist Nate Thayer. Moving between Banteay Chhmar and Thmar Puok that noon, he encountered repeated scenes of chaos. Word that the guerrillas were equipped with antitank weapons had rippled across the district, sparking a level of panic among the SOC troops that could hardly have been anticipated. Thayer snapped photos of regime soldiers surrendering by the dozens, along with several shots of KPNLF troops

Hul Sakada provides instruction on the border for the French LRAC F1 rocket, late 1989. (Author's collection)

wielding their Swedish and German rockets. As evening set in, along with a light rain, he looked to get back to the border to file his story.

As luck would have it, a vehicle approached in the fading light. When it grew close, Thayer recognized it as a Soviet Zil truck. It was filled with SOC troops, all of them seeking to defect. Thayer climbed into the cabin, bracketed by the driver and a former deputy division commander, and they set off down a muddy cart-path that led west toward the Thai frontier. But as Khuon Roeun had discovered six months earlier, vehicular travel close to the border was undertaken at one's own peril. The Zil predictably hit an antitank mine, killing the driver, three passengers in the rear, and sending Thayer for a spell at the Site 2 hospital.[10]

As for Khuon Roeun, he had fully healed from his own encounter with a mine and was back leading Special Regiment 801. His men were focusing their attention against the firebase at Kandaol. But as they approached the perimeter on 30 September, the SOC responded with a blistering volley of heavy weapons fire. The defenders rumored to be at Thmar Puok, it turned out, were actually packed into Kandaol. And even though Khuon Roeun's regiment was equipped with antitank rockets, SOC heavy weapons were keeping it well at bay.

The KPNLF, however, had another game-changer in its arsenal—this one courtesy of the CIA. Back at the start of 1989, the agency had picked a dozen promising young officers from the ANS and another dozen from the KPNLF and brought them to the Non Din Daeng training center. There a pair of CIA instructors had given them a crash course in radio intercept skills and codebreaking.

Once finished, the two units—given the codename White Pigeon—were outfitted with tactical intercept gear and returned to their respective factions. The ANS team, it turned out, never showed much determination to put its equipment into play.

The White Pigeon team from the KPNLF was different. The team leader, a young lieutenant named Srey Sangha, was no stranger to the military. His father, Srey Yar, had been a trusted Lon Nol loyalist and the commander of airborne troops for much of the Republican era. In a gut-wrenching moment, Srey Sangha, not yet a teen, had been at his father's side when he donned his general's uniform for the last time on 17 April 1975 and drove to the Ministry of Information building to offer his surrender. The young Sangha had waited outside through noon, when his father came out briefly and removed his shirt. Giving his family a final farewell, Srey Yar returned to the ministry building. He, and the other senior FANK officers who had assembled there, did not live to see that evening.

Sangha had gone on to survive the Khmer Rouge period and was quick to join the KPNLF soon after its inception.[11] Now given the opportunity to helm the Front's radio intercept unit, he was eager to make a difference. Trouble was, picking a good vantage point on the border to utilize the equipment had been harder than first imagined. Two initial sites—including one high in the Dangrek Range—were too far removed to pick up any SOC radio traffic.

Then in September, Sangha had shifted his White Pigeon team to the border opposite Banteay Chhmar. Once in place, its earphones came alive with HF and VHF military chatter. Zeroing in on the transmissions from Kandaol, the team was suddenly like a fly on the wall inside the firebase. What it heard was pivotal: "Phnom Penh was telling them that reinforcements were on the way, that ammunition was coming by chopper. But the garrison commander was not going to wait. He said that they were out of ammunition and they could not hold."[12]

With a transcript in hand, Sangha on 2 October passed this information to General Pann Thai. Thereby realizing Kandaol was at its most vulnerable, orders were given to Special Regiment 801 to redouble its efforts. On the morning of 3 October, it surged forward. The estimated 400 SOC defenders, they discovered, had already fled south. What's more, they had left behind an unprecedented amount of hardware: "We hit the jackpot at Kandaol. There were four 122mm guns with ammunition, lots of 122mm rockets, and a Zil truck. The garrison commander had claimed that he had no ammunition, but this was obviously not true."[13]

Although the KPNLF leadership was elated with the haul at Kandaol, the bat-

The KPNLF's White Pigeon radio intercept station at Thmar Puok, November 1989. Members of the Working Group and a Singaporean technician are in the background. (Courtesy Srey Sangha)

tle had put their campaign a few days behind schedule. Several other KPNLF columns had entered to the south, and though they had managed to move across Svay Chek district, the SOC was putting up fierce resistance in that district capital.

More bad news was to follow. Nate Thayer had managed to get his scoop into print, revealing that the noncommunists possessed Carl Gustav and Armbrust launchers. Driving home the point, the SOC captured three Armbrusts from the KPNLF near Svay Chek and promptly presented them to the press.[14]

The reactions from the governments of Sweden and West Germany, predictably, reflected deep concern. The Swedes, in particular, were livid over the flagrant violation of their export laws, and it did not take long before fingers were pointed in the direction of Singapore.

Panicking over the likely fallout, the Singaporeans dispatched military officers to the Thai border with orders to repossess the rockets. The CIA's Tom Fosmire, who was still monitoring logistics for the Working Group, could not help but chuckle. "The weapons were already over the border. I told one of the Singaporean majors, 'If I were the Khmer, I wouldn't give them back.'"[15]

Surprisingly, the KPNLF was somewhat cooperative. Although it had much preferred the lethal punch of the Carl Gustavs, it reluctantly returned all the

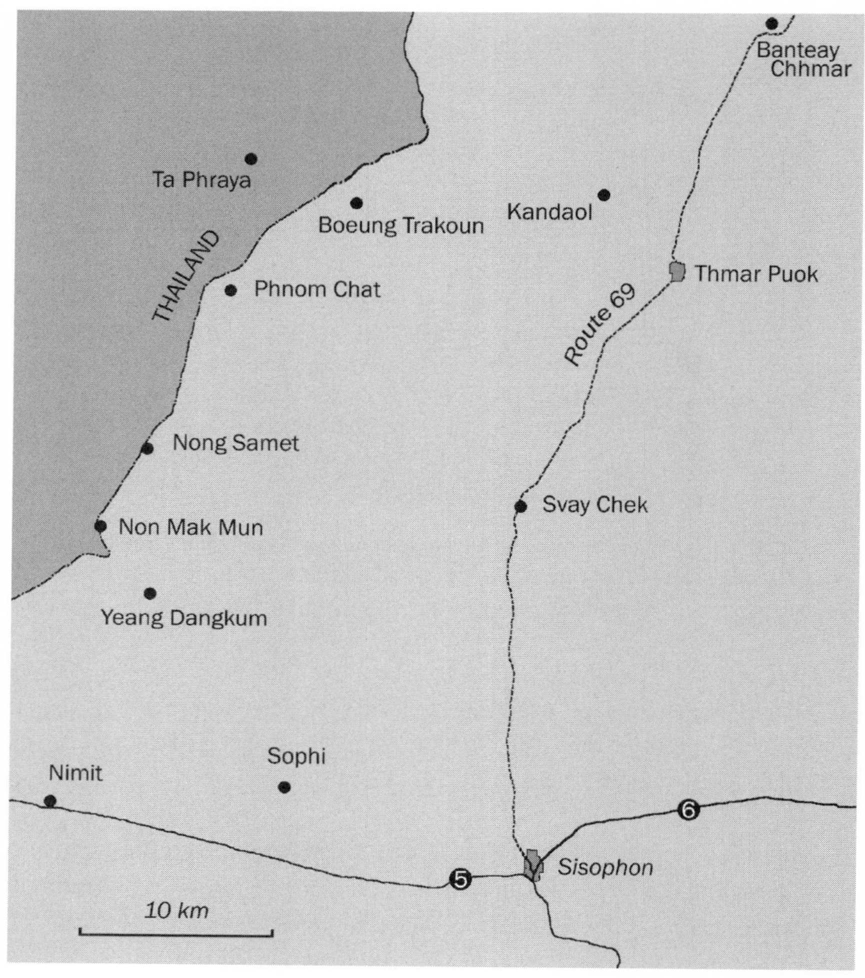

Location of key battles in Banteay Meanchey province.

Swedish launchers. Of the twelve Armbrusts, however, less than half were returned. This did not overly concern the Singaporeans, who felt the German protest held less merit as they had already purchased production rights for this weapon.

The story was almost the same for the ANS. It, too, returned its Carl Gustavs but kept several of the Armbrusts. In this case, the loss was soon offset by French largesse. Making good on a promise from earlier in the year, a representative from the French embassy in late October dropped off three F1 89mm rocket launchers at the ANS office in the Thai capital.[16] A total of twenty F1 launchers and 120 rockets were ultimately given; these were warehoused at Ranariddh's house in Surin and, from there, parceled out to ANS units as needed.[17]

As it turned out, the ANS was finding few opportunities to use its antitank rockets. The bulk of its brigades were stalled to the north in Oddar Meanchey province, where they were attempting—unsuccessfully—to evict the SOC's 286 Division from the provincial capital in Samraong. Only belatedly did it send a few hundred men down to Banteay Meanchey, where they tried—also unsuccessfully—to push across Phnom Srok, a district in the eastern quadrant of the province that was largely covered in wetlands. At neither front did these forces encounter armor.

Despite its tardy arrival in Banteay Meanchey, and what was only a token contribution at Phnom Srok, the ANS was quick to jump on the KPNLF's coattails and laud Thmar Puok as an example of successful noncommunist cooperation. Although several journalists pointed out that the ANS had been notable for its absence on the battlefield, this did not stop the Sihanoukists from insisting that one of their generals be appointed the new governor of liberated Banteay Meanchey.[18]

Such demands obviously did not endear the ANS with its KPNLF coalition partners. What's more, dueling over the right to name a new Banteay Meanchey governor was all a bit premature. After all, the KPNLF had still been unable to move into Svay Chek town as of mid-October. And even if it could get Svay Chek, the provincial capital of Sisophon promised to be a far tougher slog.

In fact, Sisophon had become even more formidable thanks to some pragmatic maneuvering on the part of the CGDK's third coalition partner, the Khmer Rouge. Until that time, Sisophon had been garrisoned by the SOC's 179 Division, while the 196 Division was posted farther south at the gem-mining town of Pailin. At the same time that the KPNLF had started its drive into Banteay Meanchey, the Khmer Rouge had initiated its own offensive against the 196th at Pailin.

Initially, the Khmer Rouge had made strong progress. Pailin was Cambodia's Wild West, both geographically and figuratively. Its gemstone reserves had a played a huge corrupting factor, with local SOC officials reportedly signing a mining agreement with a Thai businessman and government troops occasionally firing on each other for control of promising veins. Pailin, too, was bracketed by hills, like a smaller version of Dien Bien Phu. And much like the pivotal battle at Dien Bien Phu in 1954, the Khmer Rouge had been able to haul heavy weapons atop the hills to pummel the town below—all the while being careful to leave open a corridor for the SOC garrison to escape northeast to Battambang city.

Then as soon as they started, the Khmer Rouge guns mysteriously fell silent.

The KPNLF was by that time bearing down on Svay Chek, and the SOC, believing that Pailin was now in less danger, thought it safe to shift part of the 196 Division north to reinforce Sisophon.[19]

The feint worked. With the Pailin garrison at reduced strength, the Khmer Rouge resumed its onslaught in mid-October. On 22 October, troops punched their way into town, allowing the remaining defenders and residents to flee toward Battambang in order to spread defeatist rumors. This had its intended effect: Three days later, the SOC imposed a curfew in Battambang.

Sisophon, meantime, had benefited from the infusion of SOC troops. It had also managed to keep the Svay Chek garrison well stocked, with its heavy weapons holding the KPNLF at a distance through the entire month of November.

Indeed, the battle for Svay Chek had come to take on extreme symbolic significance. The SOC was vowing to hold the town; with the rains set to end at the close of November, it could make this promise knowing it would soon be able to maneuver more artillery and armor forward from Sisophon.

But the KPNLF was displaying an equal amount of determination. The Front had committed OMZ 3 and OMZ 7 to push toward the town from the east, while OMZ 6 and an assortment of commando teams had curled to the south and were staging harassment operations along the stretch of Route 69 between Svay Chek and Sisophon. Pressing down from the north was the insufferable Khuon Roeun, who at long last had been promoted to brigadier general in recognition of his exploits at Ampil Lake and Kandaol. His entire Special Regiment 801 had been upgraded, in fact, and was now known as 1 Brigade.

But even this vast array of guerrillas, as well as a steady stream of 107mm rockets being moved to the battlefront on oxcarts, could not evict the Svay Chek garrison. By the opening of December, a fully frustrated General Pann Thai was reviewing his dwindling options from a new forward headquarters at the Boeung Trakoun border crossing. Located 6 kilometers south of the old KPNLF headquarters at Ampil, Boeung Trakoun village had at one time hosted a small PAVN outpost. Pann Thai had moved there because it was midway along the border between Banteay Chhmar and Thmar Puok and close to a feeder road that led east to the latter.

It was at this point that White Pigeon's radio operators once again provided a critical piece of data. Srey Sangha had initially based his intercept team at Boeung Trakoun, but VHF signals from SOC units had grown weak as the KPNLF pushed them south to Svay Chek. In order to get a better signal, Sangha deployed his gear and men to Thmar Puok, where they once again started getting strong VHF signals.

Unfortunately for them, the SOC had read the press accounts about the KPNLF overhearing their final communications with the hapless Kandaol garrison. Realizing that the KPNLF was eavesdropping, Phnom Penh purchased some SuperStar radios in Singapore and used these for relaying important orders among the capital, Sisophon, and Svay Chek.

For its part, White Pigeon soon realized that the SOC was communicating on a frequency outside the ability of the intercept gear. The CIA quickly purchased some of its own SuperStar receivers from Singapore and rushed these out to Thmar Puok in mid-November. Two CIA officers assigned to the Working Group, along with a Singaporean technician, made a four-hour ride out to Thmar Puok at month's end to ensure White Pigeon was once again getting clear signals.[20]

At the end of the first week of December, White Pigeon struck gold. In a near repeat of the traffic intercepted at Kandaol, Sangha's team overheard a transmission from Phnom Penh promising that SOC reinforcements were to be dispatched from Sisophon the following day at 1600 hours. But before this could happen, a lucky KPNLF artillery round (fired from a 76.2mm gun captured at Kandaol) had impacted near the main bunker inside Svay Chek, killing a regimental commander from the 179 Division. The deputy regiment commander, in no mood to meet a similar fate, radioed Sisophon that he was moving his post to the rear to escape the shelling.

Bursting with excitement, Sangha had rushed to Pann Thai's hut and handed him the transcript. Having come to trust the results from White Pigeon, the general issued new orders for commando teams to lay in wait for the reinforcement column moving up Route 69. He further ordered Khuon Roeun's 1 Brigade to make one final push from the north.

As the KPNLF moved forward on the morning of 7 December, it braced for resistance. To its surprise, it found Svay Chek largely deserted. When the deputy regiment commander had tried to shift south the previous night, it had sparked a mass exodus from the town. An isolated SOC outpost to the northeast, led by a colonel who happened to be on a morale-building visit, had also fled in panic but was surrounded by KPNLF commando teams and taken prisoner.

It was almost worth the wait. In and around the town were three 122mm artillery pieces, a pair of 85mm field guns, more than 1,000 mortars and light weapons, 4,000 cases of ammunition, two T-54 tanks, four Zil trucks, a BRT-60 armored personnel carrier, and a Soviet UAZ jeep.[21] Dozens of SOC defectors, still armed, mingled with the KPNLF troops as the latter scrounged souvenir hats, pins, and scarves from corpses and bunkers.

Not all the news was good for the KPNLF, however. For one thing, thousands of SOC defenders had been able to reach Sisophon—which was already brimming with government troops.

For another thing, the ANS had once again arrived late to the front but was in a demanding mood. Since shortly after the start of the campaign, the ANS contribution had been tangential at best. Several hundred ANS troops from the 11 Brigade had tried to liberate Phnom Srok district without success—understandable given that the district was covered in marshland and was a nightmare for maneuvering and logistics. Still, the ANS had been quick to demand equal credit for the KPNLF's initial gains around the neighboring battlefield at Thmar Puok.

Then on 20 November, the ANS dispatched its 2 Brigade south from Oddar Meanchey with orders to assist the KPNLF at Svay Chek. This brigade was one of the original ANS formations, built around Toan Chay's Khleang Moeung guerrilla band. Toan Chay had since gotten his general's star and a promotion to ANS deputy chief of staff. In a conscious effort to soften the clannish nature of the ANS brigades, he had selected an officer without a Khleang Moeung background to replace him as head of 2 Brigade.

That officer, Colonel Nhek Bun Chay, was one of the more promising young turks in the ANS. Thirty-one years old, he had a cherubic face tempered by a wicked scar that ran from one ear to the corner of his mouth. During the Khmer Rouge era when he was in his late teens, he had managed to escape to the Thai border, sometimes working odd jobs in Thailand, sometimes joining the roving anticommunist guerrilla cells just inside Cambodia that mixed equal parts resistance and banditry. The Thai authorities had a fickle appetite toward such insurgents during that period, and the young Nhek had served short prison stints on ten different occasions.

After the fall of the Khmer Rouge, Nhek had joined Moulinaka at its inception. When Moulinaka was merged into the ANS and became its 1 Brigade, Nhek was named one of the brigade's battalion commanders. He had risen within the brigade over the years, eventually becoming deputy commander. Now as the newly promoted head of 2 Brigade, he symbolized the attempt to forge unity within the ANS. Most important, for this particular operation Nhek was a hometown boy: He had been born in Svay Chek and went to high school in Thmar Puok.[22]

But by the time 2 Brigade was deployed, there was not much for it to do. It maneuvered into Treas, a commune on Route 69 midway between Thmar Puok and Svay Chek, but the vicinity had already been secured by the KPNLF and there was no fighting to be had. And when Khuon Roeun made his final push into Svay Chek in early December, it was an all-KPNLF operation.

True to form, however, the ANS brigade triumphantly marched into Svay Chek after the last shots were fired. Nhek eyed the two liberated T-54 tanks and, noting that the ANS had armor officers who had recently returned from training in China, demanded one as his rightful booty. The OMZ 3 commander, Kho Chhien, was a longtime acquaintance of Nhek and reluctant to incur bad blood. Stalling for time, he radioed back to General Pann Thai at Boeung Trakoun and relayed the ANS's demand. After some eyerolling, the general relented in the name of CGDK harmony. Nhek Bun Chay got his tank, and his brigade was soon heading back north as self-styled victors.

In the north, meantime, the bulk of the ANS had been doing preciously little in Oddar Meanchey.

A few insignificant outposts had been overrun, but the main SOC base at Samraong was never in any real danger of falling. This had frustrated the Working Group to no end, and members expressed their disappointment to senior ANS officers. Ranariddh, for one, took exception. "The CIA and Singaporeans are so impatient. They want big battles, big shows," he lamented. "This is what happened when they forced the Afghan resistance to attack Jalalabad."[23]

Ranariddh's shrewd reference to Jalalabad held some merit. Back in February, the Afghan conflict had seemingly entered its final stage after the withdrawal of Soviet combat forces. With the Soviets gone, the mujahideen's foreign sponsors, especially the CIA, were optimistic they could quickly overrun the Afghan puppet government that Moscow had left behind. The CIA's most guarded estimates gave the Kabul regime no more than six months in power; its more optimistic predictions had the mujahideen marching into the capital in just three months.

To hasten the fall of Kabul, the CIA had signed off on an ambitious mujahideen operation to capture the town of Jalalabad in a conventional assault. Not only would this be a fast-track victory; it would serve to humiliate the Soviets and provide sweet revenge for America's retreat from Vietnam.

On 5 March 1989, the Jalalabad onslaught began. But when the mujahideen began to torture and execute prisoners, the Afghan government dug in. Its air force staged relentless bombing sorties (assisted by rocket support from some Soviet Scud teams secretly left behind), inflicting crippling blows on the exposed mujahideen ranks. By July, some 3,000 mujahideen casualties littered the Jalalabad battlefield; Afghan government morale was riding high as a result, dashing even the most conservative CIA estimates about their survivability.

Ranariddh saw an exact parallel with Samraong, where ANS was being pressured to assault a town in the face of heavy minefields and artillery. Rather than launching a costly frontal assault, he claimed he wanted to move into Kompong Thom and cut the SOC lines of supply running toward Oddar Meanchey—theoretically starving out Samraong. Ultimately, the ANS ended up doing virtually nothing, so much so that Sihanouk called his son from Beijing in early December and berated him for forty-five minutes. "Does he want us to take responsibility for territory we cannot defend?" complained an exasperated Ranariddh. "This is not a Hollywood movie."[24]

With just a few weeks left to 1989, the weather in Banteay Meanchey had turned dry and cool. Although the SOC should have been able to take advantage of the hardened terrain to push north from Sisophon with its armor and artillery, White Pigeon radio intercepts were painting a different picture. "The 179 Division was in chaos and the SOC tactical headquarters in Sisophon was exhausted," recalled KPNLF officer Suon Samnang, a member of the Front's headquarters staff. "They were on the verge of pulling back to Siem Reap."[25]

Realizing that Sisophon was ripe for attack, Pann Thai took stock of his available forces. OMZ 3, which had turned in a very credible performance for a solid quarter, was tired and had been tasked with administering Thmar Puok. OMZ 5 and OMZ 6 were in better condition and could have been used, but the general wanted Khuon Roeun's battle-hardened 1 Brigade, which was occupying Svay Chek, to once again spearhead the effort.

Khuon Rouen was not one to shirk from a fight. In this case, however, his men were also weary from nearly constant fighting since March. He radioed Boeung Trakoun, pleading that the brigade be given a short leave before tackling Sisophon.

Not wanting to lose momentum, Pann Thai was reluctant to grant the request. Yet despite his better judgment, he compromised and gave Khuon Roeun permission to rest his men for just two days before surging south. Upon having their leave granted, 1 Brigade promptly vacated Svay Chek and rushed back toward the border to spend time with friends and family. After a week passed, only a handful had returned. Heading toward year's end, the opportunity to move decisively against Sisophon had all but wafted away.

Sisophon aside, there was no denying that 1989 had been the KPNLF's finest year of combat operations. Its crowning achievement had been the capture of Svay Chek, a bloody two-month slog in which the SOC had blinked first. While this should have been something for celebration, the KPNLF's long-time planning chief, Gaffar Peang-Meth, was not there to see it. His departure from the scene, in fact, was a year in the making—ever since he had been the driving force behind the relaunch of the JMC the previous October.

The JMC's restructuring, of course, had mattered little in hindsight. When the KPNLF penned its 1989 offensive, the ANS had not shown up to the planning sessions. And when the two armies had met on the battlefield over the course of that year, their cooperation was fleeting and ad hoc at best.

Gaffar had seen all this and took the failure personally. On 25 October, he had sequestered himself in his hut at the JMC compound in Aranyaprathet and composed a two-page letter of resignation. A believer in the JMC until the end, he addressed the letter to his immediate JMC boss, General Toan Chay from the ANS. He cried while signing it.

That night, Toan Chay and the commander of Task Force 838 came to Gaffar's hut and reminisced into the late hours.[26] The next morning Gaffar woke early and watered the roses that Dien Del had planted along the lane. So as not to demoralize the staff, he had not revealed his planned departure. But when they saw him bidding farewell to the loyal hound that guarded the compound, they knew something was amiss. "Your Lord Buddha says nothing is permanent," were his parting words.

After a delay in Bangkok to hand over responsibilities, Gaffar headed back toward his Maryland home. On 17 November, for the first time in nearly a decade, he carved a Thanksgiving turkey alongside his wife and sons.[27]

16. Paradigm Shift

As the KPNLF's conceptualizer-in-chief, Gaffar Peang-Meth surprised few people when he left behind several irons in the fire. One of them involved yet another attempt to enter the world of espionage and special operations. Gaffar had dubbed this the Clandestine Operations Service (COS), which he envisioned as a means of secretly taking the KPNLF into the heart of Phnom Penh. Sak had signed off on the scheme, and it was ready to go operational just as Gaffar tendered his resignation.

Picked to helm the COS was Vong Tham, one of Gaffar's more able PLANA deputies. Tham had started his military career as a young FANK officer in an armored personnel carrier squadron on the outskirts of Phnom Penh. When the Republic collapsed, he had eluded the fate meted out to many fellow FANK officers and instead had been sent to tend paddies in Kampot province. He eventually managed to escape his Khmer Rouge minders and flee to Vietnam, where he stewed in a refugee camp for a couple of years.

In early 1979, Tham was thrown together with most of the other males in his camp and sent to triumphantly march back to Phnom Penh in one of the PRKAF's fledgling infantry battalions. This, too, was hardly to his liking, so he worked his way to the Thai border at year's end and joined the nascent KPNLF. He had served as one of the Front's military instructors for most of the intervening years before moving under Gaffar and helping run the APPCO program.[1]

Had Gaffar remained at the border, he might have been able to lobby for resources—both financial and personnel—to get the COS off and running. But with its patron now gone, the COS did not have the pull among the KPNLF's upper echelon to secure a meaningful budget or supplies. Realizing he would have to do miracles with what little he could muster, Tham and his skeleton crew of would-be clandestine operators debated their options.

In early November 1989, they settled on a debut mission. Rather than focus on the capital just yet, they would instead hit a soft target midway to Phnom Penh. Picking a team of agents and giving them a pair of antitank mines, Tham sent them on their way toward Kompong Chhnang province. Upon reaching the Sras Angkam Bridge, 20 kilometers west of the provincial capital, they enticed the head guard at the bridge to help them plant the mines. These cratered the bridge and, for a time, inhibited traffic. The COS team was able to escape back to the border; the bridge guard, not as fortunate, fell suspect and was carted off to a jail cell.

Spirited by this initial performance, the COS at month's end was sufficiently confident to dispatch an agent handler to Phnom Penh. He was equipped with an FT-70G manpack transceiver, rigged to work off of a car battery. The handler made it to the capital without incident, then settled in among relatives 30 kilometers to the southwest along Route 4.

A week later, the COS sent another nine agents to Phnom Penh. By this time, the Working Group had been briefed on the COS agenda and was mildly supportive. Courtesy of the Singaporean representative, the team had been supplied with a box of military-grade stun grenades and Soviet-made timers. These were basically glorified firecrackers, capable of making loud noises but otherwise nonlethal.

The team, grenades in hand, rendezvoused with the agent handler south of Phnom Penh. The latter obtained a pair of motorcycles, on which four of the agents, two per motorcycle, set off for the capital on the afternoon of 5 December. That evening, and on every evening for the next five days, the agents dropped innocuous boxes at roadside along Phnom Penh's main thoroughfares. Inside each box was a grenade with a timer set for ten minutes. These detonated at, among other places, the front of Hun Sen's residence near the Independence Monument, the Ministry of Defense building, and the Royal Palace. The results were passed to the agent handler south of the capital, who radioed the news back to the COS office on the border.[2]

If the COS intended for the stun grenades to sow fear and undermine the Phnom Penh regime, it was being far too optimistic. In fact, the SOC was busy putting a positive spin on developments since the PAVN withdrawal in September. It had fully anticipated losing up to 30 percent of its territory when the Vietnamese left, Hun Sen explained in December, but it had done better than expected.[3]

Of course, PAVN had never really left. In early 1989, in an uncanny parallel to the Mike Force contribution during the Lon Nol regime, Hanoi had started transferring Khmer Krom members from its own military to the SOC armed forces as stiffeners. Then when PAVN supposedly made their complete withdrawal in September, Front 719 quietly retained a team of specialists in Phnom Penh to advise the SOC General Staff.[4]

These relatively small violations paled in comparison to what was to take place the next month. When the SOC's 196 Division wilted and the Khmer Rouge on

22 October pushed into Pailin against relatively little resistance, Battambang city appeared in real danger of falling. This prompted Phnom Penh to make an emergency request to Hanoi for help, and PAVN five days later dispatched a reconnaissance battalion to Battambang. It was joined at month's end by part of an artillery battalion, elements of an armor battalion, and three full infantry regiments, including one from the 330 Division that had garrisoned Pailin prior to the September pullout.[5]

This deployment had its desired effect. In pitched battles throughout the month of November, PAVN troops spearheaded an SOC counterattack to reclaim territory north of Route 10 linking Battambang with Pailin. While the Khmer Rouge remained in control of Pailin as of December, it had been pushed back far enough to give Battambang city some breathing room.

Other PAVN troops were quietly introduced elsewhere to harden the SOC lines. In Siem Reap, a battalion-sized advisory element known as Group K4B was assigned in late October to assist the SOC's Military Region 4 staff. In Battambang, a similar group codenamed K5B was established to assist the Military Region 5 headquarters. During November, yet another advisory group, this one codenamed K88B, was drawn from PAVN's 308 Mechanized Infantry Division to advise the SOC's 7 Infantry Division and assist with sweeps in Kompong Speu and Kratie.[6]

As might be expected, Hanoi had a hard time keeping these deployments a secret—especially where they had critical mass along Route 10. By mid-December, almost two dozen PAVN members had been captured alive by the Khmer Rouge. Showing media savvy, the Khmer Rouge promptly paraded them in front of the media, published their details in glossy magazines, and even handed out VHS tapes of their confessions.[7]

To the north of the Pailin front, the SOC and noncommunist resistance entered 1990 with their standoff simmering just below boil.[8] At Samraong, the SOC's 286 Division engaged in the occasional heavy weapons duel with the ANS but was never in any real danger of being evicted.[9]

At Thmar Puok, meantime, the KPNLF was preoccupied with administering a sizeable liberated zone. Specifically, it had to contest with the fact that it had no existing program to buy and sell the rice harvest, which was the sole livelihood for the villagers now under its control. To help with logistics, the Working Group had hurriedly provided the Front with a pair of Unimogs, four Bedford trucks, and a dozen camouflaged Chevrolet pickups.[10]

SOC troops prepare to attack Banteay Srei district, Banteay Meanchey province, 1990. Their lack of uniform standardization is little different from the noncommunist resistance. (Author's collection)

At Svay Chek, the situation was far more dire. Because of extensive minefields left behind by the SOC, the town's 4,000 inhabitants had been unable to collect their harvest from the surrounding fields. Even without the mines, all of the draught animals had been killed by shrapnel from incoming SOC artillery rounds.[11]

Not until February did the SOC begin a belated dry-season offensive. This coincided with a new infusion of sheep-dipped PAVN troops. The largest PAVN concentration remained in Battambang, where another regiment from the 330 Division was dispatched to bolster the SOC column pushing west along Route 10.[12] In the vicinity of Sisophon, a battalion from the 5 Division—which had garrisoned that town for years—was sent to reinforce the SOC's Military Region 4. And in the eastern province of Kratie, a battalion from the 7 Division was assigned to perform static defense.[13]

Steeled by the PAVN reinforcements, the SOC surged forward. Its most dramatic move was from Sisophon, where tanks led a thrust pushing toward Svay Chek. While still equipped with Armbrusts, the KPNLF's Khuon Roeun decided discretion was the better part of valor and shifted his 1 Brigade a few kilometers north to enable the SOC to take the town on 21 February without much resistance. Though now within artillery range, the KPNLF held new defensive lines at Thmar Puok.

Two days later, Prince Sihanouk, his wife, Monique, and their pet poodle had ventured across the Thai border 8 kilometers into Oddar Meanchey province. There, in a small corner of liberated territory he dubbed Phum Sereipheap ("Freedom Village"), the prince declared his intent to remain on Cambodian soil.[14]

The prince also saw fit to ratchet up his diplomatic gymnastics. This had started back on 24 January, when he announced that—yet again—he was resigning as chairman of the CGDK. Then on 21 February, Sihanouk had sat down with Hun Sen in Bangkok and discussed the possibility of establishing the Supreme National Council (SNC), an interim ruling entity he would presumably head following a comprehensive peace agreement. Finally, in a further attempt to bolster his objectivity ahead of a possible peace deal, he signed on 27 April a decree at Phum Sereipheap removing himself from the ANS. From that time forward, his Sihanoukist army was renamed the National Army for an Independent Cambodia (Armées Nationale pour Khmer Independent, or ANKI). Ranariddh was named ANKI's supreme commander.[15]

Sihanouk had good reason for such pragmatism. While Cambodia appeared deadlocked in its seasonal cycle of war, the world around it had been changing with dizzying speed. Specifically, the Soviet Union in January 1990 had entered what appeared to be an irreversible process of weakening and disintegration. Radical political changes were already occurring across the Warsaw Pact, with several pro-Soviet governments now finding themselves out of work.

All of this obviously had a major impact on the SOC, which as of 1989 had almost 80 percent of its budget subsidized by socialist aid. Reading the tea leaves and predicting that the sources of that aid would soon disappear, Vietnam's foreign minister that December had addressed a special meeting of the SOC's ruling party and urged it to take a flexible line toward the peace process.

But the impact of a changing world was being felt far beyond the SOC. The CGDK, too, saw significant changes among its supporters.[16] China, for one, was proving itself to be especially fickle. Perhaps fearing that the Khmer Rouge would be the odd party out in a peace deal, Beijing was taking extra steps to boost its proxy. In January 1990, for instance, it secretly shipped fifteen Type 62 light tanks to Trat. From there, five were given to the Khmer Rouge at Pailin and a similar amount to the Khmer Rouge based at Anlong Veng.[17] Another five tanks were retained by the RTA.[18]

Conversely, China was no longer in an especially coddling mood toward the noncommunist resistance. As of April 1990, it unilaterally ceased material support to both noncommunist factions.[19] Beijing even went as far as to block military aid from another source, North Korea. Through that time, Pyongyang's support for Sihanouk had been rock-solid. The prince, for instance, rarely ventured abroad without his bevy of North Korean bodyguards. And when he moved to a villa in Phum Sereipheap, Kim Il-Sung had even promised five North Korean agricultural experts to live there for a year and give ANKI tips on horticulture.[20] But when Kim tried in 1990 to send a shipment of 76.2mm field guns to ANKI via China, Bejing balked and refused to forward the hardware to Thailand.[21]

The United States, too, had started to reevaluate its relationship with the noncommunists. Of course, there were still hawks in Washington—like Defense Secretary Richard Cheney and NSC Director Brent Scowcroft—who were favorably disposed toward continued support to the KPNLF and ANKI. Perhaps still feeling the sting of the Vietnam War, they were opposed to any flexibility toward Hanoi or, by extension, the Phnom Penh government.

But in the State Department, and especially on Capitol Hill, the knives were out. There were several reasons for this. First, with the Cold War winding down and America the apparent winner, the worldwide anticommunist crusade did not resonate as it once had. Rather than funding surrogates in far-flung places like Cambodia, lawmakers were more prone to declare victory and start discussions on how to spend the peace dividend.

Second, with PAVN claiming to be out of Cambodia and the SOC in a weakened state, there were fears among some in Congress that the Khmer Rouge might seize power once again. To prevent this, these members of Congress championed the SOC as the lesser of the two evils and felt that the noncommunists should be pushed into an accommodation with the Phnom Penh regime in order to head off Khmer Rouge designs.

There was a third factor at play as well. U.S. Ambassador to Thailand Daniel O'Donohue observed: "In 1990 and 1991, looking toward the 1992 presidential elections, a number of Democrats in Congress were looking for an issue and somehow thought that the matter of the Khmer Rouge in Cambodia might embarrass the Bush administration. So the whole thrust of this group of Democrats in Congress was there we were really supporting the Khmer Rouge by dealing with the noncommunist resistance!"[22]

This line of thinking became apparent in late June when Democrats on the Senate Intelligence Committee took aim at the noncommunists. Arguing that CIA covert assistance was directly or indirectly benefiting the Khmer Rouge, they

ANS Brigade 6 commander Kien Vang enters a newly captured district capital in the Phnom Kulen vicinity, Siem Reap province, 1990. The presence of an ANS honor guard on the left and a Khmer Rouge honor guard on the right speaks to the increasingly close cooperation between these two factions during the late phases of the war. (Author's collection)

voted to end that aid.[23] When it was put before the House Intelligence Committee, however, the CIA money was for the time being reinstated.

Sensitive to all this, U.S. Secretary of State James Baker ventured to Paris on 17 July for a meeting with British, Chinese, French, and Soviet counterparts to discuss a United Nations role in Cambodia. When their tryst ended the next day, Baker took to the steps of the U.S. embassy and delivered a bombshell. The United States would seek contact with the SRV to discuss Cambodia, he announced, and would no longer support the CGDK's hold over the Cambodia seat at the United Nations. While covert aid to the noncommunists would continue, Bush administration officials hinted that the $5 million in overt congressional support—heretofore given to the noncommunist resistance—could instead be directed toward the Phnom Penh government.

In making these concessions, the State Department was hoping to push the Cambodian factions closer to a compromise. Despite an initial shrill outburst from Sihanouk, it seemed to have the desired effect.[24] During August, CGDK leaders met with SOC officials in Jakarta to discuss the SNC interim government arrangement. On 17 September, they met again in Bangkok and agreed to the twelve members—six from the SOC, six from the CGDK—that would comprise the SNC. Satisfied with this progress to date, the United Nations on 12 October announced that there would be no vote on the Cambodian seat that year.

But apparently not appeased by Baker's revamped Cambodia policy, congressional critics responded in October with their own set of limitations. This was part of a larger package of restraints imposed that month on three CIA paramilitary programs that had been central to the Reagan Doctrine during the Cold War. In Afghanistan, they slashed $50 million from the agency's largest covert operation, the $300 million annual assistance effort to the mujahideen. In Angola, Congress put legal curbs on the $60 million annual program to support Jonas Savimbi's UNITA resistance.

Their harshest changes, however, were reserved for the Cambodian resistance. Following a proposal by Representative Bill Richardson, a New Mexico Democrat, House and Senate negotiators insisted that covert aid to the noncommunists no longer be channeled through the CIA but instead be done openly through other government agencies. Presumably this meant USAID, which was already administering overt congressional aid to the noncommunists. Not stopping there, a Senate provision required President Bush to produce a public report by 1 January 1991 detailing how the now redesignated humanitarian aid would be allocated as well as the extent of military cooperation between the Khmer Rouge and noncommunist resistance since 1986.

The subject of military cooperation with the Khmer Rouge was especially sensitive. On 1 May 1990, the State Department had delivered a confidential report to Congress stating that, despite requests from the Bush administration, there was no discernible decrease in Chinese military aid to the Khmer Rouge for the past six months. At the same time, the U.S. embassy in Bangkok admitted that there were increasingly close ties between the Khmer Rouge and noncommunists.

This was especially true in the case of ANKI, which had been leaning heavily on the Khmer Rouge in recent years. In some cases, this was the result of kinship that spread across factional lines. For example, Colonel Nhek Bun Chay, the ANKI brigade commander, hailed from the same extended family as Ta Su, the one-armed deputy commander of the Khmer Rouge 519 Division. Not surprisingly, Nhek's brigade and the 519 Division, based at Phnom Chat in Banteay Meanchey, conducted joint operations on more than a few occasions.[25]

In other cases, ANKI was just acknowledging realities on the battlefield. In 1990, for example, a sixty-seven-man element from the ANKI 3 Brigade had managed to reach Svay Rieng province on the SRV border only by leapfrogging between Khmer Rouge–held villages along the way.[26]

Khmer Rouge assistance was especially apparent in Kompong Thom province. This was underscored in June and July, when journalist Nate Thayer and Roland Eng, a senior Funcinpec official who was also Ranariddh's brother-in-law, made an extended trek to visit ANKI units. Arriving in Kompong Thom, they had met the ranking ANKI officer, Khan Savoeun, who dressed in white robes and had a flair for the dramatic. "He was like a warlord regent with Buddhism," summed up Thayer.[27]

But much of Khan's rising clout within ANKI was due to piggybacking on credit for Khmer Rouge gains in Kompong Thom, to include a spectacular April rocket attack on the provincial capital that had sent SOC Defense Minister Tea Banh fleeing from the city.[28] Khan's 15 Brigade had also operated alongside a far larger Khmer Rouge contingent during two separate stabs that year at Staung, a district capital in central Kompong Thom.[29]

More than just Svay Rieng or Kompong Thom, the CIA saw a Khmer Rouge nexus in virtually every battlefield where ANKI was present. "Whatever successes they had, especially in 1990–91, was due almost entirely to the Khmer Rouge providing the real muscle," assessed one CIA officer attached to the Working Group. "ANKI was mostly just window dressing for these operations."[30]

Coincidentally, an entirely new cast of CIA officers was arriving at Bangkok Station over the summer of 1990 to contend with this reality and its likely impact on aid given the restraints imposed by Congress. On 22 August, Harry Slifer, in one of his last acts as station chief, hosted an Exco meeting at the RTA Golf Club in Bangkok. By month's end, he was replaced by Billy Huff, a longtime China expert on his first CIA posting in Southeast Asia.

Under Huff were two new faces handling both of his Cambodian projects. At the Hilton, the debriefing center at Aranyaprathet, Davis Knowlton had completed his tour in mid-1990 and left the kingdom. In as the new base chief was Robert Wnukowski, a paramilitary officer who years earlier had led a regiment of Lao guerrillas. From the start, Wnukowski found the Hilton to be exceedingly quiet: The zoo was long gone and, with peace talks in the air, plans were already afoot to wind down the operation.[31]

At the Working Group, Joe Murray had also completed his assignment and was headed home. Replacing him was Barry Broman, an officer whose varied career had delved into Cambodia on several occasions. In 1963 as a stringer for the Associated Press in Bangkok, he had sometimes found himself in Phnom Penh for the occasional photo assignment. After a stint as a U.S. Marine officer, then Thai language training during graduate school, he had been recruited into the CIA. Ostensibly a commercial attaché, he was one of two undeclared agency

CIA paramilitary officer Tom Fosmire with Sak Sutsakhan, 1990. (Author's collection)

officers assigned to the U.S. embassy in Phnom Penh from 1973 through the fall of the Republic.

Broman had remained in Asia and was serving as the deputy station chief in Jakarta before getting an offer in early 1990 to run the Indochina Operations Group at headquarters. He was there only a few months before being asked by Huff, a fellow former Marine, to head the six-man CIA team on the Working Group.[32]

From the start, Broman had to balance how he would represent CIA interests at a time when ongoing covert funding was growing less likely by the month. Much, if not most, future aid would instead be passing through USAID. This was not exactly a bad thing, as the CIA and USAID had enjoyed an unusually close level of cooperation when dealing with the noncommunist resistance. For years, USAID had been handling the overt congressional funds largely used to run vocational and medical training programs for the KPNLF and ANS. As of September 1990, overt funds were also being spent on equipment to build a 21-kilometer road from the border to KPNLF-held Thmar Puok as well as a smaller road to the ANKI base at Phum Sereipheap.[33]

But even if USAID assumed a greater role, it was doubtful that it could handle all of what CIA covert funds covered. As of 1990, the agency's contribution to the Working Group was being used for a wide variety of nonlethal programs, including purchasing uniforms and communications gear, subsidizing RTA training, and running propaganda venues like the noncommunist radio stations.[34] This last category included one shortwave radio based in Chiang Mai, two medium-wave transmitters on the border, and the salary of a British technician who was with the radio program since the outset.[35]

With these funds now in jeopardy, reaction in the Working Group was predictably unfavorable. Among its RTA members, the always frank Ayupoon was quick to chide his CIA counterparts. "Just when the last stone is placed in the wall, you quit."

The Singaporeans, who had been seeking to keep the United States engaged in Southeast Asia, were equally unhappy—though their displeasure was somewhat ameliorated when their resulting position within the Working Group went up from where it had been. This came after Prime Minister Lee Kuan Yew agreed to pump more money into the program in the event CIA funding was cut. Looking ahead to a postsettlement Cambodia, Singapore's SID had also started intelligence training for a select number of noncommunists.[36]

Malaysia was unsettled about a CIA pullout for a couple of reasons. First, it did not want the CIA's withdrawal to scuttle ASEAN's position when victory was practically in sight. Second, anything that enhanced Singapore's influence was, in its eyes, not all that welcome. This was especially true after five Malaysian naval personnel were arrested in 1988 for spying on Singapore's behalf, embarrassing SID and continuing to make bilateral relations exceedingly frosty.[37]

Singapore's relative rise within the Working Group, as well as its squabbling with Malaysia, was plainly apparent near year's end during the last Exco of 1990. Symbolic of Singapore's heightened clout, the meeting was hosted by SID in its city-state. Huff and Broman had gone there to represent the CIA and afterward were invited by the Malaysians to attend the eleventh (and, in hindsight, last) graduation of noncommunist guerrillas from the jungle warfare camp in Pahang state. But as the Singapore hosts were barely on speaking terms with their Malaysian counterparts, an SID car had driven the two CIA officers halfway across the Johor-Singapore Causeway, then dropped them off and let a Malaysian car take them the rest of the way to Pahang.

Upon his return to Bangkok, Station Chief Huff had communicated to Langley the negative feedback to a CIA funding cutoff from fellow Working Group members. He was answered, for the most part, with silence: "There was not only no high-level interest in our ongoing assistance program to the noncommunist resistance, but there seemed to be diminished interest in Thailand, too. . . . We were visited by one of the Deputy Directors of Operations, but he was not enormously interested in what we were doing in Cambodia."[38] Rather, Langley, and the rest of Washington, was wholly consumed by the Iraqi invasion of Kuwait. The resultant U.S. staredown with Baghdad had started on 2 August 1990 with Operation Desert Shield, then escalated into full-blown war on 17 January 1991 with Desert Storm.

Huff soon discovered that Kuwait's direct impact extended to Bangkok. On 19 January, two days after the start of Desert Storm, a bomb had detonated in front of the U.S.-funded Thomas Jefferson Cultural Center in Manila. CIA officers in the Philippines had determined that two Iraqi nationals were behind the bombing, one of whom died in the blast. They also learned that the two had traveled on Iraqi passports issued in sequential order.

CIA stations around the world immediately began searching for other Iraqi passports in that series. Pairs of would-be bombers were soon uncovered in several Southeast Asian capitals, including two suspect Iraqis in Bangkok. The Thai authorities had quickly located both and had them deported.[39]

While the Iraqi threat in Thailand had seemingly been averted, Huff received a package at the embassy late that month. Inside was a Chinese revolver, along with a note from KPNLF General Pann Thai stating that the pistol was for his added protection. Huff smiled at the sentiment, as well as the gentle reminder that the war in Cambodia had, at least for the moment, been lost in the shuffle.

17. Parting Shots

As Desert Storm entered its second—and final—month, a Land Cruiser departed Bangkok and made its way east along Route 33 toward the Cambodian border. Upon reaching Aranyaprathet the driver pulled into Eagle House, a safe house used by the CIA members in the Working Group. There two of the passengers—Billy Huff and Barry Broman—paused briefly to empty pocket litter and pick up some weapons, then got back in the Land Cruiser and headed to the nearby JMC compound. Several four-wheel-drive vehicles were awaiting them, packed with KPNLF escorts. They formed up a convoy—the Land Cruiser tucked in the middle—and pushed another 55 kilometers northeast out of Aranyaprathet on a parallel track with the border. Upon reaching Ban Chiang Dam village in Ta Phraya district, they turned east on an unmarked dirt road. A few kilometers farther on, they were on Cambodian soil.

The two CIA officers had arrived at the KPNLF base at Boeung Trakoun, which over the previous year had taken on the trappings of a true headquarters. It now featured a manicured parade ground, a motor pool with dozens of captured and donated vehicles, and an impressive memorial to the war dead with the names of hundreds of guerrilla fatalities inscribed around its sides.[1] It had also been given a new name: Banteay Meanrit, Khmer for "Military Fort."

After marching single-file through a minefield on the outskirts of the base, the officers came upon some huts erected on the edge of some scrub. There they were treated to a live-fire demonstration of captured artillery and shown one of the captured T-54 tanks. They also saw a demonstration of the West German–made Komet MRL-80 mine-breaching system, which consisted of a detonating cord shot across a minefield by a small rocket. CIA funds had purchased this system, with training courtesy of Singaporean instructors.

From Banteay Meanrit, the CIA officers returned to their vehicles and headed to Site 2, adjacent to which was the main KPNLF hospital. Here the viewings were grim: Dozens of amputees and malarial victims were crammed into the hospital's wards. On a more positive note, the Site 2 hospital, as well as the other KPNLF field medical facilities, was well staffed with literally hundreds of Khmer nurses and health officials trained by USAID.

Back in the Thai capital by nightfall, this was the closest that Bangkok Station would come to a Cambodian victory lap. A week later, Huff called on the RTA chief, the somewhat taciturn Suchinda Kraprayoon. He informed the army com-

CIA Station Chief Billy Huff with a captured SOC T-54 tank at Boeung Trakoun, early 1991. (Courtesy Barry Broman)

mander what had already been telegraphed for months: Although some leftover funds were distributed in January, as of February 1991 the CIA had no more covert money available for the Cambodian project. The United States would still support the noncommunist resistance with humanitarian assistance channeled through USAID, but the CIA had officially ended its financial links to the program.[2]

If Suchinda had any reaction to the news, it was not betrayed on his face. "It was not his style to protest," commented Huff. "Besides, he was busy plotting against both his political and military (nominal) masters."[3]

Suchinda's scheming, in fact, had gone into overdrive. On 23 February, citing corruption in the Chatichai government, the military detained the prime minister and installed the National Peace-Keeping Council during a bloodless putsch. General Chavalit, who had already parted ways with Chatichai the previous year (he had earlier been deputy prime minister and defense minister) to form his own political party, was thought to benefit from the coup. But it was Suchinda and his powerful Class 5 that had emerged as the real powerbrokers.

The rise of General Suchinda had an immediate impact on Cambodia. The deposed Chatichai, eyeing business opportunities in Indochina, had been sympathetic toward the SOC and had pressured China into halting military support to the Khmer Rouge the previous November.

Suchinda, by contrast, looked favorably on the Khmer Rouge taking direct part in a power-sharing arrangement between the SOC and CGDK. Seeing this as an opening, Beijing immediately resumed military aid to Pol Pot's men.[4] The Khmer Rouge naturally lauded this move, then singled out Chavalit as being responsible for the rampant theft of Chinese aid under previous governments. "They said it was like someone had been pouring water over their mouths for the previous eleven years," recalled Ayupoon Karnasuta from the Working Group.[5]

The resumption of Chinese aid came just as the factions were trying to land some dry-season blows. In the vicinity of Route 10 near Pailin, both the Khmer Rouge and SOC had brought forward their tanks in February and engaged in the first armor duels of the civil war. The results were inconclusive, though the SOC later managed to stage a grisly press conference in Battambang city with three damaged Khmer Rouge tanks—including one with the charred remains of a crew inside the cupola.[6]

During the same month, the noncommunists had gone on an offensive near Svay Chek. This was an effort by the KPNLF to expand its liberated zone near Thmar Puok, where USAID was busy with roadbuilding and a range of other development projects. Not only did this effort make little headway; the SOC responded in March with a tank-led counteroffensive. This was rebuffed with some timely support from the Khmer Rouge 519 Division, resulting in four destroyed SOC tanks and the frontlines once again stabilizing just north of Svay Chek.[7]

At that point, the KPNLF and ANKI decided it was the right time to pool resources for their largest joint operation to date. Their target was Phnom Srok, the district in the northeastern quadrant of Banteay Meanchey where the Sihanoukists had staged a failed offensive in 1989. This low-lying area was normally inundated with water, and the ANS assault two years earlier had predictably bogged down in the soggy terrain. But as it was now well into the dry season, the terrain had baked into a hard crust and logistics were expected to be that much easier.

Set to participate in the main column was Nhek Bun Chay's 2 Brigade from ANKI and Kho Chhien's OMZ 3 from the KPNLF. To the south, the KPNLF's OMZ 6 under Lay Virak had pledged to cut Route 6 in order to prevent the arrival of reinforcements from Sisophon.

Eager to use its spoils of war, the KPNLF had positioned two 122mm guns at Thmar Puok with OMZ 3. For his part, Nhek Bun Chay was contributing a D-30 122mm howitzer he had captured in Oddar Meanchey. In addition, because a KPNLF agent had reported two SOC tanks in residence, both Nhek Bun Chay and Kho Chhien had assigned one T-54 apiece for the operation.

The KPNLF war memorial at Boeung Trakoun, 1991. (Courtesy Barry Broman)

Very quickly, however, Murphy's Law made an entry. Nhek Bun Chay's tank had its engine seize up and was sidelined, meaning the KPNLF tank would be going alone. The rest of the ANKI column was lagging as well, with only a fraction of the troops on hand when the operation was set to start. Compounding matters, Lay Virak suddenly showed little appetite to block Route 6 as promised.

Then when the KPNLF artillery was set to kick off the offensive with a barrage, all hell broke loose—from the opposite direction. In a perfectly timed spoiling maneuver, the SOC garrison at Phnom Srok put into play a BM-21 122mm multiple rocket launcher. This consisted of a Ural truck fitted with a bank of forty launch tubes arranged in a rectangular box in the rear. Each 2.87-meter rocket was slowly spun by rifling inside its tube as it exited, which along with stabilization fins kept it on course for up to 20 kilometers.

The forty rockets had arced toward Thmar Puok, impacting around the command post set up just behind the KPNLF artillery position. As senior officers were sent sprinting to the rear, half a dozen SOC tanks—not just two—surged forward from Phnom Srok and circled behind the forward line of noncommunist guerrillas. Dozens were killed or captured. One ANKI team was taken with three of its French-made F1 rocket launchers, which the SOC promptly displayed at a press conference in Phnom Penh. Thus, the most ambitious of joint noncommunist operations ever attempted fizzled just as soon as it started.[8]

By April, with the dry season coming to an end and all of the factions largely spent, United Nations Secretary General Javier Pérez de Cuéllar, who was fast approaching a decade in office and probably contemplating his legacy, thought it a good time to call for a Cambodian cease-fire. To the surprise of many, all of the parties agreed and a halt to fighting was theoretically enacted for the first time since 1979.

Of course, nothing of the sort actually took place. The official SOC press agency issued weekly statements about wide-ranging violations by all three CGDK factions. The SOC military, too, was hardly idle. The Military Region 4 commander in Siem Reap, General Long Sopheap, later admitted that his Dac Cong commando unit, which had been trained by PAVN counterparts, was active during this time frame against the KPNLF near Thmar Puok.[9]

Despite all this, however, there seemed to be momentum toward a negotiated settlement. In June, all four factions met under the auspices of the SNC as the Thai seaside resort town of Pattaya. Significantly, Sihanouk joined the event and acted as the meeting's chairman.[10]

But even more significant was what took place behind the scenes. General Suchinda realized that any SNC decisions that did not include the Khmer Rouge were destined to fail. And while there were two Khmer Rouge delegates in the SNC, the only one who could truly speak for that faction was Pol Pot himself. He was a pariah, however, and could not be seen in public, much less join the SNC in person.

Suchinda had a solution. He instructed Task Force 838 to fetch Pol Pot from his safe house on the border near Trat province, where he was living with a minor wife and their child. Pol Pot was lifted by chopper to Pattaya, then taken in a blacked-out van to the resort where the SNC had gathered. Tucked away inside a hotel room, he was provided with earphones and allowed to secretly listen to the deliberations taking place at an adjacent hall. His comments to the proceedings were surreptitiously fed to the Khmer Rouge delegates on the SNC, and they were thereby able to authoritatively offer their misgivings, and promises, with their leader's full knowledge and consent.[11]

Those promises proved significant. Over the course of the Pattaya meeting, all factions called for the so-called cease-fire to be extended indefinitely.[12] They also made tentative plans to cut off all external military assistance.

This second point was of special concern to Task Force 838.[13] In any future coalition, it wanted the noncommunists to balance, if not outnumber, the SOC's military. Colonel Nikorn, the head of Task Force 909,[14] was spearheading an eleventh-hour effort to drive up its numbers: "Our goal was to get ANKI up to

SOC M-113 armored personnel carriers from Military Region 4 conduct an exercise in Siem Reap province, 1991. They have been equipped with Soviet B-10 82mm recoilless rifles and DShK 12.7mm heavy machine guns. The vehicle in the center still bears its Khmer Republic–era stenciled insignia from the FANK 2 Division. (Author's collection)

about 23,000 men and the KPNLF to about 25,000. Our training camps were running non-stop to turn out Khmer fighters."[15]

In the case of ANKI, Ranariddh expanded his original four brigades into divisions. On paper, the brigades had comprised battalions, while the new divisions now had a trio of regiments apiece. Their sizes were hardly standardized, however, with Chakrapong claiming his 5 Division fielded more than 3,000 men, whereas the others pegged their strengths at only a fraction of that amount.[16]

In the KPNLF, a similar restructuring took place. With two exceptions, the OMZ commanders merely reclassified themselves as division commanders: Prum Vith became head of 1 Division at Sok Sann, Khem Sophoan now headed 2 Division near the Svay Chek frontline, Kho Chhien fielded 3 Division at Thmar Puok, Duong Sokhon controlled 4 Division along Route 5 west of Sisophon, and Lay Virak ran 5 Division at Nong Chan. Most of these divisions consisted of 2,300 men divided into three regiments, a headquarters unit, and a heavy weapons company. Khuon Roeun, meantime, still commanded his elite 1 Brigade, while two of the remaining OMZs, which had atrophied in recent years, were downgraded and converted into brigades.[17]

A pair of French LRAC F1 rockets was among the ANKI weapons captured at Phnom Srok and put on display in Phnom Penh, 25 March 1991. (Author's collection)

The wildcard in all this was the Khmer Rouge, whose size was always an enigma. Even the estimates of the most seasoned Cambodia-watchers varied widely, though most seemed to agree that its numbers had peaked in 1989 at about 40,000 fighters.[18] This dropped significantly in 1990 due to casualties and defections following the temporary cessation of Chinese aid. Task Force 838 placed the number at just 20,000 as of early 1991; although it never provided direct training support to the Khmer Rouge, 838 hoped to channel enough Chinese supplies to allow it to reach at least 30,000 guerrillas by the third quarter.[19]

These increases to the CGDK rosters came just in time. In late August, the SNC convened at Pattaya for a second time. All of the factions again agreed that foreign military assistance should cease. They further made tentative plans to demobilize 70 percent of their fighters, with the remaining 30 percent to gather inside designated cantonment areas at a time subject to further agreement.

The Cambodian factions could make these promises with the knowledge that two of the key foreign players—Vietnam and China—had reached an understanding to pull back and give negotiations a chance to unfold. On 30 August,

Generals Pann Thai and Sak review KPNLF troops at Boeung Trakoun, 1991. Note the Bedford trucks (in background) provided by the Working Group. (Courtesy Barry Broman)

almost two years after it falsely claimed to have withdrawn its troops, PAVN quietly removed its last military advisers from the SOC.[20]

In the case of China, it once again halted supplies to the Khmer Rouge in September—though with a gaping loophole when it turned over to Son Sen, the Khmer Rouge defense minister, a massive cargo ship docked at Thailand's Klong Yai port. It took little imagination to envision Son Sen dispatching the vessel to purchase weapons on the open market, then bringing them to desolate beaches along the Koh Kong coast. To be sure, the Khmer Rouge was making more than enough money selling logs and gemstones to sustain its movement even without Chinese cash infusions.[21]

Such duplicity aside, the seemingly endless rounds of negotiations finally reached a climax in Paris during October. That month, in a set of agreements signed by SNC President Sihanouk and eighteen other nations, a comprehensive peace pact took effect. This signaled the beginning of a transitional period in Cambodia that would last until the formation of a new government following free and fair elections set for the second quarter of 1993. The SNC ceded considerable power to the United Nations Transitional Authority in Cambodia

(UNTAC), which would effectively administer the country in the interim, enforce a cessation of all outside military assistance, and confirm the demobilization of 70 percent of each faction's military.

On 11 November, an advance contingent of United Nations troops landed in Phnom Penh.[22] Concurrent with this, Charles Twining, a U.S. diplomat who had previously headed the Cambodia desk at Foggy Bottom, arrived in the Cambodian capital as Washington's special representative to the SNC. This was the first official U.S. representation in Cambodia in more than sixteen years.[23]

The next day, Prince Chakrapong made a surprise appearance in the city. As one of the more colorful members of the extended, often dysfunctional Cambodian royal family, Chakrapong had been fuming ever since Ranariddh was named ANKI's Supreme Commander. Though he wore a number of hats as consolation—minister of defense, first deputy chief of staff, and commander of 5 Division—he was still unhappy with his perceived mistreatment at the hands of his half-brother. This had led him in mid-1991 to send out feelers to the Khmer Rouge warlord at Anlong Veng, Ta Mok, about him possibly defecting with the entire 5 Division. The offer was flatly rejected.[24]

Hardly fazed, Chakrapong quietly made his case with Hun Sen. Shrewdly, the Phnom Penh regime concurred. Glad to have a prominent royal on board, and potentially split ANKI in the process, Hun Sen elevated Chakrapong to vice prime minister.

Hun Sen, meantime, had flown to Beijing. There he was welcomed by Sihanouk, his wife, Monique, and Ranariddh. Sihanouk, while suffering from high blood pressure and mild diabetes, was in good spirits. On 14 November, all four boarded an Air China Boeing 707 bound for Beijing. Surrounded by North Korean bodyguards armed with cattle prods to keep crowds at bay, the prince landed in the Cambodian capital to a tumultuous welcome after a twelve-year absence.

Along the western border, the CGDK factions scrambled to adjust to the new realities under the Paris peace agreements. A so-called Blue Zone centered around Thmar Puok, home to about 75,000 civilians, was designated as the cantonment area for the KPNLF. The cantonment for ANKI was the White Zone in the vicinity of Phum Sereipheap, which it outrageously claimed had a population of 500,000—probably off by at least one decimal point. UNTAC observers would theoretically be visiting these zones in the coming months to verify the demobilization of troops.

While noncommunist combatants were ordered to start massing in their

General Sak confers an award on General Prum Vith while Dien Del (right) looks on, Boeung Trakoun, 1991. (Courtesy Barry Broman)

respective zones, leadership in these factions was suddenly in short supply. In ANKI, Ranariddh had shifted to Phnom Penh, and Chakrapong had already defected. This left it largely up to Toan Chay to run ANKI on a daily basis.

A similar situation was evident in the KPNLF. Son Sann, who occupied one of the two SNC seats allocated to the Front, went to Phnom Penh in late November to attend the council's first meeting in the capital.[25] General Sak remained in the vicinity of Site 2 and spent much of his time dabbling with plans to form a political party that would contest the 1993 elections. His deputy, Dien Del, was largely preoccupied in Aranyaprathet with his wife and baby son.

By default, this left it squarely on Pann Thai's shoulders to manage the KPNLAF. In late December, however, Pann Thai also took leave of Banteay Meanrit for Phnom Penh. This was because he had been selected as the Front's representative on the Mixed Military Working Group, the four-member body designated in the Paris peace agreements to help UNTAC resolve problems with the cease-fire.[26]

Pann Thai's departure from Banteay Meanrit was not without controversy. Situated under a parasol in front of the general's residence was a magnificent stone statue of the Hindu god Vishnu. Smugglers had stolen it from the Angkor Wat temple, but they were intercepted by KPNLF guerrillas just before crossing the

The ANKI chief of operations, General Toan Chay. (Courtesy Barry Broman)

Thai frontier. On the night before Pann Thai's departure, however, the head of the statue mysteriously disappeared. His secretary later accused the general of selling it to a Thai collector.

A second, more sinister rumor would also dog Pann Thai. Shortly before the general's arrival in Phnom Penh, the COS agent network in the capital was quietly rolled up by SOC authorities. They had been lying low since the grenade strikes of late 1989, diligently gathering information and sending it back via their handler's radio.

After their arrests, the handler was pressured into continuing radio play with Banteay Meanchit, to include requests to send more agents. These requests were passed to Dien Del—who had also gotten word that one of the COS members had evaded the dragnet and escaped via Klong Yai. Realizing the handler was communicating under duress, the general allowed the radio play to continue for another month before ceasing contact.[27]

This immediately begged the question of how the agents had been exposed. It could have been chalked up to good detective work on the part of the SOC. But the Cambodians are always game for a good conspiracy, and ever since 1988 the KPNLAF leadership had suspected a mole was active within the senior ranks. CIA officers at the Hilton had quietly stated as such, probably based on communica-

Members of the Mixed Military Working Group confer in Phnom Penh, 24 December 1991. On the right are ANKI officers Nhek Bun Chay, Krouch Yoeum, and Tes Chanthan. Later a major general in the Royal Cambodian Air Force, Tes Chanthan died in a March 1995 plane crash in Kompong Thom. (Author's collection)

tions intercepts. "We smelled a Fifth Column," said Gaffar Meang-Peth. "There were too many things that had gone wrong to blame on coincidence."[28]

Several suspects rose to the top of the list of possible traitors. Fingers initially were directed at Lay Bun Song, the Front's chief of intelligence during the later years. But Song would go on to show unceasing loyalty to the ideals of the Front, up through his death in the 1990s.

Others cast a suspicious eye toward Pok Sam An, the former chief of staff who had left Thailand on bad terms with Sak. He had suddenly reappeared in Phnom Penh in 1991 with a large amount of cash, which he promptly invested in renovating the Renakse Hotel near the Royal Palace. But Pok Sam An had been with the Front for only a short period, and most of the betrayed secrets postdated his departure.

All of this caused many to scrutinize Pann Thai. He was already tainted with charges tied to the missing Vishnu head, bringing into question his ethics. Then in 1992, after a few months on the Mixed Military Working Group, he suddenly broke ranks with the KPNLF and took a position as senior adviser to Hun Sen.

The members of the COS ring, who would languish in prison until being released by UNTAC in 1993, were convinced of his betrayal. No conclusive evidence was ever produced, however, and Pann Thai, who was reduced to a vegetative state following a severe stroke near the turn of the century, took his secrets to a living grave.

18. Aftermath

In March 1992, UNTAC formally began its interim period of governance over Cambodia. The contingent was set to grow to 22,000 foreign military and civilian personnel, last about sixteen months, and cost upward of $2 billion. It would be the largest, most ambitious United Nations operation of its kind since the organization tried to nursemaid the independence of Congo in 1960.

The challenges facing UNTAC were legion, most notably those tied to enforcing the cease-fire and demobilization of combatants. The former task was rife with danger, as the Khmer Rouge were standing firm against the provision in the Paris agreements that left the SOC government structure in place in more than 80 percent of the country. The Khmer Rouge had unsuccessfully tried to have the SNC assume control and, in frustration, was now showing little hesitation to take the occasional shot at foreign monitors.[1]

Like the Khmer Rouge, the KPNLF had also voiced trepidation over the incumbent SOC regime maintaining its infrastructure across the countryside. Once the Paris agreements went into effect, however, General Sak had abided by both the letter and spirit of the agreements. The KPNLF, in fact, was proving itself a model for demobilization. On 16 July, nearly 3,000 of the Front's guerrillas laid down arms in a ceremony at Banteay Meanrit attended by UNTAC's civilian and military chiefs. Also surrendered were the spoils taken in 1989: a pair of T-54 tanks, a BTR-60 armored personnel carrier, and an assortment of artillery. At the end of the event, Sak relinquished his own rifle and released a flock of doves with a pledge that another 5,700 men under arms would rally before month's end.

Leaving the resistance business behind, the KPNLF's leaders took their struggle—and enduring internal rift—to the political arena. As he had long planned, Sak created his own political vehicle, the Liberal Democratic Party, to contest the elections. Son Sann, meantime, established a rival Buddhist Liberal Democratic Party. Neither figure was a household name across much of Cambodia, though they theoretically had support among their guerrilla ranks and the soon-to-be-repatriated masses from Site 2.

In the case of ANKI, Ranariddh was set to run on the Funcinpec ticket. Unlike his KPNLF rivals, the prince appeared to be making strong headway by milking his royal lineage for all it was worth. To drop Funcinpec leaflets around the country, he had even cut a jungle airstrip near the ANKI cantonment in Oddar Meanchey province and purchased a French-made Socata TB 10 light plane.[2]

From Bangkok, the Working Group watched all this unfold. It was steadfastly complying with the stipulation in the Paris agreements against external military assistance, but political assistance—at least covert political assistance—was considered fair game. Its members realized that in order to defeat the SOC's candidate, Hun Sen, they could not split the noncommunist vote. And among all the noncommunist candidates—Ranariddh, Son Sann, and Sak—only Ranariddh appeared to have a good chance at winning based on name recognition alone. The Working Group decided, therefore, that it would work toward a Funcinpec victory.

There was a major problem, however. Even if UNTAC observers could ensure that the SOC did not stuff ballot boxes, much of the rural populace was illiterate and probably could not read the ballots.

Not wanting to leave anything to chance, the Thai members of the Working Group had a novel solution. In the Golden Triangle of northernmost Thailand, the Royal Thai government had often encountered uneducated constituencies that could not read a ballot. In cases where the government wanted to push a certain candidate, it had handed out measured strings ahead of the polls. When one end of a string was held flush with the top of the ballot, the other end rested atop the name of the desired candidate.

And this is exactly what happened in Cambodia. Operating behind the scenes, the Working Group obtained a sample ballot and set about cutting strings that would steer illiterate voters to the box aside Ranariddh's name. These were then distributed through the Funcinpec zone and beyond.[3]

Whether or not this was a major contributing factor, the election of 23 May 1993 very much went the Working Group's way. Ranariddh took a plurality with 45 percent of the vote, while Hun Sen placed second with 38 percent. Son Sann trailed with a paltry 3.8 percent, but even this dismal turnout shined next to Sak's 1.6 percent. The next day the Working Group threw a party, then quietly disbanded.

Though the United States could also take heart in the electoral results, the CIA was not on hand to share in the Working Group's backslapping. Barry Broman had completed his tour in 1992 and already departed Thailand. Over the rest of that year, the remainder of his team concluded their assignments and deployed elsewhere.

At the Hilton in Aranyaprathet, Robert Wnukowski had also overseen a discrete phaseout during 1992. While this meant that the CIA's window to that part of eastern Thailand was now closed, another officer had already been tapped to reopen Phnom Penh Station.

Significantly, Aranyaprathet would later factor into one of the darker footnotes in the CIA's history. Harold James Nicholson, the case officer who served at the Hilton during 1985–1987, had done a very credible job as deputy base commander. He followed this up with another good tour in Tokyo, after which his career got a push and he was promoted in 1990 to station chief in Romania. There he had again done well and was told in 1992 he would next serve as the second-ranking officer in the larger Kuala Lumpur Station.

As Nicholson was preparing to leave Bucharest, however, his wife announced she was ending their marriage. He was not particularly distressed with the news, as their relationship was strained ever since his time at Aranyaprathet. But the breakup promised to be costly: After a prolonged custody battle for their three children, he was told in 1994 to pay his former wife $12,000 in an initial divorce settlement and alimony of $650 per month.

Nicholson eyed this substantial figure and calculated it would financially sink him. With apparently little pause, his solution was to turn to the same people he had targeted for much of his CIA career: the Russians. In June 1994, as he was finishing his Kuala Lumpur tour, he walked into the Russian embassy and offered to sell secrets.

While undoubtedly suspicious, the KGB *rezident* took the bait. Over a series of four meetings before departing Malaysia, Nicholson swapped information for cash. After the last of these, he wired enough money to the United States to cover his divorce settlement.

But the KBG was looking for more, and Nicholson was game. Sweetening the pot, his next posting—as an instructor at the CIA's training facility in Williamsburg, Virginia—was obviously of intense interest to his Russian handlers. Over the next two years, the CIA turncoat gathered biographic data on four entire classes of trainees, then took trips to New Delhi, Jakarta, and Zurich for secret trysts with the KGB. The identities of 300 junior CIA officers were thus exposed to the KGB even before their first overseas assignments.

But this was not without considerable risk. By the time of his Zurich trip in December 1995, Nicholson had already started to receive scrutiny from the CIA's counterintelligence wing. Besides failing a string of routine polygraphs, he had neglected to properly hide a pattern of large spending, unusual travel, and sizable but unexplained bank deposits.

In June 1996, as his Williamsburg tour was concluding, Nicholson took a fourth overseas trip to rendezvous with the KBG. Unknown to him, a CIA team followed as he made his way to Singapore. This destination was an exceedingly poor decision on Nicholson's part, as that entire city-state was virtually wired for surveillance. Once there, the CIA, in coordination with Singaporean counterparts, monitored Nicholson as he entered a seemingly desolate parking lot, was bundled into the trunk of a Russian diplomat's car, and driven into the Russian embassy compound for a debriefing.

From Singapore, Nicholson flew to Thailand. There he called on his former secretary from Aranyaprathet, a Thai woman named Kanookwan Lehliem. The sister of the handyman employed at the Hilton, she had been only twenty years old when they worked together on the border.[4] Now ten years on, the two fast-tracked a romance and set out for a Honolulu vacation. They made tentative plans to marry, but for the moment Kanookwan returned to Thailand and Nicholson headed back to Langley.

By that time, the CIA spyhunters were convinced of Nicholson's duplicity but had not yet caught him with stolen documents. To keep him under closer observation, they arranged for his next posting to be as a branch chief at the CIA's Counterterrorism Center in Washington. After surreptitiously watching him photograph classified material, he was arrested in November 1996 as he was headed for yet another meeting with the KGB in Zurich. He pleaded guilty in March 1997 to being paid $300,000 by the Russians. Described as the highest-ranking CIA officer to be exposed as a spy, he was sentenced to 23 years and 7 months in prison.[5]

In Thailand, a sudden bout of bloody political turmoil during early 1992 briefly eclipsed Cambodia from the radar. This began in April, when General Suchinda, the leader behind the military's February 1991 power grab, went a step too far by assuming the mantle of prime minister. The Bangkok populace took to the streets in protest, with perhaps hundreds of demonstrators perishing in a subsequent crackdown. After intervention from the king, Suchinda retreated from public life and stability quickly returned.

In as the new RTA commander was General Wimol Wongwanich, a well-regarded professional who had led the Special Warfare Command during the late 1980s when it was providing manpower to Cambodian projects such as the DPPU and Task Force 838. The Cambodian situation had changed considerably since then but was still fully capable of inflicting migraines on the RTA chief. Specifically, Wimol had to perform a delicate dance with the Khmer Rouge. On the one hand, Thailand was trying to publicly distance itself from them. On the other,

Co–Prime Ministers Ranariddh and Hun Sen review the Indonesian contingent during the final withdrawal of UNTAC, September 1993. (Author's collection)

Wimol was reluctant to fully sever ties and went on record as opposing sanctions against the Khmer Rouge. His rationale: They would fail due to the self-sufficiency that the Khmer Rouge had allegedly achieved in agriculture. In reality, the general was no doubt being protective of the lucrative gemstone and timber deals those guerrillas had signed with Thai businessmen.

Eventually, the balancing act proved too much. By late 1993, the belligerent Khmer Rouge had grown increasingly isolated and Thailand was under heightened pressure to cut its vestigial links to the faction. That December, in a bout of interservice rivalry, police officers raided a heavily guarded border warehouse in Chanthaburi province, just opposite the Khmer Rouge stronghold at Pailin. Loaded with Chinese-made weapons up to and including 130mm field guns, the depot was one of three Khmer Rouge compounds established more than a decade earlier with covert support from the RTA. Embarrassed by the exposure, the RTA at long last removed the stockpiled arms and, without fanfare, disbanded Task Force 838.

With Task Force 838 now history, the RTA consolidated its Cambodian operations in 838's parent unit, TOC 315. This center not only assisted with policy-making; it also maintained an intelligence function by running agent networks into Cambodia. In 1996, during a repeat stint as defense minister, General Chavalit had assigned one of his trusted subordinates, Lieutenant General Wichit Yathip, as head of 315. Wichit had his own long history with Cambodia, all the

Sihanouk with his North Korean bodyguards arriving at Pochentong, November 1993. (Author's collection)

way back to serving as a liaison officer with the nascent noncommunist resistance during the late 1970s.

Ever ambitious, Chavalit had his eyes on bigger and better roles. That November, his New Aspiration Party won the most seats in a general election and he was at long last elevated to prime minister. It would prove a rocky pinnacle to his career: With the Thai economy battered by international currency speculators in early 1997, he was forced to resign after only a year for his failure to defend the baht and contain the kingdom's financial crisis.

Other veterans of the secret war in Cambodia would continue to play prominent roles in Thailand. In 1998, General Surayud Chulanont, the seemingly apolitical officer who had led both Task Force 838 and the Working Group, was elevated to RTA chief. On the same day of his promotion, he sacked Wichit as head of TOC 315. He would later strip 315 of its intelligence function, transferring responsibility to the Special Warfare Command where he had spent much of his career.

In 2003, Surayud, who was having strains with populist Prime Minister Thaksin Shinawatra, stepped aside as army commander and took the more senior, but largely hollow, role as Supreme Commander of the Armed Forces. More significant, he was named to the Privy Council, the King's inner ring of trusted advisers. From this position, he worked behind the scenes to get General Sonthi Boonyaratglin promoted in 2005 to head of the army.

Sonthi, who had served under Surayud in the Special Warfare Command as well as his own stint as Task Force 838 commander, was an unlikely RTA chief. Soft-spoken and mild-mannered, he never betrayed a taste for power. And as a Muslim, he seemed a long shot to rise to the top in Buddhist-majority Thailand.

Sonthi's benign demeanor would prove deceptive, however. In September 2006, following his own strains with Prime Minister Thaksin, Sonthi led the army in seizing control of the kingdom. The following month, he implored his former Special Forces boss, General Surayud, to take the reins as prime minister. Surayud, in turn, appointed his deputy at both 838 and the Working Group, General Boonrod, as defense minister. Sonthi himself retired from the military and became deputy prime minister in charge of security.

As it turned out, managing Cambodia's secret war was nothing compared to the pitfalls of politics. Though he entered office with a respectable approval rating, Surayud proved unable to revive Thailand's floundering economy. This, plus a spotty human rights record and a host of other shortcomings, led to skyrocketing criticism of his rule. After a tumultuous 16 months in office, the general and the rest of his Cambodian cabal had little choice but to step aside.

In Cambodia itself, UNTAC had finally departed in September 1993. At a cost of seventy-eight fatalities of their own and a bill of $1.62 billion, UNTAC had more or less fulfilled its mandate of monitoring a transparent election.

But problems remained in its wake, some of them glaring. Topping the list was the fact that Hun Sen's Cambodian People's Party was not happy with placing second and sulked until Funcinpec agreed to an unwieldy power-sharing arrangement in which Hun Sen and Ranariddh were named co–prime ministers in a bifurcated Royal Cambodian government. Shunted to the side in this equation was Sihanouk, who had abandoned hopes of becoming a strong French-style president and in September 1993 took the oath to become king for the second time in his life.[6]

An equally vexing problem involved the Khmer Rouge, which had both boycotted the elections and resisted the demobilization process. Even without access to arms stockpiles in Thailand, it had enough weapons in its border enclaves—which covered about 20 percent of the country—to sustain the movement for years to come.

Forced to confront the Khmer Rouge without the crutch afforded by UNTAC, the Cambodian government in late 1993 turned to the newly constituted Royal Cambodian Armed Forces (RCAF). Trouble was, the Cambodian army was barely

A frail General Sak talks with General Pol Saroeun in early April 1994, just weeks prior to his death. (Author's collection)

up to the task. Even more than the awkward coministers arrangement, the RCAF attempted to cobble together three separate entities. But rather than blending them after a decent interval of confidence-building, virtually all of the units remained segregated along factional lines. Half were filled with former SOC troops. Another quarter was composed of ex-KPNLAF guerrillas: 7 Division under Kho Chhien at Thmar Puok, 8 Division led by Khuon Roeun in his home province of Pursat, and 12 Division under Lay Virak at Poipet. ANKI veterans constituted the final quarter: 3 Division under Sim Paul in Siem Reap, 9 Division headed by Khin Yean at Oddar Meanchey, and 14 Division commanded by Long Sereyrath at Preah Vihear.[7]

There were obvious problems with such an arrangement. First, there was no standardization in equipment or training. Also, few foreign sponsors were stepping forward to provide military assistance. Even North Korea, Sihanouk's guardian angel over the decades, balked on an agreement to equip two brigades.[8]

Second, the RCAF had become arguably the most top-heavy military in the world. Each of the three factions had been given a quota of generals—which were quickly filled, then exceeded. By 1994, the RCAF was bloated with an estimated 2,000 generals. There were numerous verifiable tales of FANK veterans from the United States and France returning to their homeland where, for a modest fee, they suddenly sported stars on their shoulderboards. The vast majority of them postured in Phnom Penh with no actual position, let alone troops under their

Royal Cambodian Air Force Mi-17 prepares to hit Pailin with Russian-made 250-kilo cluster bombs on its weapons pylons, 1994. After this supply of bombs was soon exhausted, the RCAF began dropping 120mm mortar rounds bound in clusters of four. (Courtesy Leng Sochea)

command. For the average RCAF combatant, however, such rampant promotions in the capital hardly boosted morale.

Then there was the question of which RCAF units would actually bear the brunt of combat against the Khmer Rouge. After decades of fighting, few RCAF soldiers relished the idea of resuming brutal combat—especially against a hard-nosed foe like the Khmer Rouge. But because they were in close proximity along the border, and perhaps because Hun Sen wanted to mete out some poetic justice, it was decreed that the KPNLF divisions in September 1993 would spearhead the initial RCAF thrust against the Khmer Rouge enclave at Phnom Chat.

This was a bittersweet decision. No matter how reprehensible they were, the Khmer Rouge fighters at Phnom Chat had come to the assistance of the KPNLF over the years. But obeying orders, the KPNLF troops moved against their erstwhile CGDK partners and, to their surprise, sent the Khmer Rouge reeling. In revenge, Khmer Rouge farther south surrounded Sok Sann—Prum Vith's old mountaintop bastion—and massacred the villagers.

Not wanting to lose momentum, the government in early 1994 ordered the RCAF to move against the larger Khmer Rouge enclaves at Phnom Melai and Pailin. Some former SOC and ANKI units were to be used, but the bulk of the task force would again be the three KPNLF divisions. After a tough slog down

Route 10, government troops during the final week of March punched their way into Pailin.

Among those on hand to see the government's flag raised over the liberated town was General Sak. Officially calling himself an adviser to the government, Sak was still sporting his four stars. Over the ensuing three weeks, he remained around Pailin to encourage his former KPNLF guerrillas as they expanded their area of control into the surrounding hills.

For Sak, this was a rare departure. Despite rising to the top of FANK, then the KPNLF, he had always been closer to a desk than the field of combat. Now in the twilight of his career, and in failing health, he had taken to touring the frontlines in a BTR-60.

It took a toll on the general. On 28 April, a weary Sak came back to Phnom Penh and shared a drink with one of his aged contemporaries, General Nhiek Tioulong. Short of breath, he retired to his bed and died in his sleep. His cremated remains were interned at Wat Botum, the fifteenth-century temple adjacent to the palace.

After seizing Pailin, the Cambodian government exchanged stick for carrot. This was a fortuitous move, as the upper echelon of the Khmer Rouge was primed for implosion due to competition over dwindling financial resources. During the war years, the Chinese embassy in Bangkok had funneled much of its monetary assistance through the onetime Khmer Rouge foreign minister, Ieng Sary. This had given him disproportionate influence for as long as the money flowed, but it also prompted whispers of corruption from fellow senior revolutionaries.

After the Chinese financial spigot was turned off, Ieng Sary was suddenly the odd man out. Ta Mok had steady income from logging deals in the north. Pol Pot and Noun Chea were tapped into the gemstone windfall at Pailin. And Son Sen had promptly sold the transport vessel given by China, reportedly earning $1 million. Ieng Sary had tried to muscle into the Pailin gem business, but years of pent-up jealousy from his peers was now coming to the fore.[9]

Out of ideas, Ieng Sary quietly sent out a feeler to Phnom Penh. It bit, and in August 1996 he and thousands of his followers filed out of the jungle. After King Sihanouk offered a pardon for his 1979 conviction in absentia by the PRK regime, Ieng Sary was placed in charge of the new municipality declared around Pailin.

Reduced to a northern enclave around Anlong Veng, the remainder of the Khmer Rouge grew paranoid about further defections. Sickly and skittish, Pol Pot in June 1997 had Son Sen and thirteen of his family members murdered then,

A Chinese Type 62 light tank captured from the Khmer Rouge at Anlong Veng in 1994. (Courtesy Chea Chheang)

for good measure, ordered that a truck drive over their corpses. Though the remainder of the movement would cling on for another year—Pol Pot himself died of heart failure in April 1998—it had long ceased to be a serious challenge to the government.

Without the need to focus on the Khmer Rouge threat, Cambodia's leaders turned their knives inward. By 1997, the idea of co–prime ministers—not to mention mirror cabinet posts—had been confirmed as sheer folly. In early July, the marriage of convenience forced upon Funcinpec and the Cambodian People's Party devolved into a bloody divorce.

The issue precipitating this was tied to the RCAF. Although steps had been taken to integrate troops in some units, the military was still largely segregated along factional lines. Each eyed the other with suspicion, with charges that the other side was trying to integrate former Khmer Rouge fighters into the ranks.

There were also charges that units loyal to Ranariddh were stockpiling their own weapons. There was some truth to this. On a symbolic level, Ranariddh's bodyguards were the only ones in the RCAF to be equipped with FAMAS rifles, saved since the ANS days. Somewhat more substantially, Ranariddh's generals in February 1996 quietly negotiated for Taiwan to give three months of airborne and commando training to twenty Funcinpec troops and, the next year, reportedly received a secret shipment of Taiwanese arms.

On 5 July 1997, the rivalry passed the point of no return. That day, SOC units in the RCAF launched a brutal blitz against senior Funcinpec figures, prompting many to flee the capital. South of Pochentong, SOC armor attempted to block their escape route. Wielding Armbrusts they had kept hidden since 1989, a column of Funcinpec troops managed to destroy two tanks before disappearing into the countryside.[10]

Among the lucky was General Nhek Bun Chay, the former ANKI brigade commander. Fleeing to Oddar Meanchey, he set up a base of resistance near the O'Smach border pass. As this was at one time an ANS stronghold, Nhek was more than familiar with the surrounding terrain. Using this to his advantage, he and a band of Funcinpec loyalists kept RCAF units at bay for a year.[11]

Others were not as fortunate. This included Lieutenant General Krouch Yoeum, the former ANKI delegate to the Mixed Military Working Group and most recently the undersecretary of state in the Ministry of National Defense, the third highest Funcinpec official in that ministry. He was reportedly arrested by SOC commandos in Kompong Speu, then summarily executed behind a pagoda with three shots to the head and one to the chest.

Another was Chea Chhut, the notorious KPNLF camp commander at Nong Chan. Defecting to the Sihanoukists during the war, he spent the remainder of the conflict with ANKI. After 1993, he had been rewarded with the governor's slot in the newly formed province of Kep. He, too, was arrested in Kompong Speu and shot in the head.

As the smoke from the coup cleared, Hun Sen alone sat on top. With political freedoms eroded and corruption on the rise through the turn of the century, it was hard to rate Cambodia as an unqualified success story. Still, there was ample reason to see the glass as half-full. Cambodia, after all, had emerged from unspeakable internal genocide and a brutal civil war with its borders intact, a population once more on the rise, and an economy making marked gains.

For the United States, and especially for the CIA, the ties with Cambodia throughout the Cold War had been especially vexing. But in the end, Cambodian policy had seen Soviet expansionism on mainland Southeast Asia checked, America's regional friends and allies reassured, the Khmer Rouge spent, and the Cambodian noncommunists left with a foothold to build upon.

Stephen Solarz, who had been the strongest congressional supporter for the

KPNLF and Funcinpec, felt more than vindicated. “The peace process worked out better than anybody could have expected,” he would later assess. “And the noncommunists even got the most votes.”[12]

Barry Broman, the senior CIA representative on the Working Group, agreed. “The U.S. could declare its policy objectives were met,” adding, “In Cambodia, we could finally declare victory.”

Notes

1. Springtime in Cambodia

1. As might be expected of a kingdom that had lost significant amounts of territory, many ethnic Khmer were outside of Cambodia's consolidated borders: As many as 800,000 could be found in Thailand and another half-million in Vietnam's Mekong Delta.

2. His seventh wife, Monique Sihanouk, née Paule Monique Izzi, was the daughter of a French-Italian banker and a Cambodian mother. Sihanouk had two more children with her after getting married in 1952 (and undergoing a more formal wedding ceremony in 1955).

3. Despite abdicating, Sihanouk retained all the de facto powers of a king and ran the government like a royal court. When his father, Norodom Suramarit, died in April 1960, Sihanouk delayed any decision to select a new monarch and instead formally named himself to the new position of chief of state.

4. Robert C. Taber, *After Action Report: Discontinuance of U.S. MAAG Cambodia*, 14 January 1964, pp. C–4, C–5.

5. Sihanouk was incensed with South Vietnam and Thailand for their support of anti-communist Cambodian rebels, as well as the latter's territorial claim over the Preah Vihear border temple. By association, he was irate at the United States for its close ties to the governments in Saigon and Bangkok.

6. Kenton Clymer, *Troubled Relations: The United States and Cambodia since 1870* (DeKalb: Northern Illinois University Press, 2007), p. 60.

7. Dang Phong, *Kinh Te Mien Nam Viet Nam Thoi Ky 1955–1975* ["The Economy of South Vietnam during the Period 1955–1975"] (Hanoi: Social Science Publishing House, 2004), p. 572; Nguyen Viet Phuong, *Truong Son, Duong Ho Chi Minh Huyen Thoai* ["The Annamite Mountains: The Legendary Ho Chi Minh Trail"] (Ho Chi Minh City: Tre Publishing House, 2004), Volume 2, pages 15–17. The shipping arrangements were initially handled by Koch Ann, an ethnic Chinese Cambodian from Kratie province who was a close business associate of Lon Nol. He had earlier grown wealthy by shipping timber and beef to the PRC and Hong Kong. In late 1967, Koch Ann was forced to relocate to Hong Kong after being accused of smuggling. The weapon shipments were then handled by Hak Ly, which was ostensibly headed by a Cambodian of Vietnamese ethnicity but actually commanded by a PAVN officer. Interview with Sabu Bacha, 29 July 2011.

8. In February 1966, the Chinese began shipping funds for foodstuffs to be purchased on the Cambodian market and shipped to PAVN sanctuaries along the South Vietnamese border. In July 1966, PAVN established Rear Services Group 17 to coordinate the impending supply traffic through Sihanoukville. The first Chinese vessel loaded with weapons arrived in Sihanoukville during December 1966. Evidence gathered in 1970 indicated that the Cambodian military routinely sold a significant portion of its 10 percent cut to PAVN for extra cash. "Communist Deliveries to Cambodia for the VC/NVA," CIA Directorate of

Intelligence, Intelligence Memorandum, December 1970, p. 2, 10; Dang Phong, 5 *Duong Mon Ho Chi Minh* ["The Five Ho Chi Minh Trails"] (Hanoi: Intellectual Publishing House, 2008), p. 246.

9. Thomas L. Ahern Jr., "Good Questions, Wrong Answers" (Washington, D.C.: Center for the Study of Intelligence, 2004), p. 47.

10. Milton Osborne, *Sihanouk: Prince of Light, Prince of Darkness* (Honolulu: University of Hawaii Press, 1994), p. 4.

11. Milton Osborne, *Phnom Penh: A Cultural and Literary History* (Oxford: Signal Books, 2008), pp. 134–135.

12. Sihanouk could be especially testy toward the PRC. He forbid the distribution of publications with Mao Tse-Tung's thoughts and in September 1967 threatened to sever ties with Beijing if the Chinese ever attempted to export the Cultural Revolution to Cambodia. Central Intelligence Agency [CIA] Intelligence Information Cable, "Comments by Prince Sihanouk on Cambodia's Relations with the United States and China," 4 September 1968.

13. Osborne, *Sihanouk*, p. 86.

14. *Foreign Relations of the United States* [FRUS], 1969–76, Volume X (Washington, D.C.: Department of State, 2010), Document #137, "Telegram from Embassy in Cambodia to Department of State," 14 August 1974.

15. William Shawcross, *Sideshow* (New York: Simon & Schuster, 1979), pp. 60–61.

16. Steve Heder, *Cambodian Communism and the Vietnamese Model*, Vol. 1 (Bangkok: White Lotus Press, 2004), p. 98.

17. In 1964, this front became part of a larger opposition umbrella, the United Front for the Liberation of Oppressed Races (Front Uni de Lutte des Races Opprimées, or FULRO), which received significant covert support from the Cambodian government.

18. This underground movement openly agitated for ethnic Cambodians in the lower Mekong to secede from Saigon's rule. With prompting from Chau Dara, the Front recruited sympathizers among the ethnic Cambodian population in the Delta; these members occasionally crossed the border to report their findings to Cambodian government handlers.

19. In 1965, for example, twenty-five White Scarf members, all of whom had temporarily entered the monkhood, were given travel allowances to come to Cambodia ostensibly on a religious pilgrimage. While there they were debriefed by Cambodian military officers and persons claiming to be senior White Scarf cadre. They were even granted an audience with Sihanouk at his Black Palace in the hill resort of Bokor. Interview with Sovandy Kong, 30 October 2010.

20. The KKK was formed in November 1961 and initially staged attacks against South Vietnamese government targets in the Mekong Delta. But as it were opposed to Vietnamese of all political persuasions, by 1962 it had started to clash with communist Vietnamese guerrillas. During 1965–1966, large numbers of KKK switched loyalties due to a South Vietnamese amnesty program and the prospect of proper employment with South Vietnamese paramilitary forces. In late 1967, an entire battalion of former KKK was given training under U.S. Army Special Forces (USSF) auspices at the Phu Quoc Training Center and deployed to Hue. Nicknamed the Red Devil Battalion, it was assigned to the Military Assistance Command Vietnam's Special Operations Group (MACVSOG) and deployed

around the A Shau Valley. When the battalion regulars threatened mutiny to protest being separated from their dependents, they were sent back to the Delta and reassigned to the Civilian Irregular Defense Group (CIDG) program. In July 1970, two battalions of former KKK serving in the CIDG were flown to Cambodia and incorporated into the 7 Infantry Brigade. Interview with John Gebbie, 22 July 1997; Franklin J. Yurco, *Outline History of Company D, 1962–1970*, 5th Special Forces Group (Airborne), pp. 3–6.

21. Interview with Dien Del, 9 April 2011. Queen Sisowath Kossamak was the mother of Norodom Sihanouk.

22. CIA Intelligence Information Report, "Khmer Rouge and Viet Cong Activities in Ratanakiri Province," 18 September 1969, p. 1.

23. FRUS, 1969–76, Volume VI (Washington, D.C.: U.S. Department of State, 2006), Document #110, Editorial Note.

24. Radio Khmer Serei briefly broadcasted from clandestine radio stations in South Vietnam and Thailand during May 1959. After an extended hiatus, it resumed broadcasts in 1963. Taber, p. C-6.

25. Justin Corfield, *Khmers Stand Up!* (Victoria: Center of Southeast Asian Studies, 1994), p. 34.

26. By 1965, the vast majority of Khmer Serei in South Vietnam had joined the paramilitary CIDG program in III Corps; a smaller number joined the CIDG in IV Corps. In late December 1965, the South Vietnamese government reportedly sent a shipload of unrepentant Khmer Serei guerrillas to join their fellow rebels in Thailand.

Former Khmer Serei leader Lek Sam Ouen confirmed that one Khmer Serei battalion was shifted from South Vietnam to the Dangrek Mountains circa 1965. Declassified Document Reference System [DDRS], Retrospective Collection, #334F, Department of State Memorandum for Ambassadors Lodge and Martin, 30 December 1965; interview with Lek Sam Ouen, 15 June 2011.

27. Foreign Broadcast Information Service [FBIS], Asia & Pacific edition, 31 October 1969, p. H2.

28. In late October 1969, Prime Minister Lon Nol went to France for belated medical treatment for injuries sustained in a serious jeep accident three years earlier. In his absence, Sirik Matak was the acting prime minister.

29. Sak Sutsakhan, *The Khmer Republic at War and the Final Collapse* (Washington, D.C.: U.S. Army Center of Military History, 1980), p. 63.

30. The last Chinese vessel with arms had off-loaded at Sihanoukville in April 1969. The following month, Lon Nol temporarily suspended distribution of Chinese weapons to the border from a specially designated depot in Kompong Speu. As was often the case, however, the signals sent by the Cambodian government to the communists were mixed. Despite its harder line against PAVN, the Lon Nol government signed a new commerce deal with the communist Provisional Revolutionary Government (PRG) of the Republic of Vietnam in October 1969. The PRG had been formed that year to give the National Liberation Front—the so-called Viet Cong—governmental status during peace negotiations. And during the opening of 1970, there were indications that weapons once again began to flow toward the border from Kompong Speu. FBIS, Asia & Pacific edition, 31 October 1969, p. H1; Ahern, pp. 19, 26.

31. Casualties in the northeast predated the arrival of the tactical groups. On 28 May 1969, Cambodian infantry clashed with two PAVN companies in an area 3 kilometers southeast of Phum Ba Kham, Ratanakiri province. Three Cambodian troops were killed and two Vietnamese combatants were captured. CIA Intelligence Information Report, "Vietnamese Communist Involvement in Khmer Rouge Attacks on Cambodian Army Units," 8 August 1969, p. 3.

32. Albert Grandolini, "L'Aviation Royale Khmere: The First 15 Years of Cambodian Military Aviation," *Air Enthusiast*, Issue No. 37, p. 47.

33. Ian Harris, *Buddhism under Pol Pot* (Phnom Penh: Documentation Center of Cambodia, 2007), p. 25.

34. The PRG had diplomatic ties with a range of communist nations as well as several in the Nonaligned Movement, including Cambodia.

35. DDRS, 1984 collection, #758, CIA Intelligence Information Cable, "Indications of Possible Coup in Phnom Penh."

36. Heder, p. 156.

37. Grandolini, p. 47.

2. Finger in the Dike

1. FRUS, 1969–76, Vol. VI, Document #179, Memo from Kissinger to Nixon, 12 February 1970.

2. FRUS, 1969–70, Vol. VI, Document #205, Memo from Kissinger to Nixon, 19 March 1970, fn. 3.

3. The 40 Committee, a part of the executive branch, reviewed and oversaw foreign covert operations. It was chaired by the National Security Advisor and normally attended by the Secretary of Defense, Secretary of State, Chairman of the Joint Chiefs of Staff, Director of Central Intelligence (CIA), and their relevant staff members. The WSAG was also chaired by the National Security Advisor and attended by the Director of the CIA and a smaller number of staff members from other departments; it often met after 40 Committee meetings and dealt with breaking crises.

4. FRUS, 1969–76, Vol. VI, Document #203, Minutes of WSAG Meeting, 19 March 1970.

5. FRUS, 1969–76, Vol. VI, Document #204, Minutes of WSAG Meeting, 19 March 1970.

6. FRUS, 1969–76, Vol. Vl, Document #205, Memo from Kissinger to Nixon, 19 March 1970. As of 18 April, Kissinger was still referring to Sihanouk as a "political genius." He also continued to note the profits Lon Nol had reaped from the communists and was at a loss to explain the general's change of heart. See FRUS, 1969–76, Vol. VI, Document #238, Memorandum of Conversation, 18 April 1970.

7. FRUS, 1969–76, Vol. VI, Document #205, fn. 1; FRUS, 1969–76, Vol. VI, Document #206, Minutes of WSAG Meeting, 23 March 1970.

8. Ken Conboy, *FANK: A History of the Cambodian Armed Forces* (Jakarta: Equinox, 2011), p. 217.

9. The Sihanouk-era Royal Cambodian Armed Forces (*Forces Armées Royales Khmères*, or FARK) as of April 1970 had started changing its name to the National Cambodian Armed

Forces (*Forces Armées Nationales Khmères*, or FANK). By June, the term "FANK" was solely in use.

10. While attempting to cover these initial skirmishes during 5–8 April 1970, ten foreign journalists—including Sean Flynn, son of the late swashbuckling actor Errol Flynn (d. 1959)—were captured and executed by communist forces near Bavet.

11. In late 1970, Lieutenant Colonel Cheung Sayomborn, the commander of Military Region 6, which encompassed Kratie and Mondolkiri provinces, faced a military tribunal in Phnom Penh for dereliction of duty.

12. Sutsakhan, p. 61.

13. During this time frame, South African mercenary leader Mike Hoare, who had gained notoriety while commanding soldiers-for-hire in the Congo during the mid-1960s, visited Phnom Penh and offered the services of either mercenaries or foreign trainers. He was politely rebuffed by the Cambodian army. Correspondence with Mike Hoare, 24 November 1999.

14. FRUS, 1969–76, Vol. VI, Document #225, Memorandum for the Record, 10 April 1970.

15. American Embassy Phnom Penh message to Secretary of State, #495, 10 April 1970; American Embassy Phnom Penh to Secretary of State, #497, 10 April 1970.

16. State Message 053 785, for Charge from Assistant Secretary Green, 11 April 1970.

17. Also on 10 April, the CIA was instructed to explore whether the Cambodians could make an open purchase of weapons from Belgian arms dealers using U.S. funds. FRUS, 1969–76, Vol. VI, Document #225. Coincidentally, when Rives again met with the Cambodian foreign minister on the morning of 14 April, the latter wondered whether the U.S. government could "turn over stocks of communist weapons and ammunition seized in Vietnam . . . since the Cambodian army was already partially equipped with such weapons." American Embassy Phnom Penh to Secretary of State, #528, 14 April 1970.

18. Joint Chiefs of Staff (JCS) memo, Paul Kearney to Admiral McCain, #05161, 15 April 1970; JCS memo, General Wheeler to General Abrams, #05285, 17 April 1970. On 16 April, the CIA was told to arrange for a covert transfer of the AK-47s by air directly to Phnom Penh because communist troops would likely frustrate a turnover along the border. On 22 April, an initial shipment of 1,500 rifles was flown directly to Phnom Penh. FRUS, 1969–76, Vol. VI, Document #235; FRUS, 1969–76, Vol. VI, Document #253, Memo from Kissinger to Nixon, undated.

19. In April 1962, Son Ngoc Thanh received limited material and training assistance from the South Vietnamese CVTC Labor Federation. This was done with the knowledge of the South Vietnamese government, which designed the aid "merely to keep Son Ngoc Thanh on a string in case the political situation in Cambodia was to deteriorate." CIA document, "Status Report on Covert Actions in Vietnam," 18 April 1962, p. 4.

20. During 1962–1963, the RTA secretly trained three contingents of Khmer Serei officers, totaling 100 men, at Lopburi. Lek Sam Ouen interview. As of 1969, the RTA was still helping to recruit members of the Khmer Serei, including ethnic Cambodians living in Thailand as well as those from inside Cambodia. CIA Intelligence Report, "Thailand's Khmer Minority," September 1970, p. 10.

21. Interview with Lek Sam Ouen, 22 November 1996.

22. Interview with Ola Mize, 28 October 1996; interview with Ron Forrester, 30 October 1996; interview with Rinh Kien, 25 November 1996; interview with Thach Thuong, 26 November 1996. Son Ngoc Thanh, still recognized as a top leader among the Khmer Krom, maintained an office at Long Hai camp.

23. FRUS, 1969–76, Vol. VI, Document #226, Memo from Kissinger to Nixon, 9 April 1970.

24. FRUS, 1969–76, Vol. VI, Document #244, Memo from Acting Chairman of the Joint Chiefs of Staff to Secretary of Defense Laird, 21 April 1970; FRUS, 1969–76, Vol. VI, Document #249, NSC Memorandum, 22 April 1970. Apparently thinking along parallel lines, on 20 April Lon Nol asked Rives for the use of Khmer Krom in Cambodia. FRUS, 1969–76, Vol. VI, Document #240, 20 April 1970.

25. *Far Eastern Economic Review*, "Coup Questions," 13 January 1994, p. 31.

26. FRUS, 1969–76, Vol. VI, Document #219, Memo from Haig to Kissinger, 3 April 1970.

27. In late 1970, 2 Commando Brigade was expanded and divided into the 1 and 2 Autonomous Infantry Regiments. In October 1970, a second wave of former Khmer Serei CIDG was sent to Phnom Penh and used to form 3 Autonomous Infantry Regiment. Then in November 1970, a third and final wave of former Khmer Serei CIDG arrived in Cambodia and formed the 16 Autonomous Infantry Regiment. In late 1971, these four regiments were expanded, respectively, into the 43, 45, 47, and 48 Brigades. In June 1970, two battalions of former KKK CIDG (who at no point had been part of the Khmer Serei) were flown to Phnom Penh and made part of 7 Brigade.

28. To camouflage MACVSOG's true mandate, its bland cover designation was the Studies and Observations Group.

29. MACVSOG Command History 1970, Annex B, p. B-54.

30. Interview with Steve Spoerry, 9 January 1997.

31. FRUS, 1969–76, Vol. VI, Document #314, Editorial Note. In late May, the Cambodian government had requested that two Khmer Krom battalions from South Vietnam be deployed to Ba Kev. This was discussed at a WSAG meeting on 27 May but never approved. FRUS, 1969–76, Vol. VI, Document #311, Editorial Note.

32. A total of 7,571 Cambodian troops, dependents, and refugees were evacuated from Labang Siek and Ba Kev to South Vietnam during 23–26 June, many of them lifted out by U.S. helicopters. Interview with Billy Waugh, 20 December 1996; Brigadier General Tran Dinh Tho, *The Cambodian Incursion* (Washington, D.C.: U.S. Army Center for Military History, 1979), pp. 104–105. The troops evacuated from Ba Kev were given a quick retraining session at Pleiku and sent back to Phnom Penh as the newly minted 1 Shock Brigade under Lieutenant Colonel Um Savuth.

33. "Sihanouk has an . . . obsession with the CIA, which he holds responsible for much of what has happened to him," wrote U.S. Ambassador John Gunther Dean in 1975. "His book, ghost-written for him by Wilfred Burchett in 1973, entitled *My War with the CIA*, is ample proof of his deep-seated distrust of the CIA and the exaggerated role he ascribes to it in American policy direction and its execution in Cambodia." FRUS, 1969–76, Vol. X (Washington, D.C.: Government Printing Office, 2010), Document #173, Telegram from Embassy Cambodia to State, 18 February 1975.

34. FRUS, 1958–60, Vol. XVI, Document #93, Phnom Penh embassy to State, 12 January 1959.

35. Corfield, *Khmers*, p. 23.

36. David P. Chandler, *The Tragedy of Cambodian History* (New Haven: Yale University Press, 1993), p. 104.

37. Slat Peou had done a study tour in the United States in 1956, and apparently was recruited as a CIA source at that time.

38. FRUS, 1958–60, Vol. XVI, Document #95, Phnom Penh embassy to State, 16 February 1959.

39. FRUS, 1958–60, Vol. XVI, Document #125, Telegram from Embassy in Vietnam to State, 7 October 1959.

40. Interview with Ngo The Linh, 20 June 1996.

41. Clymer, p. 55; James Lilley with Jeffrey Lilley, *China Hands* (New York: PublicAffairs, 2004), p. 62.

42. Interview with Robert Myers, 29 October 1996.

43. Lilley, pp. 101–103.

44. Ahern, pp. 16–18. Lon Nol's business partner, Koch Ann, was forced to relocate to Hong Kong after an alleged business dispute in Cambodia. Still, he maintained close contact with Lon Nol through the 1970 change in governments. According to Son Sann, who was prime minister at the time, he pushed for the expulsion of Ann on smuggling charges. Son Sann, *The Memoirs of Son Sann* (Phnom Penh: Cambodia Daily Press, 2011), p. 105.

45. FRUS, 1969–76, Vol. VI, Document #42, Memorandum from Kissinger to Nixon, 17 March 1969.

46. Interview with John Stein, 9 May 2002. As of February 1970 Kissinger confirmed that, following a suggestion from Mansfield, there were no CIA personnel at the Phnom Penh embassy. FRUS, 1969–76, Vol. VI, Document #179, Memorandum from Kissinger to Nixon, 12 February 1970. At the time of the March 1970 change in governments, the U.S. embassy, which was operating out of a hotel room until proper office space could be arranged, consisted of a chargé d'affaires, a junior Foreign Service officer, an administrative officer, a budget and fiscal officer, one military attaché, a sergeant, a communicator, and two secretaries.

47. FRUS, 1969–76, Vol. VI, Document #208, Memorandum from Helms to Kissinger, 23 March 1970.

48. FRUS, 1969–76, Vol. VI, Document #217, Memorandum from Senior Military Assistant Haig to Kissinger, 1 April 1970.

49. FRUS, 1969–76, Vol. VI, Document #228, Memorandum from Kissinger to Nixon, 14 April 1970; FRUS, 1969–76, Vol. VI, Document #238, Memorandum of Conversation, 18 April 1970. The Cambodian agent indicated that Cambodia was seeking military assistance from Indonesia and the Philippines before it turned to the United States, but by the time of the Kissinger briefing the U.S. already had several forms of military assistance in the pipeline.

50. FRUS, 1969–76, Vol. VI, Document #237, Editorial Note. According to John Stein, who had been selected as the new station chief, there was an additional reason for the delayed deployment. "Many in Washington thought that Cambodia, or at least Phnom

Penh, was going to fall," he recalled, "so there was really no rush to send people there." Stein interview.

51. FRUS, 1969–76, Vol. VI, Document #237.

52. FRUS, 1969–76, Vol. VI, Document #241, Editorial Note. The CIA had initially proposed giving Lon Nol a secret installment of US$5 million, but Nixon ordered that it be doubled.

53. Interview with James Dunn, 9 April 2000.

54. Lieutenant Les Kosem conducted a 120-second freefall on 27 August 1957 and was lauded in *Cambodge* magazine (including a cover photograph) the following February. *Cambodge* (No. 2, February 1958), p. 13. Article provided courtesy of Justin Corfield.

55. As the ostensible leader of the Champa Liberation Front, Kosem used the alias Po Nagar, derived from the name of a famed Cham temple located near Nha Trang. According to a Hanoi account, FULRO maintained its headquarters at Kosem's residence on Monivong Boulevard in Phnom Penh. Ngon Vinh, *Fulro?* (Hanoi: Van Hoc Publishing House, 1982), p. 118.

56. Les Kosem also sent his paratroopers to Mondolkiri in order to forcibly dissolve the remnants of FULRO that were ensconced there in jungle camps. After the March 1970 change in governments, one battalion of former FULRO troops was taken to Phnom Penh and integrated into the 5 Infantry Brigade. Po Dharma, p. 128.

57. Ahern, p. 12. According to a Hanoi account, several Cham acquaintances of Les Kosem made trips to South Vietnam during the second half of the 1960s to pass classified documents to the CIA. Ngon Vinh, p. 9.

58. Ahern, p. 28. According to brother-in-law Sabu Bacha, Les Kosem was scared of possible government reprisals because he had helped transship Chinese weapons without any official orders from his military superiors. As a result, he hoarded documents at his home in order to have evidence that his activities were known to, and condoned by, officials such as Lon Nol. Sabu Bacha interview.

59. FRUS, 1969–76, Vol. VI, Document #233, Record of Meeting, 18 July 1970.

60. In October 1970, Phnom Penh Station was augmented by a second officer, Harry Slifer. An experienced Far East hand, Slifer had previously served in Cambodia from 1957 to 1959.

61. When PAVN was making serious gains across Cambodia in early May, Lon Nol apparently penned an appeal to Thailand asking for an urgent dispatch of RTA troops. This led to a Thai counterproposal to train two Thai-Cambodian regiments for deployment in Cambodia. On 11 May, Cambodian General Srey Saman went to Bangkok to discuss this plan. He lent support with two provisos: that the United States would be involved in planning, and that the project would be kept covert. It was on the following day that the scheme was raised during the WSAG meeting. FRUS, 1969–76, Vol. XX (Washington, D.C.: Government Printing Office, 2006), Document #63, Editorial Note; Document #66, Unger to Johnson, 21 May 1970.

62. FRUS, 1969–76, Vol. VI, Document #290, Minutes of Conversation, 12 May 1970. One Cambodian brigade was eventually trained in Thailand during mid-1970, but this was conducted outside of the discussions surrounding the Thai-Cambodian regiments and without U.S. participation.

63. FRUS, 1969–76, Vol. VI, Document #303, Editorial Note.

64. FRUS, 1969–76, Vol. XX, Document #68, Holdridge to Kissinger, 5 June 1970; Document #85, Holdridge to Kissinger, 14 August 1970. This plan was dropped because the Black Panthers would likely have ranged too far inside eastern Cambodia—and outside of the PAVN border sanctuaries—thus making it illegal for the United States to fund.

65. FRUS, 1969–76, Vol. VI, Document #304, Memorandum for the Record, 25 May 1970; Document #325, Minutes of WSAG Meeting, 12 June 1970.

66. FBIS, Asia & Pacific edition, 4 June 1970, p. K5.

67. FRUS, 1969–76, Vol. VI, Document #329, Memorandum from Kissinger to Nixon, 18 June 1970. Despite the fact that the situation had somewhat stabilized, in late June the Royal Thai government considered withdrawing its entire Black Panther Division back from South Vietnam and covertly deploying some of its forces to western Cambodia. This plan was dropped because the U.S. government would not give guarantees for tactical support in the field. FRUS, 1969–75, Vol. XX, Document #85, Holdridge to Kissinger, 14 August 1970.

68. FRUS, 1969–76, Vol. VII (Washington, D.C.: Government Printing Office, 2010), Document #7, Minutes of WSAG Meeting, 4 August 1970.

69. FRUS, 1969–76, Vol. VII, Document #22, Minutes of WSAG Meeting, 13 August 1970, fn. 5. During a conversation between Kissinger and Khoman in October, Khoman revealed that, in addition to Cambodia balking, Thailand had also soured to the plan because of constant U.S. congressional criticism and because Bangkok feared communist reprisals. FRUS, 1969–76, Vol. XX, Document #91, Memorandum of Conversation, 7 October 1970.

70. Interview with Thawon Wannachote, 12 May 2011. Although Thai documents from the period refer to the battalions as BP 41 and BP 42, the abbreviation BP is not further defined. It is believed to have stood for "Bataillon Parachutiste," a French designation used by Cambodian airborne battalions. By adopting such a designation, it could have helped the battalions better camouflage themselves in the FANK order of battle.

71. Back on 20 May 1970, the CIA had proposed creating ten SGU battalions of Thai volunteers for use in southern Laos (FRUS, 1969–76, Vol. VI, Document #300, Editorial Note). After its Cambodian deployment fell through, the CIA immediately considered rebranding the Thai-Cambodian units as SGU battalions earmarked for Laos (FRUS, 1969–76, Vol. VII, Document #36, Minutes of WSAG Meeting, 10 September 1970). This was initially opposed by Kissinger, who held hope that the regiments might still go to Cambodia. The plan also met initial resistance from Bangkok, which had promised Lon Nol that the regiments would be held as a ready reserve for use in a Cambodian emergency (FRUS, 1969–76, Vol. XX, Document #90, Backchannel from Unger to Johnson, 18 September 1970). But in November 1970, after more than a month of negotiations between the Thai and U.S. governments, BP 41 and BP 42 were recalled to Pranchinburi and told they were being redirected to Laos as the first contingent of the CIA's planned Thai SGU force. Four CIA case officers were added to the Prachinburi staff, and the battalions were each augmented by twenty-two cadre and thirty-three medical personnel from the RTA. On 15 December, both battalions were flown to the northern Bolovens Plateau on a one-year assignment. To conceal their nationalities, they were renamed Bataillon Commando

601 and Bataillon Commando 602 in order to let them blend with the French nomenclature prevalent in the Lao military. All further Thai volunteer battalions in Laos were sequentially numbered in the 600 series.

72. Lao officials had been hopeful that ties with Lon Nol would be an improvement over the chilly relations they experienced during the Sihanouk era. This disconnect had been partly because, decades earlier, the Lao monarchy had bestowed Sihanouk with a princess—but he had treated her as little more than a minor consort. It was also partly because, despite promises, Sihanouk had refused to implement laws to protect the rights of the ethnic Lao population living in northeastern Cambodia.

73. Kenneth Conboy with James Morrison, *Shadow War* (Boulder: Paladin Press, 1995), p. 281.

74. Along with the formation of FUNK on 5 May, Sihanouk (while in exile in Beijing) was declared head of state of the affiliated Royal National United Government of Kampuchea (Gouvernement Royal d'Union Nationale du Kampuchea, or GRUNK). While FUNK/GRUNK alleged to be umbrella organizations that included noncommunist opponents of Lon Nol, they were both controlled from the start by the Cambodian Communist Party, colloquially known as the Khmer Rouge.

75. Showing an appreciation for this historical animosity, Nixon had told Kissinger back on 17 April that the CIA should highlight the distrust between the Khmer and Vietnamese in its radio and leaflet propaganda themes.

76. FRUS, 1969–76, Vol. VI, Document #311, Editorial Note.

77. FRUS, 1969–76, Vol. VI, Document #340, Minutes of WSAG Meeting, 10 July 1970.

78. FRUS, 1969–76, Vol. VII, Document #4, Memorandum of Conversation, 23 July 1970.

79. FRUS, 1969–76, Vol. VII, Document #7, Minutes of WSAG Meeting, 4 August 1970.

80. Department of State Telegram, American Embassy Phnom Penh to Secretary of State, #3016, 31 March 1973.

81. Air America was a CIA proprietary airline active across mainland Southeast Asia.

82. A new camp, codenamed PS 46, was built at Wat Phu, 31 kilometers south of Pakse, to handle Lao SGU training previously conducted at PS 18.

83. Correspondence with Jonathan Clemente, 25 June 2011.

84. 3 Conboy, *Shadow War*, p. 283.

85. FRUS 1969–76, Volume VII, Document #126, Minutes of WSAG Meeting, 10 February 1971.

86. The two battalions chosen for Copper were 201 Battalion under Major Ngin Ros and 202 Battalion under Major Keth Reth. However, there already were infantry battalions numbered 201 and 202 in the Royal Lao Armed Forces. To avoid confusion, and to conceal their identity, the two Cambodian battalions were renumbered 701 and 702, respectively.

87. Conboy, *Shadow War*, p. 284.

88. On 4 June, CIA Director Helms sent Kissinger a memo stating that Project Copper had been terminated after Lon Non's battalions failed to return to Laos. He also stated that the Copper Cambodians might have been complicit in drug smuggling. FRUS 1969–76, Vol. VII, Document #212, Senior Group Review, 7 June 1971. According to CIA

paramilitary officer Malcolm Kalp, who was serving in Pakse Unit at the time, "The Cambodians had been a complete waste of time. They were mostly city hoods and students from Phnom Penh. Their leaders wanted to do 'business' things, not 'army' things, while in Laos." Interview with Malcolm Kalp, 12 May 1997.

89. On 13 June 1971, Lon Nol wrote to Admiral John McCain, commander of U.S. Forces in the Pacific, noting that the six Toro Teams had been returned to Cambodia without weapons or communications gear. The Cambodian leader requested equipment for the teams, but the United States, by now leery that the underperforming sibling Lon Non would seek to retain control, was noncommittal.

90. Department of State telegram from American Embassy Phnom Penh to Secretary of State, #3016, 31 March 1973.

91. Stein interview.

92. Interview with Kong Thann, 10 April 2008.

93. The Phitsanulok graduates were dispersed across Lon Non's infantry units, which by December 1972 had been expanded into 3 Infantry Division.

3. Finger on the Pulse

1. FRUS, 1969–76, Vol. X (Washington, D.C.: Government Printing Office, 2010), Document #137, Telegram from Embassy in Cambodia to Department of State, 14 August 1974.

2. Corfield, *Khmers*, p. 41.

3. As Lon Nol tugged at the xenophobic chords in Cambodian society, members of FANK not only moved against PAVN but also staged pogroms against the ethnic Vietnamese communities around Phnom Penh. During late April and May, some 1,000 Vietnamese living in a Catholic settlement on the Chrui Changwar Peninsula across from the capital were slaughtered, their bodies tossed into the Mekong.

4. Wilfred Deac, *Road to the Killing Fields* (College Station: Texas A&M University Press, 1997), p. 152; Clymer, p. 203; Philip Short, *Pol Pot: The History of a Nightmare* (London: John Murray, 2004), p. 196.

5. Corfield, *Khmers*, p. 151.

6. According to Dien Del, Chenla 2 was launched in August 1971 with the specific purpose of giving Sirik Matak good press during the Nixon meeting. Dien Del interview.

7. In June 1973, Sosthene was additionally named FANK commander-in-chief. However, Lon Nol elevated himself to Supreme Commander and continued to wield true power over the military.

8. Irate at these poor choices, the United States withheld material and financial support to both divisions for as long as these commanders were present.

9. PAVN's 367 *Dac Cong* (Sapper) Group, created in September 1970 to conduct special operations in Cambodia, included three sapper commando battalions, three ground sapper battalions, one maritime sapper company, and one heavy weapon support battalion. The maritime sapper company attacked the Kompong Som (formerly known as Sihanoukville) oil refinery in February 1971. This same company dispatched frogmen to

destroy vessels in Kompong Som port in May 1972 and January 1973, and cargo ships at Phnom Penh port in August 1972, November 1972, December 1972, and January 1973. U.S. Defense Attaché's Office (Phnom Penh), Monthly Assessment reports, August 1972, November 1972, December 1972, January 1973. The author is indebted to Harry Amos for granting access to these monthly assessment reports.

10. Nguyen Quoc Minh, Vu Doan Thanh, Pham Gia Khanh, and Nguyen Thanh Xuan, *Lich Su Bo Doi Dac Cong, Tap Mot* ["History of the Sapper Forces, Volume I"] (Hanoi: People's Army Publishing House, 1987), p. 249. Ten days later, the 367 Sapper Group hit the oil refinery north of Kompong Som port.

11. Corfield, *Khmers*, p. 115.

12. Deac, p. 148.

13. PAVN commandos infiltrating Phnom Penh fired 107mm rockets from pushcarts on two further occasions. On 1 December 1972, two rockets hit the Council of Ministers building but inflicted little damage. On 11 January 1973, two more went wide of the National Assembly building. U.S. Defense Attaché's Office (Phnom Penh), Monthly Assessment reports, October 1972, December 1972, January 1973.

14. Two other terrorist attacks in Phnom Penh during that period targeted American diplomats. On 26 September 1971, explosives hurled into a baseball game being played by U.S. embassy personnel resulted in two dead servicemen. Ten other embassy personnel were wounded; CIA Station Chief John Stein was blown off of third base, ruffled but otherwise unhurt. On 17 September 1972, a roadside bomb seriously damaged the car carrying Deputy Chief of Mission Thomas Enders and killed two Cambodians. It was suspected that the erratic Lon Non was behind both incidents. Deac, p. 120.

15. The DRV continued to withhold material support to Cambodian communists through the end of the decade. One exception may have occurred on 3 March 1968, when CIA sources reported that a junk with a Vietnamese-Cambodian crew had anchored off of Kampot province and made a weapons delivery to Khmer insurgents. CIA Directorate of Intelligence, Intelligence Report, "*Communism and Cambodia*," May 1972, p. 50.

16. In 1960, the KPRP had changed its name to the Worker's Party of Kampuchea in order to show solidarity with the Vietnam Worker's Party. The 1966 name change signaled a conscious shift away from the DRV and toward the PRC.

17. Heder, p. 5.

18. Interview with Tea Banh, 1 March 2009.

19. Sihanouk lived in Beijing during this period with 120 of his followers, including women and children. "He doesn't do anything except await telegrams," claimed one witness. "And when he received news of [FANK] casualties, he rejoices and throws a party." Harish C. Mehta, *Warrior Prince* (Singapore: Graham Brash, 2001), p. 34.

20. In June 1971, Kissinger lamented the fact that FANK had largely abandoned the countryside and "allowed the self-sufficent Khmer Rouge to continue organizing." Two months later when Sirik Matak met Nixon, he admitted that the Khmer Republic government had intentionally abandoned the north and northeast in order to focus on the richer and more densely populated area below. FRUS, 1969–76, Vol. VII, Document #212, Senior Review Group minutes, 7 June 1971; Document #242, Memorandum of Conversation, 10 August 1971.

21. According to the U.S. Defense Attaché's Office in Phnom Penh, the Khmer Rouge numbered only around 15,000 as of December 1971. By October 1972, the number had been revised upward to as many as 40,000 combatants (including main-force units, regional forces, mixed PAVN units, advisers, and administrators). U.S. Defense Attaché's Office (Phnom Penh), Monthly Assessment reports, December 1971, April 1972, October 1972.

22. An oft-repeated explanation for the fast growth of the Khmer Rouge is the alleged outrage registered by the Cambodian peasantry toward the U.S. bombing of PAVN sanctuaries that began in 1969. This simplistic explanation is off the mark for several reasons. First, the U.S. bombing started a full year before Sihanouk lent his name to the FUNK resistance front—and the Khmer Rouge had never been able to expand its anemic ranks during that earlier period. Second, U.S. bombing was largely directed at PAVN sanctuaries where few Cambodian citizens were present. Conversely, many of the zones where the Khmer Rouge experienced its greatest growth were in areas that received little to no U.S. bombing. Had the original premise been true, it logically holds that Laos, which was on the receiving end of a far longer and more concentrated U.S. bombing campaign, should have experienced a meteoric rise in Pathet Lao insurgents; this was never the case.

23. Kim Il-Sung feted Sihanouk and even had the Chhang Sou On palace built for him in Pyongyang. Norodom Sihanouk, edited by Julio A. Jeldres, *Shadow Over Angkor: Memoirs of His Majesty King Norodom Sihanouk of Cambodia*, Volume 1 (Phnom Penh: Monument Books, 2005), p. 153.

24. The number of PAVN deployed directly against FANK peaked at an estimated 13,000 troops in late October 1971 during the Chenla 2 campaign. U.S. Attaché's Office (Phnom Penh), Monthly Assessment report, December 1971.

25. U.S. Attaché's Office (Phnom Penh), Monthly Assessment reports, February 1972, May 1972, July 1972, November 1972.

26. FRUS, 1969–76, Vol. X, Document #9, Minutes of WSAG Meeting, 6 February 1973.

27. At a 28 March 1973 WSAG meeting, Kissinger asked if South Vietnam could survive if Cambodia fell to the communists. "If the communists range along that long border between Cambodia and South Vietnam," said the Chairman of the Joint Chiefs of Staff, Admiral Thomas Moorer, "it would be very hard for South Vietnam to survive." Kissinger later commented, "[The Thai] will turn against us if all goes bad there. Then the Indonesians will follow suit. We have a lot more at stake here than just Cambodia." FRUS, 1969–76, Vol. X, Document #36, Minutes of WSAG Meeting, 28 March 1973.

28. The Military Equipment Delivery Team–Cambodia, organized in January 1971 and led by a U.S. Army brigadier general stationed at the Phnom Penh embassy, was the U.S. military body that oversaw the requirements and usage of American equipment by FANK. Due to restrictions set out in the Cooper-Church Amendment, its members were forbidden from advising FANK personnel on strategy or tactics.

29. Named after Republican Clifford Case from New Jersey and Missouri Democrat Stuart Symington, this amendment also stated that no more than eighty-five third-country nationals could be paid by U.S. Military Assistance Program funds earmarked for Cambodia. As of late 1972, almost half of the U.S. personnel assigned to Cambodia were military. This included seventy-four in the Military Equipment Delivery Team, seventeen in

the defense attaché's office, and five military communicators. There were also forty third country nationals on a Vinnell Corporation contract that helped maintain U.S. military equipment given to FANK.

30. Interview with Mia Sovarn, 5 March 1995. Sovarn was one of the Cambodians trained at Hua Hin.

31. As of 1973, the Preah Vihear operation was placed under the administrative control of the Khmer Special Forces, FANK's unconventional warfare unit. Two Khmer Special Forces detachments were deployed to Preah Vihear, where they conducted separate but parallel forays into the lowlands.

32. TOC 315, established in 1970, was headed by an RTA special colonel (equivalent to a U.S. Army brigadier general). The first commander was Special Colonel Chalat Vongsayan.

33. Task Force 506, established in 1970, had a forward headquarters in the Thai border town of Aranyaprathet. Its first commander was Colonel Anek Boonyatee, who was concurrently the deputy commander of the RTA Special Forces.

34. Prior to deployment, a CIA officer gave a course on clandestine collection methods to the team leaders at Lopburi.

35. Interview with Aroon Chindaprasarn, 18 May 2002. Aroon was commander of the Siem Reap team from 1971 to 1973. His team had the added responsibility of coordinating tactical airstrikes in Siem Reap provided to FANK by the Royal Thai Air Force.

36. Interview with William Lair, 21 September 2002.

37. National Security Council report, "Stabilizing the Leadership in Cambodia," 3 March 1973.

38. FRUS, 1969–76, Vol. X, Document #36, Minutes of WSAG Meeting, 28 March 1973, fn 3.

39. Hythe is the name of a small British coastal market town on the south coast of Kent. It is also an old English word meaning *haven* or *sanctuary*. CIA cryptonyms are selected at random and have no intentional relationship to the country or project to which they are assigned.

40. Interview with Kinloch Bull, 11 August 2002.

41. Ibid.

42. Ibid.

43. Correspondence with Douglas Beed, 28 February 2003. Members of the Defense Attaché's Office, especially the assistant army attachés, visited FANK units in the field on a daily basis. Similar trips were made by members of the Military Equipment Delivery Team. But unlike the HYTHE officers, their trips were usually extremely brief as they were required to return to Phnom Penh every night.

44. Beed correspondence.

45. Ibid.

46. Interviw with Mike Magnani, 4 April 2002.

47. Interview with Walt Floyd, 26 April 2002.

48. Interview with Richard Boys, 20 April 2002.

49. The Special Police Service of the Technical Directorate within the National Police was an undermanned and underfunded unit that investigated subversion and espionage

in Phnom Penh. Another small military unit that reported to the Prime Minister's office known as SEDOC (Section de Documentation et de Recherche) focused on penetrating foreign missions. CIA National Intelligence Survey, "Cambodia," April 1972, p. 54.

50. Department of State telegram from American Embassy Phnom Penh to Secretary of State, #3016, 31 March 1973. Lon Non was prone to establishing special committees. In mid-1970, he created a Coordination Committee for National Defense for the purpose of managing the declaration of the Khmer Republic that October. The following year, he created the Committee for Special Coordination initially to gather political support behind his brother. This committee later expanded its mandate to special activities like penetrating the Khmer Rouge. Ros Chantrabot, *La République Khmère* (Paris: Editions L'Harmattan, 1993), p. 40.

51. One of the original responsibilities of the HYTHE officers was to gather targeting data for strategic or tactical airstrikes. But aside from the information passed by Floyd in Kompong Cham, which was never exploited, this HYTHE role was never realized. Instead, FANK created its own target selection committee, with no HYTHE involvement, to identify strategic air targets. In April 1973, the Khmer Air Force created the Direct Air Support Center—again with no HYTHE involvement—to validate and coordinate tactical air support from the U.S. and Cambodian air forces.

52. Floyd interview; correspondence with Heng Chea, 20 April 2008.

53. *Washington Star*, "U.S. Puts 'Advisors' in Cambodia," 24 July 1973. Arbuckle apparently got his scoop from CIA officer Joe Boys in Svay Rieng. The two had known each other in Laos, and the latter hosted Arbuckle when he was passing through Svay Rieng in early July.

54. FRUS, 1969–76, Vol. X, Document #86, Memorandum for the Record, 19 June 1973.

55. According to the 8 July 1973 issue of *The China Post*, the Thai government, worried about the Khmer Republic's fate after the bombing halt, had resurrected plans to raise a "Yellow Tiger Brigade" and dispatch it to Cambodia. This media report appears to have been without basis.

56. FRUS, 1969–76, Vol. X, Document #89, Memorandum from Stearman to Kissinger, 29 June 1973.

57. As of June 1973, the only PAVN unit still thought to be confronting FANK was a battalion of the 96 Artillery Regiment, which was providing heavy weapons support to the Khmer Rouge along the east bank of the Mekong. As of October 1973, less than 1,000 PAVN troops were thought to be in the Khmer Republic, and none of them were targeted against FANK. U.S. Defense Attaché's Office, Monthly Assessment reports, June 1973, October 1973.

58. FRUS, 1969–76, Vol. X, Document #92, Minutes of WSAG Meeting, 10 July 1973.

59. FRUS, 1969–76, Vol. X, Document #91, Memorandum from Moorer to Schlesinger, 5 July 1973.

60. U.S. Defense Attaché's Office (Phnom Penh), Monthly Assessment Report, August 1973.

61. On 19 November 1973, another disgruntled Khmer Air Force pilot, Pech Lim Kuon, took his T-28 over the Presidential Palace and began bombing, then flew to Khmer

Rouge–held Kratie province. Antiaircraft gunners tried to respond, but their Chinese-made weapons, not fired for three years, were hopelessly jammed. As with the March incident, Lon Nol (again, not in the palace at the time) ordered a bombing standdown and a letter of resignation from the air force commander.

62. FRUS, 1969–76, Vol. X, Document #106, Memorandum from Colby to Kissinger, 12 September 1973; interview with Barry Broman, 6 June 2009. According to Dien Del, he had support for a coup from the newly installed commanders of 1 and 3 Division. He also discussed a putsch on numerous occasions with the Cambodian naval chief, Admiral Vong Sarendy. However, plans barely progressed because Sarendy was insistent that he be named armed forces commander after Lon Nol was deposed. Dien Del interview.

63. FRUS, 1969–76, Vol. X, Document #104, Memorandum from NSC Staff to Kissinger, 31 August 1973.

64. Correspondence with Charles Hafner, 5 May 2008.

65. Beed correspondence.

66. Bull interview.

67. During WSAG meetings on 20 September and again on 2 October, the participants singled out General John Vogt for allegedly boosting FANK morale during the Kompong Cham battle. Vogt was commander of the U.S. Support Activities Group, a joint U.S. military command based in Thailand that handled contingencies for the resumption of U.S. combat activity in Indochina. Through August, a three-man team from this group was assigned to the U.S. embassy in Phnom Penh to assist with bomb targeting. Although it was true that Vogt made a tour of the FANK frontlines in August, some at the embassy hardly felt he was a linchpin at Kompong Cham. "I credited the presence of Hafner with helping save the town," said Station Chief Bull, "and [DCM] Enders agreed." FRUS, 1969–76, Vol. X, Document #107, Minutes of WSAG Meeting, 20 September 1973; FRUS, 1969–76, Vol. X, Document #109, Minutes of WSAG Meeting, 2 October 1973; Bull interview.

4. Requiem

1. U.S. Defense Attaché's Office (Phnom Penh), Monthly Assessment report, February 1974.

2. Bernard's role in Kampot was exposed in a 13 March 1974 article in the *Washington Post*.

3. FRUS, 1969–76, Vol. X, Document #127, Richard Kenney and William Smyser of NSC Staff to Kissinger, 16 May 1974.

4. These included Svay Rieng, Kompong Chhnang, Siem Reap (opened by Chuck Hafner when he briefly abandoned Kompong Cham in September 1973), Kompong Cham, Kompong Speu (opened in early 1974), Battambang (opened in early 1974), and Kompong Thom (reopened in early 1974).

5. Beed correspondence.

6. Interview with Colin Thompson, 7 December 2001.

7. Interview with Richard Boys, 20 April 2002.

8. Defense Attaché's Office (Phnom Penh), Monthly Assessment reports, August 1974, October 1974. A Khmer Air Force C-123 transport had also crashed on the Svay Rieng runway, but that was due to pilot error and not enemy fire.

9. Julio Jeldres, *The Royal House of Cambodia* (Phnom Penh: Monument Books, 2003), p. 102.

10. The Indochinese Communist Party, which had representation from Laos and Cambodia but was dominated by members from Vietnam, was formally dissolved in 1945 in order to hide its communist affiliation and was officially divided into three separate communist parties in 1951. In reality, the Vietnamese-dominated party continued to exist through the 1945–1951 time frame.

11. Heder, p. 22.

12. Short, p. 87.

13. *Les Insignes des Forces Armees au Cambodge* (Paris: L'Association Symbols et Traditions, 2002), p. 127. Helping Chantarangsey organize the 3 BAM was a former Japanese officer from the Kempeitai, the Japanese wartime secret service, who had gone native and remained in Kompong Speu.

14. Interview with Ny Van Ty, 14 September 2010.

15. Clymer, p. 135; Corfield, *Khmers*, p. 185.

16. Interview with Richard Santos, 18 March 1996. Santos had served as a paramilitary officer in northern Laos during 1967–1969, then in southern Laos for another two years.

17. During the Sihanouk period, Thach Ung had worked as a teacher and became an *assimile* officer immediately after March 1970. When 13 Brigade was first formed, he served as one of its battalion commanders. He was later promoted to chief of staff of 13 Brigade and the intelligence officer for 2 Military Region. Dien Del interview.

18. The 9 Brigade Group consisted of two brigades: 12 Brigade, which Teap Ben also commanded, plus a newly formed and lowly rated 59 Brigade. All FANK brigade group headquarters were disbanded in December 1972, but Teap Ben retained control over 12 Brigade.

19. Orr Kelly, *Never Fight Fair* (New York: Pocket Books, 1995), p. 188.

20. Correspondence with William Beck, 13 December 2001.

21. Correspondence with Phil Runfola, 8 August 2011.

22. Sek Sam Iet's career also no doubt benefited from the fact that his older sister was one of Sihanouk's wives. Interview with Sisowath Sirirath, 11 October 2012.

23. Interview with George Kenning, 14 January 1999.

24. The pressure Dean could bring to bear was overwhelming. By 1974, Cambodian domestic revenues accounted for just 2.2 percent of the annual budget for the Khmer Republic; U.S. aid, by contrast, accounted for 95.1 percent. The remainder was aid from other nations.

25. In August 1974, to alleviate command and control problems, Pursat was removed from Military Region 3 and placed under a new Military Region 9 headquartered in Kompong Chhnang.

26. Interview with Mike Ingham, 3 December 1996.

27. Interview with Robert Baskett, 5 December 1996. Middling results were also seen at the Alpha post at Kompong Chhnang. Posted there beginning in September 1974 was

Malcolm Kalp, who had run CIA interrogation centers at Pakse and Savannakhet in Laos during 1970–1973. His time at the Savannakhet center was especially successful, with the CIA eventually able to double almost a dozen PAVN soldiers and send them back to the Ho Chi Minh Trail to capture others. Kalp had even put his skills to use in Thailand when he interrogated a PAVN commando captured after an abortive attack on Udorn airbase on 3 October 1972. Kalp was later on the receiving end of an extended interrogation when he was among the U.S. embassy members taken hostage in Teheran in 1979. Interview with Malcolm Kalp, 12 May 1997.

28. Four senior officers, including Lieutenant General Sosthene Fernandez, were awarded the Grand Officer of the Order of the Republic (the country's second highest award), seven were named Commander of the Order of the Republic (the third highest award), eight were named Officer of the Order of the Republic (the fourth highest award), five were named Chevalier of the Order of the Republic (the fifth highest award), and three received the National Defense Medal.

29. Correspondence with Alan Armstrong, 5 December 2011.

30. FRUS, 1969–76, Vol. X, Document #137, Telegram from Embassy in Cambodia to Department of State, 14 August 1974.

31. U.S. Defense Attaché's Office (Phnom Penh), Monthly Assessment report, November 1974.

32. The head of the Second Bureau for the Kompong Cham Military Sub-Division was Thann's former high-school student. The head of the Second Bureau for Military Region 1 (which included Kompong Cham) had gone for a military intelligence course in Okinawa in 1971, during which time Kong Thann had served as interpreter. In addition, his deputy was Kong Thann's elementary school classmate.

33. During the royalist era, the military police had been known as the Gendarmerie. After March 1970, its name had officially been changed to Prévôté Militaire and its numbers increased from a few hunded to several thousand.

34. The East Zone consisted of Prey Veng, Svay Rieng, Kandal, and Kompong Cham provinces.

35. Correspondence with Barry Broman, 26 April 2011.

36. Deac, p. 211.

37. Interview with Son Sen, 15 June 1990.

38. End of Tour Report, MEDT-C, Brigadier General William W. Palmer, February 1974–April 1975, p. B-12.

39. Kenning interview.

40. In the third quarter of 1974, the U.S. Air Force had sought a civilian airline to handle supply airdrops in Cambodia. Although Air America and Continental Air Services had a long history of such operations, the Thai government rejected their involvement because of their public association with the CIA's paramilitary operation in Laos. Instead, William Bird, who had run an airline in Laos the previous decade, was enticed to create BirdAir to handle the Cambodian assignment and in October 1974 leased five C-130 transports from the U.S. Air Force. Unmarked except for small tail numbers and based at Utapao Royal Thai Air Force Base, they began dropping supplies to besieged outposts across Cambodia. In February 1975, when BirdAir began landing directly at Pochentong, the number of

leased C-130s was increased to ten. Interview with William Bird, 8 January 1997; interview with Harry Aderholt, 8 July 1997.

41. Bird interview.

42. FRUS, 1969–76, Vol. X, Document #174, Memo from William Stearman of the National Security Council to Secretary of State Kissinger, 19 February 1975.

43. Hopkins had served two tours in South Vietnam, one advising the Vietnamese Marine Corps and the other as an operations officer for a U.S. Marine battalion. From 1968 to 1974, he served at the Special Operations Center under the U.S. European Command, then as a U.S. Marine battalion commander at Camp Pendleton.

44. When Sosthene was relieved, the position of FANK commander-in-chief was abolished. In addition, the chief of the General Staff was now to report to the government, not the president.

45. The marshal's grip on reality continued to erode until the end. Earlier that month, he had ordered air force helicopters to drop consecrated sand around the Phnom Penh perimeter in order to form a supernatural barrier against the advancing communists.

46. CIA report, "A Look at the Khmer Communists," 1 April 1975, p. 3.

47. FRUS, 1969–76, Vol. X, Document #196, Minutes of National Security Council Meeting, 28 March 1975.

48. FRUS, 1969–76, Volume E-12, Document #64, CIA Intelligence Memorandum, 30 January 1975.

49. This is excerpted from an eight-page letter Antippas sent to conservative commentator William F. Buckley in order to clarify and correct views offered during a 23 March 1975 session of *Firing Line*.

50. Heng Chea correspondence.

51. Interview with John Sullivan, 2 July 2011. A CIA polygrapher, Sullivan went to Phnom Penh in late February to interview two of the would-be stay-behind agents.

52. Interview with Chheang Ly, 20 November 2008.

53. Samay Mom was later the subject of a *Washington Post* article that chronicled her hard luck as a refugee. She claimed to have married her CIA case officer in a traditional Cambodian wedding at Svay Rieng, only to learn in April 1975 he had a wife waiting in Bangkok. Moving to the United States, she met and married a former Khmer Air Force pilot in 1976. The following year, however, the pilot learned that his original wife, thought to have died under the Khmer Rouge, was in fact alive and intented on joining him in the United States. Samay Mom, for a second time, was thus forced out on her own. See *Washington Post*, "What Can I Do?" 12 November 1979, p. A1.

54. Kong Thann interview.

55. One of the only other senior FANK members to make a premature departure from the Khmer Republic was Brigadier General Les Kosem, the same pragmatic Cham officer who had been instrumental in shipping Chinese weapons to the border—then turning over documentation to the CIA. On 8 April, Kosem took a flight to Bangkok with his family, ostensibly to seek eleventh-hour assistance for the Republic from diplomats at the Libyan embassy. Sabu Bacha interview.

56. Osborne, *Prince of Light*, p. 226.

5. Arrested Development

1. Dien Del interview.

2. From 1 January through 14 April, more than 2,500 artillery rounds and 107mm rockets impacted on Pochentong. The United States continued to perform airdrops over Phnom Penh after Pochentong was closed; the final six drops were conducted on 16 April.

3. Correspondence with Brian O'Connor, 5 July 2001.

4. FBIS, Asia & Pacific edition, 14 April 1975, p. H9.

5. O'Connor correspondence.

6. Chheang Ly interview.

7. Using the alias Thach Nih, Thach Reng was the Secretary General of the Khmer Krom Liberation Front. Interview with Thach Reng, 3 March 1995.

8. According to General Palmer in 1975, "There is no indication of corruption in the Khmer Special Forces; the use of 'phantoms' was not indicated, and it is believed that this stemmed from Brigadier General Thach Reng's personal integrity." Palmer End-of-Tour Report, Appendix 5 to Annex B, "Special Forces."

9. This misuse of the Khmer Special Forces was not because they were ill prepared for their intended role. During 1971–1973, three cycles of Khmer Special Forces students were trained at Lopburi, Thailand, by instructors from the U.S. Army Special Forces and RTA Special Forces. From 15 November 1971 through 10 January 1972, Thach Reng himself was put through the paces of unconventional warfare and airborne training under U.S. Army Special Forces auspices at Nha Trang and Long Thanh, South Vietnam.

10. Thach Reng claimed that General Sosthene and armor commander Yai Sindy were planning a November 1974 putsch. Thach Reng interview.

11. Palmer End-of-Tour report, "Special Forces."

12. Thach Reng interview.

13. Photographs taken after the fall of the Khmer Republic clearly show six UH-1 choppers still parked inside the Olympic Stadium. It is probable that Long Boret forfeited his chance at escape because there were not enough pilots, or enough helicopters in flyable condition, to carry out his entire entourage. Long Boret and Sirik Matak would later become two of the most prominent Cambodian leaders to be immediately executed by the Khmer Rouge after Phnom Penh fell.

14. FBIS, Asia and Pacific edition, 27 March 1975, p. H1. The two main opposition parties boycotted the September 1972 legislative election to protest unfair electoral rules. As a result, all 126 candidates fielded by Lon Nol's Social Republican Party won. Ten other candidates were unsuccessfully fielded by the upstart Pracheachon group—which was reportedly created by Lon Non to offer token opposition during the vote.

15. The minor wife in Phnom Penh, Minh Chin, survived the war. *Phnom Penh Post*, "Cambodia's Prince of Mystery," 13 December 2010.

16. Shawcross gives a garbled account of the final radio transmissions from the Khmer Republic, confusing the messages sent by Thach Ung in Kompong Speu and Kon Vorrot in Kompong Cham. William Shawcross, *Sideshow* (New York: Simon & Schuster, 1979), p. 372.

17. Hafner correspondence. Operations Assistant Nop Prang had also elected to remain behind at the Kompong Cham villa. He disappeared along with Kon Vorrot.

18. The two officers were Special Colonel Wichit Artkumvong, who had recently taken command over Task Force 506, and another 506 officer, Lieutenant Colonel Kasem Thammakul. Task Force 506 ran the radio teams that had been positioned across the Khmer Republic. Interview with Kasem Thammakul, 13 July 2002.

19. O'Connor interview; Elizabeth Becker, *When the War Was Over*, revised edition (New York: PublicAffairs, 1998), p. 194.

20. Interview with Chhuon Sam Ol, 24 May 2009.

21. Over the course of 17 April, a steady stream of Khmer Air Force planes had fled to Utapao. This included five T-28s, one C-123, one Au-24A, one AC-47, and 109 passengers and crewmen.

22. Interview with Tea Chamrat, 30 July 2011. P-111 was later reflagged and used by the Philippine navy.

23. FBIS, Asia and Pacific edition, 20 May 1975, p. H1.

24. Correspondence with Kim Sakun, 19 October 2007.

25. Ben Kiernan, *The Pol Pot Regime*, third edition (New Haven: Yale University Press, 2008), p. 33; Osborne, *Phnom Penh*, p. 146; Short, p. 287.

26. *Testimonies on Genocide in Cambodia*, compiled by Bernard Hamel and Soth Polin, pp. 48–49.

27. *Paris Le Figaro*, "Cambodia: Witch Hunt," 11 February 1977.

28. Short, p. 271.

29. Sullivan interview. The information on the Soviet ambassador was passed by Stanislav Levchenko, a KGB major who defected in 1979 and was interviewed by CIA polygrapher Sullivan.

30. The bulk of the officers assigned to the Shadow Station had arrived in Bangkok immediately after Eagle Pull on 12 April. Two officers—Chuck Hafner and Bear, from Kompong Speu—had briefly gone to Saigon to help coordinate further evacuations from Cambodia. Both Hafner and Bear arrived in Bangkok on 26 April aboard the last Air Vietnam flight out of Tan Son Nhut.

31. O'Connor interview. Khmer Rouge radio on 22 May conjured an excuse for the abandoned vehicles: "Our fighters tried to drive these automobiles and armored cars and park them properly but could not because they were surrounded by large amounts of people, especially youths and children, along the streets." FBIS, Asia and Pacific edition, 28 May 1975, p. H1.

32. FRUS, 1969–76, Volume E-12, Document #67, Memorandum for Kissinger, 2 May 1975.

33. Kong Thann interview; interview with Savan Koy, 8 November 2002. Savan Koy was the only ethnic Cambodian operations assistant to work for the CIA in Laos, where he operated out of Pakse prior to 1973. He then shifted to the Alpha Program and assisted the post at Kompong Speu before moving to Battambang.

34. The CIA was so desperate to gain insights into the Khmer Rouge that they dispatched Snake and George Kenning to Paris in late 1975 to contact Khieu Pauline, the

younger sister of prominent Khmer Rouge personality Khieu Samphan. Pauline had married a government bureaucrat during the Sihanouk regime and moved to France during the Republican era. But as she had long fallen out with her older brother, she could offer no meaningful insights into Khieu Samphan or the Khmer Rouge upper echelon. Kenning interview; additional information provided by Steve Heder, 6 August 2011.

35. Runfola correspondence.

36. Kong Thann interview.

37. When CIA officer Snake first joined the Alpha Program, he was sent to Koh Kong province in an effort to exploit his Khmer linguistic ability. He was thoroughly frustrated after two weeks. "If you want to send somebody who can speak the language in Koh Kong," he reported to Phnom Penh, "send somebody who speaks Thai."

38. Two days after the 25 February 1976 explosions, Democratic Kampuchean radio reported that U.S. aircraft had conducted two bombing runs in Siem Reap, five hours apart. This report perplexed Cambodia-watchers, who for years speculated as to whether the bombings were conducted by U.S., Thai, Vietnamese, or perhaps even Cambodian aircraft. It was only much later that Khmer Rouge leader Ieng Sary admitted it was an uprising and not a bombing. Short, p. 354.

39. In April 1975, Ny Van Ty, a former battalion commander from Chantarangsey's 13 Brigade, took to the forest near the Kompong Speu provincial capital with thirty followers. Although they had the Khmer words for "Khmer Revolution" tattooed on their forearms, they were of no discernible political persuasion and lived as brigands through early 1979. Ny Van Ty interview.

40. FBIS, Asia and Pacific edition, 23 April 1975, p. H1.

41. Despite a near perfect record of defeats as a brigade commander, Ith Suong was promoted in December 1972 to lead the 1 Infantry Division due to his slavish devotion to Lon Nol. Replaced following heavy U.S. pressure, in April 1974 he was picked to lead the new 9 Infantry Division. This formation never came to full strength, but was retained within Phnom Penh as part of Lon Nol's anticoup insurance.

42. As the senior FANK liaison officer at Thailand's Supreme Command, Chudett was theoretically responsible for commanding FANK training programs in Thailand and representing Khmer interests with Thailand with regard to that training. According to General Palmer, he was "consistently and wholly derelict in both functions." Palmer End-of-Tour report, Appendix 3 to Annex A, p. 2.

43. Correspondence with Ian Harris, 12 February 2010; interview with Ea Chuor Kimmeng, 16 January 2010.

44. Chamnian reportedly cut an identical deal with anticommunist Lao rebels in May 1976: he offered low-level support in exchange for intelligence gathered by the guerrillas. CIA Intelligence Information Cable, 314/01261–76, 5 May 1976.

45. Within two weeks after the fall of Phnom Penh, the Thai government was referring to FANK remnants along its border as the Khmer Serei. FBIS, Asia and Pacific edition, 28 April 1975, p. J5.

46. FBIS, Asia and Pacific edition, 28 April 1975, p. J5; *Bangkok Post*, 14 May 1975, p. 3.

47. FBIS, Asian and Pacific edition, 3 November 1975, p. J4.

48. In fact, the RTA's relations with the Cambodian resistance grew somewhat schitzophrenic immediately after the January 1977 Khmer Rouge raid. The new RTA commander, the rather indecisive Soem Nan Nakhon, ostensibly ordered the army that March not to forge ties with the resistance for fear of inviting further reprisals. Nhek Bun Chhay, a nineteen-year-old anti–Khmer Rouge insurgent staging from just inside Chanthaburi province, confirmed there was an RTA crackdown against smaller guerrilla bands after January. At the same time, however, TOC 315 courted other resistance elements.

49. Interview with Chavalit Yongchaiyud, 31 July 2009.

50. Tea Banh interview.

51. Interview with Ea Nguon, 15 June 2009.

52. In late April 1975, Ea Nguon purchased eleven shotguns from Thai troops posted along the frontier. The following month, he offered large baht rewards for Cambodians who ventured across the border and captured weapons from the Khmer Rouge.

53. CIA Intelligence Information Cable, DB-315/03493–77, 28 March 1977.

54. Ea Chuor Kimmeng interview.

55. Interview with CIA officer Snake, 5 July 2011.

56. Interview with Ben Vy, 7 December 2009; Bernard Hamel, *Resistances au Vietnam, Cambodge, et Laos* (Paris: Editions L'Harmattan, 1994), p. 103.

57. Ea Chuor Kimmeng interview.

58. The two majors were Youk Man and Kan Vanna. Chantrabot, p. 141; Kong Thann interview; Ben Vy interview; Ea Chuor Kimmeng interview.

6. Trading Places

1. CIA Intelligence Information Cable, DB-315/03493–77, 28 March 1977.

2. While Ly Tieng Chek was embraced by TOC 315, other guerrilla bands in nearby Surin province did not fare as well. One of the largest among them was near the O'Smach border crossing, where former FANK Captain Svy Thoeun by early 1977 had gathered several hundred guerrillas. For a time, they provided intelligence to Task Force 506 in exchange for food and permission to operate from Thai territory. But as with the Ea Nguon front, they came under heavy RTA pressure later that year. Svy Thoeun was spared jail time, probably because he had several well-connected relatives, including a senior RTA officer, a Thai legislator, and Chhay Ek Thang, an influential businessman in Surin. Interview with Nguon Ponn, 10 December 2009; interview with Nhem Peoung, 30 October 2010. Both Ponn and Peoung were deputies to Svy Thoeun.

3. Kiernan, p. 367.

4. Kasem Thammakul interview.

5. The RTA Special Forces traced its lineage back to June 1954 when the RTA activated an airborne battalion at Lopburi. In 1965, this battalion was expanded into a Special Forces Group. In January 1966, the Special Warfare Center was founded at Lopburi; it consisted of the Special Forces Group, a psychological warfare company, and an airborne infantry battalion. As of 1972, the Special Warfare Center, headed by a major general, had grown

to four Special Forces Groups, a psychological warfare battalion, an airborne infantry battalion, an airborne quartermaster battalion, a long-range reconnaissance company, and a special warfare training battalion.

6. Interview with Wannah Mungkhalee, 7 June 2003. Task Force 506 had grown to 200 men by that time, many of them drawn from the RTA Special Forces. However, only Alpha 77 was mandated with training resistance forces.

7. Kasem Thammakul interview.

8. Kasem Thammakul interview; Wannah Mungkhalee interview.

9. Nguyen Van Hong, *Cuoc Chien Tranh Bat Buoc: Hoi Uc* ["The Unwanted War: A Memoir"] (Ho Chi Minh City: Tre Publishing House, 2004), pp. 21–22.

10. Margaret Slocomb, *The People's Republic of Kampuchea, 1979–1989* (Chieng Mai: Silkworm Books, 2003), p. 17.

11. Justin Corfield, *A History of the Cambodian Non-Communist Resistance, 1975–1983* (Victoria, Australia: Centre of Southeast Asian Studies, Monash Asia Institute, 1991), p. 6.

12. Son Sann cited the death of his eldest son in a June 1968 car accident as his reason for stepping down from most of his government posts. However, it was a scandal at the Cambodian Commercial Bank that forced him to resign as head of the National Bank two months later.

13. Clymer, p. 120.

14. Son Sann toured France with a classical Cambodian dancing troupe to raise money for the resistance. *Phnom Penh Post*, November 16–27, 2007, p. 2.

15. Dien Del interview.

16. In late 1977, however, some Cambodian donors in France, probably through the Liaison Committee, sent funds to Ly Tieng Chek and his fledgling guerrilla band.

17. General Staff–Combat Operations Department, *Lich Su Cuc Tac Chien 1945–2000* ["History of the Combat Operations Department 1945–2000"] (Hanoi: People's Army Publishing House, 2005), p. 381.

18. Interview with Huy Keo, 23 February 1994.

19. Interview with Pou Saboddy, 2 August 2008.

20. This 200-man unit was known as Group 125, a reference to its establishment on 12 May. This was referenced in a speech by Cambodian Prime Minister Hun Sen reprinted in the *Quan Doi Nhan Dan* newspaper, 2 January 2012.

21. Phung Dinh Am (ed.), *Mat Tran 479, Tren Dat Nuoc Angkor* ["Front 479, In the Nation of Angkor"] (Ho Chi Minh City: Tre Publishing House, 2006), p. 32.

22. Interview with Long Sopheap, 4 March 1995. Long Sopheap, a nephew of the late Prime Minister Long Boret, had been a young Khmer Rumdoh political officer as of 1972. During that year, he had been taken into the PAVN 367 Sapper Group. He was on the fifteen-man team that walked for thirty-two days into Kompong Cham beginning in October 1978.

23. C-130 bombers hit the Neak Luong ferry crossing on 3 January 1979, the Siem Reap runway on 7 January, and the Battambang runway on 9 January. Nguyen Ngoc Hung, *Lich Su Trung Doan Khong Quan 918 (1975–2005)* ["History of the 918th Air Force Regiment (1975–2005)"] (Hanoi: People's Army Publishing House, 2005). To a very limited degree, the Khmer Rouge also used airpower. On 26 December, two of its T-28 aircraft bombed

a convoy of troops from 5 Division near Kratie city, killing sixty new recruits and a regimental chief of staff.

24. During a visit to Japan in 1980, Tran Danh Thuyen, an SRV national assemblyman and vice chairman of the Foreign Relations Committee of the Vietnamese Communist Party, claimed that there had been three earlier PAVN plans to abduct Sihanouk and whisk him out of Democratic Kampuchea by helicopter. As PAVN could not guarantee success, Tran alleged that the SRV Politburo nixed all of the schemes.

25. Dinh Kinh, *Lich Su Doan Dac cong Hai quan 126 (1966–2006)* ["History of the 126th Navy Sapper Group (1966–2006)"] (Hanoi: People's Army Publishing House, 2006), p. 246.

26. Pou Saboddy interview.

27. Nguyen Ngoc Lien, *Lich Su Doan Dac Cong Biet Dong 1(1968–2008)* ["History of Sapper/Commando Group 1 (1968–2008)"] (Hanoi: People's Army Publishing House, 2008). Journalist Nayan Chanda was the first to allude to this failed raid in his *Brother Enemy* (New York: Macmillan Publishing Company, 1986).

28. Pou Saboddy interview; Huy Keo interview.

29. Although the exact figure will never be known and estimates vary considerably, Cambodian scholar Ben Kiernan makes a compelling case that at least 1.5 million Cambodians—more than a fifth of the population—died in less than three years during the Khmer Rouge reign. Kiernan, pp. 460–461.

30. Accompanying the PAVN troops that seized Koh Kong was longtime Cambodian revolutionary Tea Banh. Himself a former Khmer Rouge from Koh Kong, he had earlier escaped to Thailand's Trat province ahead of a purge by Southwest Zone purists. Rebuffing an appeal by Chavalit to join other anti–Khmer Rouge rebels massing along the Thai-Cambodian border, Tea Banh and several fellow Koh Kong refugees in mid-1977 had instead radioed the SRV for assistance. Not wishing at the time to further antagonize the Khmer Rouge, Hanoi rejected their request and another sixteen radioed pleas that followed. In an eighteenth attempt, Tea Banh crossed by fishing boat from Trat to Ho Chi Minh City in late 1978. This time he was warmly embraced by PAVN; choppered back to Kompong Som in January 1979, he was integrated into the fledgling PRK armed forces. Tea Banh interview.

31. Ho Son Dai, *Lich Su Su Doan Bo Binh 5 (1965–2005)* ["History of the 5th Infantry Division (1965–2005)"] (Hanoi: People's Army Publishing House, 2005).

32. Dinh Thu Xuan, *Lich Su Bo Doi Tang-Thiet Giap Quan Giai Phong Mien Nam va Quan Khu 7* ["History of South Vietnamese Liberation Army and Military Region 7 Tank-Armored Troops"] (Hanoi: People's Army Publishing House, 2003).

33. After the Pathet Lao took power in 1975, Laos became increasingly important to the CPT. But starting in late 1977, Laos put pressure on their Thai comrades to support Vietnam over China. In November 1978, they went so far as to give the CPT a one-month ultimatum to endorse Vietnam's position on China and the Khmer Rouge or withdraw from bases in Laos. Sukhumbhand Paribatra, *From Enmity to Alignment: Thailand's Evolving Relations with China* (Bangkok, ISIS Chulalongkorn University, 1987), p. 16.

34. *Undeclared War Against the People's Republic of Kampuchea* (Phnom Penh: Ministry of Foreign Affairs Press Department, 1985), p. 13.

35. As before, Task Force 506, which was headquartered in an annex to an RTA infantry battalion camp at Aranyaprathet, would remain responsible for covert intelligence collection inside Cambodia.

36. Chavalit Yongchaiyud interview; Kasem Thammakul interview; Short, p. 402.

37. Short, p. 405. During the meeting with Kriangsak, Geng Biao agreed that eight Chinese diplomats would go back to Cambodia and form a jungle "embassy" accredited to the Khmer Rouge government. They returned in early February and established a camp in the forest east of Pailin. After several close encounters with PAVN patrols, the diplomats decided to leave Cambodian soil on 11 April. They were escorted to the Thai border by such senior Khmer Rouge personalities as Pol Pot, Khieu Samphan, and Ieng Sary.

38. Paribatra, p. 5.

39. To get around these restrictions, Cambodians had resorted to bribing Thai consular officials in France to get visas. In another case, a Cambodian had routed a trip from the United States to Europe via Bangkok, then had feigned illness at Don Muang and slipped into Bangkok while being taken to the hospital.

40. Chavalit Yongchaiyud interview; Dien Del interview.

7. Fratricide

1. Later in February, Son Sann dispatched Nguon Pythoureth, the same former colonel who had cobbled together the first association of Cambodian expatriates in Paris back in 1975, to assist Dien Del along the border. As a former pro-Sihanouk army officer, he balanced Del's Republican leanings. Their egos clashed, however, and Nguon elected to recuse himself from the insurgency and return to France in early 1980.

2. Im Chudett remained in Sisaket province only briefly. By March 1980, he had shifted to a new camp near the O'Bok border crossing opposite Thailand's Buriram province.

3. Ta Maing, a former farmer from Svay Chek, had since 1977 commanded a guerrilla band called the "Cobras" in the Ampil vicinity. To raise funds, he made and sold charcoal to Thai border traders. Ta Luot was a former FANK sergeant from Sisophon.

4. Dien Del interview. The general was insistent that a civilian be the commander-in-chief, as in the United States and France.

5. Created in 1967, ASEAN was the noncommunist grouping in Southeast Asia comprising Brunei, Indonesia, Malaysia, the Philippines, Singapore, and Thailand.

6. By 16 January, the Khmer Rouge radio team that was evacuated from Poipet was already in southern China and had resumed Khmer Rouge radio broadcasts. By the second quarter of 1979, the Khmer Rouge leadership was coordinating the delivery of Chinese military supplies from a new jungle headquarters established just inside Thailand's Trat province.

7. There is considerable debate as to which side bested the other in the Sino-Vietnamese War. Though China failed in forcing PAVN to withdraw from Cambodia, it is equally true that the reduced number of PAVN remaining in Cambodia were only able to conduct an anemic dry-season offensive in late 1979, thus buying much-needed time for

the Khmer Rouge to rebuild. And though official statistics have never been released, it is believed that PAVN suffered more than twice the casualties of the Chinese military.

8. Dien Del interview.

9. Journalist Jacques Bekaert claimed that Kong Sileah entered the French Foreign Legion in 1975 with the rank of captain and remained there until 1977. However, a search of personnel records of former Legionnaires revealed that no Cambodian with his name or fitting Kong Sileah's description served in the Foreign Legion during that time frame. Jacques Bekaert, *Cambodian Diary, Tales of a Divided Nation, 1983–1986* (Bangkok: White Lotus, 1997), p. 33; correspondence with Christophe Boutonnier, 15 October 2010.

10. Kong Sileah for years reportedly harbored intense feelings against the Vietnamese, not uncommon for Svay Rieng natives during the 1960s and early 1970s. Starting in late April 1970 and lasting through May, he allegedly helped orchestrate the killing of hundreds of Vietnamese citizens living on the Chrui Chhangwar Peninsula near Cambodia's main naval base. Dien Del interview.

11. Nhem Sophon was the younger brother of Neak Moneang Kanhol, Sihanouk's former wife and the mother of Prince Ranariddh and Princess Bopha Devi.

12. The media incorrectly reported Nhem Sophon was a former FANK paratrooper, and Nhem himself apparently repeated this claim on several occasions. In fact, he was an infantry officer and never served in an airborne unit.

13. Interview with Duong Khem, 29 May 2010.

14. FBIS, Asia & Pacific edition, 15 August 1979, p. H1.

15. The two most prominent attendees were former Prime Minister In Tam and the former president of the National Assembly, Cheng Heng. Both had been key conspirators in the removal of Sihanouk in March 1970, and both had been on the Khmer Rouge list of traitors threatened with immediate execution in 1975. Each had been associated with Son Sann through early 1979.

16. Though largely consumed with his resistance plans, Sihanouk managed to find time for banalities. He concluded one rant with Japanese journalists by noting he would soon be heading from Pyongyang to Beijing to celebrate his birthday on 31 October. "President Kim Il-Sung has agreed to this," he chimed, "and I am going to enjoy my birthday in China." FBIS, Asia & Pacific edition, 9 October 1979, p. H3, H7, H9.

17. *Phnom Penh Post*, 16–29 November 2007, p. 2.

18. Almost a dozen more resistance groups had queued up to merge under the KPNLAF. None of these were consequential in terms of number or fighting ability, many counting just a few dozen men apiece.

19. Sok Sann—literally, "Camp of Harmony"—was actually the civilian camp under Prum Vith's control. His guerrillas dug their emplacements on Phnom Bantoat ("Mountain of Rulers"), the crest to the immediate east.

20. Son Sann claims that he wanted the proclamation to take place on 5 October—his birthday—but Thai authorities had insisted on the delay. Son Sann, p. 129.

21. Cambodia's bumper wet season crop had been only partially harvested when PAVN invaded in late 1978. The remainder of the harvest had either been torched by the retreating Khmer Rouge, or abandoned when the newly liberated population left the fields in

search of their former lives. As a result, it was estimated that perhaps 10 percent of the population starved to death during 1979. Slocomb, pp. 93–94.

22. Corfield, *Khmers*, p. 177.

23. Concocting a completely false backstory, Soryavong claimed to be the son of Norodom Kantol, the prime minister during 1962–1966. Sihanouk went out of his way to debunk Soryavong's alleged royal lineage.

24. According to Hindu myth, Reahou was an ogre that attempted to drink an elixir for immortality. The sun and moon gods spotted Reahou and notified the diety Vishnu, who promptly chopped Reahou in half at the armpit. Because the elixir had already passed his throat, Reahou had become immortal—but only from the shoulders up. Taking his revenge on the moon and sun gods, the truncated form of Reahou often tries to eat them, thus causing eclipses.

25. Kong Sileah had formally established Moulinaka on 31 August. Van Saren declared himself prime minister at Non Mak Mun on 3 October, and the Angkor National Liberation Movement at Nong Samet was declared on 5 October.

26. After Kong Sileah moved out from Non Mak Mun, Camp Reahou received the additional nickname of "Old Camp," and Camp 007 was nicknamed "New Camp."

27. From the time of the Khmer Rouge takeover in 1975 until the PAVN invasion in late 1978, an estimated 34,000 Khmer had fled to the Thai border. Though large, this number could be accommodated by humanitarian groups. During 1979–1981, however, a deluge of 1 million Cambodians sought refuge along the border.

28. Interview with Suon Samnang, 2 August 2008.

29. At the time, sizable Khmer Rouge and PAVN units were located not far from Ampil. On 13 March 1980, the Khmer Rouge staged a ferocious, unsuccessful attack against elements of the PAVN 5 Division holding the nearby Ampil Lake.

30. Front 479 was specifically responsible for Siem Reap and Battambang provinces. After 1988, it was additionally responsible for Banteay Meanchey when that province was carved off from northern Battambang.

31. The numerical designations of the two fronts were derived from the month and year in which they were formed. Two other fronts in Cambodia—579 and 979—were established in 1981 in the northeastern and southern provinces, respectively. PAVN had apparently opted to continue numbering them in the "79" series, rather than the year in which the latter two were created. Correspondence with Merle Pribbenow, 4 April 2010.

32. On occasion, Front 479 was reinforced by the 317 Division. Phung Dinh Am, p. 10.

33. The PAVN headquarters in Cambodia under Major General Le Duc Anh was established in 1979, though it was not officially designated as Front 719 until July 1981. On 24 August 1979, the Central Committee of Vietnam's Communist Party had additionally placed Le Duc Anh in command of a party section overseeing Cambodian operations.

34. In April 1980, PAVN elements also engaged KPNLF units around Ampil Lake. PAVN suffered moderate casualties before withdrawing from the vicinity.

35. Nguyen Thanh Hong, Nguyen Phi Yen, and Nguyen Van Thang, *Su Doan Song Lam* ["The Song Lam Division"] (Hanoi: People's Army Publishing House, 1984), pp. 336–339.

36. Most of the noncommunist Cambodian guerrillas wore camouflage, as opposed to the Spartan olive or black uniforms associated with the Khmer Rouge. This was because

such uniforms were readily available on the Thai market, because some of the guerrillas traced their lineage back to FANK (which favored the use of camouflage), and because they wanted to differentiate themselves from the communists. As it was rumored that several former FANK paratroopers were among the first recruits into the KPNLF and Moulinaka, and because they reasoned that paratroopers often wore camouflage uniforms, PAVN used the slang term *para* when referring to all the noncommunist resistance.

37. The insurgents at Camp Reahou were aware that PAVN was approaching because a resident Khmer Krom guerrilla—fluent in Vietnamese—had been monitoring its radio transmissions. They were taken by surprise, however, by the direction of the attack.

38. Interview with Amporn Chewtapootih, 22 September 2002. Chewtapootih, who went by the callsign "Kitti" (Thai for "Honor"), was the commander of Task Force 80, the RTA unit in charge of protecting refugee camps along the border.

39. One enterprising guerrilla later recovered the tailrotor off the H-34 and, claiming it contained a precious alloy, tried to sell it in the local market. Suon Samnang interview.

40. Hoang Nghia Khanh, *Duong Len Co Quan Tong Hanh Dinh* ["The Road to the Staff of the General Headquarters"] (Hanoi: People's Army Publishing House, 2008), p. 235.

41. Suon Samnang interview. Zone 201 was responsible for the area around Ampil. Though also temporarily based at Ampil, Zone 202 was theoretically responsible for eastern Battambang province and Zone 203 was responsible for Phnom Srok district in northeastern Battambang.

42. A fourth was established at Nong Samet by the opening of 1981.

43. Along with Ta Luot's Battalion 206, Battalion 208 had been sent from Ampil to help seize control over Nong Samet. Interview with Khem Sophoan, 11 April 2008; interview with Khuon Roeun, 22 May 2009.

44. Battalion 213 under Chhit Van Chhou proved to be a hard-luck unit. A couple months after being inducted into the KPNLF, Chhou decided to defect to the PRK. Showing little mercy, PAVN immediately placed the battalion members under arrest.

45. Suon Samnang interview.

46. An exception to ASEAN unanimity was Indonesia, which since February 1979 had counseled against support for anti-Vietnamese resistance forces in Cambodia and instead pushed a noticeably softer line toward the SRV. This was grounded in two factors. First, Indonesia had adopted a staunch anti-China policy after a failed 1965 communist coup in that country; by association, Jakarta was also opposed to Beijing's proxy in Cambodia, the Khmer Rouge. Second, Indonesia had long felt a special kinship toward Vietnam as the only other nation in Southeast Asia that had successfully fought a European colonial power to gain independence.

47. In late 1979, Pol Pot had ostensibly been demoted to commander of the Khmer Rouge guerrilla forces, while the relatively more moderate Khieu Samphan took over as prime minister of their exiled government. At the time, Lon Nol was still living quietly in Hawaii and there is no evidence he made his peace with Sihanouk; the marshal died in November 1985 in California.

48. Dien Del interview; interview with Gaffar Peang-Meth, 4 April 2009.

49. Dien Del interview.

50. In a familiar refrain, Sihanouk in 1980 had once more started dabbling in direct-

ing movies while in North Korea. See *Les Archives de Norodom Sihanouk* (Paris: Ecole francaise d'Extreme Orient, 2010), p. XXIV.

51. Short, p. 415.

52. Sihanouk, p. 280.

53. Aside from the six existing guerrilla battalions in the central sector, Battalion 111 and 112 had been created in the northern sector by January 1981.

54. The six new units outfitted with Chinese weapons were Battalion 214 at Nong Chan, Battalion 215 at Camp Rithysen, and Battalions 216, 217, 218, and 219 at Ampil. Suon Samnang interview; interview with Khem Sophoan, 11 April 2008; interview with Duong Sokhon, 28 May 2010. Sophoan was commander of Battalion 215; Sokhon was commander of Battalion 216.

55. Gaffar Peang-Meth interview.

8. Parity

1. In July 1982, Son Sann openly discussed the Chinese arms deliveries to the media. FBIS, Asia & Pacific edition, 23 July 1982, p. H1.

2. Duong Khem interview.

3. Duong Khem interview; Dien Del interview. Sihanouk supporters, and Sihanouk himself, were fast to weave a conspiracy around Kong Sileah's death, variously claiming he was poisoned by KPNLF members or the RTA. For example, see Sihanouk, p. 153.

4. In their own official publications, Funcinpec members occasionally translated "ANS" as the Sihanoukist Nationalist Army (Armée Nationaliste Sihanoukienne). Ranariddh himself preferred the translation "Sihanoukian National Army."

5. FBIS, Asia & Pacific edition, 26 March 1981, p. H1.

6. Joining Sihanouk in Beijing was Bour Hell, his cousin and the former general manager of the national air carrier Air Cambodge. Meeting with Chinese Foreign Minister Huang Hua, Hell was told that the promise of 3,000 Chinese weapons was contingent on approval of, and coordination with, the royal Thai government. Hell was subsequently named Sihanouk's permanent representative in Bangkok.

7. Defense Intelligence Agency [DIA] Information Report, from USDAO [U.S. Defense Attaché's Office] Bangkok to DIA, 27 May 1981.

8. Three other minor groups gravitating toward the ANS were going by the names Black Eagle (*Entry Khmao*), White Elephant with Blue Tusks (*Damrei Sar Phluk Khiev*), and Khmer Soul (*Proleung Khmer*). Black Eagle, led by Chuon Chai Ky, had been at Camp 007 but was independent of the Khmer Angkor movement. Although some of his loyalists opted for the ANS, Chuon Chai Ky later pledged loyalty to the KPNLF and his men became the core of Battalion 243 at Camp Rithysen. Khmer Soul had engaged in a whispering campaign advocating civil disobedience in Siem Reap during the first half of 1979. PAVN subsequently arrested seventeen members of the group—including leader Hem Kroeusna—and gave them excessive prison sentences. The remaining handful eventually made their way to the border and joined the ANS.

9. DIA Information Report, 27 May 1981.

10. Joining Teap Ben was the gruff Tea Chamrat. Trained by the U.S. Marines at Quantico and Coronado during 1973–1974, Chamrat had returned to Cambodia near the end of the war to take over a marine battalion at Ream. Escaping to the United States in 1975, he had been working odd jobs—including as a gasoline attendant in Pomona, California—before accompanying Teap Ben on the flight to Bangkok. Tea Chamrat interview.

11. Since the end of Chinese support in early 1979, the CPT had largely atrophied. From 4,144 violent clashes in 1978, CPT insurgents were tied to just 1,891 incidents in 1980. This fell further to 353 acts in 1983. Paribatra, p. 21.

12. Chavalit Yongchaiyud interview. The Five Tigers were the army chief, deputy army chief, two assistant army chiefs, and the army chief of staff.

13. Kasem Thammakul interview. Pol Pot had shifted to Office 131, the secret Khmer Rouge headquarters just inside Cambodian territory opposite Trat province. Members of Task Force 838 reportedly guarded the paths leading into Office 131 from Thailand.

14. Worawit, who went by the callsign "*Khwan*" (Thai for "Axe"), had spent seven years in Laos during the 1960s running roadwatch and intelligence teams in coordination with the CIA. As deputy commander of Task Force 506, he had not only run RTA agent networks into Cambodia by land; he also operated a small fleet of fishing vessels that collected information off the coast of Koh Kong.

15. When the KPNLF formed Battalion 206 in late 1980, four RTA Special Forces trainers from Task Force 838 provided assistance. Also starting in late 1980, RTA Special Forces advisers from Task Force 838 began assisting Prum Vith at Sok Sann. Interview with Lay Khek, 10 January 1993.

16. ASEAN had been virtually unanimous in its public opposition to the PAVN invasion. The exception continued to be Indonesia, whose foreign minister in December 1981 claimed that ASEAN was not hostile to the SRV and was opposed to arming anti-SRV groups in Cambodia. Sihanouk, p. 244.

17. The first coordination session at Chavalit's Bangkok residence, held at the opening of 1979, was attended by Chavalit, Air Chief Marshal Siddhi Savetsila (secretary-general of Thailand's National Security Council), SID Director S. R. Nathan, Lim Hang Hing (SID representative at the Singapore embassy in Bangkok), and three RTA logistics officers assigned to TOC 315. Beginning in mid-1979, subsequent Bangkok meetings were attended by the new SID director, the Oxford-educated Eddie Teo. Interview with Lim Hang Hing, 20 September 2002.

18. Malaysia's foreign intelligence agency is officially titled the Research Division of the Prime Minister's Department. Unofficially it is known as the Malaysian External Intelligence Organization, often abbreviated as ME-10. Beginning in 1983, an ME-10 director was dispatched from Kuala Lumpur to attend the Bangkok meetings. Interview with Mohamed Jawhar, 25 September 2002; interview with Datuk Zakaria Abdul Hamid, 16 December 2002.

19. Jawhar interview.

20. CIA Intelligence Information Cable, TDFIRDB-315/09542–81, 26 May 1981.

21. FBIS, Asia & Pacific edition, 4 September 1981, p. H1. Relations between the three

guerrilla factions remained frosty, with constant bickering between Moulinaka and the KNPLF at Nong Chan. In addition, the Khmer Rouge occasionally clashed with the KPNLF at Nong Samet and at Nam Yuen.

22. Soon after the CGDK was formed, representatives from the Brunei embassy in Bangkok handed over $50,000 to the KPNLF. This was the first, and last, incident of largesse to the CGDK on the part of Brunei.

23. The Southeast Asia Treaty Organization (SEATO), which was established with the 1954 Manila Pact and included the United States and Thailand as founding members, was a collective defense treaty against communist expansionism in Asia. Although SEATO was formally dissolved in July 1977, Bangkok was insistent that Washington's Manila Pact obligations remained in force.

24. Clymer, p. 168.

25. According to Bangkok Station Chief Dan Arnold, who ended his tour on 30 June 1979, Bangkok Station conducted no activities with the noncommunist resistance during his tenure in Bangkok.

26. In mid-1981, the Reagan Administration began a shrill campaign accusing the Soviet Union, and proxies like the SRV, of using weaponized mycotoxins dubbed "Yellow Rain." Although some Cambodian resistance fighters, especially among the Khmer Rouge, claimed to have anecdotal evidence of PAVN using poison gas, Yellow Rain was never a reporting priority for Kong Thann and his Nong Samet network. Later, a September 1985 article in *Scientific American* determined that Yellow Rain samples collected from various cold-war hotspots were nothing more than bee feces; in hindsight, the allegations that PAVN was using mycotoxins in Cambodia were almost certainly unfounded. Kong Thann interview; correspondence with Merle Pribbenow, 2 April 2009.

27. The Khmer Rouge had printed paper currency in China during its reign but had never put it into circulation.

28. Slocomb, p. 133.

29. Eight groups were raised by PAVN's Military Region 7 and assigned to provinces in the north and northwest. Four were raised by PAVN's Military Region 5 and assigned to provinces in the northeast; seven more were raised by Military Region 9 and assigned to the provinces in the southern part of the country.

30. The numerical designations chosen for the first three PRKAF divisions held historical significance tied to the pro-Vietnamese portion of the Cambodian communist movement. The 196 Division referred to 19 June, the date in 1951 when Son Ngoc Minh founded Cambodia's first revolutionary armed force. The 286 Division was a reference to 28 June, the date in 1951 when the Khmer People's Revolutionary Party was established. The 179 Division was an allusion to January 1979, when Phnom Penh was liberated from the Khmer Rouge. Ironically, the weapons and uniforms provided to these PRKAF infantry divisions by the Soviet bloc were usually of far better quality than those used by their PAVN counterparts.

31. The 196 Division operated in the vicinity of Pailin. The 179 Division was paired with the PAVN 5 Division near Ampil. The 286 Division operated alongside the PAVN 302 Division to the north near the Dangrek Range against the ANS and Khmer Rouge. The 8 Divi-

sion (later renumbered as the 6 Division) was raised in Kampot in 1982 but soon shifted to Battambang province. Hong, p. 159.

32. Not all of the deserters were draftees. In late 1979, PAVN Captain Nguyen Van Quan, the deputy chief of staff of the 28 Artillery Regiment, defected to Thailand after a romantic dalliance with a Cambodian woman. He later allegedly gave information to the RTA that helped them plan counterbattery fire during the June 1980 attack at Non Mak Mun.

33. Kong Thann interview; Chheang Ly interview.

34. FBIS, Asia & Pacific edition, 7 January 1982, p. H8.

35. The donut trade was exceedingly popular among Cambodian refugees in the United States. None was more prominent in this industry than Sak Sutsakhan's brother-in-law, Tek Ngoy, who owned fifty shops across California.

36. Voice of the National Army of Democratic Kampuchea did not start broadcasting under this name until 14 February 1983. FBIS, Asia & Pacific edition, 15 February 1983, p. H14. The Khmer Rouge wielded its radio station to good psychological effect, using PAVN prisoners and deserters to appeal to their countymen to oppose the war. It also broadcast so-called yellow music—romantic songs from pre-1975 South Vietnam—which were banned at the time in the SRV.

37. An-26 planes were used to bomb the Khmer Rouge at Phnom Malai in late December 1981, to little effect. FBIS, Asia & Pacific edition, 5 January 1982, p. H10.

38. In one of the more enduring mysteries of the war, on 11 February 1982 a PAVN An-26 transport plane from Pochentong headed northwest and crashed into a paddy on the Thai side of the border. The plane was carrying a crew of five plus eight military passengers. One flight mechanic died of injuries during the emergency landing. His cremated ashes, plus the surviving crew and passengers, were returned to the SRV embassy in Bangkok in May. After an exhaustive inquiry, the Thai government concluded that the plane's compass was malfunctioning and the pilot was on the exact opposite heading of his intended destination, Tan Son Nhut. However, U.S. embassy officials noted that many of the passengers were from a radio intercept unit and speculated that the plane may have been on an electronic eavesdropping flight.

39. After Khieu Samphan and Sihanouk showed up in Beijing in mid-February, Son Sann dragged his feet in France until Samphan and the prince departed China in frustration during early March. Son Sann would later claim that he could not attend because Gaffar was in the hospital with malaria (which he contracted during a visit to Sok Sann), and Dien Del was busy on the border. FBIS, Asia & Pacific edition, 15 March 1982, p. J1 and 1 April 1982, p. J2.

40. FBIS, Asia & Pacific edition, 29 June 1982, p. H1.

41. While at Khao I Dang, Sihanouk presented a delegation of Buddhist monks with $10,000 in cash, which he announced was a gift from North Korean leader Kim Il-Sung. FBIS, Asia & Pacific edition, 8 July 1982, p. H1.

42. FBIS, Asia & Pacific edition, 26 July 1982, p. J1.

43. Soon after the CGDK was formed, Malaysia arranged for Gaffar to visit representatives from Arab National Bank in Jeddah, Saudi Arabia, to make a pitch for funding. The bank officers professed sympathy but offered nothing more than pencils and paper for

Khmer children in the border refugee camps. There was also a KPNLF overture toward Israel, similarly unsuccessful.

44. In November 1979, the U.S. Department of State established the Khmer Emergency Group (KEG) to administer U.S. Agency for International Development (USAID) funds used for World Food Program aid to Khmer refugees. Three U.S. officials were associated with KEG: Lionel Rosenblatt, the former head of the refugee section at the U.S. embassy in Bangkok; U.S. Army Lieutenant Colonel Michael Eiland; and MacAlan Thompson, a USAID official. In addition, two Cambodians that were longtime U.S. residents—one of them arriving on a USAID scholarship in 1962, the other a recipient of an Asia Foundation scholarship in 1960—were hired by KEG to collect refugee information from along the border. Some media reports inaccurately claimed that KEG, which operated until 1983, was associated with paramilitary operations along the Cambodian frontier; in fact, it was a State Department operation that had no connection to the CIA or resistance activities. Correspondence with MacAlan Thompson, 25 March 2002; interview with Sieng Lapresse, 8 February 2009.

45. Lee Kuan Yew, *From Third World to First* (Singapore: Times Media Private Limited, 2000), p. 378; Bob Woodward, *Veil* (New York: Simon and Schuster, 1987), p. 216. Classified presidential findings are regulated by the Hughes-Ryan Amendment to the Foreign Assistance Act of 1974. This amendment prohibits the CIA from spending funds on covert operations until and unless the president declares the activities important to national security and reports the description and scope of such activities in a timely fashion to the congressional intelligence committees.

46. Journalist Bertil Lintner gave slightly different dates for the first cycle of Malaysian training, claiming it took place from September 1982 through January 1983. Bertil Lintner, "Letter from Tum Ba Chan," *Far Eastern Economic Review*, 12 September 1984.

47. Suon Samnang interview.

48. Interview with Hul Sakada, 27 April 2012. Sakada, a member of the ANS, attended the Malaysian course on two occasions, once as a guerrilla instructor and then as a guerrilla commander.

49. Interview with Lay Bun Song, 25 April 1996.

50. Yew, p. 378; FBIS, Asia & Pacific edition, 27 October 1982, p. H2.

51. This pledge came after a fact-finding journey to Aranyaprathet by Singapore's deputy prime minister, Goh Keng Swee. RTA officers from TOC 315 and Task Force 80, as well as the KPNLF's Gaffar and Prum Vith, briefed Goh.

52. There is photographic evidence of at least one M-16S1 in the hands of Moulinaka guerrillas in September 1979. It is not certain how this weapon reached the Thai-Cambodian border during that early date.

53. FBIS, Asia & Pacific edition, 14 December 1982, p. H1.

54. Reflecting Dien Del's conventional mindset, he had revamped the upper echelon of the KPNLAF over the course of 1982. In July, he had appointed officers in charge of artillery (or, more accurately, mortars), engineers, and signals. On 7 September, he restructured the General Staff by naming several former FANK officers as his deputies: Colonel Thou Thip in charge of training, Colonel Keth Reth in charge of personnel, and Brigadier General Thach Reng in charge of operations.

55. Suon Samnang interview.

56. FBIS, Asia & Pacific edition, 18 October 1982, p. J2.

57. Dien Del interview.

58. FBIS, Asia & Pacific edition, 30 December 1982, p. J1.

9. Pyrrhic Victories

1. CIA Intelligence Assessment, "Kampuchea: The Impasse Continues," December 1983.

2. Bekaert, *Divided Nation*, p. 43.

3. Shortly after arriving at Tatum, Moulinaka commander Nhem Sophon died of malaria. Moulinaka's new military commander, and subsequently the commander of 1 Brigade, was the former FANK airborne battalion commander Duong Khem. The insignia for 1 Brigade featured *hongsa*, a mythical goose that Cambodians often associate with banks and finance. This was chosen because the founder of Moulinaka, Kong Sileah, had been the navy's finance officer. Duong Khem interview.

4. Formation of the three brigades had started at O'Smach but did not truly come to fruition until the ANS consolidated at Tatum.

5. He had also inherited his father's libido, having four wives and ten children by 1975. He would ultimately add at least three more wives, including one Thai national.

6. Interview with Norodom Chakrapong, 21 November 2008.

7. The CGDK had four coordinating commissions with one minister from each of the three factions. Chakrapong was Funcinpec's designated minister on the commission dealing with health and social affairs.

8. Norodom Chakrapong interview.

9. *New Cambodge*, September 1971, p. 5.

10. Mehta, p. 39.

11. Mehta, p. 65.

12. Bekaert, *Divided Nation*, p. 43.

13. Much of that time was spent at the commando training center in Phitsanulok, where Surayud helped train, among others, Cambodians from the Khmer Republic. Because of this, he was awarded the First Class Freedom Fighter Medal issued for Cambodian operations during the 1969–1972 time frame.

14. Prior to 1982, 1 Special Forces Regiment was known as 1 Special Forces Group. During mid-1982, this regiment, along with 2 and 3 Special Forces Regiments, was placed under the 1 Special Forces Division based at Lopburi. In 1983, 1 Special Forces Division was subordinated to the new Special Warfare Command. It was joined under the command by 2 Special Forces Division, which consisted of 4 and 5 Special Forces Regiments. In a geographic division of responsibility, 1 Special Forces Regiment was targeted toward Cambodian assignments, 2 Special Forces covered Laos, 4 Special Forces was assigned to the restive southern provinces, and 5 Special Forces was active along the Burmese border. The 3 Special Forces Regiment circa 1985 was briefly given maritime tasks in the Gulf of Thailand, then was stationed at Lopburi and assigned with supporting the Special Warfare School.

15. While serving as head of Task Force 838, Surayud used the cover name *Witchu*, sometimes transliterated as *Vitiu*.

16. In 1983, escorts from Task Force 838 took Pol Pot to Bangkok for a medical checkup, where it was determined he had Hodgkin's lymphoma. This did not stop him from returning to the border and marrying a twenty-two-year-old Khmer Rouge porter in 1985. Also in 1983, members of Task Force 838 flew Khmer Rouge chieftain Ta Mok to a Bangkok hospital after he lost the lower part of a leg to a landmine.

17. Lay Bun Song interview.

18. Although the Vz-58 externally appears almost identical to the AK-47, internally it features a wholly different design that does not have the gas blowback system of the Soviet model. Both solid-stock and folding-stock versions were supplied to the Cambodian guerrillas. Singapore reportedly shipped these rifles via Zimbabwe and Somalia. *Asiaweek*, 10 August 1984, p. 26.

19. In August 1983, General Sak asked that the Exco increase its stipend for KPNLF guerrillas from half a baht a day per soldier to 5 baht a day. No decision was made until 1986, when the rate was increased to 3 baht a day, then again to 6.6 baht a day in 1988.

20. Interview with Francis Sherry, 7 April 2001.

21. Sherry was assigned to monitor the Groupement de Commandos Mixtes Aéroportés (Mixed Airborne Commando Group), a French-led guerrilla organization run almost identically to the CIDG program later run by the U.S. Army Special Forces in South Vietnam.

22. Correspondence with David Zogbaum, 4 November 1998.

23. Phillip Agee, *Inside the Company: CIA Diary* (New York: Bantam, 1975), p. 546.

24. In addition to the personnel at the Hilton base, Bangkok Station since 1983 had also periodically dispatched an intelligence officer—who happened to be one of their most gifted Vietnamese linguists—to the border specifically to gather information on PAVN (from deserters and prisoners) and the noncommunist factions. With only a few gaps, this officer would see his border deployments extend through 1992.

25. Parker's exploits during the fall of Vietnam are recounted in his autobiographical *Last Man Out* (New York: Ballantine, 1996).

26. Interview with Brian Dougherty, 17 May 2002.

27. Interview with Tepi Ros, 28 April 2012.

28. Given his background and linguistic talents, Phong often assisted with interviewing PAVN defectors. Some 1,015 PAVN defectors reportedly entered Thailand between 1980 and April 1986. Khien Theeravit, "Research Report on the Vietnamese Army Defectors," Institute of Asian Students (Bangkok: Chulalongkorn University, July 1987).

29. Under pressure by the Vietnamese diaspora to show results after years of fundraising, the National United Front belatedly tried to infiltrate into the SRV three times between May 1986 and August 1987. While attempting to cross the Lao panhandle on their third attempt, they were hit hard by a PAVN task force. Hoang Co Minh himself was among the fatalities; another seventy-seven were taken prisoner.

30. In 1975, Brigadier General Chuc was the head of the South Vietnamese Corps of Engineers. The Vietnamese diaspora in the United States pinned much blame on him for

the collapse of the Central Highlands because he had not arranged for pontoon bridges to assist the retreating troops, leading to their rout.

31. Correspondence with Nguyen Van Chuc, 3 July 2009.

32. PAVN came to know of the infiltration of the team into An Giang after a Khmer Rouge rallier in Takeo province alerted a local PAVN advisory team in January 1981 that he had helped escort the United Front commandos across southern Cambodia.

33. This radio play is detailed in Kenneth Conboy and Dale Andrade, *Spies and Commandos* (Lawrence: University Press of Kansas, 2001).

34. On 8 February 1982, Le Quoc Tuy reportedly sent a forty-five-man company to Minh Hai province by sea. Intercepted upon landing, seven were killed and thirty-eight arrested. *Lich su Cong an Thanh pho Ho Chi Minh (1975–1985)* ["History of Ho Chi Minh People's Public Security (1975–1985)"] (Hanoi: National Political Publishing House, 2006), pp. 148–152.

35. Though thoroughly discredited by the December 1984 trials, Le Quoc Tuy for another three years continued to talk up his alleged resistance exploits in Europe and the United States. He also maintained close ties to the KPNLF leadership. In November 1986, Voice of the Khmer radio claimed that Tuy was going to cooperate with Son Sann in helping find U.S. prisoners of war (see FBIS, Asia & Pacific edition, 13 November 1986, p. H4). Tuy reportedly died of food poisoning in Paris in January 1988.

36. During this same time frame, many combatants at the KPNLF camp at O'Bok abandoned that site due to high instances of malaria. These guerrillas shifted to Ampil, where they were formed into the new 220 Battalion.

37. Bekaert, *Divided Nation*, p. 78.

38. He was not the only PAVN officer lost during the campaign. Major Pham Quang Kien, the acting commander of 16 Regiment/5 Division, was captured on 23 April when he got lost while scouting forward positions around Ampil Lake. The KPNLF brought its prisoner back to Thailand and turned him over to Task Force 506. During a press conference on 6 May, the RTA claimed that Kien was captured inside Thailand on a spying mission. *The Nation Review*, 7 May 1984, "VN Captives Admit Spying Missions."

39. Slocomb, p. 160.

40. Of the other three military regions, Military Region 1 was in the north and northeast, Military Region 2 covered the east, and Military Region 3, corresponding to Front 979 in Kompong Speu, covered the southwestern and coastal provinces.

41. According to the ranking Soviet military adviser to the SRV, General Fedot Krivda, he first proposed that the entire Thai-Cambodian border be sealed during consultations with senior PAVN and PRKAF officers in late 1982. The 600-kilometer border that Laos and Vietnam shared with China had already been sealed, so Krivda reasoned that it would be even easier to close the 400-kilometer border between Thailand and the PRK. Krivda further proposed that an elite regiment of heliborne assault troops be raised in the PRKAF in order to quickly respond to incursions detected along the border buffer zone.

42. Slocomb, pp. 230–231.

43. In May 1981, the KPNLF had started sporadic broadcasts. In July 1983, Voice of the KPNLF began more regular border broadcasts over a transmitter provided by Singapore.

In November 1983, the KPNLF agreed to cooperate with Funcinpec in operating a joint medium-wave station. During 1984, a dozen more KPNLF students, plus a dozen from Funcinpec, went to Singapore for a broadcasting course taught by British instructors. FBIS, East Asia edition, 7 November 1991, p. 31.

44. *Bangkok Post*, 29 October 1985, p. 4.

45. Military assistance from the Exco was more than matched by aid supplied by China. At the start of 1984, a Chinese arms package was delivered to the ANS. And after Son Sann trekked to Beijing that July to request supplies to replace those expended around Ampil Lake, China in early November promised to arm 2,000 guerrillas from each of the three CGDK factions.

46. FBIS, Asia & Pacific edition, 22 March 1983, p. H2; 29 March 1983, p. H3.

47. Bekaert, *Divided Nation*, p. 101.

48. Ibid., p. 105.

10. Event Horizon

1. Aside from the three original ANS brigades, Prince Chakrapong expanded the Royal Guard company into the new 5 Brigade under his command. In addition, a large group of ethnic Khmer Krom combatants from 1 Brigade (formerly Moulinaka) were split off to form 6 Brigade under Kieng Vang.

2. The PAVN advance was aided by the fact that they had conducted thirteen reconnaissance missions against Nong Chan since September, to include one foray personally led by the 9 Division commander, Senior Colonel Tran Quang Trieu.

3. *Bangkok Post*, 5 January 1985, p. 1.

4. In 1984, PAVN Dac Cong instructors had helped raise a 120-man commando unit for the PRKAF's Military Region 4 in Siem Reap. This unit's first mission was to infiltrate behind KPNLF lines and strike Ampil from the rear during the January 1985 dry-season offensive. However, the base collapsed too quickly for them to have any significant impact on the outcome of the battle. Long Sopheap interview.

5. Dien Del interview.

6. Two of the most recent additions to the KPNLF order of battle ceased to exist after the Ampil battle. The 220 Battalion, which was composed of guerrillas that had regrouped at Ampil from the Dangrek Range, was dissolved soon after the KPNLF headquarters was overrun. The 221 Battalion, which was formed the previous year from soldiers that had defected from the PRKAF, decided to redefect back to the Phnom Penh government after Ampil fell.

7. Lê Anh Dung, ed., *Nhung Chang Duong Chien Dau: Thuong Tuong, Anh Hung Nguyen Chon* ["Steps in a Combat Career: Colonel General and Hero Nguyen Chon"] (Hanoi: People's Army Publishing House, 2008), p. 288. Also overrun near the 801 Division base camp was a satellite camp of Lao guerrillas fighting against the Pathet Lao and remnants of the FULRO hilltribe movement that had been opposed to the Vietnamese authorities since the Vietnam War.

8. Interview with Nhek Bun Chay, 3 March 2009.

9. Interview with Sonthi Boonyaratglin, 14 December 2008.

10. In mid-1984, King Men was also placed in charge of Permico's Department of Operations.

11. Sherry interview. Besides being fearful of the hazards involved, King Men's wife wanted him away from the border because he had reportedly fathered children from two other women in the ANS camps. In part because of her incessant pressure, King Men did return to the United States for several weeks in early 1985. This sojourn was also due to exile politics: Sosthene Fernandez, the former FANK commander, had recently created a Republican Party among the Cambodian diaspora and recruited King Men's brother as his deputy. King Men met with his brother in California to discuss the party, but declined to join and in late February headed back to Tatum. Tum Sambol interview.

12. The tennis court at the headquarters of 1 Special Forces Regiment in Lopburi is dedicated in memory of Major Jong Buranasompob.

13. Nhek Bun Chay interview.

14. Ibid.

15. The *Bangkok Post* ran a photo of the funeral on 14 March in which Fleischer is visible in the background. The CIA reportedly funneled funds to underwrite the publication (in both French and German versions) of a short book that documented King Men's life and death at Tatum. Sherry interview.

16. Interview with Srey Sangha, 29 April 2012.

17. Pann Thai and his Special Forces went to the nearby abandoned camp at O'Ksach, which at one time had been occupied by ANS troops under Toan Chay.

18. On the Thai side of the border was the village of Ban Naeng Mut in Surin province.

19. In early 1989, U.S. Army Colonel Denny Lane, who was seconded to the United Nations, identified thirty-seven border camps and supply bases under Khmer Rouge control. It was conservatively estimated that at least 153,200 Khmer were living in these camps.

20. In order to provide more disciplined security for Khmer refugees, the RTA in 1980 formed Task Force 80 at Aranyaprathet to protect the first two camps established inside Thai territory. Led by Special Colonel Amporn Chewtapootih, better known on the border by his nom de guerre Colonel Kitti, this unarmed task force, manned by regular RTA soldiers, initially earned high marks. In 1984, Kitti was reassigned and his unit was renamed Task Force 88. The massive influx of refugees in 1985 far outstripped what Task Force 88 could effectively guard, and the supplemental security provided by the Rangers received increased negative comment. Desmond Ball, *The Boys in Black* (Bangkok: White Lotus, 2004), p. 30; Amporn Chewtapootih interview.

21. Clymer, p. 168.

22. Clymer, p. 171.

23. Interview with Stephen Solarz, 26 August 2002.

24. Solarz claimed he was not aware of CIA covert assistance when he pushed for overt aid. However, there were already media references to the CIA program; for example, a front-page mention in the 8 July 1985 edition of the *Washington Post*. To think that Solarz, who was arguably the best-informed congressman on the Cambodian situation, had not learned of such covert assistance strains credulity. More likely, he was insistent on overt

aid to boost the morale of the noncommunists and offer a tangible congressional rebuke of both the Khmer Rouge and Vietnamese.

25. *Washington Post*, 4 April 1985, p. A6.

26. Chakrapong claimed to have added three more battalions to his 5 Brigade by this time, bringing it to a total of six battalions and 3,000 troops. Norodom Chakrapong interview.

27. Correspondence with Gary Fleischer, 16 September 2008.

28. Mehta, p. 74.

29. Norodom Chakrapong interview. A further class for another thirty KPNLF and ANS officers was held at the end of the year.

30. Lay Bun Song interview.

31. Suon Samnang interview. Samnang, a member of the KPNLF, participated in several of the SAS training cycles, both as a student and translator.

32. Bekaert, *Divided Nation*, p. 214. The ANS became fixated on attacking the Siem Reap provincial capital with the SAS graduates. In early 1987, thirty-six of them were assigned with hitting Siem Reap with seven Chinese-made 107mm rockets. They aborted the mission after running into a PAVN ambush. A few months later, another thirty-six graduates of the SAS course managed to get close enough to fire three 107mm rockets, but all went wide. Hul Sakada interview.

11. Dry Rot

1. An estimated 300–500 tons of material—everything from firearms to ammunition to uniforms—was being sent by China to the Khmer Rouge every month. Paribatra, p. 18.

2. Son Sann was irate with Gaffar—and Dien Del—for an additional reason: Both had disagreed with Son Sann's apparent desire to directly appoint his son, Son Soubert, as the next KPNLF president. Rather, Gaffar and Dien Del insisted that the succession issue be voted upon by the KPNLF's leadership committee. Gaffar Peang-Meth interview; Dien Del interview.

3. Gaffar Peang-Meth interview.

4. FBIS, Asia & Pacific edition, 5 June 1985, p. H4; *The Nation Review*, 26 June 1985, p. 2.

5. *The Nation*, 13 June 1985, p. 3.

6. *Bangkok Post*, 1 August 1985, p. 5.

7. FBIS, Asia & Pacific edition, 30 August 1985, p. H2.

8. FBIS, Asia & Pacific edition, 26 August 1985, p. H2.

9. Chhuon Sam Ol interview. Chhuon was present at the safe house during the meeting.

10. Palmer End of Tour Report, Part Two, Section D (Air Force), Sub-Section 3, p. 6.

11. Bekaert, *Divided Nation*, p. 230.

12. Judging that Thach Reng shared much of the blame for the rift, the RTA in late December 1985 gave him 48 hours to vacate the country. This was the second time he was expelled from Thailand in as many years. FBIS, Asia & Pacific edition, 3 July 1986, p. H5.

13. FBIS, Asia & Pacific edition, 20 December 1985, p. H1; *Bangkok Post*, 24 December

1985, p. 1. Liv Ne's participation in the PCCS lasted just days, as he soon declared his support for Son Sann.

14. Sensing opportunity for his Republican Party, former FANK commander Sosthene Fernandez began touring the United States at the end of 1985. The general let it be known he was recruiting a new anticommunist guerrilla army as an alternative to the ANS and the rift-ridden KPNLF. His offer did not spark any enthusiasm, however, and he soon disappeared from the scene.

15. FBIS, Asia & Pacific edition, 4 February 1986, p. H4.

16. FBIS, Asia & Pacific edition, 21 February 1986, p. H5.

17. *Bangkok Post*, 8 February 1986, p. 3.

18. Within the KPNLF compound at Aranyaprathet, the JMC was allocated one office, a small barracks, and a residence for Teap Ben.

19. "Ranariddh was not about to accept being second to Sak in the JMC," observed Gaffar, "so Teap Ben continued to be a convenient and useful figure in the JMC. Although Teap Ben was the JMC deputy commander, Sak and I were still dealing with Ranariddh on important policy issues. We had to do this without squashing Teap Ben's dignity—a balancing act that gave me headaches."

20. Kong Thann interview.

21. Gaffar Peang-Meth interview.

22. *The Nation*, 5 February 1986, p. 2.

23. FBIS, Asia & Pacific edition, 10 April 1986, p. H6; FBIS, Asia & Pacific edition, 22 April 1986, p. H3.

24. When Ta Luot was assassinated in 1982, Liv Ne took over as the camp commander at Rithysen.

25. Perhaps in an attempt to deflect attention from the human rights charges leveled against him, Liv Ne in September 1986 claimed to have found remains of a U.S. soldier and journalist, both allegedly killed in 1972, in Kompong Cham province. His claims were quickly discounted as a fabrication. FBIS, Asia & Pacific edition, 22 September 1986, p. H2.

26. Journalist Bekaert scoffed at Santoli's misappropriation of blame, calling it more "fairy tale than reality." Bekaert, *Divided Nation*, p. 318.

27. *Bangkok World*, 24 December 1986, p. 34.

28. General Staff–Combat Operations Department, pp. 399–400.

29. Slocomb, p. 206.

30. Evan Gottesman, *Cambodia After the Khmer Rouge* (New Haven, CT: Yale University Press, 2003), p. 227.

31. Slocomb, p. 238.

32. PAVN's heavy use of choppers continued through the second half of 1986. One notable incident took place on 24 September, when copilot Vu Anh Tuan attempted to hijack at gunpoint (presumably to head for Thailand) an Mi-8 on a medical evacuation mission in Kompong Chhnang province. He forced four crew members to jump from an altitude of 150 meters, killing two, after which he wrestled with the pilot for control. During their struggle, the aircraft plunged into the Tonle Sap. Vu Anh Tuan was arrested and the pilot, Senior Captain Nguyen Minh Tuan, received the Combat Achievement Medal.

33. During one of those engagements in late November, a company from the 4 Regi-

ment of the PAVN 5 Division ran up against an estimated 600 Khmer Rouge guerrillas. Save for one survivor, the company was wiped out and many of the bodies desecrated.

34. Interview with Ek Sereywath, 26 October 2002.

35. In the fourth quarter of 1985, the SAS had run another commando course for forty-eight ANS guerrillas. It had concurrently conducted a 15-day class on the use of video cameras at Phitsanulok, run in part by a former BBC cameraman.

36. Interview with Lay Khek, 10 January 1993; Nhek Bun Chay interview.

37. Nicholson was reportedly having marital strains at the time, and some of his colleagues speculated that this fueled his desire to forgo monthly leaves and remain in Aranyaprathet for long stretches.

38. Dean Almy was also the ranking CIA officer in Nha Trang in 1969 when eight U.S. Army Special Forces members in that city were accused of murdering a suspected PAVN double agent working as one of their interpreters.

39. Interview with Steve Almy, 18 June 2002.

40. David Barnett had worked for the CIA through 1970, including time at Jakarta Station. Switching to the private sector, he amassed $80,000 in debts. To rectify this, he approached KGB officers in Jakarta (including Piguzov) and offered to sell the names of CIA assets. He eventually turned over information collected during his earlier CIA career, getting paid more than $90,000 by the Soviets. In 1979, Barnett was rehired by the CIA as a contract officer and may have gone on to expose more secrets—but was uncovered due to information provided by Piguzov. He was convicted on espionage charges in 1980 and sentenced to 18 years in a plea bargain.

41. Correspondence with CIA officer J. P., 5 December 2005.

42. Piguzov, whose CIA codename was JOGGER, was fingered by CIA turncoat Alrich "Rick" Ames in mid-1985. The KBG delayed arresting him for a year while its counterintelligence chief meticulously pulled together a case. He was put before a secret tribunal in 1987 and executed.

43. By 1985, the Exco meetings were normally attended by the chiefs of intelligence and logistics from the Singapore army, the head of SID, a senior MEIO officer dispatched from Kuala Lumpur, a senior officer from Thailand's National Intelligence Agency, and a handful of top officers from the RTA.

44. In July 1985, Thailand's Central Intelligence Department, which reported to the prime minister, was expanded into the National Intelligence Agency. Piya Chakkaphak was its first director.

45. Ted was hardly alone in being drawn into Chavalit's orbit. "Chavalit had a way of showing attention; you are the center of his world," a longtime CIA officer in Thailand would later remark. "He swayed lots of people, including diplomats and intelligence officers." Interview with M. E., 27 February 2004.

46. Often attending these meetings with Slifer was CIA officer Charlie Bulner. Born to a Sri Lankan father (working in Thailand on a Dutch teak concession) and a Thai mother, Charlie Bhunchelee joined the U.S. Marines and, upon becoming a naturalized citizen, changed his name to Bulner. A native Thai speaker, Bulner joined the CIA and worked on various paramilitary programs in Thailand, but he later fell under a cloud due to his overly close ties to General Chavalit. Interview with Prawit Sukawiboon, 30 November 2002.

47. Clymer, p. 188.

48. Prior to 1985, the two field hospitals were at Ampil and Tatum. After these base areas were destroyed, new hospitals were built on Thai soil near Site 2 and Site B. At that point, funding of these hospitals passed from the CIA to USAID.

49. Correspondence with William Erdahl, 8 October 2002.

50. Interview with Ayupoon Karnasuta, 12 July 2002.

51. The author has previously detailed Fosmire's exploits in Laos and Thailand in *Shadow War* (Paladin Press, 1995), his Indonesia assignment in *Feet to the Fire* (Naval Institute Press, 1999), and his training of Tibetan guerrillas in *The CIA's Secret War in Tibet* (University Press of Kansas, 2002).

52. Interview with Thomas Fosmire, 21 March 2002.

12. Détente

1. Gaffar Peang-Meth interview. Gaffar was among the few members of the noncommunist resistance who was present during Lee's Aranyaprathet briefing. Lee Kuan Yew mentions his discrete visit to the border in *From Third World to First*, p. 367. It is also mentioned in Francis Deron, *Le Procès des Khmer Rouges* (Paris: Gallimard, 2009), p. 249.

2. Aside from Son Sann and Prum Vith (who had the rare beer just to be social), virtually all of the military leaders in the KPNLF and ANS publicly, and often, drank to excess. Arguably the most infamous was Dien Del, whose drunken tirades against subordinates were legendary. By contrast, Sak kept a bottle of scotch on hand and drank to relieve stress—though he made a point of never being publicly intoxicated.

3. In 1993, the eastern six districts of Prachinburi, including Ta Phraya, were carved off to form Sa Kaeo province.

4. In the months immediately after Ampil was overrun in early 1985, Dien Del established a temporary headquarters high in the Dangrek Range. By early 1986, he had abandoned the Dangrek position and shifted to a new forward headquarters at Chieng Daoy, inside Thai territory just 2 kilometers west of Site 2. While Dien Del set up his office at Chieng Daoy, Sak and the other KNPLAF leaders divided their time between their Bangkok safe house and the KPNLF compound in Aranyaprathet. In late 1986, Chieng Daoy was abandoned and the KPNLAF leadership shifted to its new headquarters at Klang Dong.

5. Some of the corruption within the KPNLF took unusual forms. One senior member, who had taken out a sizable life insurance policy in the United States, had his wife falsely claim he had been killed on a mission. After an insurance investigator arrived at the KPNLF safe house in Bangkok, the fraud was exposed and he was unable to return to the United States for fear of arrest.

6. Thou Thip had disappeared for much of 1986. Irate at the constant infighting among his superiors, he had taken a small band of guerrillas and quietly infiltrated all the way to Kompong Cham province. There he had lived off the land for months, eluding PAVN patrols but also doing nothing to draw their ire. He had made his way back just as quietly near year's end, placing a call from Aranyaprathet to the Soi Saisin safe house to announce his triumphant return. As Sak was on leave in California, Gaffar scrounged up several

thousand baht and raced toward the border. Thou Thip was disappointed by what he viewed as this lackluster reception. "I spent more time soothing his sore ego than debriefing him on his stay in the interior," admitted Gaffar.

7. The nine military regions announced in March 1987 were as follows: Military Region 1 under Major General Thou Thip covered Kompong Cham, Prey Veng, and Svay Rieng; Military Region 2 under Brigadier General Sopheak Rachana covered Kandal and Kompong Chhnang; Military Region 3 under Major General Liv Ne covered Takeo, Kampot, and Kompong Speu; Military Region 4 under Major General Prum Vith covered Koh Kong and Kompong Som; Military Region 5 under Chea Chhut covered Battambang and Pursat; Military Region 6 under Major General Ta Maing covered Battambang east of Route 5 and Pursat south of Route 6; Military Region 7 under Chum Cheang covered Oddar Meanchey, Battambang, and Siem Reap; Military Region 8 under Major General Keo Chuon covered Preah Vihear, Stung Treng, and Ratanakiri; and Military Region 9 under Major General Pann Thai covered Siem Reap, Kompong Thom, Kratie, and Mondolkiri.

8. Thou Thip and Pann Thai were firmly in Sak's camp. Sopheak Rachana was a rank opportunist who straddled the fence.

9. Men Pheng had formerly been with Zone 202. He was a close friend of Toan Chay, which probably contributed to his desire to join the ANS.

10. From its office at Site 2, KISA theoretically still performed a range of tactical intelligence duties. In reality, it focused solely on rooting out agents dispatched by the PRK to mingle among the refugees. It continued to perform this role until disbanded in 1991.

11. The original BIRD commander was Van Sar, the undersecretary of state for security in 1974 and the Republic's final minister of national security in 1975. His BIRD tenure lasted a couple of weeks before he determined that life on the border was not to his liking and returned to the United States.

12. Kim Sakun was involved in a serious jeep accident on the border in January 1989. Left paralyzed with a head injury, he returned to the United States and was replaced by his deputy, Chay Kim Moeung. Previously, Chay had spent several years working as a staff member at the Hilton.

13. The four deputy chiefs of staff were Pann Thai for operations, Chak Bory for personnel and logistics, Ea Chhor Kimmeng for training, and Hing Kunthon for civilian affairs. All four became major generals. When Pann Thai became a deputy chief of staff, command of Military Region 9 was passed to his deputy, the newly promoted Brigadier General Duong Sokhon. Mention of the reorganization is found in FBIS, Asia & Pacific edition, 21 July 1987, p. I5.

14. *Norasing* is a Hindu deity featuring the head of the lion and the body of human. In the mid-1970s, Boonrad had been an aide to RTA Deputy Commander Chalard Hiranyasiri. In March 1977, Chalard staged a failed coup during the course of which he killed a fellow general—who happened to be a palace favorite. For this indiscretion, Chalard was put before a firing squad the next month, becoming the only RTA general ever to be executed for a putsch.

15. Interview with Nikorn Hamcumpai, 16 June 2002.

16. KPNLAF document, "Meeting on 11 January 1987 at Klang Dong," provided by Kong Thann.

17. By that time, the British SAS had trained several cycles of KPNLF students in sabotage and demolition techniques at Phitsanulok. Although the KPNLF claimed in late 1986 that it had formed a special sabotage unit, apparently with these graduates, in reality the Phitsanulok alumni were never utilized in the field but were instead retained as trainers at the KPNLAF officer course at Klang Dong. "Sabotage Unit Deployed," *Far Eastern Economic Review*, 6 November 1986, p. 43; Lay Bun Song interview.

18. Gaffar Peang-Meth interview.

19. In September 1985, Pol Pot announced he had reached the compulsory retirement age of sixty and was stepping down as commander. He ostensibly handed over the title to Son Sen, while Khieu Samphan became president of the civilian wing.

20. FBIS, Asia & Pacific edition, 17 June 1987, p. I2.

21. Even the KPNLF's overseas representation had divided their loyalties. For example, the Front's lobbyist in Washington, D.C., Delopez Sanguar, was a staunch Son Sann supporter. By late 1986, he had been replaced by Lapresse Sieng, previously a Khmer language broadcaster for Voice of America, who continued to back Son Sann. Concurrently, a separate lobbying office in Washington, known as the Committee for a Free Cambodia, supported Sak. At the United Nations as well, there were KPNLF delegates falling on either side of the rift.

22. Present during Sak's breakdown were Kim Sakun, Gaffar, and Captain Bantoon Tipayanon. Going by the callsign "*Nantasak*," Bantoon was the chief of staff for Task Force 838.

23. Gottesman, p. 224.

24. Doan Khue commanded Front 719 only through year's end when he was sent back to Hanoi to become deputy minister of defense and chief of the General Staff. He was replaced by Le Ngoc Hien.

25. According to the Thai media, radio intercepts indicated that Hanoi in May urged Laos to initiate friction along the Thai border in the vicinity of Phitsanulok in order to draw attention away from PAVN's prolonged offensive in Cambodia. The Lao military began sporadic border skirmishes in August. Ball, p. 20.

26. The Non Din Daeng site was codenamed Camp 215. Non Din Daeng was not upgraded to a district until 1993.

27. In late 1985, Task Force 838 had set up a temporary ANS training camp near the provincial capital of Ubon Ratchathani. This camp, which had been used by the CIA to train guerrillas during its paramilitary campaign in Laos more than a decade earlier, was closed down when Non Din Daeng was established. Hul Sakada interview.

28. Hul Sakada interview. Remnants of the CPT had also been encountered by the KPNLF when they were building Klang Dong. These communist holdouts, too, begged the Cambodians not to reveal their location to the RTA.

29. The Khmer Rouge officer who defected to the ANS with a fully armed company, Som Narin, had been a bodyguard for the infamous Khmer Rouge leader Ta Mok.

30. Norodom Chakrapong interview.

31. Jacques Bekaert, *Cambodian Diary: A Long Road to Peace* (Bangkok: White Lotus Press, 1998), p. 71.

32. Slocomb, p. 150.

13. Limelight

1. Military Region 1 was still commanded by Major General Thou Thip. Military Region 2, which held a toehold in the Dangrek Range in the northwest, was commanded by Brigadier General Duong Sokhon. Military Region 3 was held by Brigadier General Kho Chhean, a former schoolteacher who took over from the late Ta Maing. Military Region 4 was still commanded by Prum Vith at Sok Sann. Newly promoted Brigadier General Khem Sophoan took over Military Region 5 near Rithysen from Liv Ne. Lay Virak, who had also been given his first star, took over Military Region 6 at Nong Chan from Chea Chhut. Major General Chum Cheang had Military Region 7, but he soon took a leave of absence at Site 2; his region then went to his deputy, Colonel Kem Cheng.

2. The KPNLF reportedly reduced the number of military regions (and, later, operational military zones) to seven in order to better correspond to the ANS organizational structure. The ANS did, in fact, have seven military regions, but its breakdown in territory in no way corresponded to that of the KPNLF. For example, Military Region 4 of the ANS covered the substantial northern arc from Oddar Meanchey to Preah Vihear. OMZ 4 in the KPNLF, by contrast, covered the equally substantial southern arc from Koh Kong to Takeo.

3. The Special Forces previously commanded by Pann Thai, which had never lived up to its promise, was disbanded and its men split between OMZ 1 and OMZ 2.

4. All of the regiments were given three-digit designations, with the first digit corresponding to the number of the operational military zone. For example, the largest was OMZ 2 with Regiments 211, 212, 213, 214, and 215. The smallest was OMZ 4, with just Regiments 411 and 412.

5. The commander of PAVN's 88 Regiment reportedly obtained one of the APPCO radios and used the solar cells to power his cassette player.

6. Judging the size of the ANS was often more of an art than a science. In 1987, Sihanouk himself claimed that it fielded 7,000 troops, while Ranariddh put the figure at 11,000. In March 1988, Ranariddh claimed that it already had 17,500 men, of which 11,500 were operating inside Cambodia. Ranariddh letter to author, 11 March 1988.

7. The 6 Brigade, numbering just 370 men and led by Colonel Kieng Vang, largely comprised Khmer Krom. Of the 120 men who reached Kampot, several were killed or arrested in late November. They allegedly were planning to conduct spoiler attacks in Phnom Penh on the ten-year anniversary of the PRK in January 1989. Bekaert, *Long Road to Peace*, p. 164.

8. FBIS, East Asia edition, 5 April 1988, p. 22.

9. Ek Sereywath interview.

10. Although the DPPU ostensibly answered to the Supreme Command, all of its officers came from the RTA Special Forces and, like Task Force 838, were primarily responsive to the Special Warfare Command at Lopburi.

11. Correspondence with C. Dennison Lane, 30 March 2012.

12. Interview with Davis Knowlton, 1 April 2002.

13. Erdahl correspondence.

14. Correspondence with Bill McCollum, 29 December 2008.

15. Paribatra, p. 60.

16. Francis Sherry, the first officer in charge of Cambodian operations at Bangkok Sta-

tion, retired in early 1987. A second officer took up the post in the interim before Murray assumed the assignment.

17. Interview with Joe Murray, 12 August 2002.

18. Later media reports, and the recollections of some CIA officers, put the level of CIA covert funds far higher than $12 million in Fiscal Year 1988, probably reaching at least $20 million.

19. Ayupoon Karnasuta interview.

20. Creation of the Working Group headed by Surayud was first made public in the 3 November 1988 edition of the *Bangkok Post* (FBIS, East Asia edition, 3 November 1988, p. 36).

21. Correspondence with Scott Malone, 11 August 2008.

22. FBIS, East Asia edition, 2 November 1988, pp. 47, 49; 3 November 1988, p. 34.

23. *Bangkok Post*, 7 November 1988.

24. Lair interview.

25. In the days immediately before the July legislative elections that would ultimately bring Chatichai to power, the PRK had extended an olive branch to Thailand by releasing ten RTA prisoners captured over the previous six years. Most had been taken during clashes along the ill-defined border, though two were paramilitary rangers who had gotten drunk and walked toward Sisophon on an ill-conceived peace mission. *Bangkok Post*, 21 July 1988, p. 1.

26. There were eight promotions of A3 cadre in the SRV between 1983 and 1988. Every province had its own A3 battalion, which were rated as mediocre at best. Far more competent were the five A3 reserve battalions—assigned to Battambang, Kampot, Kompong Speu, Kompong Thom, and Poipet—which were larger than the standard PRKAF infantry battalion and had organic heavy weapon support.

27. In addition, another 30,000 Vietnamese had died during the 1977–1978 border war with Democratic Kampuchea. See Bekaert, *Long Road to Peace*, p. 116. This total number of fatalities roughly corresponds to figures given by Gottesman, who claims some 55,300 Vietnamese died in Cambodia from 1978 through 1989, slightly more than the number of U.S. servicemen who died in the Second Indochina War. Gottesman, p. 143.

28. Gaffar finalized the twenty-nine-page Operational Plan during a marathon typing session in late October. It was signed by both Sak and Teap Ben on 29 October.

29. *Funcinpec ANS Bulletin* (April–May 1988, No. 29), p. 4.

30. Sihanouk again ostensibly left the CGDK presidency due to clashes between the Khmer Rouge and ANS. He also complained that China had not made good on promises six months earlier to send heavier weapons to his guerrillas. He may actually have left, as during the previous year, in order to give himself greater leeway in negotiating a settlement. However, he ended the year hardly in a negotiating mood: During a Funcinpec congress in Paris during December, Sihanouk disparaged Hun Sen as "one-eyed," a "traitor," and a "Quisling." See Raoul M. Jennar, *Cambodian Chronicles 1* (Bangkok: White Lotus, 1998), p. 3.

31. Laos and Thailand had long squabbled over the exact border demarcation near Phitsanulok, the result of a disputed 1907 French survey. This prompted a round of heavy fighting between December 1987 and February 1988. Of the 1,000 casualties suffered in total, Thailand got the worst of it.

32. The Saraburi site was codenamed Camp 256.

33. Powpong had also been the head of the first RTA Special Force contingent to be trained by the SAS at Phitsanulok in 1984.

34. Nikorn Hamcumpai interview.

14. Phnom Penh Spring

1. Son Sann announced on 17 February during a trip to Jakarta that he was dismissing Sak and taking over as KPNLF military commander. He allegedly did this after the renegade Chea Chhut sent him an appeal on 6 February to wrest back the top slot. Chhut, already stripped of his rank by Sak, ultimately joined the ANS. FBIS, East Asia edition, 7 March 1989, p. 41.

2. During 1989, the number of noncommunist resistance members trained with Solarz aid soared to 3,168 people—triple the amount trained two years earlier. Courses offered that year focused on carpentry and blacksmithing. Erdahl correspondence.

3. Later in the year, a third regiment under the Special OMZ, Special Regiment 807, was established under Colonel Men Vichet.

4. In January 1989, Pann Thai had overseen the deployment of a second wave of twenty-five APPCO teams to Battambang, Kompong Cham, Kompong Thom, and Siem Reap. Like the first wave, the results were middling.

5. Suon Samnang interview; Khuon Roeun interview.

6. KPNLAF Briefing Sheet, 19 June 1989.

7. A KPNLF communiqué on 26 March 1989 incorrectly stated that PRKAF Major General Hul Savoan was killed by the mine. In fact, he, along with an accompanying PAVN adviser, walked away with only wounds. FBIS, East Asia edition, 27 March 1989, p. 60.

8. Ironically, one of the authors of the SOC constitution was the ANS founder, In Tam. Profoundly disappointed with Sihanouk after resigning from the ANS in 1985, In Tam once again proved himself a chameleon and requested a visa to the PRK. After a series of rejections, he was finally granted one in early 1989 and was on hand for the PRK's tenth anniversary celebrations. He was then appointed deputy chairman of the commission assigned with revamping the constitution.

9. Ranariddh began his Washington visit on 14 March. Solarz landed in Phnom Penh on 29 March.

10. "Interview with Ambassador Daniel A. O'Donohue," Association for Diplomatic Student and Training, 28 May 1996, p. 142.

11. Clymer, pp. 192–193.

12. By this time, the Son Sann faction was virtually excised out of the monthly KPNLF allotment of Working Group funds. During May 1989, in recognition of the Liberation One success, Sak was allocated nearly 8 million baht—a fourfold increase over the same month the previous year.

13. In 1989, Malaysia also began a combat intelligence course for mixed KPNLF/ANS classes.

14. The Singaporeans normally sent the weapons via ship to Bangkok, where they were

disguised as supplies for Singaporean troops conducting live-fire exercises at Kanchanaburi.

15. Ek Sereywath interview.

16. Yew, p. 379.

17. Of the two noncommunist factions, the ANS benefitted slightly more from Chinese largesse. A Chinese general attached to their embassy in Bangkok even began making monthly visits to the ANS border camps to assess their needs. Ek Sereywath interview.

18. In November 1989, two dozen ANS students departed for six months of engineering training near Nanjing. During this same time frame, China also gave heavy weapons training to one KPNLAF contingent and heavy weapons maintenance training to a small group of ANS students. Nhek Bun Chay interview; correspondence with Tum Sambol, 11 June 2012; Ek Sereywath interview.

19. Correspondence with Nate Thayer, 7 June 2012.

20. North Korea and Democratic Kampuchea shared a unique ideological bond. As Kiernan notes, Democratic Kampuchea was the only communist regime to make punishable by death the use of minority or foreign languages. Similarly, North Korea had long pursued a "no minority" policy, even though North Korea had no ethnic minority population. North Korea thus might have provided Pol Pot with a model of ethnic as well as ideological purity. Kiernan, p. xxx.

21. The North Korean pistols became prestige items wielded by ANS officers—as well as souvenir collectibles sought by CIA officers at Bangkok Station.

22. Hul Sakada interview.

23. Ibid.

24. Interview with Hun Phoeung, 2 October 2009.

25. This is not to be confused with the Royal Guard company originally created by Chakrapong in 1983, which had been expanded into his 5 Brigade. Although Chakrapong still liked to refer to his brigade as "Royal Guards," they did not have any role as bodyguards.

26. Interview with Dennis Gallwey, 25 July 2002. In October 1990, a heated debate broke out in the British House of Commons when opposition politicians mistakenly accused the SAS of having trained members of the Khmer Rouge.

27. Hul Sakada interview. Sakada was a senior officer in the Royal Guard.

28. Ek Sereywath interview.

29. Bekaert, *Long Road to Peace*, p. 171.

30. Not until 1993, well after the war was over, were the FAMAS rifles distributed to Ranariddh's bodyguards.

31. Transcript of interview conducted by Colonel Dennison Lane with Major General Toan Chay, 12 August 1989.

32. The Khmer Rouge representative to the Higher Council was their defense minister Son Sen. The ANS was represented by Prince Chakrapong, though Ranariddh made occasional appearances. The KPNLF's Son Sann insisted that his faction fill the Front's seat; he selected Im Chudett as his representative.

33. On 23 March, the Khmer Rouge reportedly hit a noncommunist patrol in Prey Veng province, killing two.

15. White Pigeon

1. In hindsight, the impact of the Stinger may have been exaggerated. Over the ensuing three years after its introduction, perhaps 150 Soviet aircraft were taken down with this missile, less in overall numbers to the losses attributed to mujahideen heavy machine guns. Still, there is no denying the significant boost to morale the Stinger gave to both the Afghan guerrillas and their foreign backers.

2. PAVN, which did not have any specialized air assault units in its order of battle, unsurprisingly did not conduct any air assault operations in Cambodia. In December 1982, the senior Soviet military advisor to PAVN, General Fedot Krivda, who was concurrently in charge of the Soviet military advisory groups in the PRK and Laos, had urged senior PRK officials to establish a composite helicopter regiment with an elite unit of air-assault troops that could be used as a nationwide strike force. This was a pipedream, of course, as the PRKAF had a hard enough time maintaining conventional infantry units, let alone elite formations.

3. Ironically, PAVN's Mi-24 fleet had been absent from the Cambodian battlefield since early 1987 after a training accident killed a crew near Ho Chi Minh City.

4. Apart from some Chinese-made MiG-19 fighters left behind by Demcratic Kampuchea, the PRK/SOC armed forces never had much of an air wing. In June 1989, the SOC's first squadron of MiG-21s arrived at Pochentong. Its pilot contingent had been training for four years in the Soviet Union, then another four in the SRV. There is no evidence these SOC jets were ever used against CGDK guerrillas.

5. These charges were detailed by journalist Bertil Lintner in "Passing in the Dark," *Far Eastern Economic Review* (3 November 1988).

6. FBIS, East Asia edition, 11 September 1989, p. 37.

7. Penn Thola was the youngest son of Penn Nuth, a former prime minister under Sihanouk and ostensibly prime minister of the GRUNK rebel coalition against Lon Nol. Despite his father's reputation as a staunch Sihanoukist, Penn Thola had joined the KPNLF in 1983.

8. Much like the varying estimates about the size of the ANS, the size of the KPNLAF was equally mysterious. In June 1989, Son Sann met Sak and urged the general to increase the size of the KPNLAF to more than 15,000 combatants. To this, Sak responded that he already had 18,000 men under arms. The very next day in a conversation with U.S. Army Colonel Denny Lane, Pann Thai claimed the actual size of his military was 15,000. Report by Dennison Lane, "Security and the KPNLF: A Soliloquy," July 1989.

9. The events on 30 September 1989 were detailed in a KPNLF publication entitled *A Visit to Banteay Chhmar: Reaching the Khmer Soul* by M. H. Lao (Khmer Buddhist Association, 1989).

10. Thayer received shrapnel to the feet and a fractured rib. Correspondence with Nate Thayer, 17 August 2002.

11. Sangha and his family had sought sanctuary in Pursat province. His mother, two brothers, and sister did not survive Democratic Kampuchea.

12. Suon Samnang interview.

13. Ibid. A KPNLF communiqué on 6 October claimed that seven 82mm mortars were also taken at Kandaol. FBIS, East Asia edition, 10 October 1989, p. 44.

14. For reasons not apparent, Dien Del erroneously told an Associated Press reporter in early October that the United States had provided the KPNLF with M47 Dragon antitank missiles. KPNLF spokesman Gaffar was forced to issue repeated denials of this claim. FBIS, East Asia edition, 12 October 1989, p. 39 and 16 October 1989, p. 34.

15. Fosmire interview. Fosmire's attempt to monitor logistics was often a losing battle. In June 1989, a flood of KPNLF equipment, much of it with stencils of unit numbers, showed up in markets across Bangkok. Rucksacks were especially prevalent. FBIS, East Asia edition, 14 December 1989, p. 32; Lane report, "Security and the KPNLF."

16. The F1 delivery was reported in the media on 3 November. FBIS, East Asia edition, 3 November 1989, p. 39.

17. The French remained especially coy about their military support to the ANS. In January 1990, General Toan Chay announced that a follow-on French shipment—to have consisted of handheld 60mm mortars—had been cancelled due to media leaks over the F1 launchers. Hul Sakada interview; Ek Sereywath interview.

18. The ANS insisted that the new governor be General Krouch Yoeum. A former high-school principal during the Sihanouk era, Yoeum had joined FANK and was assigned to an airborne brigade. The ANS publicly claimed, without basis, that he was in charge of joint noncommunist units as of 1989 and had allegedly planned the Banteay Meanchey operation at the JMC.

19. Khmer Rouge military commander Son Sen told Ranariddh about their Pailin strategy during a private conversation in late November 1989, the details of which were passed to journalist Al Santoli on 3 December.

20. Srey Sangha interview.

21. The haul around Svay Chek was detailed over Voice of the Khmer on 6 December. FBIS, East Asia edition, 7 December 1989, p. 40.

22. Nhek Bun Chay recounted his background in a self-published autobiography titled *A Single Piece of Luck Among a Thousand Dangers*.

23. Ranariddh made these comments during an interview with journalist Al Santoli on 3 December 1989. Santoli provided his notes from this conversation to the author.

24. Ibid.

25. Suon Samnang interview. At twenty-seven years old, Suon had seen more than his share of hardship over the years. His father, the deputy governor of Ratanakiri province, had gone missing in March 1970 and was apparently killed during the initial PAVN land-grab after the fall of Sihanouk. His older brother had joined FANK in Battambang but on 20 April 1975 was taken outside the city limits and executed. Suon had managed to reach the Thai border in April 1979 and joined the KPNLF shortly after its inception. See *The Globe and Mail*, 3 January 1987, p. D5.

26. The fact that Task Force 838 played a major role in overseeing the resistance was an open secret on both sides of the border. In an apparent poke at the task force, the SOC announced that it had put 838 guerrillas out of action in October 1989, then announced that it had also put another 838 out of action in November. FBIS, East Asia edition, 22 November 1989, p. 48 and 1 December 1989, p. 50.

27. In 1991, Gaffar joined the staff of the University of Guam as a professor of political science. He remained there for more than a decade.

16. Paradigm Shift

1. Interview with Vong Tham, 16 January 2010.

2. The explosions were reported on Voice of the Khmer radio. See FBIS, East Asia edition, 11 January 1990, p. 38. Grenade attacks in Phnom Penh were not exactly uncommon. On 21 November 1989, the Khmer Rouge claimed to have thrown four grenades in the capital. Another set of six noise grenades were set off around Phnom Penh on 6 January 1990, one day before the regime celebrated the liberation of the city from the Khmer Rouge. Journalists noted that some of the grenade attacks were attributed to frustrated war invalids not getting enough compensation from the SOC government. FBIS, East Asia edition, 29 November 1989, p. 49 and 30 November 1989, p. 30.

3. Gottesman, p. 309.

4. General Staff–Combat Operations Department, p. 432.

5. The three regiments were 1 Regiment of the 330 Division, 9 Regiment of the 339 Division, and 20 Regiment of the 4 Division. Tran Ba Diem, ed., *Lich Su Su Doan Bo Binh 330 Quan Khu 9* [History of the 330 Infantry Division/Military Region 9] (Hanoi: People's Army Publishing House, 2004), pp. 119–121.

6. Phung Dinh Am, p. 37; Pham Duc Hoan, *Lich su Quan doan 1* [History of the 1 Corps] (Hanoi: People's Army Publishing House, 2003); Phan Chi Nhan, Le Kim, Le Huy Toan and Nguyen Dinh Khuong, *Su Doan 308 Quan Tien Phong* [308 Vanguard Division] (Hanoi: People's Army Publishing House, 1999), pp. 319–320. The SOC's 7 Division, which was based at Longvek and acted as a strategic reserve, was officially inaugurated in February 1990.

7. The Khmer Rouge since 1986 published a glossy bimonthly magazine titled *National Army of Democratic Kampuchea*. A special edition, titled *Evidences: Vietnamese Soldiers Captured by the Cambodian National Resistance After September 26, 1989*, was published in December 1989.

8. The standoff between Son Sann and Sak was also simmering near boil. On 16 February, Son Sann ventured to Banteay Chhmar and held a press conference—during which time he lashed out at the KPNLAF for abuse and said it was worse than the Khmer Rouge. FBIS, East Asia edition, p. 55.

9. On 28 December 1989, the ANS used its T-54 tank for the first time to help overrun two SOC outposts in Ampil district, Oddar Meanchey province. FBIS, East Asia edition, 29 December 1989, p. 45.

10. In a time honored tradition among Khmer combatants, KPNLF guerrillas at Thmar Puok expended tens of thousands of rounds into the sky during a total lunar eclipse on 9 February.

11. FBIS, East Asia edition, 14 February 1990, p. 56.

12. On the morning of 6 January 1990, Khmer Rouge teams had briefly gotten close enough to launch rockets into Battambang city.

13. The battalion from the 7 Division remained in Kratie through July 1990. Reference to its brief deployment can be found in Tran Xuan Ban, chief editor, *Lich su Su doan bo binh 7, 1966–2006* [History of the 7 Infantry Division] (Hanoi: People's Army Publishing House, 2006).

14. Phum Sereipheap, previously known as Romchong village, was located in Banteay Ampil district, Oddar Meanchey district.

15. Three days before he signed the decree forming ANKI, Sihanouk signed another decree in which Chakrapong's 2,150-man 5 Brigade was declared an autonomous formation under the ANS/ANKI umbrella. While it was still administered by ANKI, the brigade theoretically was beholden only to its own commander for operational orders. This was done to assuage the ambitious Chakrapong, who was bickering constantly with half-brother Ranariddh and would not have abided serving in ANKI with Ranariddh as Supreme Commander. Norodom Chakrapong interview.

16. In January 1990, the CGDK announced it was officially changing its name to the National Government of Cambodia. This new term never entered into popular usage.

17. The Type 62 light tank is a scaled-down version of the Type 59 medium tank, which in turn is a Chinese copy of the Soviet T-54. In June 1990, the Khmer Rouge created the Armor Regiment at Pailin. This consisted of the five Type 62s supplied by China, plus a total of fourteen T-54s it eventually captured from the SOC. Interview with Huot Sotha, 22 May 2009.

18. Ayupoon Karnasuta interview.

19. Two months earlier, the KPNLF had already claimed that it had run out of ammunition for its Chinese-made heavy weapons. FBIS, East Asia edition, 26 February 1990, p. 55.

20. Tea Chamrat interview. Despite promises, the North Korean agricultural experts never showed up.

21. Ek Sereywath interview; Nhek Bun Chay interview.

22. Association for Diplomatic Studies and Training, Interview with Ambassador Daniel A. O'Donohue, p. 144.

23. In April 1990, ABC News had aired a Peter Jennings documentary titled "Reporting from the Killing Fields." In it, Jennings hinted that a U.S. intelligence unit in Thailand had ties to the Khmer Rouge. The documentary singled out U.S. Army Colonel Dennison Lane as a member of this alleged unit and even went as far as featuring hidden-camera footage of Lane. In fact, Lane had agreed to provide background information about the Thai border to an ABC reporter making the documentary—and the reporter had secretly filmed him during their meeting at an outdoor Washington café. Far from the insinuations in the Jennings documentary, Lane had not served in any secret U.S. intelligence unit in Thailand; rather, he had been seconded to the United Nations to serve on an overt, multinational team training Khmer policemen at Thai refugee camps.

24. On 19 July, speaking from his palace in Pyongyang, Sihanouk called the U.S. decision to end support for the CGDK seat at the United Nations a "grave injustice."

25. Nhek Bun Chay interview. Ta Su, forty-three years old, was considerably more educated than the normal Khmer Rouge cadre. Fluent in French, he had studied to be a teacher at the University of Phnom Penh during the Sihanouk era, then joined the communists and lost his right arm below the elbow fighting against FANK in 1973.

26. Hul Sakada interview.

27. Khan Savoeun had served in the Transportation Directorate in FANK. After surviving Khmer Rouge rule, he had joined the fledgling PRK police force in 1979. In 1981,

Moulinaka commander Nhem Sophon had been captured during a cross-border foray into Pursat but Khan had liberated him from his PRK police cell and the two then fled to the border. Khan subsequently joined Moulinaka and had remained with the ANS ever since. Interview with Khan Savoeun, 9 October 2012.

28. The 24 April rocket attack had been conducted by the Khmer Rouge 616 Division. The 616 Division was arguably the best in the Khmer Rouge order of battle; nearly all of its cadre had been trained in China. Tea Banh interview.

29. Further blurring lines, the deputy commander in 15 Brigade, Som Narin, was himself a former Khmer Rouge officer who had been the bodyguard for the notorious Ta Mok before defecting to the ANS in 1988.

30. Correspondence with CIA paramilitary officer assigned to the Working Group, 3 October 2008.

31. Correspondence with Robert Wnukowski, 13 November 2002. When Brian Dougherty completed his three-year assignment in June 1989, he donated the last member of the Hilton's animal collection, a 3-meter-long python named Cleopatra, to the Dusit Zoo in Bangkok.

32. In the diplomatic parlance at the time, Station Chief Huff was officially listed as the special assistant to the ambassador. Broman, in turn, was the special assistant to the special assistant. The six-man CIA team assigned to the Working Group consisted of Broman, his deputy, a logistics officer, a finance officer, and two paramilitary specialists.

33. The road to Thmar Puok was nicknamed the Erdahl Highway in honor of William Erdahl, the USAID officer who administered the overt nonlethal aid program.

34. The Working Group in September 1989 had started underwriting the quarterly publication of a glossy magazine titled *NCR Bulletin*. After five issues, publication ceased following the halt to CIA covert funding.

35. Interview with Ung Tea Seam, 28 November 2002. The shortwave radio had started broadcasts on 6 November 1986.

36. In September 1990, SID gave a month of intelligence training to a class of four ANS and six KPNLF operatives. Ek Sereywath interview; Lay Bun Song interview; Tum Sambol interview.

37. Two Singaporean agent handlers were also arrested by the Malaysians. In 1998, the Singapore government belatedly detained one of its citizens for betraying the spy ring. Though never proven, an SID officer, who had earlier served on the Working Group, was also thought to have abetted the betrayal for financial gain.

38. Correspondence with Billy Huff, 10 April 2002.

39. Reference to their deportation can be found in *Washington Post*, 25 January 1991, p. A25.

17. Parting Shots

1. Though the KPNLF did not retain personnel records for many of its earlier years, it was estimated that the Front's military wing had suffered 7,000 fatalities over the course of the war.

2. "U.S. Quietly Terminates Covert Program that Aided Cambodia Resistance Forces," *Asian Wall Street Journal*, 20 May 1991.

3. Huff correspondence.

4. Kyodo News reported on 26 February that a Japanese diplomat visiting Beijing was told that Chinese arms had once again started flowing to the Khmer Rouge. FBIS, East Asia edition, 27 February 1991, p. 30.

5. Ayupoon Karnasuta interview. Suchinda soon promoted Ayupoon up and out of the Working Group, naming him as the three-star head of the National Intelligence Agency.

6. Joint Publications Research Service-SEA-91–013, 20 May 1991, p. 5.

7. Ibid., pp. 3–4.

8. Suon Samnang interview.

9. Long Sopheap interview.

10. Sihanouk was officially designated as the SNC President in July.

11. Ayupoon Karnasuta interview.

12. The cease-fire was still a sham. On the night of 1 July, the SOC accused the Khmer Rouge of using artillery and armor along Route 10. Late that same month, it accused ANKI of provocations in northern Siem Reap province.

13. The head of Task Force 838 during this period was Special Colonel Sonthi Boonyaratglin, who had previously worked closely with the ANS in Surin during an earlier assignment with the task force. Sonthi used the callsign "*Navik*" (a contraction of the Thai word for "navy") because his father had once served in the navy. Sonthi Boonyaratglin interview.

14. Task Force 909, which consisted of nearly 100 members from the RTA Special Forces, had been formed under Task Force 838 to accompany the noncommunists into Cambodia and improve their combat performance in the field. By late 1990, Task Force 909's members were instead being used primarily as instructors at Thai-based training sites. After the Paris agreement, Task Force 909 was disbanded and its members folded back into Task Force 838.

15. Nikorn Hamcumpai interview.

16. Duong Khem interview; Nhek Bun Chay interview; Norodom Chakrapong interview.

17. Duong Sokhon interview; Suon Samnang interview. OMZ 1 was downgraded into 2 Brigade. OMZ 7, plus the men from the two other special regiments fielded since 1988, were combined to form 3 Brigade.

18. In a detailed 1989 analysis, U.S. Army Colonel Denny Lane, who spent considerable time visiting Khmer Rouge camps while assigned to the United Nations, concluded that the Khmer Rouge probably fielded 45,000 combatants. Its appeal, he wrote, was a "combination of intense nationalism, chauvinism, discipline, organization, leadership, and an apparent ability of late, at least, to take better care of their followers." Dennison Lane, "Dealing with Khmer Rouge Numbers."

19. Nikorn Hamcumpai interview.

20. Advisory Groups K88B and K4B departed the SOC around July. Advisory Group K5B left on 25 August. The final team of advisers, which directly supported the SOC General Staff in Phnom Penh, left Cambodian soil on 30 August. Tran Ba Diem, Ho Van Sanh, and Tran Nhu Phuong, p. 126; Phung Dinh Am, p. 108.

21. Gemstone proceeds from the Pailin vicinity were split among Pol Pot, Ieng Sary, and Noun Chea, while logs sold to Thai timber companies funded Ta Mok in the Anlong Veng vicinity. In September 1991, the *Washington Post* estimated that the Khmer Rouge had earned $300 million from the sale of gemstones since taking Pailin in late 1989.

22. This contingent belonged to United Nations Advance Mission in Cambodia (UNAMIC), which was tasked with preparing the way for the arrival of the main UNTAC contingent in March 1992. UNAMIC would eventually total 1,090 military personnel from 24 countries.

23. FBIS, East Asia edition, 12 November 1991, p. 39.

24. Nate Thayer correspondence.

25. Son Sann landed in Phnom Penh on 21 November. Escorting him was Delopez Sanguar, the KPNLF representative in Washington during the mid-1980s, who was now sporting the stars of a general and claimed to be chief of staff of the KPNLF. FBIS, East Asia edition, 21 November 1991, p. 37 and 3 December 1991, p. 30.

26. The other members of the Mixed Military Working Group were Lieutenant General Ke Kimyan from the SOC, Major General Krouch Yoeum from ANKI, and the Khmer Rouge economic and finance minister Mak Ben.

27. Vong Tham interview.

28. Gaffar Meang-Peth interview.

18. Aftermath

1. Khmer Rouge frustration was stoked when its representative to the SNC, Khieu Samphan, had flown to Phnom Penh on 27 November 1991 but, after nearly being lynched by a mob, had hurried back to Thailand the same day.

2. On its very first landing at the jungle strip, the Cambodian pilot wrecked the plane. Ranariddh then rented a second prop-plane with two European pilots for the leaflet missions. Hul Sakada interview.

3. Ayupoon Karnasuta interview.

4. Correspondence with Dennis Elmore, 11 July 2002.

5. David Wise, "The Spy Who Sold the Farm," *GQ*, March 1998. While behind bars from 2006 through December 2008, Nicholson, with the assistance of son Nathaniel, continued to pass information to the Russians and received cash for past espionage. For this added infraction, in January 2011 he had his sentence extended by eight more years.

6. Sihanouk went into self-imposed exile in 2004, first to Pyongyang, then to Beijing. Undergoing treatment for a host of ailments, including a series of cancers, he abdicated later that same year. Sihanouk died after a heart attack in Beijing on 15 October 2012.

7. Suon Samnang interview; Duong Sokhon interview.

8. In March 1994, Cambodia's coministers of defense went to Pyongyang and received a pledge from the North Koreans to equip two Royal Guard brigades. For reasons never made clear, no equipment was ever sent.

9. Nate Thayer correspondence.

10. The RCAF General Staff later ordered an investigation into who had provided the Armbrusts. While the answer was hardly a secret, the case officially remained unresolved.

11. Proving himself an adroit political gymnast, Nhek helped engineer the 2006 ouster of Ranariddh from Funcinpec, then took the position of party secretary-general for himself. In 2008, he came to an accommodation with Hun Sen and was named deputy prime minister.

12. Solarz interview.

A Note on Sources

Among written sources, several collections were used extensively in this book. Many of the CIA intelligence reports from the pre-1975 period were found in the *Declassified Documents Reference System*. Post-1975 CIA and DIA documents were mostly found at the online Vietnam Center and Archive maintained by Texas Tech University.

White House and NCS documents primarily came from the *Foreign Relations of the United States* series compiled by the U.S. Department of State.

Media reports, especially from Thai newspapers, were taken from the *Foreign Broadcast Information Service* and its sister *Joint Publications Research Service*.

I was especially fortunate to gain access to the monthly assessment reports written by the U.S. Defense Attaché's office in Phnom Penh from 1971 through December 1974. Unclassified versions of these reports had been retained by retired Colonel Harry Amos, who had assisted General Sak Sutsakhan when the latter was writing a monograph in the late 1970s for the U.S. Army Center of Military History. These reports provided fantastic snapshots of the deteriorating military situation across the Khmer Republic during most of the war.

I was also fortunate to gain access to a series of unclassified reports written by Colonel Denny Lane when he visited Khmer refugee camps during a United Nations deployment in 1989. These provided invaluable insights into conditions at these camps, including those run by the Khmer Rouge—insights that often ran against the views held by many Cambodia-watchers during that period.

Among Vietnamese-language sources, I am indebted to Merle Pribbenow for translations of his extensive collection of PAVN unit histories and memoirs. Even today I am amazed by the level to which PAVN has candidly documented its recent military campaigns, especially its decade-long occupation of Cambodia.

Among Khmer written sources, a self-published history of the KPNLF by Kong Thann was very helpful. Equally helpful was another self-published, and closely held, history of the KPNLF written by an active-duty RCAF officer who served in several intelligence positions during the 1980s. These were supplemented by the author's own collection of *Funcinpec-ANS Bulletins*, *NCR Bulletins*, KPNLF newsletters, and magazines of the *National Army of Democratic Kampuchea*.

Among oral sources, interviews were conducted across four continents over the course of nearly three decades. Many of the primary sources were former or active members of intelligence services—primarily from the CIA, but also from Australia, Malaysia, Singapore, and Thailand. Despite the passage of time, some insisted on complete anonymity. Others did not object to being identified as intelligence officers but did not want to be associated with specific anecdotes or quotes. I have honored their requests.

Index